BLUME • STEIN

FRENCH

FIRST YEAR

Second Edition

WORKBOOK

ELI BLUME

Former Chairman of the Foreign Language Department
Forest Hills High School
New York City

GAIL STEIN

Foreign Language Department
New York City Schools

AMSCO

Amsco School Publications, Inc.,
a division of Perfection Learning®

Cover design by Meghan Shupe
Cover photograph: Métro Entrance, Paris, France, by Radius Images / jupiterimages

Illustrations by Steven Duquette
Additional illustrations by Ed Malsberg / Noel Malsberg
Maps by Susan Dietrich / Hadel Studio
Electronic composition by Compset, Inc.

Please visit our Web sites at:
www.amscopub.com and *www.perfectionlearning.com*

When ordering this book, please specify either **13477** or
BLUME/STEIN FRENCH FIRST YEAR, SECOND EDITION, WORKBOOK

ISBN 978-1-56765-338-0

Printed in the United States of America

7 8 9 10 EBM 21 20 19 18

Preface

The new BLUME / STEIN FRENCH FIRST YEAR, Second Edition, is designed to give students a comprehensive review and thorough introductory understanding of the elements of the French language and the highlights of French culture. The book was revised to incorporate and reflect the National Standards for Foreign Language Learning in the 21st century, also known as the five Cs: cultural competence, comparisons, connections, communities, and communication. This book demonstrates how the acquisition of French is connected and interwoven with the principles of critical thinking, learning strategies, and the mastery of other subject areas. It also reflects how French is used not only in France, but throughout the world.

ORGANIZATION

For ease of study and reference, the book is divided into five Parts. Parts One to Three are organized around related grammatical topics. Part Four, Word Study, is devoted to vocabulary: synonyms, antonyms and lists of topical vocabulary. An updated Part Five covers the culture of France, dealing with language, geography, history, life-style, literature, film, music, song, art, architecture, science, and *la francophonie* (French as it is spoken and used throughout the world).

GRAMMAR

Each grammatical chapter deals fully with one major grammatical topic or several closely related ones. Explanations of structure are brief and clear. All points of grammar are illustrated by many examples, in which the key elements are typographically highlighted.

This first year-review of French covers a basic grammatical sequence. Care has been taken, especially in the critical *Part One: Verb Structures*, to avoid the use of complex structural elements. To enable students to concentrate on the structural practice, the vocabulary has been carefully controlled and systematically "recycled" throughout the grammatical chapters.

EXERCISES

For maximum efficiency in learning, the exercises directly follow the points of grammar to which they apply. Carefully graded, the exercises proceed from simple assimilation to more challenging manipulation of elements and communication. To provide functional continuity of a grammatical topic, the exercises are set in communicative contexts. Many are also personalized to stimulate student response.

While the contents of the exercises afford extensive oral practice and cultural information, the book's format also encourages reinforcement through written student responses. The English to French exercises, once included in the student's book, have now been moved to the Teacher's Manual to allow for more extensive updated exercises. The grammatical chapters conclude with Mastery Exercises, in which all grammatical aspects in the chapter are again practiced in recombinations of previously covered elements. English is used to describe communicative situations, while simple specific directions to the exercises are in French.

FLEXIBILITY

The topical organization and the integrated completeness of each chapter permit the teacher to follow any sequence suitable to the objectives of the course and the needs of the students. This flexibility is facilitated by the detailed table of contents at the front of the book and the comprehensive grammatical index at the back. Teachers as well as students will also find the book useful as a reference source.

CULTURE

The cultural chapters in Part Five are in English. Every effort was made to keep the narratives clear and readable and to provide a wealth of cultural information. Each cultural chapter includes an exercise to test comprehension and a selection of portfolio exercises, which allow the student to pursue his or her own particular interests.

OTHER FEATURES

The Appendix features model verb tables and the principal parts of common irregular verbs, common reflexive verbs, prepositions, popular French search engines and Web sites, and basic rules of French punctuation and syllabication as well as a guide to pronunciation. French-English and English-French vocabularies, a glossary of grammatical terms, and a comprehensive Index complete the book.

The BLUME / STEIN FRENCH FIRST YEAR, Second Edition, is a thoroughly revised and updated edition. With its comprehensive coverage of the elements of level-one French, clear and concise explanations, extensive practice materials, functional vocabulary, and readable cultural narratives, the book clearly incorporates the National Standards for Foreign Language Learning in the 21st century, thus enabling students to improve and strengthen their skills in the French language. As students pursue proficiency, they will also gain valuable insights into the culture of France and the other *francophone* nations.

Gail Stein

Contents

Part One
Verb Structures

Part Two
Noun Structures; Pronoun Structures; Prepositions

Part Three
Adjective/Adverb and Related Structures

Part Four
Word Study

Part Five
Civilization

Part One

Verb Structures

Chapter 1
Present Tense of -er Verbs

[1] AFFIRMATIVE CONSTRUCTIONS

The present tense of regular -er verbs is formed by dropping the infinitive ending (-er) and adding the personal endings (-e, -es, -e, -ons, -ez, -ent).

chanter *to sing*		
SINGULAR	**je chante**	*I sing, I am singing*
	tu chantes	*you sing, you are singing*
	il chante	*he sings, he is singing*
	elle chante	*she sings, she is singing*
PLURAL	**nous chantons**	*we sing, we are singing*
	vous chantez	*you sing, you are singing*
	ils chantent	*they sing, they are singing*
	elles chantent	*they sing, they are singing*

NOTES:

1. *Tu* is generally used to address someone with whom the speaker is on familiar terms: a relative, a friend, a child. *Vous* is a more formal and respectful way to address an individual. To address two or more persons, *vous* is always used.

2. The *e* of *je* is dropped when the next word begins with a vowel or silent *h*.

   j'arrive   *I come, I am coming*

   j'habite   *I live, I am living*

3. The third-person pronouns *il, elle, ils, elles* refer to both persons and things. To refer to nouns of different genders, *ils* is used.

   Le garçon et la fille chantent   *The boy and the girl sing a song.*
      une chanson.

   Ils chantent une chanson.   *They sing a song.*

Common -er verbs

accompagner *to accompany*	chauffer *to heat, warm*	cuisiner *to cook*
aider *to help*	chercher *to look for*	danser *to dance*
aimer *to like, love*	collectionner *to collect*	décorer *to decorate*
ajouter *to add*	commander *to order*	déjeuner *to eat lunch*
allumer *to light, turn on*	comparer *to compare*	demander *to ask (for)*
apporter *to bring*	composer *to compose*	dépenser *to spend*
arriver *to arrive*	compter *to count*	(money)
bavarder *to chat*	continuer *to continue*	désirer *to desire*
camper *to camp*	coûter *to cost*	dîner *to dine*
chanter *to sing*	crier *to shout*	donner *to give*

écouter *to listen (to)*	montrer *to show*	prêter *to lend*
emprunter *to borrow*	noter *to note*	raconter *to tell*
entrer *to enter*	organiser *to organize*	regarder *to look at, watch*
étudier *to study*	oublier *to forget*	rentrer *to return*
expliquer *to explain*	parler *to speak*	réparer *to repair*
fermer *to close*	participer *to participate*	respecter *to respect*
gagner *to win*	passer *to pass; to spend*	rester *to stay, remain*
garder *to keep; to take care of*	(time)	retourner *to return*
	patiner *to skate*	téléphoner *to phone*
habiter *to live (in)*	pêcher *to fish*	toucher *to touch*
indiquer *to indicate*	penser *to think*	travailler *to work*
inviter *to invite*	porter *to carry; to wear*	trouver *to find*
jouer *to play*	pousser *to push; to grow*	utiliser *to use*
laver *to wash*	préparer *to prepare*	vider *to empty*
marcher *to walk*	présenter *to introduce*	voler *to fly; to steal*
monter *to go up*		

EXERCICE A

Henri is telling his cousin what he and his friends do after school. *Exprimez ce qu'il dit* (says).

EXEMPLE: Grégoire / parler avec des amis
Grégoire **parle** avec des amis.

1. Lise / téléphoner à des copines

_____

2. je / jouer au basket

_____

3. Robert et Lucien / réparer les voitures

_____

4. tu / collectionner les bandes dessinées *(comic books)*

_____

5. nous / regarder la télévision

_____

6. vous / écouter des cassettes

_____

7. Jean et moi / travailler dans une pharmacie

_____

8. Paul et Georgette / bavarder au café

_____

EXERCICE B

Mme Lamont is describing the weekly chores assigned to each family member. *Exprimez ce qu'elle dit.*

EXEMPLE: laver la voiture (Pierre)
Pierre **lave** la voiture.

1. vider les ordures (tu)

_____

2. passer l'aspirateur (Papa)

_____

3. ranger le salon (André et Odette)

_____

4. travailler dans le jardin (vous)

_____

5. préparer les repas (je)

_____

6. garder le bébé (Janine et moi)

_____

EXERCICE C

Catherine and Isabelle live near Paris; they are 14 years old and are in the same class. They and some friends are planning a party. Describe what each one is doing. *Utilisez les suggestions.*

aider avec tous les détails   décorer le salon
apporter les boissons   inviter des amis
chercher des disques compacts   préparer des sandwiches
cuisiner

EXEMPLE: Chantal **aide** avec tous les détails.

1. Lise _____ .

2. Tu _____ .

3. Pierre _____ .

4. Vous _____ .

5. Nous _____ .

6. Je _____ .

EXERCICE D

You received this postcard from a friend who is traveling in France. *Complétez le texte avec les mots qui manquent (the missing words).*

adorer	bavarder	désirer	penser	trouver
apporter	coûter	parler	rester	visiter

Chère Patricia,

Salut de Paris! J'_____ cette ville. Ma famille et moi, nous _____
       1.   **2.**
tous les monuments importants. Mes parents _____ que la vie ici
                                            3.
_____ assez cher. Nous _____ dans un hôtel luxueux et notre
    4.   **5.**
concierge _____ français avec un drôle d'accent. Je _____ cet
            6.   **7.**
homme très intéressant. Je _____ un peu avec lui tous les jours en français.
                            8.
Qu'est-ce que tu _____ comme souvenir? Je t'_____ un cadeau
                   9.   **10.**
typique, d'accord ?

Grosses bises,

Anaïs

[2]   NEGATIVE CONSTRUCTIONS

In a negative construction, *ne* precedes the verb and *pas* follows it.

Je **ne** parle **pas** italien.	*I don't speak Italian.*
Luc **ne** joue **pas** au football.	*Luc isn't playing soccer.*

Ne becomes *n'* before a vowel or a silent *h*.

Vous **n'**écoutez **pas**.	*You aren't listening.*
Ils **n'**habitent **pas** loin.	*They don't live far.*

EXERCICE E

The bad weather is ruining everybody's vacation. *Exprimez ce que ces personnes ne font pas (are not doing).*

EXEMPLE: Je joue au volley-ball.
           Je ne joue pas au volley-ball.

1. Nous jouons au tennis.

_____ .

2. Claude nage dans la mer.

_____ .

3. Tu campes en plein air.

_____ .

4. Annick et Christine marchent sur la plage.

_____ .

5. Je participe à un match de basket.

_____ .

6. Lucie pêche dans l'océan.

_____ .

7. Vous patinez dans le parc.

_____ .

8. Jean et Michel déjeunent sur l'herbe.

_____ .

EXERCICE F

Exprimez ce que les personnes suivantes ne font pas.

EXEMPLE:

Pierre ne joue pas au football.

1.

Les amies _____ .

2.

Il _____ .

3.

Vous _____ .

4.

Nous _____ .

5.

6.

Tu _____ .   Je _____ .

EXERCICE G

Make a list of six things that you do not do in class.

1. _____
2. _____
3. _____
4. _____
5. _____
6. _____

[3] INTERROGATIVE CONSTRUCTIONS USING INTONATION ONLY

In spoken French nowadays, an interrogative intonation (shown, in writing, by a question mark) is often all that is needed to change a statement into a question. This is especially the case for questions that can be answered by yes or no.

Tu joues au tennis?   *Do you play tennis?*

Oui, bien sûr!   *Yes, of course!*

EXERCICE H

Your French friends, Catherine and Isabelle, and their classmate Pierre are curious about you and life in the United States. *Répondez (answer) à leurs questions avec des phrases complètes.*

EXEMPLE: Tu joues au tennis?

Oui, je joue au tennis.

OR: **Non, je ne joue pas** au tennis.

1. Tu dînes avec la famille le soir?

_____

2. Tu déjeunes à l'école tous les jours?

_____

3. En Amérique vous aimez les sports?

_____

4. Les parents américains donnent beaucoup de liberté aux enfants?

_____

5. Les élèves parlent français avec le professeur?

_____

6. Nous bavardons trop?

_____

[4] INTERROGATIVE CONSTRUCTIONS USING *EST-CE QUE*

A question may also be formed by beginning a statement with *est-ce que,* which becomes *est-ce qu'* before a vowel or silent *h*.

Tu parles français.	*Est-ce que* **tu parles** français?
Elles dansent bien.	*Est-ce qu'***elles dansent** bien?
Henri invite Michelle.	*Est-ce qu'***Henri invite** Michelle?

EXERCICE I

A Canadian family has moved into your neighborhood. Ask Babette questions about herself and her family. Utilisez *est-ce que.*

EXEMPLE: tu / aimer notre ville
Est-ce que tu aimes notre ville?

1. vous / habiter la maison bleue

_____ ?

2. je / parler bien le français

_____ ?

3. ton père / travailler en ville

_____ ?

4. tes sœurs / étudier l'anglais

_____ ?

5. tu / préparer des plats typiques

_____ ?

6. nous / jouer aux mêmes sports

_____ ?

EXERCICE J

You are president of the French club, which is planning a French festival. Write the questions your fellow students asked, based on the answers you received. Utilisez *est-ce que.*

EXEMPLE: Oui, Pierre pense aider les autres.
Est-ce que Pierre pense aider les autres?

1. _____ ?

Oui, le club prépare un repas.

2. _____ ?

Oui, Jules et Luc empruntent des CD aux membres du club.

3. _____ ?

Oui, Marie chauffe tous les plats.

4. _____ ?

Oui, la cuisinière aide les étudiants.

5. _____ ?

Oui, les filles décorent la salle de classe.

6. _____ ?

Oui, Charles et Jeanne dépensent beaucoup d'argent.

[5] INTERROGATIVE CONSTRUCTIONS USING INVERSION

A question may also be formed by reversing the order of the subject pronoun and the conjugated verb and joining them with a hyphen.

Tu travailles beaucoup.	**Travailles-tu** beaucoup?
Vous patinez bien.	**Patinez-vous** bien?

NOTES:

1. This construction is very rare in the first person singular (*je*). Use *est-ce que* to form questions with *je*.

2. Inversion is less frequent in spoken French. It is more formal, except in some common expressions such as *Quelle heure est-il? Comment allez-vous?*

3. With *il, elle,* or *on* and an *-er* verb form, *-t-* is added between the verb and the pronoun to separate the vowels.

Elle étudie les sciences.	**Étudie-*t*-elle** les sciences?
Il cherche son ami.	**Cherche-*t*-il** son ami?
On aime nager.	**Aime-*t*-on** nager?

4. When the subject of a question is a noun, the noun is retained before the inverted verb and pronoun.

Claudine travaille bien.	**Claudine travaille-*t*-elle** bien
Les garçons jouent au ballon.	**Les garçons jouent-ils** au ballon.

EXERCICE K

Ask your friends what you are going to do today. *Demandez à vos amis ce que vous allez faire aujourd'hui.*

EXEMPLE: nous/déjeuner ensemble
Déjeunons-nous ensemble?

1. tu / inviter Laurent au cinéma

_____ .

2. tu / accompagner Marie au magasin

_____ .

3. nous / patiner à deux heures

_____ .

4. vous / dîner au restaurant

_____ .

5. elle / jouer au tennis

_____ .

6. il / rentrer à pied

_____ .

[6] NEGATIVE INTERROGATIVE CONSTRUCTIONS

A negative question can be formed using intonation.

Tu n'aimes pas la viande?	*Don't you like meat?*
Pierre ne vient pas?	*Isn't Pierre coming?*

A negative question can also be formed with *est-ce que.*

Est-ce que je travaille bien?	*Do I work well?*
Est-ce que je ne travaille pas bien?	*Don't I work well?*

NOTE: The word *si* is used to give an affirmative response to a negative question.

Est-ce qu'il ne travaille pas bien?	*Doesn't he work well?*
Si, il travaille bien.	*Yes, he works well.*

EXERCICE L

You are surprised by some of the negative things you've heard about your friends. Ask for more information. *Exprimez vos questions.*

EXEMPLE: Patrick/étudier beaucoup
Patrick n'étudie pas beaucoup?

1. Janine / aider ses parents

_____ ?

2. Berthe et Michelle / jouer avec leurs sœurs

_____ ?

3. Henri / collectionner les cartes postales

_____ ?

4. Paul et Lucien / travailler consciencieusement

_____ ?

5. Alice et Charles / danser souvent

_____ ?

6. Hélène / aimer ses leçons de piano

_____ ?

M A S T E R Y   E X E R C I S E S

EXERCICE M

You took pictures while vacationing in Martinique. _Décrivez_ (describe) _**les photos à vos amis.**_

EXEMPLE:

Christine **marche** dans le parc.

1.

Je _____ le bateau.

2.

Nous _____ .

3.

Jean, Arthur et Luc _____ .

4.

Odette _____ de l'argent.

5.

Tu _____ .

6.

Vous _____ .

7.

Henri _____ .

8.

Barbara et Éric _____ .

EXERCICE N

Isabelle's parents are asking her questions about herself and her friends. *Exprimez ses réponses comme dans l'exemple.*

EXEMPLE: Tu arrives toujours à l'heure? (non)
                      Non, **je n'arrive pas** toujours à l'heure.

1. Tu déjeunes avec des amis tous les jours ? (oui)

_____ ?

2. Vous aimez jouer au tennis avec Catherine ? (non)

_____ ?

3. Est-ce que vous bavardez continuellement ? (oui)

_____ ?

4. Est-ce que Nicole aide à étudier les leçons ? (non)

_____ ?

5. Est-ce que Catherine et Lise habitent près d'ici ? (oui)

_____ ?

6. Tu invites Pierre à danser ? (non)

_____ ?

7. Est-ce que Pierre travaille bien ? (oui)

_____ ?

8. Posons-nous trop de questions ? (oui)

_____ ?

EXERCICE O

You have just made a new friend at school. Write a note in which you ask five personal questions to help you get to know him/her better. You may wish to include:

- where he/she lives
- if he/she speaks French
- what sports he/she likes
- at what time he/she eats lunch
- what type of music he/she listens to

Chapter 2
Present Tense of *-ir* Verbs

[1] AFFIRMATIVE CONSTRUCTIONS

The present tense of regular *-ir* verbs is formed by dropping the infinitive ending (*-ir*) and adding the personal endings (*-is, -is, -it, -issons, -issez, -issent*).

finir *to finish*		
SINGULAR	**je** fin**is**	*I finish, I am finishing*
	tu fin**is**	*you finish, you are finishing*
	il fin**it**	*he finishes, he is finishing*
	elle fin**it**	*she finishes, she is finishing*
PLURAL	**nous** fin**issons**	*we finish, we are finishing*
	vous fin**issez**	*you finish, you are finishing*
	ils fin**issent**	*they finish, they are finishing*
	elles fin**issent**	*they finish, they are finishing*

Common *-ir* verbs

bâtir *to build*	grossir *to become fat*	remplir *to fill*
choisir *to choose*	guérir *to cure*	réussir *to succeed*
désobéir *to disobey*	maigrir *to become thin*	rôtir *to roast*
finir *to finish*	obéir *to obey*	rougir *to blush*
grandir *to grow*	punir *to punish*	saisir *to seize, grab*

EXERCICE A

Anne and a friend describe their first day at school. *Exprimez ce qu'elles disent.*

1. je / rougir souvent

   _____

2. vous / obéir au professeur

   _____

3. deux élèves / désobéir

   _____

4. le professeur / punir un mauvais élève

   _____

5. Georges et moi / réussir à donner des réponses correctes

   _____

6. tu / choisir une bonne place

_____

7. Marie / finir tous les exercices

_____

8. nous / remplir les cartes de renseignements

_____

EXERCICE B

Say what each person is doing in the pictures below.

1.

Le docteur _____ le malade.

2.

Je _____ le verre d'eau.

3.

Tu _____ le dîner.

4.

Nous _____ .

5.

Vous _____ un chien.

6.

Les ingénieurs _____ un pont.

EXERCICE C

Tell what each person is doing. _Utilisez un élément de chaque colonne._

elles	bâtir	la balle
Henri	choisir	le livre
je	finir	le poulet
le chef	obéir	le verre
nous	remplir	toujours
tu	rôtir	un bon CD
vous	saisir	une grande maison

EXEMPLE: **Henri finit le livre**.

1. _____

2. _____

3. _____

4. _____

5. _____

6. _____

[2] NEGATIVE AND INTERROGATIVE CONSTRUCTIONS

Negative, interrogative, and negative interrogative constructions with *-ir* verbs follow the same rules as with *-er* verbs.

Il ne finit pas son travail.	*He doesn't finish his work.*

Il finit son travail ?	
Est-ce qu'il finit son travail ?	*Does he finish his work?*
Finit-il son travail ?	

Il ne finit pas son travail ?	*Doesn't he finish his work?*
Est-ce qu'il ne finit pas son travail ?	

EXERCICE D

Tell what these people do not do. *Donnez la forme négative correcte du verbe qui convient* (*fits*).

choisir	grossir	obéir	rougir
finir	maigrir	réussir	

EXEMPLE: Une personne qui mange très peu **ne grossit pas.**

1. Un élève qui n'étudie pas _____ la réponse correcte.

2. Une personne qui mange beaucoup de bonbons _____ .

3. Quand vous travaillez lentement, vous _____ vite le travail.

4. Si je _____ à mes parents, ils me punissent.

5. Si tu n'es pas embarrassé, tu _____ .

6. Nous _____ si nous n'étudions pas.

EXERCICE E

Write questions based on the pictures below.

EXEMPLE:

vous

Grandissez-vous?

1.

il / le voleur

_____

2.

tu / le livre

_____

3.

nous / les verres

_____

4.

il / le chien

_____

5.

elles / un chateau de sable

_____

6.

elle

_____

EXERCICE F

Write questions that express your surprise, and supply your friend's affirmative or negative answers.

EXEMPLE:

Paul / réussir en classe
Paul **ne réussit pas** en classe?   *OR*   Paul **ne réussit pas** en classe?
Si, il réussit en classe.   **Non, il ne réussit pas** en classe.

1.

Yvette / maigrir

_____

_____

2.

les garçons / obéir en classe

_____

_____

3.

vous / finir toujours les devoirs

_____

_____

4.

tu / grandir vite

_____

_____

5.

Antoine / choisir bien ses amis

_____

_____

6.

les filles / saisir l'occasion de réussir

_____

_____

EXERCICE G

Janine conducted a survey of students in her class. Unfortunately she has lost the paper with her questions. *Exprimez ses questions d'après les réponses (based upon the answers) des élèves.*

EXEMPLES: **Mais oui,** le docteur Blois guérit les malades.
Est-ce que le docteur Blois **guérit** les malades?

OR: **Mais si,** le docteur Blois guérit les malades.
Est-ce que le docteur Blois **ne guérit pas** les malades?

1. Mais si, les adolescents d'aujourd'hui obéissent à leurs parents.

   _____

2. Mais oui, nous réussissons dans toutes nos classes.

   _____

3. Mais oui, je grossis un peu.

   _____

4. Mais si, Marc grandit rapidement.

   _____

5. Mais si, Lucie finit toujours son travail.

   _____

6. Mais oui, je saisis toujours une bonne occasion.

   _____

MASTERY EXERCISES

EXERCICE H

Françoise likes to chat with everyone. Complete the conversations she has with people waiting for the bus. *Donnez la forme correcte du verbe.*

1. (*rougir*) _____-vous souvent? Moi, je _____ tout le temps. Mais

   ma sœur Christine, elle ne _____ jamais !

2. (*grandir*) Mon frère et moi, nous _____ vite. Comment est-ce que votre petit-fils

   _____ ? Généralement, les garçons _____ plus vite que les filles.

3. (*finir*) À quelle heure _____-tu ton travail ? D'habitude je _____

   tout avant neuf heures. Malheureusement, le travail de ma mère ne _____ jamais.

4. (*choisir*) Quand _____-vous vos vêtements pour la journée ? Mon frère et moi,

   nous _____ toujours au dernier moment. Moi, je _____ la

   couleur d'abord. Ma sœur _____ le soir avant d'aller au lit.

EXERCICE I

You are explaining why our friends from Meudon act the way they do. *Choisissez le verbe qui convient sur la liste ci-dessous et donnez la forme correcte.*

bâtir	désobéir	grossir	maigrir	rôtir
choisir	finir	guérir	réussir	rougir

Catherine _____ parce qu'elle aime beaucoup les gâteaux. Au contraire, Isabelle
 1.

_____ parce qu'elle déteste les desserts et ne mange pas beaucoup.
 2.

Nicole, la sœur d'Isabelle, _____ bien ses vêtements parce qu'elle désire
 3.

être admirée. Pierre et Claude _____ leur travail rapidement parce qu'ils
 4.

sont très sérieux. Le père de Catherine _____ les malades parce qu'il est
 5.

médecin. Sa mère _____ des maisons parce qu'elle est architecte.
 6.

La mère d'Isabelle _____ un poulet tous les dimanches parce que toute
 7.

la famille aime le poulet. Michel et Jacques _____ souvent parce qu'ils ne
 8.

sont pas sages. Chantal _____ quand elle parle à son professeur parce qu'elle
 9.

est timide. « Nous _____ très bien dans nos études, expliquent les grands, parce que
 10.

nous sommes intelligents et parce que nous travaillons bien. »

EXERCICE J

A new exchange student at your school is asking questions about you, your friends, and the school. *Donnez des réponses négatives.*

EXEMPLE: Réussissez-vous toujours ?
 Je ne réussis pas toujours.

1. Est-ce que les étudiants choisissent leurs classes ?

_____

2. Obéissez-vous toujours au professeur ?

_____

3. Désobéissez-vous au règlement ?

_____

4. Est-ce que le directeur punit beaucoup d'élèves ?

_____

5. Est-ce que les élèves finissent toujours leurs devoirs ?

_____

6. Choisis-tu toujours les bonnes réponses aux questions ?

_____

EXERCICE K

Your class has to remain after school because certain students misbehaved. Write an e-mail to your parents explaining what happened using as many _–ir_ verbs as possible. You may wish to include:

• who is punishing the class
• the reason why the class must stay
• how you act in class
• what you will finish when you remain in class
• how students succeed in class

_____

_____

_____

_____

_____

_____

_____

_____

Chapter 3
Present Tense of *-re* Verbs

[1] AFFIRMATIVE CONSTRUCTIONS

The present tense of regular *-re* verbs is formed by dropping the infinitive ending (*-re*) and adding the personal endings (*-s, -s, -, -ons, -ez, -ent*).

vendre *to sell*		
SINGULAR	**je vends**	*I sell, I am selling*
	tu vends	*you sell, you are selling*
	il vend	*he sells, he is selling*
	elle vend	*she sells, she is selling*
PLURAL	**nous vendons**	*we sell, we are selling*
	vous vendez	*you sell, you are selling*
	ils vendent	*they sell, they are selling*
	elles vendent	*they sell, they are selling*

Common *-re* verbs

attendre *to wait (for)*   perdre *to lose*
correspondre *to correspond; to exchange letters*   rendre *to give back, return*
defendre *to defend*   répondre (à) *to answer*
descendre *to go down; to take down*   vendre *to sell*
entendre *to hear*

EXERCICE A

Berthe describes the people she knows. *Exprimez ce qu'elle dit.*

1. M. Lamont / perdre patience facilement

   _____

2. Anne / correspondre avec une amie française

   _____

3. je / attendre toujours mes amis

   _____

4. vous / défendre vos amis

   _____

5. Luc et Paul / répondre à toutes les questions de leurs parents

   _____

6. Les Dupont / vendre des bijoux dans un magasin

_____

7. Jean et moi / rendre ce que nous empruntons

_____

8. tu / descendre souvent chez tes amis

_____

EXERCICE B

The French club is trying to increase its membership. _Exprimez ce que chaque membre fait pour aider._

attendre les questions du public	descendre chercher des brochures
correspondre avec les élèves	répondre à toutes les questions
défendre la langue française	vendre des affiches sur la France

1. Pierre _____ .

2. Nous _____ .

3. Vous _____ .

4. Les jeunes filles _____ .

5. Je _____ .

6. Tu _____ .

EXERCICE C

Someone asks you questions. _Répondez en français._

1. Qui attendez-vous après l'école ?

_____

2. Votre ami et vous, quand descendez-vous en ville ?

_____

3. Qui défendez-vous ?

_____

4. Qui répond souvent au téléphone chez vous ?

_____

5. Quand perdez-vous patience ?

_____

[2] NEGATIVE AND INTERROGATIVE CONSTRUCTIONS

Negative, interrogative, and negative interrogative constructions of *-re* verbs follow the same rules as *-er* and *-ir* verbs.

Il ne répond pas au téléphone.	*He doesn't answer the phone.*
Il répond au téléphone ?	
Est-ce qu'il répond au téléphone ?	*Does he answer the phone?*
Répond-il au téléphone ?	
Il ne répond pas au téléphone ?	*Doesn't he answer the phone?*
Est-ce qu'il ne répond pas au téléphone ?	

EXERCICE D

Write that the following people are not doing what is shown in the pictures.

EXEMPLE:

Luc **ne répond pas** au téléphone.

1.

Les filles _____ l'autobus.

2.

Nous _____ la musique.

3.

Je _____ l'escalier.

4.

Tu _____ la voiture.

5.    **6.**

Le professeur _____ les devoirs.   Vous _____ votre argent.

EXERCICE E

Ask your friends what they do after school. *Utilisez* **est-ce que.**

EXEMPLE: (Paul) perdre son temps

          Est-ce que Paul perd son temps

1. (Marie et Alice) défendre leur position dans un débat

_____

2. (Cécile) descendre en ville

_____

3. (les garçons) rendre la voiture de M. Rousseau

_____

4. (Jean) vendre des glaces

_____

5. (vous) répondre aux questions de vos parents

_____

6. (tu) entendre le rapport du président du club

_____

EXERCICE F

A new student is asking questions about various people. *Exprimez ce qu'il dit en suivant l'exemple.*

EXEMPLE: (tu) attendre tes amis après les classes

          Attends-tu tes amis après les classes ?

1. (elles) vendre des affiches françaises

_____

2. (tu) correspondre avec un copain

_____

3. (nous) répondre bien en français

_____

4. (vous) rendre ce que vous empruntez

_____

5. (ils) perdre souvent leurs matches de football

_____

6. (elle) descendre en ville de temps en temps

_____

EXERCICE G

Detective Marcel Boirot asks many leading questions in the course of his investigation. *Exprimez ses questions selon l'exemple.*

EXEMPLE: il / descendre souvent en ville
           Il ne descend pas souvent en ville ?

1. la femme / perdre souvent ses clefs

_____

2. vous / attendre le train de Paris

_____

3. nous / répondre à toutes les questions

_____

4. tu / vendre ta voiture

_____

5. Charles / défendre bien ses idées

_____

6. Charles et Jacques / correspondre depuis longtemps

_____

MASTERY EXERCISES

EXERCICE H

Complétez les conversations ci-dessous avec les formes correctes des verbes.

1. (*attendre*)

— Qui _____-vous après l'école ?

— Moi, j' _____ tous mes amis. Et quand j'arrive en retard, ils m' _____.

2. (*vendre*)

— _____-vous des gâteaux au chocolat ?

— Oui, nous _____ toutes sortes de gâteaux. Toutes nos pâtisseries

_____ des gâteaux de la meilleure qualité.

3. (*correspondre*)

—Tu _____ avec ton ami africain ?

— Oui, bien sûr. Je _____ avec lui et il _____ avec moi

tout le temps.

EXERCICE I

Complete this story of an incident in our French friends' lives. *Écrivez la forme correcte d'un verbe choisi dans la liste suivante.*

attendre   descendre   entendre   perdre
rendre   répondre   vendre

Après l'école, Isabelle _____ son amie Catherine. Les deux filles _____
₁   ₂

en ville en bus. Elles entrent à la bibliothèque et _____ des livres. Catherine cherche un
₃

livre en anglais. Tout à coup elles _____ leurs camarades Claude et Pierre. «Vous
₄

_____ votre temps!» Pierre crie, «Vous _____ ?» Catherine
₅   ₆

_____ à Pierre: «Tu parles trop vite! Je n' _____ pas.» Les amis
₇   ₈

_____ ensemble dans la rue et entrent dans une librairie. « _____-vous
₉   ₁₀

des livres en anglais ?» demande Catherine. Le vendeur _____: «Mais non, Mademoiselle,
₁₁

nous habitons la France ! Alors nous ne _____ pas de livres anglais !»
₁₂

EXERCICE J

Ask if the following people are doing certain things and then respond negatively. *Employez l'inversion.*

EXEMPLE: ils / rendre les livres.
Rendent-ils les livres?
Ils ne rendent pas les livres.

1. elles / descendre en ville

_____

_____

2. il / défendre son ami

_____

_____

3. tu / vendre ta voiture

_____

_____

4. nous / entendre bien

_____

_____

5. vous / attendre le bus

_____

_____

6. ils / répondre au professeur

_____

_____

EXERCICE K

You are writing a paragraph about your correspondence with a foreign pen pal as part of an assignment for your French class. Write the paragraph using as many _–re_ verbs as possible. You may wish to include:

- the name of the person with whom you correspond
- how frequently you answer your pen pal's letters
- if you patiently wait for a response
- where you go (down) to send your letters
- one piece of information about your friend

_____

_____

_____

_____

_____

_____

_____

Chapter 4
Spelling Changes in Certain -er Verbs

[1] -CER VERBS

Verbs ending in -cer change c to ç before a or o to retain the soft c sound. Thus, the first person plural form of the present tense ends in -çons.

commencer *to begin*	
je commence	nous commen**ç**ons
tu commences	vous commencez
il commence	ils commencent
elle commence	elles commencent

Other verbs ending in -cer

annoncer *to announce*	lancer *to throw*	prononcer *to pronounce*
avancer *to advance*	menacer *to threaten*	remplacer *to replace*
effacer *to erase*	placer *to place, set*	renoncer (à) *to give up*

EXERCICE A

Describe how each person expresses anger. *Employez un élément de chaque colonne.*

nous	avancer	crier
je	commencer à	des boules de papier
vous	effacer	des insultes
Lise	lancer	le tableau avec colère
tu	menacer de	parler gentiment
les garçons	prononcer	partir
Jean et moi	renoncer à	vers la porte

EXEMPLE: Lise renonce à parler gentiment.

1. _____
2. _____
3. _____
4. _____
5. _____
6. _____

EXERCICE B

Ask your friends what they do before school begins. *Notez leurs réponses.*

EXEMPLE: menacer de faire l'école buissonnière (*cut classes*) (non)
VOUS: **Menacez–vous** de faire l'école buissonnière?
VOS AMIS: Non, **nous ne menaçons pa**s de faire l'école buissonnière.

1. lancer des papiers par la fenêtre (non)

VOUS: _____

VOS AMIS: _____

2. placer vos livres sur le pupitre (oui)

VOUS: _____

VOS AMIS: _____

3. commencer à étudier (oui)

VOUS: _____

VOS AMIS: _____

4. menacer les autres élèves (non)

VOUS: _____

VOS AMIS: _____

5. prononcer les mots de vocabulaire (oui)

VOUS: _____

VOS AMIS: _____

6. effacer le tableau (oui)

VOUS: _____

VOS AMIS: _____

[2] *-GER* VERBS

Verbs ending in *-ger* insert a silent *e* between *g* and *a* or *o* to keep the soft *g* sound. Thus, the *nous* form of the present tense ends in *-eons*.

manger *to eat*	
je mange	nous mang*eons*
tu manges	vous mangez
il mange	ils mangent
elle mange	elles mangent

Other verbs ending in –ger

arranger *to arrange*	déranger *to disturb*	partager *to share, divide*
bouger *to move*	diriger *to direct*	plonger *to plunge, dive*
changer *to change*	mélanger *to mix*	ranger *to put away; to put*
corriger *to correct*	nager *to swim*	*in order*
déménager *to move* (to	neiger *to snow*	songer (à) *to think (of)*
another residence)	obliger *to oblige, compel*	voyager *to travel*

EXERCICE C

Exprimez ce qui se passe (what is happening) dans chaque image.

1.

Nous _____ .

2.

Elles _____ .

3.

Il _____ .

4.

Vous _____ .

5.

Je _____ .

6.

Tu _____ .

EXERCICE D

Your friends are bragging about things they do. *Exprimez ce qu'ils disent.*

EXEMPLE: plonger bien
            Nous plongeons bien.

1. manger énormément

_____

2. partager tout

_____

3. nager tous les jours

_____

4. corriger toutes nos fautes

_____

5. ranger la maison

_____

6. changer nos habitudes

_____

[3]   -YER VERBS

Verbs ending in -*yer* change *y* to *i* before a silent *e*. Verbs of this type are often called "shoe" verbs because the *je, tu, il, elle, ils, elles* forms, which have the same stem, form the profile of a shoe.

employer *to use*	
j'emploie	nous employons
tu emploies	vous employez
il emploie	ils emploient
elle emploie	elles emploient

Other verbs ending in -*yer*

ennuyer *to bore, bother*	essuyer *to wipe*	renvoyer *to send back; to fire*
envoyer *to send*	nettoyer *to clean*	

NOTE: This change of *y* to *i* is optional for verbs whose infinitive ends in -*ayer*.

payer *to pay*	
je paie (je paye)	nous payons
tu paies (tu payes)	vous payez
il paie (il paye)	ils paient (ils payent)
elle paie (elle paye)	elles paient (elles payent)

Another verb ending in -*ayer*
essayer (de) *to try*

EXERCICE E

Raoul is graduating and is receiving many gifts. *Exprimez ce que chaque personne lui envoie.*

EXEMPLE: tante Lise / de l'argent
Tante Lise lui **envoie** de l'argent.

1. ses grands-parents / une montre

_____

2. je/une carte

_____

3. vous/un livre

_____

4. oncle Jules/un portefeuille

_____

5. tu/une serviette

_____

6. nous/des vêtements

_____

EXERCICE F

Exprimez ce que ces personnes font aujourd'hui (today) en donnant la forme correcte du verbe qui convient.

ennuyer	essayer	payer
envoyer	nettoyer	renvoyer

1. Je _____ la maison.

2. Elle _____ les services du jardinier.

3. Tu _____ ton petit frère.

4. Nous _____ de finir notre travail scolaire.

5. Pierre et Jacques _____ un paquet en France.

6. M. Legrand _____ son secrétaire.

[4] E + CONSONANT + -ER VERBS

Verbs like *acheter* change the silent e before the infinitive ending to è in the je, tu, il, elle, ils, elles forms in the present tense. Here, too, you will notice the "shoe" pattern in the present tense.

acheter *to buy*	
j'achète	nous achetons
tu achètes	vous achetez
il achète	ils achètent
elle achète	elles achètent

Other *e* + consonant + *er* verbs

achever *to complete*	enlever *to remove, take off*	peser *to weigh*
amener *to bring, lead to*	geler *to freeze*	promener *to walk*
élever *to bring up, raise*	lever *to raise, lift*	ramener *to bring back*
emmener *to take away, lead away*	mener *to lead*	

EXERCICE G

Your French class is planning a typical French picnic. *Exprimez ce que chaque personne achète.*

EXEMPLE: Lucien/du pâté
Lucien **achète** du pâté.

1. nous/une baguette

_____

2. Paul et Georgette/du fromage

_____

3. je/des boissons

_____

4. vous/un gâteau

_____

5. tu/de la salade

_____

6. Jacques/de la viande

_____

EXERCICE H

Complete the story about M. Constant and his dog. *Écrivez la forme correcte du verbe qui manque (missing).*

achever	enlever	lever	promener
élever	emmener	peser	ramener

M. Constant _____ un très petit chien, Prince, qui _____ seulement
       1   *2*

trois kilos. Chaque jour il _____ Prince au parc où il le _____
                               3   *4*

pendant une demi-heure. Après, quand ils _____ leur promenade, M. Constant
                                                       5

_____ le chien à la maison. Quand ils arrivent chez eux, M. Constant
      6

_____ la laisse *(the leash)* attachée au cou de Prince. Prince est très content et il
      7

_____ une de ses pattes pour le remercier.
      8

[5] *APPELER* AND *JETER*

Two "shoe" verbs with silent *e, appeler* and *jeter,* double the consonant instead of changing *e* to *è.*

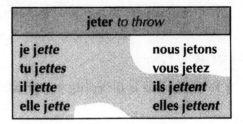

appeler *to call*	
j'app**elle**	nous app**elons**
tu app**elles**	vous app**elez**
il app**elle**	ils app**ellent**
elle app**elle**	elles app**ellent**

jeter *to throw*	
je j**ette**	nous j**etons**
tu j**ettes**	vous j**etez**
il j**ette**	ils j**ettent**
elle j**ette**	elles j**ettent**

EXERCICE I

The telephone is ringing everywhere. *Dites qui appelle qui.*

EXEMPLE: Luc/Régine
            Luc **appelle** Régine.

1. Nancy/Sophie

_____

2. nous/le docteur

_____

3. je/le professeur

_____

4. vous/vos parents

_____

5. les garçons/leurs amis

_____

6. tu/Éric

_____

EXERCICE J

Dites ce que *(what)* **les personnes suivantes jettent.**

1. Le bébé _____ une balle.

2. Les secrétaires _____ les papiers inutiles.

3. Je _____ un coup d'œil *(a glance)* par là.

4. Nous _____ les mauvais fruits.

5. Tu _____ ton stylo.

6. Vous _____ la robe usée.

[6] É + Consonant + -ER Verbs

Verbs with *é* in the syllable before the infinitive ending change *é* to *è* before the silent endings *-e*, *-es*, *-ent* and thus are "shoe" verbs.

préférer *to prefer*	
je préfère	nous préférons
tu préfères	vous préférez
il préfère	ils préfèrent
elle préfère	elles préfèrent

Other verbs ending in *é* + consonant + *-er*

céder *to yield*	espérer *to hope*	protéger *to protect*
célébrer *to celebrate*	posséder *to possess, own*	répéter *to repeat*

EXERCICE K

What do you do to relax? *Dites ce que vos amis et vous préférez faire.*

EXEMPLE:

Douglas **préfère** jouer au golf.

1.

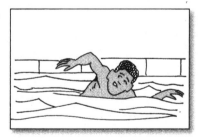

Michel _____ .

2.

Vous _____ .

3.

Tu _____ .

4.

Elles _____ .

5.

Nous _____ .

6.

Je _____ .

EXERCICE L

A classmate asks you and some of your friends to answer a few questions for a school survey. *Exprimez vos réponses en employant le verbe indiqué.*

1. (*préférer*)

   — Quel genre d'émission de télévision _____-vous?

   — Je _____ les dessins animés.

   — Nous _____ les drames policiers.

2. (*espérer*)

   — Qu'est-ce que vous _____ devenir?

   — J'_____ devenir médecin.

   — Nous _____ devenir avocats.

3. (*célébrer*)

   — Quelle fête _____—vous en décembre?

   — Je _____ mon anniversaire.

   — Nous _____ Noël.

4. (*posséder*)

   — Combien de voitures _____-vous?

   — Je _____ une voiture.

   — Nous _____ aussi une voiture.

5. (*répéter*)

   — Qu'est-ce que vous _____ souvent en classe?

   — Je _____ les mots de vocabulaire.

   — Nous _____ des poèmes.

MASTERY EXERCISES

EXERCICE M

Who does what? *Dites ce que font les personnes suivantes.*

élever des animaux   peser la vérité
employer un ordinateur   promener les enfants
jeter la balle   protéger le public
nettoyer la maison   répéter la leçon

1. Un joueur de base-ball _____ .

2. Un professeur _____ .

3. Une mère _____ .

4. Un agent de police _____ .

5. Un fermier _____ .

6. Un programmeur _____ .

7. Un juge _____ .

8. Une femme de ménage _____ .

EXERCICE N

Your teacher is curious about your household chores. *Écrivez ses questions et vos réponses selon l'exemple.*

EXEMPLE: arranger les meubles (non)
            Vous arrangez les meubles ?
            Non, je n'arrange pas les meubles.

1. promener le chien (oui)

_____

_____

2. changer les draps (non)

_____

_____

3. acheter les provisions (non)

_____

_____

4. nettoyer la maison (non)

_____

_____

5. renoncer à être paresseux/paresseuse (oui)

_____

_____

6. jeter les ordures (oui)

_____

_____

7. préférer travailler vite (oui)

_____

_____

8. payer les factures (non)

_____

_____

EXERCICE O

Your are a guest in a French home. Your host parents would like to know about your family habits. Practice writing what you plan on telling them. You may want to include:

- at what time you and your sister(s)/brother(s) begin your homework
- what you and your family eat for dinner
- the holidays you celebrate
- the sports you prefer
- where you travel

_____

_____

_____

_____

_____

Chapter 5
Verbs Irregular in the Present Tense

The following verbs are irregular in the present tense and must be memorized.

aller	écrire	lire	partir	recevoir	venir
avoir	être	mettre	pouvoir	savoir	voir
dire	faire	ouvrir	prendre	sortir	vouloir

NOTES:

1. For all irregular verbs, negative, interrogative, and negative interrogative constructions follow the same rules as regular verbs.

Pierre va en France cet été.	*Pierre is going to France this summer.*
Il ne voit pas bien.	*He does not see well.*
Claire vient ce soir ?	*Claire is coming tonight?*
Est-ce que tu le connais ?	*Do you know him?*
Est-elle intelligente ?	*Is she intelligent?*
Paul sort-il demain ?	*Is Paul going out tomorrow?*
Tu ne vas pas chez Anne ?	*Aren't you going to Anne's?*
Est-ce que tu ne sors pas ?	*Don't you go out?*

2. Verbs that end in a vowel in the third person singular add -*t*- before the pronoun *il, elle,* or *on* to separate the vowels in the inverted interrogative construction.

Où va-t-il ?	*Where is he going?*
A-t-elle le temps de venir ?	*Does she have time to come?*
Pourquoi ouvre-t-il la porte ?	*Why does he open the door?*

[1] *ALLER*: TO GO

je *vais*	nous allons
tu *vas*	vous allez
il/elle *va*	ils/elles *vont*

Je vais en France cet été.	*I am going to France this summer.*
Allez-vous en France cet été?	*Are you going to France this summer?*
Nous n'allons pas en France.	*We are not going to France.*

NOTE: Although the form *vais-je?* exists, it is rarely used.

a. Common expressions with *aller*:

aller + adverb *to feel, to be* (describing a state of health or a situation)

Comment allez-vous?	*How are you?*
Je vais bien.	*I'm fine.*
Les affaires vont mal.	*Business is bad.*

aller à pied *to walk, go on foot*

Je vais à l'école à pied.	*I walk to school.*

aller à la pêche *to go fishing*
aller en voiture *to go by car*

b. Forms of *aller* followed by an infinitive express a future action.

Je vais étudier.	*I am going to study.*
Qu'est-ce que tu vas faire?	*What are you going to do?*

EXERCICE A

The Lenoirs are shopping for their party tomorrow. *Dites dans quelles boutiques ils vont.*

EXEMPLE: Alice/au supermarché
            Alice **va** au supermarché.

1. M. et Mme Lenoir / à la boucherie

_____.

2. Geneviève / au marché

_____.

3. je / à la fruiterie

_____.

4. Maryse et moi, nous / à la boulangerie

_____.

5. tu / à la pâtisserie

_____.

6. vous / à la charcuterie

_____.

EXERCICE B

What shall we do today? *Utilisez les expressions données et dites ce que chacun va faire.*

M. Arnaud	aller au cinéma
je	dîner au restaurant
tu	écouter des CD
nous	jouer au basket
les garçons	regarder la télévision
vous	téléphoner à des copains
Jean	travailler

EXEMPLE: Jean **va** jouer au basket.

1. _____

2. _____

3. _____

4. _____

5. _____

6. _____

[2]   *AVOIR*: TO HAVE

j'*ai*	**nous avons**
tu *as*	**vous avez**
il/elle *a*	**ils/elles *ont***

J'ai un gros chien.	*I have a big dog.*
Je n'ai pas sommeil.	*I am not sleepy.*
Est-ce qu'elle a un frère ?	*Does she have a brother?*

NOTE: **Although the form *ai-je?* exists, it is rarely used.**

a. Common expressions with *avoir*:

avoir . . . ans *to be . . . years old.*

Quel âge as-tu?	*How old are you?*
J'ai vingt ans.	*I'm 20 years old.*

avoir besoin de *to need*

Elle a besoin d'un stylo.	*She needs a pen.*

avoir chaud *to be hot* (of persons)

Il a bien chaud.	*He is quite hot.*

avoir envie de *to desire, want*
    J'ai envie de rire.   *I want to laugh.*

avoir faim *to be hungry*
    J'ai toujours faim.   *I'm always hungry.*

avoir froid *to be cold* (of persons)
    Ce bébé a très froid.   *This baby is very cold.*

avoir honte (de) *to be ashamed of*
    Ils n'ont pas honte de leur faute.   *They aren't ashamed of their mistake.*

avoir mal à *to have an ache in*
    J'ai mal à la tête.   *I have a headache.*

avoir peur (de) *to be afraid (of)*
    Avez-vous peur des chiens?   *Are you afraid of dogs?*

avoir raison *to be right*
    Vous savez que j'ai raison.   *You know I'm right.*

avoir soif *to be thirsty*
    Donne-lui de l'eau. Il a soif.   *Give him some water. He's thirsty.*

avoir sommeil *to be sleepy*
    Éric n'a jamais sommeil.   *Eric is never sleepy.*

avoir tort *to be wrong*
    Il dit que nous avons tort.   *He says that we're wrong.*

b. Impersonal use of *avoir*

il y a *there is, there are*

y a-t-il? *is there?, are there?*

il n'y a pas *there is not, there are not*

n'y a-t-il pas? *isn't there?, aren't there?*

EXERCICE C

Your new French pen pal, Lise, has written her first letter to you. *Complétez la lettre avec la forme correcte du verbe* **avoir.**

Chère Renée

J' _____ treize ans et j' _____ envie d'avoir une amie américaine.
                1   2

Quel âge _____-tu? Ma sœur _____ dix ans et mon frère
                  3   4

_____ huit ans. Ma famille et moi, nous _____ une grande maison à
                    5   6

la campagne. Est-ce que vous _____ un appartement ou une maison?
                              7

_____-vous un jardin? Mes amies Nicole et Isabelle _____ des
                    8   9

cousins à New York. Elles désirent aller aux États-Unis, mais elles _____ peur
                                                                                      10

d'aller en avion; moi, je n' _____ pas peur et j'espère te rencontrer. À bientôt.
                            11

Lise

EXERCICE D

Décrivez les personnes suivantes.

1.

Il _____ .

2.

Nous _____ .

3.

Elles _____ .

4.

Vous _____ .

5.

Il _____

6.

Tu _____

EXERCICE E

Janine just arrived at the home of her friend. Replace the pictures with the correct words and fill in the appropriate form of *il y a* to describe what she sees.

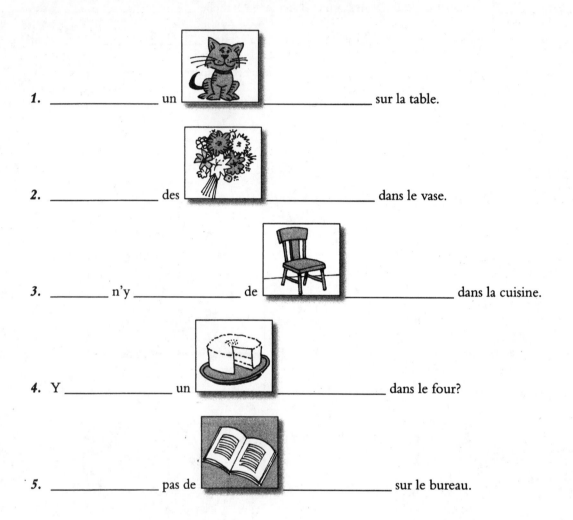

1. _____ un [cat] _____ sur la table.

2. _____ des [flowers] _____ dans le vase.

3. _____ n'y _____ de [chair] _____ dans la cuisine.

4. Y _____ un [cake] _____ dans le four?

5. _____ pas de [book] _____ sur le bureau.

[3]   *ÊTRE:* TO BE

je *suis*	nous *sommes*
tu *es*	vous *êtes*
il/elle *est*	ils/elles *sont*

Nous sommes prêts.   *We are ready.*

Ils ne sont pas contents.   *They are not pleased.*

Au moins es-tu heureux ?   *Are you happy at least?*

NOTE: Although the form *suis-je?* exists, it is rarely used.

Common expressions with *être*:

être à *to belong to*

À qui est cette montre ?   *Whose watch is this?*
Elle est à moi.   *It belongs to me.*

être en train de *to be (in the act of) doing something*

Je suis en train d'étudier.   *I'm studying.*

EXERCICE F

*Décrivez les personnes suivantes en employant la forme correcte du verbe **être**.*

1. Je _____ heureuse.

2. Elle _____ élégante.

3. Nous _____ intelligents.

4. Ils _____ charmants.

5. Vous _____ amusant.

6. Danielle et Anne _____ sociables.

7. Joseph _____ sympathique.

8. Tu _____ sérieux.

EXERCICE G

Describe what these people are doing by using the correct form of the expression *être en train de*.

EXEMPLE:

Paul et François **sont en train de jouer** au tennis.

1.

Anne and Nicole _____

_____ .

2.

Je _____

_____ .

3.

Vous _____

_____ .

4.

Ils _____

_____ .

5.

Tu _____

_____ .

6.

Grand-père _____

_____ .

[4] *FAIRE:* TO MAKE, DO

je *fais*	nous *faisons*
tu *fais*	vous *faites*
il/elle *fait*	ils/elles *font*

Maman fait un gâteau.   *Mom is making a cake.*
Il ne fait pas bien son travail.   *He does not do his work well.*
Fait-il un dessin?   *Is he making a drawing?*

a. Another verb conjugated like *faire*

refaire   *to redo*

b. Common expressions with *faire:*

faire attention (à) *to pay attention (to)*

Elle fait attention à la leçon.   *She pays attention to the lesson.*

faire des courses *to go shopping*

Il fait des courses avec sa mère.   *He goes shopping with his mother.*

faire une promenade *to go for a walk*

Mes parents font une
    promenade tous les soirs.

My parents go for a walk every
    evening.

faire un voyage (en avion, en voiture) *to take a trip (by plane, by car)*

Nous faisons un voyage en voiture.

We are taking a trip by car.

faire with weather expressions:

Quel temps fait-il?   *How's the weather?*
Il fait beau (temps).   *It's nice.*
Il fait mauvais (temps).   *It's bad weather.*
Il fait froid.   *It's cold.*
Il fait chaud.   *It's warm/hot.*
Il fait frais.   *It's cool.*
Il fait du vent.   *It's windy.*
Il fait du soleil.   *It's sunny.*

faire with sports expressions:

Nous faisons de la bicyclette.   *We go bicycling.*
Nous allons faire du basket.   *We are going to play basketball.*

EXERCICE H

What's happening today? *Exprimez ce que fait chacune des personnes suivantes.*

1. Philippe et Victor / faire un voyage en France

_____ .

2. je / faire des courses

_____ .

3. Régine / faire un voyage en voiture

_____ .

4. nous / faire une promenade

_____ .

5. vous / faire du bowling

_____ .

6. tu / faire attention en classe

_____ .

7. Lucien / faire du football

_____ .

8. les jeunes filles / faire du volley-ball

_____ .

EXERCICE I

Complete each sentence with an appropriate weather expression.

1. Quand il fait _____ , je marche dans le parc.

2. Quand il fait très _____ , je vais à la plage.

3. Quand il fait _____ , je fais du feu dans la cheminée.

4. Quand il fait _____ , je mets des lunettes de soleil.

[5]   *METTRE*: TO PUT (ON)

je *mets*	nous mettons
tu *mets*	vous mettez
il/elle *met*	ils/elles mettent

Je mets une robe verte.	*I put on a green dress.*
Mettons-nous le couvert?	*Do we set the table?*
Je ne mets pas le pain sur l'assiette.	*I do not put the bread on the plate.*

Other verbs conjugated like *mettre*:

permettre   *to allow*   remettre   *to put back; to deliver*

EXERCICE J

Décrivez les vêtements (clothes) *que les étudiants mettent pour aller danser à l'école.*

EXEMPLE:

Marie **met** un survêtement.

1.

2.

Ils _____ .   Janine _____ .

3.

Tu _____ .

4.

Nous _____ .

5.

Je _____ .

6.

Vous _____ .

[6] *OUVRIR*: TO OPEN

j'*ouvre*	**nous ouvrons**
tu *ouvres*	**vous ouvrez**
il/elle *ouvre*	**ils/elles ouvrent**

Le magasin ouvre à dix heures.	*The store opens at ten o'clock.*
Elle ouvre une boîte de thon.	*She opens a can of tuna fish.*
Est-ce que Pierre ouvre la porte?	*Does Pierre open the door?*

Another verb conjugated like *ouvrir*

découvrir   *to discover*

EXERCICE K

Your French class is having a party. Combine one element from each column. *Exprimez ce que chaque élève ouvre pour offrir à ses camarades.*

Claude et moi	un sac de chips
tu	une bouteille de soda
vous	une boîte de pâté
je	un paquet de bonbons
André	une corbeille de fruits
Anne et Sylvie	une barre de chocolat

1. _____ .
2. _____ .
3. _____ .
4. _____ .
5. _____ .
6. _____ .

[7] *PRENDRE*: TO TAKE

je prends	nous *prenons*
tu prends	vous *prenez*
il/elle prend	ils/elles *prennent*

Je prends du café le matin.	*I have coffee in the morning.*
Est-ce que tu prends le train?	*Do you take the train?*
Il ne prend pas la voiture ce matin.	*He's not taking the car this morning.*

Other verbs conjugated like *prendre*:

apprendre   *to learn*

comprendre   *to understand*

EXERCICE L

Dites comment chaque personne va à son travail.

EXEMPLE:

Jean **prend la bicyclette**.

1.

Vous _____ .

2.

Je _____ .

3.

Jean-Luc _____ .

4.

Nous _____ .

5.

Tu _____ .

6.

Alice et Berthe _____ .

[8]   *RECEVOIR:* TO RECEIVE

je *reçois*	nous recevons
tu *reçois*	vous recevez
il/elle *reçoit*	ils/elles *reçoivent*

Nous recevons le paquet. *We receive the package.*
Il ne reçoit pas la lettre. *He does not receive the letter.*
Est-ce qu'elle reçoit une récompense? *Does she receive a reward?*

EXERCICE M

C'est Noël! Dites ce que reçoit chaque membre de la famille Manet.

1.

Marianne _____

_____ .

2.

M. et Mme Manet _____

_____ .

3.

Je _____

_____ .

4.

Ma sœur et moi _____

_____ .

5.

Vous _____

_____ .

6.

Tu _____

_____ .

[9] *SAVOIR*: TO KNOW (HOW)

je *sais*	nous savons
tu *sais*	vous savez
il/elle *sait*	ils/elles savent

Claude sait la leçon. *Claude knows the lesson.*

Colette ne sait pas nager. *Colette does not know how to swim.*

Ne sais-tu pas la fin de l'histoire? *Don't you know how the story ends?*

NOTE: Although the form *sais-je?* exists, it is rarely used.

EXERCICE N

What can the following persons do? *Utilisez les suggestions ci-dessous.*

chanter   danser   parler français   préparer une mousse au chocolat
cuisiner   jouer au tennis   patiner

EXEMPLE: Ma sœur **sait** patiner.

1. Mes parents _____ .

2. Je _____ .

3. Mon ami et moi _____ .

4. Ma mère _____ .

5. Mon ami et vous _____ .

6. Tu _____ .

[*10*] *VENIR*: TO COME

je *viens*	**nous venons**
tu *viens*	**vous venez**
il/elle *vient*	ils/elles *viennent*

Stéphane vient ce soir.   *Stéphane is coming tonight.*

Est-ce que tes amis viennent?   *Are your friends coming?*

Vous ne venez pas avec nous.   *You are not coming with us.*

Other verbs conjugated like *venir*:

devenir   *to become*   revenir   *to come back*

EXERCICE O

Exprimez à quelle heure ces personnes viennent travailler.

EXEMPLE:

M. Dupont **vient à dix heures**.

1.

Je _____ .

2.

Mme Leclerc _____ .

3.

Vous _____ .

4.

Tu _____ .

5.

Les Martin _____ .

6.

Nous _____ .

[11] *VOIR*: TO SEE

je vois	nous *voyons*
tu vois	vous *voyez*
il/elle voit	ils/elles voient

Nous voyons des nuages noirs.   *We see black clouds.*
Le chat ne voit pas la souris.   *The cat does not see the mouse.*
Vois-tu le bateau sur le lac ?   *Do you see the boat on the lake?*

EXERCICE P

What do the Chenets and the Renauds see on their trip to Paris?

EXEMPLE: Lucien / le musée d'Orsay
              Lucien **voit** le musée d'Orsay.

1. nous / le Sacré-Cœur

_____

2. tu / les Invalides

_____

3. Mme Renaud / la tour Eiffel

_____

4. je / Notre-Dame

_____

5. vous / le Louvre

_____

6. les Chenet / l'Arc de Triomphe.

_____

[12] *POUVOIR*: TO BE ABLE TO, CAN / *VOULOIR*: TO WANT

je *peux*	nous pouvons
tu *peux*	vous pouvez
il/elle *peut*	ils/elles *peuvent*

je *veux*	nous voulons
tu *veux*	vous voulez
il/elle *veut*	ils/elles *veulent*

Pouvez–vous venir me voir?   *Can you come see me?*

Je peux venir demain, si tu veux.   *I can come tomorrow if you want.*

Ne peut-il pas comprendre?   *Can't he understand?*

Elle ne veut pas me parler.   *She does not want to speak to me.*

EXERCICE Q

Dites ce que chaque personne veut, mais ne peut pas, faire.

EXEMPLE: je / jouer de la guitare
                Je veux jouer de la guitare, mais **je ne peux pas.**

1. nous / aller au cinéma

_____

2. tu / lire des bandes dessinées

_____

3. Lucien / sortir jusqu'à minuit

_____

4. je / aller à la plage

_____

5. vous / faire du camping

_____

6. les garçons / écouter la radio

_____

7. Je / manger du chocolat

_____

8. Anne et Françoise / acheter des robes neuves

_____

[13] *PARTIR*: TO LEAVE, GO AWAY / *SORTIR*: TO GO OUT, TAKE OUT

je *pars*	nous partons
tu *pars*	vous partez
il/elle part	ils/elles partent

je *sors*	nous sortons
tu *sors*	vous sortez
il/elle sort	ils/elles sortent

Les Martin partent demain.	*The Martins are leaving tomorrow.*
Après tout, je ne pars pas.	*After all, I am not leaving.*
Ils ne partent pas demain?	*Aren't they leaving tomorrow?*
Vous sortez trop souvent.	*You go out too often.*
Sortez-vous ce soir?	*Are you going out tonight?*

EXERCICE R

Tell what each person is doing and when. *Donnez les formes correctes des verbes* partir *et* sortir.

EXEMPLE: je / danser / dans une heure
Je sors danser. Je pars dans une heure.

1. Sylvie / samedi soir / à sept heures

_____

2. vous / dîner / dans vingt minutes

_____

3. nous / au cinéma/à six heures

_____

4. Pierre / avec ses copains/dans quelques minutes

_____

5. tu / en auto / dans dix minutes

_____

6. elles / voir des amies / dans une demi-heure

_____

[14] *DIRE*: TO SAY / *ÉCRIRE*: TO WRITE / *LIRE*: TO READ

je dis	nous *disons*		j'écris	nous *écrivons*
tu dis	vous *dites*		tu écris	vous *écrivez*
il/elle dit	ils/elles *disent*		il/elle écrit	ils/elles *écrivent*

je lis	nous *lisons*
tu lis	vous *lisez*
il/elle lit	ils/elles *lisent*

Qu'est-ce que tu dis?	*What are you saying?*
Il ne dit jamais bonjour.	*He never says good morning.*
M. Brun lit un livre dans le train.	*Mr. Brun reads a book on the train.*
Je ne lis pas le journal.	*I don't read the newspaper.*
L'écrivain écrit chaque jour.	*The writer writes every day.*
Écrivez-vous à vos amis?	*Do you write to your friends?*

EXERCICE S

Complétez le texte suivant avec la forme correcte du verbe qui convient: **dire, écrire,** *ou* **lire.**

1. Je quitte la maison et je _____ «au revoir» à mes parents. Je _____ un journal en attendant le bus. J'_____ensuite une lettre à l'éditeur du journal.

2. Nous _____ un article. Nous _____ qu'il est injuste. Nous _____ à l'auteur.

3. Ils _____ à leurs correspondants. Ils _____ ce qu'ils font à l'école. Ils _____ leurs lettres au professeur.

4. Vous _____ le livre parce que vous _____ une composition pour la classe d'anglais. Vous _____ que le livre est intéressant.

5. Elle _____ des poèmes qu'elle _____ à ses amis. Ils _____ qu'ils sont excellents.

6. Tu _____ à ton oncle; tu lui _____ que tu _____ un livre extraordinaire.

MASTERY EXERCISES

EXERCICE T

We want to get to know you. *Répondez aux questions avec des phrases complètes.*

1. À quelle heure venez-vous à l'école?

_____

2. Que faites-vous le week-end?

_____

3. Où allez-vous passer les vacances?

_____

4. Combien de frères et de sœurs avez-vous?

_____

5. Quand êtes-vous content(e)?

_____

6. Savez-vous bien parler français?

_____

7. Quelle note recevez-vous dans la classe de français?

_____

8. À qui écrivez-vous des lettres?

_____

9. Quel moyen de transport prenez-vous pour aller à l'école?

_____

10. Qu'est-ce que vous voulez faire après les classes aujourd'hui?

_____

EXERCICE U

Complétez cette histoire avec les formes correctes des verbes indiqués.

Nous _____ un examen dans la classe de maths aujourd'hui et je ne
        1. (avoir)

_____ pas très content(e). Je _____ que les examens
        2. (être)   **3.** (savoir)

de maths sont toujours difficiles. Je _____ de ma maison à sept heures.
                                      4. (partir)

Je _____ le train et je _____ à l'école de très bonne heure.
      5. (prendre)   **6.** (aller)

J'arrive à la salle de classe et j' _____ tranquillement la porte. Je
                                    7. (ouvrir)

_____ mes livres sur mon pupitre. Je _____ étudier mais je ne
    8. (mettre)   **9.** (vouloir)

_____ pas parce que je _____ deux de mes amis en train de parler
   10. (pouvoir)   **11.** (voir)

et de rire. Je leur _____ que je _____ de mon mieux pour étudier.
                    12. (dire)   **13.** (faire)

Je _____ toutes mes notes. Je _____ un stylo. J' _____
    14. (lire)   **15.** (prendre)   **16.** (écrire)

des exemples dans mon cahier. À huit heures et demie le professeur et tous les autres élèves

_____ dans la classe et l'examen commence. Je _____ mon examen;
   17. (venir)   **18.** (recevoir)

je le regarde et je pousse un soupir de soulagement car il est très facile.

EXERCICE V

Express what the people do by choosing the missing verb from the list provided. _Conjuguez le verbe._

aller	avoir	écrire	être	faire
partir	pouvoir	prendre	recevoir	venir

1. Nous _____ en train de faire nos devoirs.

2. Vous _____ souvent une promenade.

3. Je _____ toujours à l'école à pied.

4. Elle _____ très bien parler français.

5. Tu _____ besoin d'un dictionnaire pour finir tes devoirs.

6. Ils _____ du thé le matin.

7. Les garçons _____ un article pour le journal scolaire.

8. Je _____ une lettre de ma correspondante.

9. Les Leduc _____ pour la France demain.

10. Lise _____ chez moi cet après-midi.

EXERCICE W

You are looking for a job with a French firm. Write a short note in French to the personnel director in which you tell him about yourself. You may want to include:

- your age
- what you want to do
- languages you read and write
- other things you know how to do
- questions about your responsibilities
- your personality traits

_____

_____

_____

_____

_____

_____

Chapter 6
Imperative

The imperative is a verb form used to give commands or suggestions.

1. IMPERATIVE OF REGULAR VERBS

a. Forms of the imperative

Most are the same as the corresponding forms of the present tense, except for the omission of the subject pronouns *tu*, *vous*, and *nous*.

FAMILIAR / SINGULAR		FORMAL / PLURAL		FIRST PERSON PLURAL	
Joue!	*Play!*	Jouez!	*Play!*	Jouons!	*Let's play!*
Finis!	*Finish!*	Finissez!	*Finish!*	Finissons!	*Let's finish!*
Descends!	*Go down!*	Descendez!	*Go down!*	Descendons!	*Let's do down!*

NOTE: The familiar imperative of *-er* verbs drops the final *-s* of the present tense form.

Tu joues bien.	**Joue** bien!	*Play well!*
Tu écoutes la radio.	**Écoute** la radio!	*Listen to the radio!*
Tu travailles vite.	**Travaille** vite!	*Work quickly!*

EXERCICE A

Your parents are leaving on vacation and you are staying home alone. *Exprimez leurs instructions.*

EXEMPLE: cuisiner les repas tous les jours
Cuisine les repas tous les jours!

1. parler à tes grands-parents chaque jour

_____

2. donner à manger au chien

_____

3. dîner avec ta sœur et ton frère

_____

4. rentrer tout de suite après l'école

_____

5. vider les ordures tous les jours

_____

6. téléphoner à notre hôtel en cas de problème

7. garder ta sœur et ton frère

_____

8. aider ton frère avec ses devoirs

_____

EXERCICE B

Your friends are going away to college. *Quels conseils (advice) leur donnez-vous?*

EXEMPLE: (*bâtir*) **Bâtissez** des amitiés solides.

1. (*obéir*) _____ à tous les règlements.
2. (*remplir*) _____ toujours tous les formulaires nécessaires.
3. (*réussir*) _____ en tout.
4. (*saisir*) _____ chaque occasion.
5. (*finir*) _____ tout ce que vous commencez.
6. (*choisir*) _____ des cours intéressants.

EXERCICE C

You are going away to France as an exchange student. *Exprimez les conseils de vos parents.*

EXEMPLE: perdre ton accent américain
  Perds ton accent américain!

1. répondre à toutes les questions de tes hôtes

_____

2. descendre souvent en ville

_____

3. défendre tes idées

_____

4. correspondre avec tes amis

_____

5. rendre tout ce que tu empruntes

_____

6. attendre le succès avec patience

_____

EXERCICE D

Nicole is babysitting for her little brother and sister. *Dites ce qu'elle leur dit de faire.*

EXEMPLE:

Sautons à la corde!

1.

_____ une ronde!

2.

_____ une chanson!

3.

_____ ce compact!

4.

_____ nos croissants!

5.

_____ notre verre de lait!

6.

_____ la télévision!

b. Negative imperative constructions

In the negative imperative, _ne_ and _pas_ surround the verb.

Ne parle pas si fort!	_Don't speak so loudly!_
Ne désobéissez pas!	_Don't disobey!_
Ne marchons pas si vite!	_Let's not walk so fast!_

EXERCICE E

You have been hired as a cashier in a department store. *Exprimez ce que le directeur vous dit.*

EXEMPLE: parler trop
Ne parlez pas trop!

1. vendre la marchandise au rabais *(discounted)*

_____

2. désobéir au règlement du magasin

_____

3. arriver en retard

_____

4. oublier d'être poli avec tous les clients

_____

5. rougir quand vous parlez aux clients

_____

6. acheter tout ce que vous voulez

_____

7. perdre patience avec les clients

_____

8. menacer les clients

_____

EXERCICE F

You are working as a secretary and want to make sure that you are doing what you are supposed to. *Écrivez la réponse de votre patron (boss) à chacune de vos questions.*

EXEMPLES: Je travaille jusqu'à 5 heures ? (oui)
Oui, travaillez jusqu'à 5 heures !

Je travaille jusqu'à 5 heures ? (non)
Non, ne travaillez pas jusqu'à 5 heures.

1. J'attends toujours des instructions? (oui)

_____

2. Je remplis ces formulaires? (non)

_____

3. Je garde ces papiers dans mon bureau? (non)

_____

4. Je saisis chaque occasion de réussir? (oui)

_____

5. Je copie ces documents? (non)

_____

6. Je finis le travail de M. Dumont? (oui)

_____

7. Je corresponds avec les clients? (non)

_____

8. Je rends ces livres à Mme Bertrand? (oui)

_____

9. J'emploie cette machine à écrire? (non)

_____

10. Je répète ces phrases? (oui)

_____

EXERCICE G

You and your friends are making plans for the French club's food festival. Your friend makes some suggestions that you don't like. _Menez le dialogue suivant avec un(e) camarade._

EXEMPLE: donner les recettes aux participants
VOTRE AMI(E): **Donnons** les recettes aux participants !
VOUS: **Non, ne donnons pas** les recettes aux participants !

1. vendre trois sortes de boissons

    VOTRE AMI(E): _____

    VOUS: _____

2. finir tout le travail au dernier moment

    VOTRE AMI(E): _____

    VOUS: _____

3. acheter beaucoup de desserts

    VOTRE AMI(E): _____

    VOUS: _____

4. rôtir beaucoup de viandes différentes

    VOTRE AMI(E): _____

    VOUS: _____

5. amener nos parents à la fête

    VOTRE AMI(E): _____

    VOUS: _____

6. décorer la salle de fête

    VOTRE AMI(E): _____

    VOUS: _____

[2] IMPERATIVE OF IRREGULAR VERBS

The imperative of irregular verbs generally follows the same pattern as regular verbs.

lire	*to read*	*lis, lisez, lisons*
faire	*to do*	*fais, faites, faisons*
partir	*to leave*	*pars, partez, partons*
venir	*to come*	*viens, venez, venons*

NOTES:

1. Verbs conjugated like *-er* verbs in the present tense and the verb *aller* drop the final *-s* in the familiar command form.

    Tu ouvres le cadeau.   **Ouvre** le cadeau!   *Open the gift!*

    Tu vas au magasin.   **Va** au magasin!   *Go to the store!*

2. The verbs *avoir*, *être*, and *savoir* have irregular forms in the imperative.

avoir	*to have*	**aie, ayez, ayons**
être	*to be*	**sois, soyez, soyons**
savoir	*to know*	**sache, sachez, sachons**

EXERCICE H

You are going to visit friends for the weekend and your mother gives you some instructions. *Exprimez ce qu'elle vous dit.*

EXEMPLE: (*nettoyer*) **Nettoie** ta chambre.

1. (*être*) _____ toujours poli(e)!

2. (*acheter*) _____ des fleurs pour l'hôtesse!

3. (*mettre*) _____ la table!

4. (*avoir*) _____ la gentillesse d'aider la famille!

5. (*faire*) _____ ton lit tous les jours!

6. (*prendre*) _____ soin de tes affaires!

EXERCICE I

You and your sister are helping in the kitchen while your mother hurries to finish preparing a special dinner. *Exprimez ce que votre mère vous dit de faire.*

EXEMPLE: préparer la salade
            Préparez la salade!

1. prendre un plat dans le placard (*cabinet*)

2. faire le dessert

_____

3. aller au marché

_____

4. mettre les légumes dans le réfrigérateur

_____

5. lire la recette

_____

6. ouvrir une boîte de conserves

_____

7. sortir de la cuisine

_____

8. dire bonjour aux invités

_____

EXERCICE J

You're going out on your first date and your parents have some advice for you. _Exprimez ce qu'ils disent._

EXEMPLE: parler trop
          Ne parle pas trop!

1. être timide

_____

2. avoir peur

_____

3. faire le clown

_____

4. prétendre tout savoir

_____

5. revenir tard

_____

6. dire: «Je t'aime»

_____

EXERCICE K

You are on a tour with other students and the counselor gives the group the following instructions before leaving the airport. _Exprimez ce qu'il dit._

EXEMPLE: venir ici
Venez ici!

1. mettre les valises dans le car *(tour bus)*

_____

2. monter rapidement dans le car

_____

3. être responsables

_____

4. écouter le conducteur

_____

5. obéir à tous les règlements

_____

6. prendre soin de votre appareil photo

_____

7. lire l'itinéraire avec attention

_____

8. dire «merci» au conducteur

_____

EXERCICE L

You and some friends are in Québec for *Carnaval.* **The hotel manager gives you some advice.**
Exprimez ce qu'il dit.

EXEMPLE: On apporte beaucoup d'argent? (non)
Non, **n'apportez pas** beaucoup d'argent!

1. On emploie un guide? (oui)

_____

2. On achète des masques? (oui)

_____

3. On va à pied? (oui)

_____

4. On a peur? (non)

_____

5. On est prêt à quitter l'hôtel à 8 heures? (oui)

_____

6. On prend le bus? (non)

_____

7. On fait le tour de la ville? (non)

_____

8. On voit tout? (oui)

_____

9. On met des costumes? (oui)

_____

10. On rentre à deux heures du matin? (non)

_____

EXERCICE M

You are trying to make vacation plans with a friend who can't make up his/her mind. _Exprimez ses réponses quand vous suggérez certaines activités._

EXEMPLE: camper dans les montagnes:
          VOUS: **Campons** dans les montagnes !
          VOTRE AMI(E): **Ne campons pas** dans les montagnes !

1. aller au bord de la mer

    VOUS: _____

    VOTRE AMI(E): _____

2. nager dans un lac

    VOUS: _____

    VOTRE AMI(E): _____

3. faire le tour du monde

    VOUS: _____

    VOTRE AMI(E): _____

4. sortir tous les soirs

    VOUS: _____

    VOTRE AMI(E): _____

5. voir les îles Caraïbes

    VOUS: _____

    VOTRE AMI(E): _____

6. prendre l'avion à Nice

    VOUS: _____

    VOTRE AMI(E): _____

M A S T E R Y   E X E R C I S E S

EXERCICE N

Your friends always ask you for advice. *Exprimez ce que vous leur dites.*

EXEMPLE: La voiture de Richard ne marche pas.
           (emprunter la voiture de ton frère)
           Emprunte la voiture de ton frère!

1. Georgette veut résoudre les problèmes de l'atmosphère.

    (prendre ta bicyclette)

    _____

2. La petite amie de Georges ne veut pas aller à la fête de Michel.

    (aller tout seul)

    _____

3. Robert perd toujours quelque chose.

    (faire attention)

    _____

4. Alice ne veut pas aller patiner parce que ses amies n'y vont pas.

    (être plus indépendante)

    _____

5. Suzanne travaille et vient de toucher son premier chèque.

    (mettre de l'argent à la banque)

    _____

6. Philippe voudrait aller en France mais il n'a pas assez d'argent.

    (avoir un peu de patience)

    _____

EXERCICE O

You are moving into a new house and the moving van has arrived. The movers ask you questions. *Exprimez vos réponses.*

EXEMPLE: Je monte cette chaise ? (non)
           Non, **ne montez pas** cette chaise!

1. Je descends ce carton ? (oui)

    _____

2. Je ferme cette porte ? (non)

    _____

3. Je mets le divan ici ? (non)

    _____

4. Je sors cette lampe de la cuisine ? (oui)

_____

5. J'enlève cette couverture en plastique ? (oui)

_____

6. Je vais dans le garage ? (non)

_____

7. J'essuie ce miroir? (oui)

_____

8. Je jette cette boîte ? (oui)

_____

9. Je fais le nettoyage ? (non)

_____

10. J'ouvre ce paquet ? (non)

_____

EXERCICE P

Your friend is going on an interview. Give him/her advice. You may want to include the following:

- what (not) to wear
- what (not) to say
- how (not) to act
- when (not) to arrive
- what paperwork to bring along

_____

_____

_____

_____

_____

_____

_____

_____

Chapter 7
Passé composé of Regular *avoir* Verbs

[1] AFFIRMATIVE CONSTRUCTIONS

The *passé composé* is a past tense composed of two parts: the present tense of the auxiliary (or 'helping') verb and the past participle of the main verb. For most verbs, the auxiliary verb is *avoir* (to have).

chanter *to sing*	**finir** *to finish*	**vendre** *to sell*
I sang, I have sung	*I finished, I have finished*	*I sold, I have sold*
j' *ai* chanté	j' *ai* fin*i*	j' *ai* vend*u*
tu *as* chanté	tu *as* fin*i*	tu *as* vend*u*
il/elle *a* chanté	il/elle *a* fin*i*	il/elle *a* vend*u*
nous *avons* chanté	nous *avons* fin*i*	nous *avons* vend*u*
vous *avez* chanté	vous *avez* fin*i*	vous *avez* vend*u*
ils/elles *ont* chanté	ils/elles *ont* fin*i*	ils/elles *ont* vend*u*

NOTES:

1. The past participle of *-er* verbs is formed by dropping *-er* and adding *-é*.

Tu as parlé à Marie.	*You spoke to Marie.*
Il a écouté des CD.	*He listened to CDs.*
Vous avez ennuyé Luc.	*You bothered Luc.*
Elles ont acheté des robes.	*They bought dresses.*

2. The past participle of *-ir* verbs is formed by dropping the *-r*.

J'ai fin*i* mes devoirs.	*I finished my work.*
Nous avons maigr*i*.	*We have become thin.*
Vous avez rempl*i* le verre.	*You have filled the glass.*
Elles ont désobé*i*.	*They disobeyed.*

3. The past participle of *-re* verbs is formed by dropping *-re* and adding *-u*.

J'ai vend*u* ma maison.	*I have sold my house.*
Tu as perd*u* ton livre.	*You have lost your book.*
Vous avez défend*u* vos amis.	*You defended your friends.*
Ils ont rend*u* mon argent.	*They gave back my money.*

EXERCICE A

Exprimez ce que Pierre et sa famille ont fait (did) hier soir.

EXEMPLE: Lucien/jouer au tennis
Lucien **a joué** au tennis.

1. je / patiner

_____

2. papa / travailler

_____

3. Jules et moi / regarder une émission à la télévision

_____

4. maman / préparer le dîner

_____

5. vous / téléphoner à des copains

_____

6. mes parents / écouter les informations

_____

7. tu / ranger ta chambre

_____

8. Louise et Gabrielle / dîner au restaurant

_____

EXERCICE B

M. Dumas had to go away on business. *Racontez ce que ses amis ont fait (did)* **pour *l'aider pendant son absence.***

1. (*laver*) Jean et Paul _____ sa voiture.

2. (*vider*) J'_____ les ordures.

3. (*promener*) Lucienne _____ son chien.

4. (*passer*) Nous _____ l'aspirateur.

5. (*nettoyer*) Tu _____ la maison.

6. (*ranger*) Lise et Cécile _____ le salon.

7. (*placer*) Vous _____ le courrier sur la table.

8. (*donner*) Henri _____ à manger à ses poissons.

EXERCICE C

Exprimez ce que ces personnes ont fait (did) hier matin.

1. (*finir*) J' _____ mon travail tôt.

2. (*obéir*) Les enfants _____ à leurs parents.

3. (*choisir*) Nous _____ d'aller en France.

4. (*punir*) Le professeur _____ le mauvais élève.

5. (*guérir*) Vous _____ le malade.

6. (*réussir*) Tu _____ à ton examen.

EXERCICE D

Exprimez ce que ces personnes ont fait (did) avant-hier.

EXEMPLE: Michel / rendre de l'argent à Jacques
            Michel **a rendu** de l'argent à Jacques.

1. Jean / perdre son portefeuille

   _____

2. Annette et René / entendre de bonnes nouvelles

   _____

3. je / attendre mon ami pendant une heure

   _____

4. vous / défendre à Victor de sortir

   _____

5. nous / répondre à une annonce publicitaire

   _____

6. tu / vendre ta bicyclette

   _____

[2] USES OF THE *PASSÉ COMPOSÉ*

The *passé composé* **is used to narrate an action or event completed in the past. It has several English equivalents.**

J'ai téléphoné à mes amis.	*I (have) called my friends.*
Nous avons écouté des disques.	*We listened to records.*
Elle a déjà parlé à Claude.	*She has already spoken to Claude.*

NOTE: **Some expressions that are often used with the** *passé composé* **are:**

l'année passée, l'année dernière   last year

avant-hier   the day before yesterday

hier   yesterday

hier soir   last night

le mois passé, le mois dernier   last month

la semaine passée, la semaine dernière   last week

EXERCICE E

Complete this letter that Hélène wrote to a friend while in Canada. *Écrivez la forme correcte des verbes au passé composé.*

Chère Gabrielle,

Hier soir j' _____ à une fête chez mon amie Lucienne. Tout le monde
       1. (assister)

_____ l'anniversaire de sa sœur cadette, Denise. Beaucoup de personnes
   2. (célébrer)

_____ à la fête et Denise _____ de joie à voir tous les cadeaux
   3. (assister)   4. (crier)

pour elle. La fête _____ le soir après le dîner. À neuf heures précises,
                        5. (commencer)

j' _____ ses amis. Ils _____ «Bon anniversaire» à Denise et après,
   6. (entendre)   7. (chanter)

tout le monde _____ à danser. Nous _____ des spécialités
                   8. (commencer)   9. (manger)

canadiennes. Sa mère _____ tous les plats et elle _____ un grand
                          10. (cuisiner)   11. (préparer)

gâteau au chocolat. Je suis sûre que j' _____ parce que j' _____
                                            12. (grossir)   13. (finir)

tout ce que j' _____ . J' _____ la fin de la fête avant de rentrer.
                  14. (choisir)   15. (attendre)

Quelle fête formidable! à très bientôt.

Grosses bises,

Hélène

EXERCICE F

Last year Catherine, Isabelle, Pierre, and Claude went with their classmates to the Alps to attend a 'snow class' (*une classe de neige*). *Racontez leur voyage avec le passé composé des verbes indiqués.*

attendre	durer	finir	neiger	réussir
choisir	écouter	habiter	partager	voyager
commencer	entendre	montrer	passer	

1. Tous les élèves _____ ce voyage avec joie.

2. Les élèves et les professeurs _____ en train.

3. Le voyage _____ à la gare de Lyon à Paris.

4. Le voyage _____ six heures.

5. Les élèves et les professeurs _____ un chalet sur la montagne.

6. Catherine et Isabelle _____ une chambre avec Lise.

7. Pierre et Claude _____ le dortoir des garçons.

8. Quand ils _____ le dîner, ils _____
   à dormir malgré leur excitation.

9. Il _____ toute la nuit.

10. Un professeur _____ comment skier prudemment et les élèves
_____ attentivement.

11. Plus tard, ils _____ un programme sur les montagnes.

12. Ils _____ deux semaines merveilleuses aux sports d'hiver.
La classe de neige est une idée formidable.

[3] NEGATIVE AND INTERROGATIVE CONSTRUCTIONS

a. In a negative sentence in the passé composé, *ne* precedes the helping verb and *pas* follows it.

Il *n*'a *pas* expliqué le problème.   *He did not explain the problem.*
Vous *n*'avez *pas* réussi.   *You did not succeed.*
Nous *n*'avons *pas* encore vendu la maison.   *We have not yet sold the house.*

EXERCICE G

You and your friends are comparing what you've accomplished so far. *Exprimez ce que vous n'avez pas encore fait.*

camper dans les montagnes   répondre à toutes les questions
choisir où habiter   réussir à tous les examens
entendre mon chanteur favori   visiter Paris
gagner le championnat de tennis   voyager au Canada
jouer du piano dans un concert

EXEMPLE: Nous **n'avons pas** encore **visité** Paris.

1. Les garçons _____ .

2. Vous _____ .

3. Annick _____ .

4. Je _____ .

5. Louise et Janine _____ .

6. Tu _____ .

7. Pierre _____

8. Serge et moi _____

EXERCICE H

Your mother has invited some friends to celebrate Bastille Day. She is worried that everything is not yet ready. *Écrivez ce qu'elle dit.*

EXEMPLE: je / finir / tous les préparatifs
    Je n'ai pas fini tous les préparatifs.

1. les filles / nettoyer / la salle de bains

_____

2. Pierre / cueillir / les fleurs

_____

3. Christine / tondre / la pelouse (*lawn*)

_____

4. vous / acheter / les boissons

_____

5. nous / descendre / les chaises dans le jardin

_____

6. tu / amener / les chiens chez les voisins

_____

7. la cuisinière / rôtir / les poulets

_____

8. Marie et toi / apporter / les patisseries

_____

    b. **A question may be indicated with intonation alone, or it can be formed by beginning the sentence with *est-ce que*.**

Tu as répondu à sa lettre?	*Have you answered her letter?*
Est-ce que tu as lavé la vaisselle?	*Did you wash the dishes?*
Est-ce qu'elle a fini ses devoirs?	*Has she finished her homework?*

    Inversion may also be used in the *passé composé* by inverting the subject pronoun and the auxiliary verb.

As-tu étudié la grammaire?	*Did you study the grammar?*
As-tu fini tes devoirs?	*Have you finished your homework?*
Ont-elles répondu à la lettre?	*Have they answered the letter?*

EXERCICE I

Demandez à vos amis ce qu'ils ont fait pendant leurs vacances.

EXEMPLE: Luc / pêcher dans le lac
             Est-ce que Luc **a pêché** dans le lac?

1. Lise / patiner

_____

2. Arnaud et Jean / réussir à courir le marathon

_____

3. Les Lelong / dîner dans un restaurant élégant

_____

4. Joséphine et Marie / choisir de voyager en avion

_____

5. Pierre / attendre ses amis pour partir

_____

6. M. et Mme Carré / camper au Canada

_____

EXERCICE J

You have just returned from a trip to France. Answer the questions your friend asks you. *Utilisez les indications données.*

1. Quel pays as-tu visité ? (la France)

_____

2. Avec qui as-tu voyagé ? (ma famille)

_____

3. Combien de temps avez-vous passé en France ? (quinze jours)

_____

4. Qui a choisi d'aller en France ? (mes parents)

_____

5. Quel moyen de transport avez-vous employé en France ? (le train)

_____

6. Quel endroit as-tu préféré ? (la Provence)

_____

EXERCICE K

Your parents gave you a list of things to do while they were away. *Exprimez leurs questions et vos réponses basées sur la liste suivante.*

ranger le salon	chauffer le dîner
laver la voiture ✓	finir le jardinage ✓
trouver les clefs	promener le chien
fermer toutes les fenêtres	descendre les bagages ✓
téléphoner à l'électricien ✓	nettoyer la cuisine ✓

80   Chapter 7

EXEMPLES: **As-tu rangé** le salon?
Non, je n'ai pas encore rangé le salon.

As-tu lavé la voiture?
Oui, j'ai déjà lavé la voiture.

1. _____

_____

2. _____

_____

3. _____

_____

4. _____

_____

5. _____

_____

6. _____

_____

7. _____

_____

8. _____

_____

   c. A negative interrogative sentence in the *passé composé* may be indicated
   with intonation alone, or it can be formed by beginning the sentence
   with *est-ce que.*

   Jean **n'a pas** dansé?   *Didn't Jean dance?*
   Est-ce que Jean **n'a pas** dansé?   *Didn't Jean dance?*

EXERCICE L

You are looking through your brother's yearbook. *Posez des questions (ask questions) sur certains étudiants.*

EXEMPLE: Claude Delbart / étudier la médecine
Est-ce que Claude Delbart **n'a pas étudié** la médicine?

1. Bernard Besset / gagner à la loterie

_____

2. Ginette Fleurat / épouser le professeur de biologie

_____

3. Jean Legrand / participer aux Jeux Olympiques

_____

4. Nicolas Loiseau / dépenser une fortune en bandes dessinées *(comic books)*

_____

5. Aimée Savin / finir ses études

_____

6. Catherine Fleury / réussir une chanson populaire

_____

M A S T E R Y   E X E R C I S E S

EXERCICE M

You and some friends spent a weekend in another city. *Racontez ce que vous avez fait.*

1. nous / oublier tous nos problèmes

_____

2. je / dépenser beaucoup d'argent

_____

3. vous / choisir de visiter des musées

_____

4. tu / envoyer des cartes postales à des amis

_____

5. Anne et Jacques / jouer au volley-ball

_____

6. Claire / répondre à beaucoup de questions

_____

7. Henri et Jeanne / acheter des affiches

_____

8. Robert / perdre un peu d'argent

_____

EXERCICE N

While visiting Montreal, you run into someone who spent a year at your school as an exchange student. You bring her up to date about yourself and other people she knew, and you ask about herself. *Utilisez le passé composé.*

EXEMPLES: Édouard / réussir à son examen.
            Édouard a réussi à son examen.

            Tu / choisir une université?
            Tu as choisi une université?

1. M. Lecomte / changer de travail

_____

2. je / commencer à conduire une voiture

_____

3. Lucie et moi / voyager à l'étranger

_____

4. tu / finir ton bac?

_____

5. le directeur / renvoyer M. Lechat

_____

6. Lola / gagner une bourse?

_____

7. Mlle Legrand / annoncer sa retraite

_____

8. M. Pierrot / vendre sa vieille motocyclette

_____

9. Tu / décider où travailler?

_____

10. Michel et Charles / choisir de devenir avocats

_____

EXERCICE O

Dites ce qui s'est passé (happened) hier.

EXEMPLE: écouter son CD préféré (non)
           François **n'a pas écouté** son CD préféré hier.

1. envoyer une lettre à Georgette (oui)

   Paul _____ .

2. réussir à l'examen de chimie (oui)

   Lise et Marie _____ .

3. achever un grand projet scientifique (oui)

   Paul et moi _____ .

4. perdre son sac (non)

   Berthe _____ .

5. changer vos chaussettes (non)

   Vous _____ .

6. célébrer mon anniversaire (oui)

   J'_____ .

7. attendre l'autobus après l'école (non)

   Jean et Luc _____ .

8. déjeuner sur l'herbe (non)

   Tu _____ .

EXERCICE P

Your friend had a party that you could not attend because you were away. Write him / her a note asking about it. You may want to ask:

- whom he/she invited
- the CDs everyone listened to
- who danced with whom
- what food was served
- at what time the guests left
- what gifts he/she received

_____

_____

_____

_____

_____

_____

_____

_____

Chapter 8
Verbs Irregular in the *passé composé*

All irregular verbs follow the same rules as regular verbs for negative, interrogative, and negative interrogative constructions in the *passé composé*.

The following verbs have irregular past participles:

apprendre	dire	faire	ouvrir	recevoir	voir
avoir	écrire	lire	pouvoir	savoir	vouloir
comprendre	être	mettre	prendre		

[1] PAST PARTICIPLES ENDING IN -U

avoir	to have	**eu**	**savoir**	to know	**su**
lire	to read	**lu**	**voir**	to see	**vu**
pouvoir	to be able to	**pu**	**vouloir**	to want	**voulu**
recevoir	to receive	**reçu**			

Paul a reçu deux lettres.	*Paul received two letters.*
Je n'ai pas vu ce film.	*I haven't seen this film.*
Avez-vous lu ce livre?	*Did you read this book?*

EXERCICE A

Each of the following students was absent yesterday. *Exprimez pourquoi.*

EXEMPLE: Jean / mal à l'estomac
Jean **a eu** mal à l'estomac.

1. je / mal à la gorge

_____

2. vous / la grippe

_____

3. ils / de la fièvre

_____

4. nous / mal au ventre

_____

EXERCICE B

Tell what each person read before going to bed last night. *Employez les suggestions ci-dessous.*

des bandes dessinées   une histoire d'amour
des poèmes   un roman policier
le journal

EXEMPLE: J'**ai lu** des poèmes.

1. Claire _____

2. Vous _____

3. Tu _____

4. Les jeunes filles _____

EXERCICE C

These students had to study for a test yesterday. *Dites ce qu'ils n'ont pas pu faire.*

EXEMPLE: Marc **n'a pas pu** aller dans une discothèque.

1. Vous _____ jouer au tennis.

2. Nous _____ descendre en ville.

3. Tu _____ dîner au restaurant.

4. Michel et Éric _____ finir leurs devoirs.

EXERCICE D

Each person received a gift for his/her birthday this year. *Dites ce que chacun a reçu.*

EXEMPLE:

Jean **a reçu une bicyclette.**

1.

Grand-père _____

_____.

2.

Émile et Henri _____

_____.

3.

Tu _____

_____ .

4.

Je _____

_____ .

EXERCICE E

The following students were finalists in a contest. *Dites ce qu'ils ont su.*

EXEMPLE: Marie / le nom de la capitale du Maroc.
Marie **a su** le nom de la capitale du Maroc.

1. je / épeler «théâtre»

_____

2. Paul / répondre à toutes les questions

_____

3. vous/jouer du violon

_____

4. nous/la table de multiplication par 9

_____

EXERCICE F

Each person saw something in René's backyard. *Dites ce que chacun a vu.*

EXEMPLE:

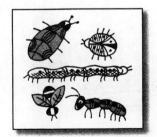

Vous **avez vu des insectes.**

1.

Nous _____

_____ .

2.

Tu _____

_____ .

3.

J' _____

_____ .

4.

Fernande et Simone _____

_____ .

EXERCICE G

Tell what each person wanted to do last Saturday. *Employez les suggestions ci-dessous.*

marcher dans le parc	rester à la maison	voir un film
partir à la campagne	sortir avec des copains	

EXEMPLE: nous/partir à la campagne
Nous avons voulu partir à la campagne.

1. Simon et Luc _____

2. Sylvie et moi _____

3. Tu _____

4. Vous _____

[2] PAST PARTICIPLES ENDING IN *-IS*

apprendre	*to learn*	*appris*	mettre	*to put*	*mis*
comprendre	*to understand*	*compris*	prendre	*to take*	*pris*

L'élève a bien appris la leçon.   *The pupil has learned the lesson well.*
Les enfants n'ont pas compris.   *The children did not understand.*
Avez-vous pris le livre?   *Did you take the book?*

EXERCICE H

Exprimez ce que ces élèves ont mis dans leur cartable (school bag).

EXEMPLE: Sylvie **a mis** des papiers.

1. J'_____ .

2. Vous _____ .

3. Josette et Colette _____ .

4. Tu _____ .

EXERCICE I

The following travelers forgot to pack certain things. *Dites ce qu'ils ont oublié.*

EXEMPLE: tu/tes chèques de voyage
   Tu n'as pas pris tes chèques de voyage.

1. Yvonne/sa brosse à dents

_____

2. je/mon permis de conduire

_____

3. vous/votre appareil photo

_____

4. Solange et moi/nos cartes de crédit

_____

[3] PAST PARTICIPLES ENDING IN *-IT*

dire *to say*	*dit*	écrire *to write*	*écrit*

Il a écrit une lettre à sa mère. — *He wrote a letter to his mother.*
Vous n'avez pas dit merci! — *You did not say "Thank you"!*
A-t-il écrit un roman? — *Did he write a novel?*

EXERCICE J

Paul has been accepted by a top university. *Exprimez ce que ses amis lui ont dit en employant les suggestions données.*

bonne chance	c'est magnifique	félicitations
c'est formidable	c'est super	

EXEMPLE: Raymond **a dit:** «C'est magnifique!»

1. Vous _____ .
2. J' _____ .
3. Tu _____ .
4. Nadine et Colette _____ .

EXERCICE K

Ask questions about work that was submitted for publication in the school magazine.

EXEMPLE: Denis/un bon livre
Est-ce que Denis a écrit un bon livre?

1. Roger et moi/de bons poèmes

_____

2. vous/un article intéressant

_____

3. tu/une histoire romantique

_____

4. Bruno /un éditorial intelligent

_____

[4] OTHER IRREGULAR PAST PARTICIPLES

être *to be*	*été*	ouvrir *to open*	*ouvert*
faire *to do*	*fait*		

Michel n'a pas été malade.	*Michel has not been sick.*
Vous avez fait une erreur.	*You made a mistake.*
A-t-il ouvert la fenêtre?	*Did he open the window?*

EXERCICE L

Exprimez quel sport les personnes suivantes ont pratiqué.

EXEMPLE: Vous **avez fait** du patin.

1. Tu _____.

2. Joseph et Maurice _____.

3. Je _____.

4. Christine _____.

EXERCICE M

Say where each person has not gone. *Employez les suggestions ci-dessous.*

Guy	à la Martinique
je	au Canada
Isabelle et moi	en Afrique
Patricia et Brigitte	en Bretagne
tu	en Grèce

EXEMPLE: **Tu n'as pas été** en Grèce.

1. _____
2. _____
3. _____
4. _____

EXERCICE N

The following persons are on a commuter train. *Exprimez ce qu'elles ont ouvert.*

EXEMPLE: Georges/une bouteille d'eau minérale
            Georges **a ouvert** une bouteille d'eau minérale.

1. Paulette/son sac

   _____

2. vous/le journal

   _____

3. tu/un livre

   _____

4. Nicole et Jacqueline/un paquet de bonbons

   _____

MASTERY EXERCISES

EXERCICE O

You and your friends had some spare time. *Exprimez ce que vous avez fait.*

EXEMPLE: Suzette/préparer un gâteau
            Suzette **a préparé** un gâteau.

1. Rose/lire un roman

   _____

2. je/écrire des lettres à des amis

_____

3. tu/être à un concert

_____

4. Éric et Émile/faire des courses

_____

5. vous/voir un film

_____

6. Henri et moi/avoir une boum

_____

EXERCICE P

Complete Catherine's entry in her diary. *Employez les formes correctes du passé composé des verbes indiqués.*

Ce matin j' _____ chez mon amie Isabelle. Son père _____ une
          1. (être)   *2.* (bâtir)
maison de poupées pour sa petite sœur Chantal, qui _____ neuf ans hier.
                                                        3. (avoir)
Elle _____ ce cadeau de ses grands-parents. M. Dupont _____
        4. (recevoir)   *5.* (lire)
avec soin toutes les instructions. Mais il n' _____ pas _____ tout comprendre
                                                                    6. (pouvoir)
et il n' _____ pas _____ comment finir le projet. J' _____ le regret
              7. (savoir)   *8.* (voir)
dans les yeux de Chantal et j' _____ aider. J' _____ tous les
                                    9. (vouloir)   *10.* (prendre)
morceaux de bois et j' _____ tout en place. Enfin j'_____ :
                            11. (mettre)   *12.* (dire)
« Voilà. J' _____ ». Tout le monde _____ .
              13. (finir)   *14.* (applaudir)

EXERCICE Q

Continue reading Catherine's diary, but this time change the verbs from the present tense to the *passé composé*.

1. Je *(finis)* _____ donc de construire la maison de poupées et tout le monde

  (applaudit) _____ .

2. J'*(ai)* _____ beaucoup de plaisir à aider M. Dupont et je *(suis)*

  _____ très contente.

3. Chantal *(prend)* _____ ma main et me *(dit)* _____ : « Tu *(es)*

  _____ formidable et tu *(sais)* _____ tout faire! »

4. Isabelle *(demande)* _____ : « Où *(apprends-tu)* _____ à construire

  des maisons ? »

5. Je *(réponds)* _____ : «Je *(réfléchis)* _____ et je *(comprends)*
_____ comment faire.

6. Ça *(n'est pas)* _____ très difficile et je *(veux)* _____ être architecte depuis longtemps ! »

EXERCICE R

Dites si vous avez fait les choses suivantes la semaine dernière.

jouer au tennis	voir un bon film	faire des courses
lire un magazine	prendre l'avion	avoir une bonne semaine
écrire une lettre	recevoir une bonne note	être au théâtre

EXEMPLE: **J'ai joué** au tennis
Je n'ai pas joué au tennis.

1. _____

2. _____

3. _____

4. _____

5. _____

6. _____

7. _____

8. _____

EXERCICE S

**Write a note to a friend expressing things you did and didn't do last week. You may want to
include:**

• a sport you played
• a TV program you didn't see
• something you read
• a chore you forgot to do
• an after-school activity in which you participated
• something you didn't do over the week-end

_____

_____

_____

_____

_____

_____

_____

Chapter 9

Passé composé of *être* Verbs

[1] VERBS CONJUGATED WITH *ÊTRE*

Sixteen common verbs use the helping verb *être* instead of *avoir*. Their passé composé is formed by combining the present tense of *être* and the past participle of the verb. Most of these verbs express motion or change of place or state.

INFINITIVE	PAST PARTICIPLE	INFINITIVE	PAST PARTICIPLE
aller *to go*	*allé*	**naître** *to be born*	*né*
venir *to come*	*venu*	**mourir** *to die*	*mort*
arriver *to arrive*	*arrivé*	**rentrer** *to go in again, return*	*rentré*
partir *to leave, go away*	*parti*	**retourner** *to go back, return*	*retourné*
		revenir *to come back*	*revenu*
entrer *to go in, enter*	*entré*		
sortir *to go out, leave*	*sorti*	**tomber** *to fall*	*tombé*
monter *to go up, come up*	*monté*	**rester** *to remain, stay*	*resté*
descendre *to go down*	*descendu*	**devenir** *to become*	*devenu*

[2] AGREEMENT

Past participles of verbs conjugated with *être* agree in gender (masculine or feminine) and number (singular or plural) with the subject.

MASCULINE SUBJECTS	FEMININE SUBJECTS	
je suis allé	**je suis allée**	*I went*
tu es allé	**tu es allée**	*you went*
il est allé	**elle est allée**	*he/she went*
nous sommes allés	**nous sommes allées**	*we went*
vous êtes allé(s)	**vous êtes allée(s)**	*you went*
ils sont allés	**elles sont allées**	*they went*

Elles sont arrivées en retard.   *They arrived late.*

Où es-tu née, Marie?   *Where were you born, Marie?*

NOTES:

1. When the subject is both masculine and feminine, the past participle is masculine plural.

   Paul et Marie sont partis.   *Paul and Marie left.*

2. Since the pronouns *je, tu, nous,* and *vous* may be masculine or feminine, and *vous* may be singular or plural, the past participles used with them vary in endings.

3. Interrogative, negative and negative interrogative forms of the *passé composé* of verbs conjugated with *être* are:

Elle n'est pas partie.	*She didn't leave.*
Elle est partie? Est-elle partie? Est-ce qu'elle est partie?	} *Did she leave?*
Elle n'est pas partie? Est-ce qu'elle n'est pas partie?	} *Didn't she leave?*

EXERCICE A

Say where Catherine, Isabelle, and their families went on Bastille Day (*le 14 juillet*).

EXEMPLE: **Nous sommes allé(e)s** en ville.

1. Je _____ à la tour Eiffel.

2. Les Dupont _____ danser à Montmartre.

3. Tu (Henri) _____ sur les quais de la Seine.

4. Vous (Hervé et Jacques) _____ à une fête.

5. Nous (trois copines) _____ à la place de la Bastille.

6. Catherine et Isabelle _____ chez des amies.

EXERCICE B

Dites quand les personnes suivantes sont sorties.

EXEMPLE: je / à midi
   Je suis sorti(e) à midi

1. François/à cinq heures

_____

2. tu (Rose) / trop tard

_____

3. nous (les Martin) / très tôt le matin

_____

4. Joseph et Claude / dans l'après midi

_____

5. vous (quatre cousines) /à minuit

_____

6. Catherine / à six heures du soir

_____

EXERCICE C

Say at what time the guests came to Liliane's party. *Suivez l'exemple.*

EXEMPLE: **Lise est venue** à neuf heures.

1. Thierry _____ .

2. Nous (René et Michel) _____ .

3. Tu (Anne) _____ .

4. Vous (les Martin) _____ .

5. Je _____ .

6. Charline et Claire _____ .

EXERCICE D

Yesterday was a holiday and everyone had the day off. Explain what the following people did. *Employez les suggestions données.*

aller au zoo

descendre en ville

partir pour la campagne

rentrer tard le soir

rester au lit

retourner à un musée favori

sortir avec des copains

EXEMPLE: **Vous êtes descendu(e)(s) en ville.**

1. Les filles Birot _____ .

2. Tu (Jacques) _____ .

3. Colette _____ .

4. Je _____ .

5. Bernard et Richard _____ .

6. Alain et moi _____ .

EXERCICE E

Your friend moved to a new neighborhood. When you meet again, he/she has many questions for you. *Répondez négativement.*

EXEMPLE: Est-ce que Jean Legrand est resté dans le quartier?
     Non, **il n'est pas resté** dans le quartier.

1. Es-tu arrivé(e) à apprendre à patiner?

_____

2. Est-ce que les grands-parents de Sylvie sont venus en France?

_____

3. Est-ce que Mme Cassard et sa fille sont parties pour l'Angleterre?

_____

4. Chantal et toi, vous êtes sorti(e)s ensemble?

_____

5. Est-ce que Lise Martin est devenue professeur?

_____

6. M. Smith est rentré aux États-Unis?

_____

EXERCICE F

You just came back from vacation. Your friend wants to know all about your trip. *Exprimez ses questions et vos réponses.*

EXEMPLE: aller à la montagne (non)
     Es-tu allé(e) à la montagne?
     Non, **je ne suis pas allé(e)** à la montagne.

1. partir en bateau (non)

   _____

   _____

2. sortir avec tes parents (oui)

   _____

   _____

3. descendre en ville (non)

   _____

   _____

4. aller à la plage tous les jours (oui)

   _____

   _____

5. devenir expert(e) en ski nautique (non)

   _____

   _____

6. arriver à apprendre à faire du surf? (oui)

   _____

   _____

EXERCICE G

Your friend wants to gossip about what happened at a party you both attended. *Exprimez ses questions comme dans l'exemple.*

EXEMPLE: Paul et moi / venir à l'heure
          Est-ce que Paul et moi ne sommes pas venus à l'heure?

1. Louise / rester avec Robert

   _____

2. Pierre et moi / arriver à très bien danser ensemble

   _____

3. tu / sortir prendre l'air

4. Marc et Michel / devenir jaloux

_____

5. Lucie / tomber amoureuse de Claude

_____

6. Chantal et Christine / partir à minuit

_____

M A S T E R Y   E X E R C I S E S

EXERCICE H

Describe a trip you took. Répondez aux questions en employant le *passé composé.*

1. Où es-tu allé(e) ?

_____

2. Avec qui es-tu parti(e) ?

_____

3. Quand êtes-vous arrivé(e)s ?

_____

4. À quel hôtel êtes-vous descendu(e)s ?

_____

5. Qu'est-ce que vous avez visité ?

_____

6. Qu'est-ce que tu as acheté comme souvenir ?

_____

7. De quoi as-tu pris des photos ?

_____

8. Quand êtes-vous rentré(e)s ?

_____

EXERCICE I

Complete the following sentences about what you did, using the verbs given in parentheses. Be careful to use the appropriate helping verb. *Suivez l'exemple.*

EXEMPLE: La semaine dernière **je suis allé(e)** chez des amis.

1. Pendant le week-end (*sortir*) _____ .

2. Samedi passé (*aller*) _____ .

3. Hier (*rester*) _____ .

4. Avant-hier (*étudier*) _____ .

5. Ce matin (*déjeuner*) _____ .

6. L'année dernière (*travailler*) _____ .

EXERCICE J

Tell what the following people did last week. Be careful to use the appropriate helping verb.

1. nous (trois cousins) / aller voir des amies

_____

2. je *(f.)* / aller chez le dentiste.

_____

3. Les Dupont / choisir d'aller voir un film

_____

4. Lisette et Marie / faire des courses

_____

5. Mme Legrand / descendre en ville

_____

6. Tu (Paulette) / acheter un cadeau à une amie

_____

7. Patrick / patiner

_____

8. Gisèle / arriver à l'école en retard

_____

9. vous (Claudine et Lucienne) / téléphoner à vos grands-parents

_____

10. Grégoire et Arthur / revenir tard le soir

_____

EXERCICE K

Express what you did and didn't do on vacation. You may want to include:

- where you went
- when you left
- what you saw
- where you stayed and for how long
- why you went there
- what souvenirs you bought
- when you returned

_____

_____

_____

_____

_____

_____

_____

Chapter 10
Imperfect Tense

1. REGULAR VERBS

The imperfect tense (*l'imparfait*) of regular verbs is formed by dropping the *-ons* ending of the *nous* form of the present tense and adding the imperfect tense endings (*-ais, -ais, -ait, -ions, -iez, -aient*).

danser *to dance* nous dans**ons**	rougir *to blush* nous rougiss**ons**	vendre *to sell* nous vend**ons**
I danced, I was dancing, I used to dance, etc.	*I blushed, I was blushing, used to blush, etc.*	*I sold, I was selling, I used to sell, etc.*
je dans**ais** tu dans**ais** il/elle dans**ait** nous dans**ions** vous dans**iez** ils/elles dans**aient**	je rougiss**ais** tu rougiss**ais** il/elle rougiss**ait** nous rougiss**ions** vous rougiss**iez** ils/elles rougiss**aient**	je vend**ais** tu vend**ais** il/elle vend**ait** nous vend**ions** vous vend**iez** ils/elles vend**aient**

NOTES:

1. Verbs ending in *-ions* and *-iez* in the present tense end in *-iions* and *-iiez* in the imperfect tense: *nous étudiions, vous étudiiez.*

2. Negative, interrogative, and negative interrogative constructions in the imperfect follow the same rules as in the present tense.

Pierre ne chantait pas.	*Pierre was not singing.*
Elle rougissait ?	*Was she blushing?*
Attendiez-vous le soleil ?	*Were you waiting for the sun?*
Est-ce que Michel jouait ?	*Did Michel play?*
Tu n'aimais pas jouer au basket ?	*Didn't you like to play basketball?*
Est-ce qu'il ne chantait pas ?	*Didn't he sing?*

EXERCICE A

At a high school reunion, some friends are remembering where they worked after school. *Exprimez ce qu'ils disent.*

EXEMPLE: Ils / travailler à la fruiterie
Ils **travaillaient** à la fruiterie

1. Louis et Georges/aider dans une pharmacie

_____

2. tu/organiser les produits au supermarché

3. Richard et moi/ nettoyer à l'hôpital

_____

4. je/cuisiner à la pâtisserie

_____

5. vous/travailler à la boucherie

_____

6. Jean/jouer de la guitare dans un café

_____

EXERCICE B

André and some of his friends have given up sweets. *Dites ce qu'ils avaient l'habitude de choisir comme dessert.*

Pierre	de la crème caramel
Thomas	de la glace
Carole et moi	de la mousse au chocolat
Arthur et Nicolas	des bonbons
tu	des profiteroles
vous	des tartes à la crème
je	du chocolat

EXEMPLE: Pierre **choisissait** de la glace.

1. _____

2. _____

3. _____

4. _____

5. _____

6. _____

EXERCICE C

Some friends are discussing what they used to sell in the flea market. *Exprimez ce qu'ils disent.*

EXEMPLE: Jean **vendait** des plantes vertes.

1. Suzanne et Laurent _____.

2. Je _____.

3. Tu _____.

4. Gilles _____.

5. Vous _____.

6. Paul et moi _____.

EXERCICE D

Roger describes what his life was like when he was ten years old. *Exprimez ce qu'il dit en employant l'imparfait.*

1. je/habiter à Paris

_____

2. mes frères/jouer au football avec moi

_____

3. ma mère/travailler

_____

4. toute la famille/visiter mes grands-parents le samedi

_____

5. ma grand-mère/attendre nos visites avec impatience

_____

6. mes frères et moi/obéir toujours à nos parents

_____

7. je/correspondre avec un garçon au Canada

_____

8. mes sœurs/rougir tout le temps

_____

EXERCICE E

Your little brother asks your grandfather questions about his life. Write the answers to his questions. *Employez l'imparfait et les indications données.*

1. Où habitais-tu à mon âge ? (un petit village)

_____

2. Tes frères et toi, à quel sport jouiez-vous ? (au base-ball)

_____

3. Quel sujet préférais-tu à l'école ? (l'histoire)

_____

4. Avec qui correspondais-tu ? (avec ta grand-mère)

_____

5. Qui aidais-tu ? (tout le monde)

_____

6. Quel genre de livre choisissais-tu ? (des livres d'aventures)

_____

[2] SPELLING CHANGES IN CERTAIN -ER VERBS

a. Verbs ending in -cer change c to ç before a or o to keep the soft c sound.

avancer *to advance, move forward*	
j'avançais	nous avancions
tu avançais	vous avanciez
il/elle avançait	ils/elles avançaient

b. Verbs ending in -ger insert silent e between g and a or o to keep the soft g sound.

manger *to eat*	
je mangeais	nous mangions
tu mangeais	vous mangiez
il/elle mangeait	ils/elles mangeaient

EXERCICE F

Say what used to happen in Mme Barrat's French class. *Mettez le verbe approprié à l'imparfait.*

annoncer	lancer	placer
effacer	menacer	prononcer

1. Tu _____ mal les mots.

2. Les garçons _____ des papiers dans la corbeille.

3. Je (J') _____ le tableau.

4. Claire et moi _____ nos bandes dessinées dans nos pupitres.

5. Le professeur _____ les examens au dernier moment.

6. Vous _____ de ne pas faire les devoirs.

EXERCICE G

Tell what these people did habitually in the past. *Employez l'imparfait.*

1. Luc et moi/nager dans l'équipe de notre école

_____

2. tu/manger au même restaurant tous les jours

_____

3. je/songer à devenir astronaute

_____

4. vous/déménager chaque année

_____

5. Liliane et Patricia/voyager à travers le monde

_____

6. M. Jouet/diriger les affaires d'une grande société

_____

[3] IMPERFECT OF IRREGULAR VERBS

The imperfect of irregular verbs, with few exceptions, is formed in the same way as the imperfect of regular verbs.

INFINITIVE	PRESENT *nous* FORM	IMPERFECT
avoir *to have*	avons	j'avais, tu avais, il/elle avait nous avions, vous aviez, ils/elles avaient
aller *to go*	allons	j'allais, tu allais, il/elle allait nous allions, vous alliez, ils/elles allaient
faire *to do*	faisons	je faisais, tu faisais, il/elle faisait nous faisions, vous faisiez, ils/elles faisaient
venir *to come*	venons	je venais, tu venais, il/elle venait nous venions, vous veniez, ils/elles venaient
voir *to see*	voyons	je voyais, tu voyais, il/elle voyait nous voyions, vous voyiez, ils/elles voyaient

NOTE: In the imperfect, *être (to be)* is the only irregular verb and adds regular endings to an irregular stem.

j'étais	nous étions
tu étais	vous étiez
il/elle était	ils/elles étaient

EXERCICE H

Explain how these people felt in the following circumstances. *Employez l'imparfait.*

EXEMPLE: Pauline a gagné un prix. (contente)
Elle était contente.

1. Jean allait passer un examen. (nerveux)

_____

2. J'avais peur de ne pas réussir. (anxieux)

_____

3. Janine et moi, nous allions être en retard. (pressés)

_____

4. Vous avez perdu votre portefeuille. (triste)

_____

5. Tu as trouvé un billet de cent francs. (heureux)

_____

6. Les garçons ont perdu le match. (fâchés)

_____

EXERCICE I

Who used to do this? *Employez l'imparfait dans vos réponses.*

1. Tu/ dire la vérité à tout le monde

_____ .

2. Nous/écrire des bandes dessinées pour le journal de l'école

_____ .

3. Monique/prendre une limousine pour aller à une fête .

_____ .

4. Daniel et Denis/étudier jusqu'à trois heures du matin .

_____ .

5. Vous/lire des poèmes d'amour à haute voix

_____ .

6. Je/regarder le coucher du soleil

_____ .

7. Yvette et Marie/ faire du ski nautique chaque été

_____ .

8. Gérard/ aller au cirque au printemps

_____ .

[4] USES OF THE IMPERFECT

The imperfect tense expresses actions, circumstances, events, and situations which are continuing, repeated, or habitual in the past.

a. The imperfect describes what was happening, used to happen, or happened repeatedly in the past.

Les enfants jouaient.	*The children were playing.*
J'habitais Paris.	*I lived (used to live) in Paris.*
Elle lisait un livre chaque jour.	*She read (would read, used to read) a book every day.*

NOTE: The imperfect tense is usually equivalent to *was/were* + *-ing* form of verb, *used to,* and *would* (meaning *used to*) in English.

b. The imperfect describes persons, things, or conditions in the past.

Il était beau.	*He was handsome.*
La fenêtre était ouverte.	*The window was open.*
Il faisait froid.	*It was cold.*

c. The imperfect is used to express the day, the month, and the time of day in the past.

C'était samedi.	*It was Saturday.*
C'était le mois de juin.	*It was June.*
Il était neuf heures.	*It was nine o'clock.*

d. The imperfect describes a situation or circumstance that was going on in the past when some single action or event occurred; this action or event is expressed in the *passé composé.*

Je réparais le moteur quand le téléphone a sonné.	*I was fixing the motor when the telephone rang.*
Il pleuvait quand j'ai ouvert la porte.	*It was raining when I opened the door.*

NOTE: Two actions going on simultaneously in the past are both expressed in the imperfect.

Il jouait pendant que j'étudiais.	*He played while I studied.*
	He was playing while I was studying.
Pendant que je parlais, elle riait beaucoup.	*While I was talking, she was laughing a lot.*

EXERCICE J

Describe what the Moreaus used to do. *Employez l'imparfait.*

1. Je (*faire*) _____ un voyage à l'étranger pendant l'été.
2. Cécile et Odette (*recevoir*)_____ de bonnes notes à l'école.
3. Tu (*voir*)_____ les matches de football le samedi.
4. Papa (*prendre*)_____ la nouvelle voiture tout le temps.
5. Vous (*partir*)_____ à la campagne le week-end.
6. Maman et moi (*aller*)_____ au cinéma le samedi soir.

EXERCICE K

M. Chabrol just bought a new video camera. His daughter Catherine is describing what his first video showed. *Employez l'imparfait.*

EXEMPLE: les oiseaux/voler dans le ciel
Les oiseaux **volaient** dans le ciel.

1. il/neiger

_____

2. le ciel/ être gris

_____

3. Claudine/avoir froid

_____

4. je/bâtir un bonhomme de neige

_____

5. Pierre et Jacques/jeter des boules de neige

_____

6. François/faire du patin à glace

_____

7. tu/manger un cornet de neige

_____

8. Maman et moi/préparer du chocolat

_____

EXERCICE L

What was everybody doing during the following weather conditions? *Employez l'imparfait dans vos réponses.*

EXEMPLE:

Il **allait** au cinéma quand **il pleuvait**.

Nous _____

1. _____

2.

Elle _____

_____

3.

Vous _____

_____

4.

Je _____

_____

5.

Ils _____

_____

6.

Tu _____

_____

EXERCICE M

How were the following people interrupted in what they were doing ? Employez *l'imparfait* **ou le** *passé composé.*

EXEMPLE: je / parler au téléphone / mon père / dire bonjour
Je parlais au téléphone quand mon père **a dit** bonjour.

1. Hélène/sortir/le téléphone/sonner

_____

2. ma mère/faire le dîner/elle/voir une souris

_____

3. je/regarder la télévision/je/entendre mes amis dehors

_____

4. Vincent et moi/faire une promenade/il/commencer à pleuvoir

_____

5. tu/avancer vers la maison/Janine/ouvrir la porte

_____

6. ils/lire un livre/maman/téléphoner

_____

7. Jean et Georges/patiner sur le lac/la glace/craquer

_____

8. les filles/rôtir un poulet/leurs invités/sonner à la porte

_____

MASTERY EXERCISES

EXERCICE N

Using the expressions given, describe what each person used to do. *Employez l'imparfait.*

| le week-end | le samedi matin | deux fois par semaine |
| trois fois par jour | tous les jours | chaque après-midi |

EXEMPLE:
Les jeunes filles **jouaient** au volley-ball le mercredi.

1.

Je _____.

2.

Jacques et moi _____.

3.

Vous _____.

4.

Tu _____.

5.

M. Robert _____.

6.

Les garçons _____ .

EXERCICE O

Rewrite the story in the imperfect tense.

C'est la fin du semestre. Il **est** une heure du matin. J'**ai** une composition à écrire pour ma classe d'anglais. Je **songe** au sujet qui n'**est** pas du tout intéressant. Je **passe** beaucoup de temps à marcher de long en large dans ma chambre. De temps en temps je **mange** des chips et des biscuits. J'**espère** trouver de l'inspiration. Malheureusement, l'inspiration nécessaire ne **vient** pas à mon esprit. Je ne **sais** pas pourquoi. Je **réussis** toujours dans cette classe. D'habitude j'**écris** d'excellentes compositions. J'**ai** de très bonnes notes et je **fais** de grands progrès. Je **saisis** chaque occasion de parler anglais. Le professeur **dit** que je **suis** un excellent élève. Pourquoi est-ce qu'il **est** tellement impossible d'écrire quelque chose de brillant aujourd'hui ? Il **est** quatre heures, cinq heures, six heures du matin. Ma mère **entre** dans ma chambre pendant que mon réveil **sonne**. Elle **dit** que je **rêve** et que je **vais** être en retard pour le déjeuner chez grand-mère. C'est dimanche.

_____

_____

_____

_____

_____

_____

_____

_____

_____

_____

_____

_____

_____

_____

_____

EXERCICE P

Who was your hero or heroine when you were younger? *Décrivez-le (-la) en employant l'imparfait.*

EXEMPLE: Mon héroïne **était** ma tante. **Elle était** grande et **elle avait** les cheveux noirs. **Elle cuisi-nait** très bien et **nous passions** de très bons moments ensemble.

_____

_____

_____

_____

EXERCICE Q

You are looking in a photo album. Describe one of the pictures. You may want to include:

- who is in the photo
- the weather conditions
- where the person(s) was (were)
- what they were doing
- what they were wearing
- what you thought of the activity

_____

_____

_____

_____

_____

_____

Chapter 11
Future Tense

[1]   ALLER + INFINITIVE

In French as in English, the near future may be expressed with a form of the present tense of the verb *aller* (*to be going to*) plus the infinitive.

Je vais danser.	*I am going to dance.*
Je vais aller au cinéma.	*I'm going to go to the movies.*

The negative construction is:

Je ne vais pas aller au cinéma.	*I am not going to go to the movies.*

The interrogative constructions are:

Tu vas jouer au tennis?	*Are you going to play tennis?*
Qu'est-ce que tu vas faire?	*What are you going to do?*
Où vas-tu aller?	*Where are you going to go?*

EXERCICE A

Georges is curious about what his friends are going to do after school. *Écrivez ses questions et les réponses de ses amis.*

EXEMPLE: tu / jouer au football
            Tu vas jouer au football?
            Oui, **je vais jouer** au football.
    OR: Non, **je ne vais pas jouer** au football.

1. Denis et Paul/écouter des disques

   _____

   _____

2. Charline/lire un livre

   _____

   _____

3. tu/rester à la maison

   _____

   _____

4. Jean et vous/jouer du piano

   _____

   _____

5. Claude/participer au cercle français

   _____

   _____

6. vous et moi/aller au concert

_____

_____

7. tu/écrire à ton correspondant français

_____

_____

8. Marie et Suzanne/faire des courses

_____

_____

EXERCICE B

What jobs are the following people sure they are not going to do? *Employez* **aller** *et l'infinitif.*

Paul	diriger les affaires d'une grande société
je	garder les enfants
vous	laver les voitures
les garçons	nettoyer les maisons des autres
Claire et moi	parler au téléphone toute la journée
tu	travailler dans un supermarché
Marianne	vendre dans un magasin

EXEMPLE: Paul **ne va pas vendre** dans un magasin.

1. _____

2. _____

3. _____

4. _____

5. _____

6. _____

EXERCICE C

It is the end of the day. Tell what you, your family, and your friends are going to do now. *Écrivez six phrases selon l'exemple.*

EXEMPLE: Paul **va dormir**.

1. _____

2. _____

3. _____

4. _____

5. _____

6. _____

EXERCICE D

The weather often affects what we are going to do. *Dites ce que vous allez faire dans les circonstances suivantes.*

EXEMPLE: S'il fait frais, **je vais jouer au football**.

1.   S'il fait du soleil, _____ .

2.   S'il fait froid, _____ .

3.   S'il pleut, _____ .

4.   S'il fait chaud, _____ .

5. S'il neige, _____ .

6. S'il fait beau, _____ .

[2] FUTURE TENSE OF REGULAR VERBS

The future tense is formed by adding the following endings to the infinitive: *-ai, -as, -a, -ons, -ez, -ont.*

parler *to speak*	**choisir** *to choose*	**vendre** *to sell*
I will speak	*I will choose*	*I will sell*
je parler*ai*	je choisir*ai*	je vendr*ai*
tu parler*as*	tu choisir*as*	tu vendr*as*
il/elle parler*a*	il/elle choisir*a*	il/elle vendr*a*
nous parler*ons*	nous choisir*ons*	nous vendr*ons*
vous parler*ez*	vous choisir*ez*	vous vendr*ez*
ils/elles parler*ont*	ils/elles choisir*ont*	ils/elles vendr*ont*

NOTES:

1. Verbs ending in *-re* drop the final *e* before the future ending.

   vendre   je vend*rai*
   prendre je prend*rai*

2. Negative, interrogative, and negative interrogative constructions in the future follow the same rules as in the present tense.

Je ne parlerai pas avec Nicole.	*I will not speak with Nicole.*
Tu parleras avec Nicole?	
Est-ce que tu parleras avec Nicole?	*Will you speak with Nicole?*
Parleras-tu avec Nicole?	
Vous ne vendrez pas la maison?	*You won't sell the house?*
Est-ce que vous ne vendrez pas la maison?	*Won't you sell the house?*

EXERCICE E

What do the following people promise to do as part of their New Year's resolutions? *Employez le futur.*

1. *(donner)* Laurent et moi _____ nos vieux vêtements aux pauvres.

2. *(maigrir)* Suzanne _____ .

3. *(répondre)* Guy _____ poliment à tout le monde.

4. *(obéir)* Vous _____ toujours à vos parents.

5. *(perdre)* Catherine et Denise _____ leurs mauvaises habitudes.

6. *(prendre)* Tu _____ soin de ton petit frère.

7. *(ranger)* Je _____ régulièrement ma chambre.

8. *(mettre)* Charles et Joseph _____ leurs affaires en ordre.

EXERCICE F

Un ami curieux vous pose des questions. Répondez-lui.

1. Qu'est-ce que tu donneras à ton/ta meilleur(e) ami(e) comme cadeau d'anniversaire ?

   _____

2. Avec qui correspondras-tu plus tard ?

   _____

3. En quelle année finiras-tu tes études universitaires ?

   _____

4. À qui téléphoneras-tu ce soir ?

   _____

5. Où choisiras-tu de vivre ?

   _____

6. Où aimeras-tu voyager ?

   _____

[3] SPELLING CHANGES IN THE FUTURE TENSE

a. Most verbs with infinitives ending in *-yer* change *y* to *i* in the future.

ennuyer *to annoy; to bore*	
j'ennuierai	nous ennuierons
tu ennuieras	vous ennuierez
il/elle ennuiera	ils/elles ennuieront

nettoyer *to clean*	
je nettoierai	nous nettoierons
tu nettoieras	vous nettoierez
il/elle nettoiera	ils/elles nettoieront

NOTES:

1. Verbs with infinitives ending in *-ayer* may or may not change the *y* to *i* in all forms of the future.

   payer *to pay*

   je paierai (payerai), tu paieras (payeras), il/elle paiera (payera),
   nous paierons (payerons), vous paierez (payerez), ils/elles paieront (payeront)

2. The verb *envoyer* is irregular in the future.

   envoyer *to send*

   j'enverrai, tu enverras, il/elle enverra,
   nous enverrons, vous enverrez, ils/elles enverront

EXERCICE G

What will each student use to complete an art project? *Employez le futur du verbe* **employer.**

1. Paul et moi _____ une gomme.

2. Vous _____ un stylo.

3. J' _____ une règle.

4. Tu _____ du papier.

5. Gilles _____ de l'encre.

6. Marie et Louise _____ un bâton de craie.

   b. Verbs with silent *e* in the syllable before the infinitive ending change silent *e* to *è* in the future.

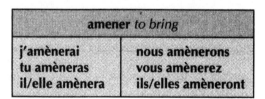

amener *to bring*	
j'amènerai	nous amènerons
tu amèneras	vous amènerez
il/elle amènera	ils/elles amèneront

EXERCICE H

What will you and your friends buy Henriette as a going-away present? *Employez le futur.*

EXEMPLE: Les filles lui **achèteront** une affiche.

1. Lucie _____

2. Nous _____

3. Vous _____

4. Les garçons _____

5. Tu _____

6. Je _____

c. Verbs with silent *e* like *appeler* and *jeter* double the consonant preceding the infinitive ending in the future.

appeler *to call*	
j'appellerai	nous appellerons
tu appelleras	vous appellerez
il/elle appellera	ils/elles appelleront

jeter *to throw*	
je jetterai	nous jetterons
tu jetteras	vous jetterez
il/elle jettera	ils/elles jetteront

EXERCICE I

Describe what will happen at the class picnic. *Employez le futur.*

acheter des sandwiches
amener un copain
appeler des amis à haute voix
commencer à jouer de la guitare

jeter une balle
manger beaucoup
essayer le pâté
ennuyer Marc

1. Je _____

2. Antoinette et Ginette _____

3. Nous _____

4. Juliette _____

5. Vous _____

6. Pierre et Jules _____

7. Tu _____

8. Gilbert _____

[4] VERBS IRREGULAR IN THE FUTURE

The following verbs have irregular stems in the future.

INFINITIVE	FUTURE	INFINITIVE	FUTURE
aller *to go*	j'irai	pouvoir *to be able to*	je pourrai
avoir *to have*	j'aurai	recevoir *to receive*	je recevrai
envoyer *to send*	j'enverrai	savoir *to know*	je saurai
être *to be*	je serai	venir *to come*	je viendrai
faire *to do*	je ferai	voir *to see*	je verrai
mourir *to die*	je mourrai	vouloir *to want*	je voudrai

EXERCICE J

What does Aunt Zoé predict for the following people? *Employez le futur.*

EXEMPLE: tu / travailler dans une station-service
            Tu travailleras dans une station-service.

1. je / faire le tour du monde

   _____

2. Henri / être avocat

   _____

3. vous / envoyer des fusées dans l'espace

   _____

4. Chantal et Marie / vouloir quitter la France

   _____

5. M. Legros / voir le président des États-Unis

   _____

6. tu / savoir tout réussir

   _____

7. le fils Vautrin / venir à Paris

   _____

8. nous / recevoir une grosse somme d'argent

   _____

9. Lise / avoir trois enfants

   _____

10. Pierre et Lucien / aller en Afrique

    _____

11. Mme Beaujour / mourir à l'âge de 100 ans

    _____

12. Claude et moi / pouvoir voyager beaucoup

    _____

EXERCICE K

Catherine and Isabelle are talking about their summer plans. *Exprimez ce qu'elles disent en mettant les verbes au futur.*

— Cet été je _____ un grand voyage avec mes parents. Nous _____
                    1. (faire)   *2. (aller)*
en Grèce. Mon frère François ne _____ pas.
                                    3. (venir)

— Où _____ François ?
      4. (aller)

— Il _____ avec des copains camper à la montagne. Je _____ un
   5. (partir)   *6.* (être)

  peu triste sans lui, mais j' _____ beaucoup de plaisir avec mes parents.
                                    7. (avoir)

— Comment _____-vous ?
            8. (voyager)

— Nous _____ l'avion, puis papa _____ une voiture. Nous
     9. (prendre)   *10.* (louer)

  _____ tous les endroits célèbres. Ensuite nous _____ sur un
   11. (visiter)   *12.* (monter)

  bateau et nous _____ par une croisière (*cruise*) pour visiter les îles. Et toi, Isabelle?
            13. (finir)

  Que _____-tu?
      14. (faire)

— Je _____ visite à des amis de mes parents en Angleterre et puis je _____
   15. (rendre)   *16.* (passer)

  trois semaines dans une école internationale pour parler anglais. Ma sœur Nicole _____
                                        17. (travailler)

  dans un magasin à Paris et maman _____ les gosses, Chantal et Michel, en colonie
                       18. (envoyer)

  de vacances. Mes parents _____ ici et ils _____ heureux.
             19. (rester)   *20.* (être)

MASTERY EXERCISES

EXERCICE L

Consider the following developments and tell whether or not they are likely to occur in the future. What is your opinion? *Répondez affirmativement ou négativement en suivant les exemples.*

EXEMPLES: les femmes / gagner plus d'argent
        Oui, les femmes **gagneront** plus d'argent.
   OR: Non, les femmes **ne gagneront pas** plus d'argent.

        le monde / avoir moins de problèmes
        Oui, le monde **aura** moins de problèmes.
   OR: Non, le monde **n'aura pas** moins de problèmes.

1. les astronautes / faire plus d'explorations dans l'espace

_____

2. je / essayer plus de nouveaux produits alimentaires

_____

3. nous/envoyer moins d'aide aux pays pauvres

_____

4. les Américains/acheter moins de produits étrangers

_____

5. vous/manger plus de viande

_____

6. les gens/avoir moins de maladies contagieuses

_____

7. les hommes/protéger mieux l'environnement

_____

8. la société/employer moins d'énergie

_____

9. le monde/avoir plus de paix

_____

EXERCICE M

Where are the following people going to go and what are they not going to do? _Employez_
aller _comme l'exemple._

Michel	au gymnase	danser
Joseph	au zoo	jouer au basket-ball
Hervé et moi	au stade	lire longtemps
tu	au restaurant	participer à un match de football
Liliane et Marie	à la discothèque	aimer le film
vous	à la plage	écouter la musique
je	à la bibliothèque	nager
Georges et Guy	au concert	dîner
Marthe	au cinéma	observer les animaux

EXEMPLE: Michel **va aller** au gymnase, mais **il ne va pas jouer** au basket-ball.

1. _____

_____

2. _____

_____

3. _____

_____

4. _____

_____

5. _____

_____

6. _____

_____

7. _____

_____

8. _____

_____

EXERCICE N

Your French assignment is to write about your future plans to your French penpal. You may want to include:

- where you will live
- what your job will be
- things you will buy
- a description of the type of person you would like to marry
- how many children you will have
- how you will feel about life

_____

_____

_____

_____

_____

_____

_____

_____

_____

Chapter 12
Reflexive Verbs

[1] REFLEXIVE VERBS IN SIMPLE TENSES

a. In a reflexive construction, the action is performed by the subject on itself. The reflexive verb has a reflexive pronoun as its object. Thus, the subject and the pronoun object refer to the same person(s) or thing(s). The reflexive pronouns (*me, te, se, nous, vous*) generally precede the verb.

PRESENT TENSE	
je *me* lave	*I wash (am washing) myself*
tu *te* laves	*you wash (are washing) yourself*
il/elle *se* lave	*he/she washes (is washing) himself/herself*
nous *nous* lavons	*we wash (are washing) ourselves*
vous *vous* lavez	*you wash (are washing) yourself/yourselves*
ils/elles *se* lavent	*they wash (are washing) themselves*

IMPERFECT TENSE	
je *me* lavais	*I washed (was washing) myself*
tu *te* lavais	*you washed (were washing) yourself*
il/elle *se* lavait	*he/she washed (was washing) himself/herself*
nous *nous* lavions	*we washed (were washing) ourselves*
vous *vous* laviez	*you washed (were washing) yourself/yourselves*
ils/elles *se* lavaient	*they washed (were washing) themselves*

FUTURE TENSE	
je *me* laverai	*I will wash myself*
tu *te* laveras	*you will wash yourself*
il/elle *se* lavera	*he/she will wash himself/herself*
nous *nous* laverons	*we will wash ourselves*
vous *vous* laverez	*you will wash yourself/yourselves*
ils/elles *se* laveront	*they will wash themselves*

b. Negative, interrogative, and negative interrogative constructions follow the same rules as regular verbs. The reflexive pronouns remain before the verb.

Ils ne se lèvent pas.	*They aren't getting up.*
Jeanne se lève?	
Jeanne se lève-t-elle?	*Is Jeanne getting up?*
Est-ce que je me lève?	*Do I get up?*
Se lèvent-ils?	*Are they getting up?*
Ils ne se lèvent pas?	
Est-ce qu'ils ne se lèvent pas?	*Aren't they getting up?*
Est-ce que tu t'amuses?	*Do you have a good time?*

T'amuses-tu toujours?	*Do you always have a good time?*
Tu ne t'amuses pas toujours.	*You don't always have a good time.*
Est-ce que les enfants s'amusent?	*Do the children have a good time?*

c. Common reflexive verbs

s'amuser *to have a good time, enjoy oneself*	se lever *to get up; to rise*
s'appeler *to be called*	se maquiller *to put on make-up*
se brosser *to brush oneself*	se mettre en route *to start out*
se coucher *to lie down; to go to bed*	se peigner *to comb one's hair*
se dépêcher *to hurry*	se préparer *to prepare oneself*
se déshabiller *to get undressed*	se promener *to take a walk*
s'ennuyer *to get bored*	se rappeler *to remember*
s'habiller *to get dressed*	se raser *to shave oneself*
se laver *to wash (oneself), get washed*	se réveiller *to wake up*

NOTES:

1. *Me, te,* and *se* become *m', t',* and *s'* before a verb beginning with a vowel or a silent *h*:

   elle s'amuse *(she has fun)*   je m'habille *(I dress myself)*

2. **Remember the spelling changes in the following reflexive verbs:**

   s'appeler (ll), s'ennuyer (uie), se lever (è), se promener (è)

3. **A verb that is reflexive in French is not necessarily reflexive in English.**

Nous nous habillons.	*We are getting dressed.*
Il se couche de bonne heure.	*He goes to bed early.*
Elle se lève.	*She gets up.*

4. **Some reflexive verbs may be used with a direct object in addition to the reflexive pronoun. This direct object often denotes a part of the body.**

Jeanne se lave.	*Jeanne washes herself.*
Jeanne se lave les mains.	*Jeanne washes her hands.*

5. **Most transitive verbs can become reflexive verbs when used with the reflexive pronoun.**

   s'acheter *to buy oneself (something)*

Elle s'achète une robe.	*She buys herself a dress.*

EXERCICE A

Each person has a daily routine. *Exprimez ce que chacun fait.*

EXEMPLE: Lucie/se brosser trois fois les dents
Lucie **se brosse** trois fois les dents.

1. je/s'habiller avec soin

_____

2. Fabien/se laver avec de l'eau froide

_____

3. Marie et Louise/se brosser 100 fois les cheveux

_____

4. tu/se lever à 6 heures

_____

5. nous/se coucher tard

_____

6. vous/se déshabiller vite

_____

7. Jules et Guy/se raser avant de manger

_____

8. Carine/se maquiller bien

_____

EXERCICE B

What will the following people not do while on vacation? _Employez le futur._

EXEMPLE: Jacques quittera l'hôtel à 11 heures du matin.
              (se mettre en route de bonne heure)
              Il ne se mettra pas en route de bonne heure.

1. Janine oubliera son rouge à lèvres. (se maquiller)

_____

2. Pierre et Luc ne rencontreront pas de copains. (s'amuser)

_____

3. Je n'entendrai pas mon réveil. (se lever tôt)

_____

4. Nous serons toujours en retard. (se dépêcher)

_____

5. Tu danseras jusqu'à 2 h du matin. (se coucher avant minuit)

_____

6. Sylvie et vous sortirez tous les soirs. (s'ennuyer)

_____

EXERCICE C

You are trying to remember what you and your friends used to do at camp. _Employez l'imparfait pour exprimer vos questions._

Albert	s'amuser tous les jours
Janine et Anne	se maquiller jour et nuit
vous	se coucher très tôt
tu	se brosser rarement les dents
André	s'ennuyer tout le temps
Robert et moi	s'habiller sans faire attention
Annick	se promener tard le soir

EXEMPLE: **Est-ce qu'Albert se couchait très tôt?**

1. _____

2. _____

3. _____

4. _____

5. _____

6. _____

EXERCICE D

Some of your friends are always late. *Demandez-leur pourquoi.*

EXEMPLE: tu/se coucher trop tard
           Tu ne te couches pas trop tard?

1. Berthe/se préparer à l'avance

_____

2. tu/se réveiller tôt

_____

3. Jean et Fabien/se lever tout de suite

_____

4. vous/se mettre en route à l'heure

_____

5. Nicolas/s'habiller rapidement

_____

6. vous/se laver en cinq minutes

_____

[2] REFLEXIVE CONSTRUCTIONS WITH INFINITIVES

When used with an infinitive, the reflexive pronoun precedes the infinitive and agrees
with the subject of the sentence.

Paul veut toujours s'amuser.	*Paul always wants to have fun.*
Je ne peux pas me lever.	*I cannot get up.*
Elle va s'acheter une robe.	*She is going to buy herself a dress.*

EXERCICE E

You and your friends just came back from a picnic. *Dites ce que chacun veut faire maintenant.*

EXEMPLE:

Nous voulons **nous laver**.

1.

Louise _____

2.

Je _____

3.

Serge et Joseph _____

4.

Vous _____

5.

Tu _____

6.

Pierre et moi _____

EXERCICE F

You are on a camping trip with some friends. *Exprimez ce que vous ne pouvez pas faire pendant ce voyage.*

EXEMPLE: Lucie n'a pas de peigne. (se peigner)
Elle ne peut pas **se peigner**.

1. Jean est trop fatigué. (se réveiller)

_____

2. Je n'ai pas de brosse à dents. (se brosser les dents)

_____

3. Paul et moi n'avons pas de rasoir. (se raser)

_____

4. Vous avez peur du noir. (se coucher)

_____

5. Tu n'as pas de savon. (se laver)

_____

6. Les filles ont oublié leur rouge à lèvres. (se maquiller)

_____

[3] REFLEXIVE COMMANDS

In affirmative commands, reflexive pronouns follow the verb. After the verb, *toi* is used instead of *te*. In negative commands, reflexive pronouns precede the verb.

AFFIRMATIVE IMPERATIVE	
Lève-toi	*Get up!*
Levez-vous!	*Get up!*
Levons-nous!	*Let's get up!*

NEGATIVE IMPERATIVE	
Ne te lève pas!	*Don't get up!*
Ne vous levez pas!	*Don't get up!*
Ne nous levons pas!	*Let's not get up!*

EXERCICE G

You promised to wake up very early and help your father do some work around the house. You're tired and you'd really like to stay in bed a little longer. *Exprimez le débat que vous avez avec votre conscience.*

EXEMPLE: se réveiller
Réveille-toi!   **Ne te réveille pas!**

1. se lever

_____

_____

2. se dépêcher

_____

_____

3. se laver

_____

_____

4. se préparer

_____

_____

5. s'habiller

_____

_____

6. se peigner

_____

_____

EXERCICE H

Pierre has become very bossy, and he is ordering everybody around. What does he says to his friends? _Utilisez les suggestions ci-dessous._

s'amuser	s'habiller	se peigner
se coucher	se laver	se raser
se dépêcher		

EXEMPLE: Vous êtes décoiffé.   **Peignez-vous!**

1. Vous avez les mains sales.

_____

2. Vous êtes fatigué.

_____

3. Vous vous ennuyez.

_____

4. Vous êtes en pyjama à midi.

_____

5. Vous êtes en retard.

_____

6. Votre moustache est trop longue.

_____

EXERCICE I

Exprimez ce que Mme Dupont dit à ses filles de ne pas faire.

EXEMPLE: se maquiller dans la cuisine
        Ne vous maquillez pas dans la cuisine!

1. s'amuser dans le salon

_____

2. se brosser les dents dans la salle à manger

_____

3. se peigner dans la chambre

_____

4. se laver dans la cuisine

_____

5. se coucher dans la salle de séjour *(living room)*

_____

6. s'habiller dans la salle de bains

_____

EXERCICE J

Quelles suggestions faites-vous à votre ami(e) pour bien commencer la journée ?

EXEMPLES: se réveiller à 6 h (oui)
          Réveillons-nous à 6 heures!

          se réveiller à 6 heures (non)
          Ne nous réveillons pas à 6 heures!

1. se lever tout de suite (oui)

_____

2. se laver vite (oui)

_____

3. s'habiller lentement (non)

_____

4. se préparer un grand déjeuner (non)

_____

5. se brosser bien les dents (oui)

_____

6. se peigner pendant une demi-heure (non)

_____

7. se maquiller vite (oui)

_____

8. se mettre en route après deux heures (non)

_____

MASTERY EXERCISES

EXERCICE K

Répondez à ces questions très personnelles.

1. Comment t'appelles-tu ?

_____

2. À quelle heure te mets-tu en route pour l'école ?

_____

3. Qu'est-ce que tu t'amuses à faire ?

_____

4. À quelle heure te réveilles-tu le samedi matin ?

_____

5. Quand te dépêches-tu ?

_____

6. Combien de fois par jour te brosses-tu les dents ?

_____

EXERCICE L

Catherine, Isabelle, and Lise are at a slumber party at Lise's house. It is morning. *Complétez leur conversation avec les formes correctes des verbes indiqués.*

LISE: _____ , mes amies. Il est déjà 9 heures.
1. (se réveiller)

ISABELLE: Je ne veux pas _____ tout de suite. _____ si tu veux.
2. (se lever)   3. (se lever)

Moi, je reste au lit.

CATHERINE: Tant pis pour toi. Puisque je _____ la première, je peux
4. (se lever)

_____ vite.
5. (se laver)

LISE: Pendant que tu _____ , je _____ . Isabelle,
6. (se laver)   7. (se peigner)

_____ .Vite, debout! Nous pouvons _____ ensemble.
8. (se réveiller)   9. (se maquiller)

ISABELLE: Vous pouvez _____ vous deux; moi, je _____ .
10. (se préparer)   11. (se coucher)

CATHERINE: Ne _____ pas de nouveau. _____ et
12. (se coucher)   13. (se laver)

tu vas _____ .Tu vas voir.
14. (se réveiller)

LISE: Catherine, s'il te plaît, ne _____ pas ici dans la chambre.
15. (se maquiller)

_____ dans la salle de bains.
16. (se maquiller)

CATHERINE: D'accord. Lise , tu _____ dans la salle de bains maintenant ?
17. (s'habiller)

LISE: Non. Entre, si tu veux. Est-ce qu'Isabelle _____ de sortir du lit ?
18. (se dépêcher)

CATHERINE: Je ne sais pas! Tu _____ ? Tu _____ ? Mais non !
19. (se lever)   20. (se préparer)

Regarde ! Elle ne _____ pas ! Cette fille est impossible. Qu'est-ce
21. (se réveiller)

qu'on va faire d'elle ?

EXERCICE M

Write a note to a friend saying what you do in the morning to prepare for school. You may want to include:

- the time you wake up
- when you wash
- what you eat for breakfast
- what you generally wear to school
- what other personal hygiene needs you attend to before leaving the house
- when you hurry to school

_____

_____

_____

_____

_____

_____

_____

Chapter 13
Negation

[1] NEGATIVE FORMS

a. The most common negatives are:

ne... jamais	*never*
ne... pas	*not*
ne... personne	*no one, nobody*
ne... plus	*no longer, no more*
ne... rien	*nothing, not . . . anything*

b. Position of negatives

In simple tenses and in the *passé composé, ne* comes before the conjugated verb and object pronouns, if there are any; the second part of the negative generally comes after the conjugated verb (or the subject pronoun in inverted questions).

Elle *n'*est *pas* contente.	*She isn't happy.*
*N'*est-elle *pas* contente ?	*Isn't she happy ?*
Tu *ne la* connais *pas.*	*You don't know her.*
Nous *n'*avons *jamais* lu ce livre.	*We have never read that book.*
Ils *ne* veulent *rien* manger.	*They don't want to eat anything.*
Je *ne* connaissais *personne.*	*I didn't know anyone.*
Vous *n'*aurez *plus de* problèmes.	*You won't have any more problems.*
Tu *n'*as *rien* mangé ? *N'*as-tu *rien* mangé ?	} *Didn't you eat anything?*

NOTE: *Personne* follows the infinitive and the past participle.

Je ne veux voir *personne.*	*I don't want to see anyone.*
Il n'a vu *personne.*	*He didn't see anyone.*

EXERCICE A

Exprimez en phrases négatives ce que les personnes suivantes ne font pas.

EXEMPLE: Patricia / obéir à son frère tout le temps
Patricia **n'obéit pas** à son frère tout le temps.

1. vous / aller d'habitude au cinéma le week-end.

_____

2. tu / sortir souvent avec tes amis

_____

3. Odette / préférer la musique rock

_____

4. Dominique et moi / manger beaucoup le matin

_____

5. je / faire le ménage tous les jours

_____

6. Odile et Grégoire / venir toujours en retard

_____

EXERCICE B

M. Richard is retiring and his co-workers are throwing a farewell party for him. *Expliquez pourquoi.*

EXEMPLE:　ennuyer
Il n'ennuyait personne.

1. irriter

_____

2. menacer

_____

3. trahir

_____

4. renvoyer

_____

5. punir

_____

6. déranger

_____

EXERCICE C

Pierre is in a bad mood and is accusing everybody, including himself, of various crimes and misdemeanors. *Exprimez comment ses amis lui répondent.*

EXEMPLE:　Tu as pris mon argent.
Je n'ai jamais pris ton argent.

1. Tu as lu mon journal intime.

_____

2. Claude est sorti avec ma petite amie !

_____

3. Claude et toi, vous êtes allés au cinéma sans moi !

_____

4. Nicole et François ont utilisé mon ordinateur.

_____

5. J'ai trahi mes amis.

_____

6. Toi et moi, nous avons dérangé les parents.

_____

7. Papa et maman sont entrés dans ma chambre.

_____

8. Mes sœurs ont pris ma voiture !

_____

EXERCICE D

You and your friends say you will no longer do certain things. _Employez le futur et les suggestions ci-dessous._

Marc	critiquer les amis
nous	parler toute la journée
Guy et Cécile	ennuyer les gens
vous	désobéir
je	être paresseux
tu	perdre patience
Lise	emprunter de l'argent

EXEMPLE: Marc **n'empruntera plus d'argent.**

1. _____

2. _____

3. _____

4. _____

5. _____

6. _____

EXERCICE E

Les personnes suivantes sont malades. Exprimez ce qu'elles ne font pas.

EXEMPLE: papa / pouvoir / sortir
Papa **ne peut pas** sortir.

1. Sylvie et Cécile / aller / parler

_____

2. Denise et moi / vouloir / aller à l'école

_____

3. je / préférer / faire le ménage

_____

4. vous / compter / jouer au tennis

_____

5. tu / aimer / manger beaucoup

_____

6. Richard / désirer / rester dans sa chambre

_____

EXERCICE F

You and your friends are being punished. *Dites ce que vous ne pouvez pas faire.*

EXEMPLE: Lucien (pas parler au téléphone)
            Lucien **ne peut pas parler** au téléphone.

1. je (rien regarder à la télévision)

_____

2. vous (plus écouter la radio)

_____

3. les garçons (voir personne)

_____

4. Régine (pas aller au cinéma)

_____

5. tu (jamais sortir seul)

_____

6. Christine et moi (rien acheter au magasin)

_____

    c. *Rien* and *personne* may be used as subjects, preceding the verb;
    ne remains before the conjugated verb.

    Rien ne m'intéresse.   *Nothing interests me.*
    Personne n'écoutait.   *Nobody was listening.*

EXERCICE G

M. Benoît is a pessimist. Exprimez ce qu'il pense.

EXEMPLE: intéressant
            Rien n'est intéressant.
    OR: **Personne n'est** intéressant.

1. facile

_____

2. amusant

_____

3. comique

_____

4. magnifique

_____

5. parfait

_____

6. joli

_____

EXERCICE H

Mme Charlier wanted to organize a talent show at the school, but there was a lack of enthusiasm. *Expliquez pourquoi.*

EXEMPLE: vouloir chanter
            Personne ne voulait chanter.

1. aimer danser

_____

2. désirer rester après les classes

_____

3. savoir organiser le spectacle

_____

4. avoir le temps de préparer le programme

_____

5. pouvoir aider avec la publicité

_____

6. vouloir participer

_____

d. *Jamais* used by itself and in the construction *ne... jamais* means *never*. But *jamais* in a clause without *ne* means *ever*.

Es-tu jamais allé en France ?   *Have you ever gone to France?*

— Non, **je ne suis jamais allé** en France.   — *No, I've never gone to France.*

— **Jamais ?**   — *Never?*

EXERCICE I

You are playing "truth or dare" with a friend. *Exprimez vos questions et ses réponses négatives, en employant le passé composé.*

EXEMPLE: dépenser trop d'argent
— **As-tu jamais dépensé** trop d'argent ?
— Non, **je n'ai jamais dépensé** trop d'argent.

1. trahir les amis

_____

_____

2. faire l'école buissonnière

_____

_____

3. voir un film interdit aux moins de dix-huit ans.

_____

_____

4. désobéir aux parents

_____

_____

5. dire de terribles mensonges

_____

_____

6. danser jusqu'à quatre heures du matin

_____

_____

e. The second part of a negative may be used alone. (*Pas* and *plus* need a modifier.)

— Qui va t'accompagner?	*Who will go with you?*
— **Personne**.	*Nobody.*
— Qu'est-ce que tu manges?	*What are you eating?*
— **Rien.**	*Nothing.*
— Est-il allé en Floride?	*Did he go to Florida?*
— **Jamais**.	*Never.*
— Tu fais du vélo?	*Do you ride a bicycle?*
— **Pas souvent.**	*Not often.*

EXERCICE J

Répondez aux questions suivantes en employant un seul mot négatif.

EXEMPLE: Qui t'aide?   — **Personne**.

1. Quand vas-tu ranger ta chambre ?

_____

2. Qui t'a téléphoné hier soir ?

_____

3. Qu'est-ce que tu as acheté ?

_____

4. Qui sonne à la porte ?

_____

5. Qu'est-ce que tu veux faire ?

_____

6. Quand changeras-tu tes habitudes ?

_____

   f. *Si* (*yes*) is used to contradict a negative statement or question.

   — Il n'est pas intelligent.   *He isn't smart.*
   — **Si,** il est très intelligent   *Yes, he's very smart.*
   — Elle ne travaille pas bien?   *Doesn't she work well?*
   — **Mais si!**   *Yes, she does!*

EXERCICE K

A friend tries to find similarities between the two of you. *Répondez affirmativement à ses questions.*

EXEMPLE: Tu n'aimes pas les concerts de rock?
            Mais si, j'aime les concerts de rock.

1. Tu n'adores pas la mousse au chocolat ?

_____

2. Tu n'aimes pas aller à la plage ?

_____

3. Tu ne travailles pas après l'école ?

_____

4. Tu ne joues pas avec l'ordinateur ?

_____

5. Tu ne lis pas les romans de science-fiction ?

_____

6. Tu ne préfères pas jouer au tennis ?

_____

[2] COMMON NEGATIVE EXPRESSIONS

Ça ne fait rien   _It doesn't matter_

Il est parti sans nous.   _He left without us._

— Ça ne fait rien.   — _It doesn't matter._

de rien / il n'y a pas de quoi   _you're welcome_

Merci de ton aide.   _Thank you for your help._

— De rien.   —_You're welcome._

Merci beaucoup.   _Thanks a lot._

— Il n'y a pas de quoi.   — _You're welcome._

jamais de la vie!   _never! out of the question! not on your life!_

Voulez-vous une cigarette ?   _Do you want a cigarette?_

— Jamais de la vie!   — _Never!_

pas du tout   _not at all_

Aimes-tu cette robe ?   _Do you like this dress?_

— Pas du tout.   — _Not at all._

pas encore   _not yet_

Est-elle prête ?   _Is she ready?_

— Pas encore.   —_Not yet._

pas maintenant   _not now_

Veux-tu voir ce film ?   _Do you want to see this film?_

— Pas maintenant.   —_Not now._

pas aujourd'hui   _not today_

Tu viens chez moi ?   _Are you coming over?_

— Pas aujourd'hui.   — _Not today._

EXERCICE L

Employez une des expressions négatives ci-dessus (above) en réponse dans les situations suivantes.

1. Votre mère demande si vous avez déjà rangé votre chambre.

Vous répondez: _____

2. Votre ami(e) vous dit merci de toute votre aide.

Vous répondez: _____

3. Votre sœur vous demande si vous voulez aller au cinéma, mais vous êtes trop fatigué(e).

Vous répondez: _____

4. Votre ami(e) vous demande si ça vous ennuie qu'il/elle écoute des disques quand vous parlez au téléphone.

   Vous répondez: _____

5. Votre ami(e) vous explique qu'il/elle ne peut pas vous accompagner au théâtre ce soir.

   Vous répondez: _____

6. Votre ami(e) vous demande si vous voulez acheter sa vieille voiture.

   Vous répondez: _____

MASTERY EXERCISES

EXERCICE M

Répondez négativement aux questions de votre ami(e).

1. Es-tu jamais allé(e) en Europe ?

   _____

2. Préfères-tu les histoires d'amour ?

   _____

3. As-tu perdu quelque chose ?

   _____

4. Menaces-tu toujours ton frère ?

   _____

5. Amènes-tu quelqu'un au bal ?

   _____

6. Vas-tu manger quelque chose ?

   _____

7. Aimais-tu faire du ski ?

   _____

8. As-tu jamais ennuyé tes amis ?

   _____

9. Arriveras-tu toujours en retard ?

   _____

10. Regardes-tu quelqu'un ?

    _____

EXERCICE N

Complétez l'histoire en ajoutant le mot négatif approprié.

Mme Chabrol n'aime _____ faire le ménage, _____ du tout. «C'est
                              1.   2.

ennuyeux!», dit elle. _____ ne l'aide avec les travaux ménagers. Son fils François ne fait
                                   3.

absolument _____ parce qu'il est toujours occupé avec ses amis.
                       4.

Est-ce que sa fille Catherine range quelquefois sa chambre? Non! _____ ! Autre-
                                                                                          5.

fois, M. Chabrol aidait un peu sa femme, mais aujourd'hui il ne fait _____ ce qu'il
                                                                                    6.

faisait alors. Un soir, Mme Chabrol déclare qu'elle ne fera _____ tout le travail si les
                                                                          7.

autres ne veulent _____ l'aider. Et un jour, les Chabrol rentrent et _____
                            8.   9.

n'est heureux. La maison est sale. Ils demandent: «Pourquoi?» à Mme Chabrol, mais elle ne dit

_____ . Le jour suivant, quand elle se lève, elle voit tout le monde en train de ranger la
            10.

maison. Elle n'avait _____ cru cela possible. _____ n'est plus
                                 11.   12.

heureux que Mme Chabrol ce jour-là.

EXERCICE O

**You are having a bad day. Write a note to a friend expressing your negative feelings. You may
want to include:**

- whom you find too selfish
- something you don't do any more
- a food you never eat
- a sport you do not like
- something you find impossible to do

_____

_____

_____

_____

_____

_____

_____

_____

Part Two

Noun Structures; Pronoun Structures; Prepositions

Chapter 14
Definite Article and Nouns

[1] FORMS OF THE DEFINITE ARTICLE

a. In English, the definite article is always *the*. In French, the definite article, has four forms: *le, la, l', les.*

	MASCULINE	FEMININE
SINGULAR	*le* livre *l'*étudiant	*la* règle *l'*étudiante
PLURAL	*les* livres *les* étudiants	*les* règles *les* étudiantes

NOTES:

1. The form *l'* is used before a singular noun of either gender beginning with a vowel or silent *h*.

   l'homme   *the man*

2. In French, the article is expressed before each noun, even though it may be omitted in English.

   les garçons et les fille   *boys and girls*

b. Contractions with the definite article

The prepositions *à* and *de* contract with *le* and *les*, becoming *au* and *aux, du* and *des*.

à + le cousin = au cousin	*to the cousin*
à + les dames = aux dames	*to the ladies*
de + le cousin = du cousin	*of the cousin*
de + les dames = des dames	*of the ladies*

NOTE: There is no contraction with *la* or *l'*.

à la mère	*to the mother*	de la mère	*of the mother*
à l'élève	*to the student*	de l'élève	*of the student*

EXERCICE A

You are looking around the classroom. *Dites ce que vous voyez.*

EXEMPLE: bureau *(m.)* **Je vois le bureau.**

1. examen *(m.)* _____

2. devoirs *(m. pl.)* _____

3. livre *(m.)* _____

4. règle *(f.)* _____

5. cahiers *(m. pl.)* _____

6. stylo *(m.)* _____

7. exercice *(m.)* _____

8. leçon *(f.)* _____

9. crayons *(m. pl.)* _____

10. étudiante *(f.)* _____

11. tableau *(m.)* _____

12. craie *(f.)* _____

13. sac *(m.)* _____

14. élèves *(m. / f. pl.)* _____

15. classe *(f.)* _____

16. trousse *(f.)* _____

[2] USES OF THE DEFINITE ARTICLE

The definite article is used to indicate a specific being or thing (*le chat*), as in English (*the cat*). It is also used in the following constructions where English does not use the article.

a. With nouns used in a general or abstract sense.

La vie continue.	*Life goes on.*
J'aime les chiens.	*I like dogs.*

b. With names of languages and subjects, except directly after *parler*, after *en*, and in an adjective phrase with *de*.

Étudiez-vous le français ?	*Are you studying French?*
Le japonais n'est pas facile.	*Japanese isn't easy.*
Tu parles bien l'italien.	*You speak Italian well.*
Pierre adore le dessin.	*Pierre loves drawing.*
BUT	
Je parle espagnol.	*I speak Spanish.*
Le roman est écrit en russe.	*The novel is written in Russian.*
Regarde mon livre de français.	*Look at my French book.*
Pierre est très fort en dessin.	*Pierre is very good in drawing.*

c. In place of the possessive adjective, with parts of the body when the possessor is clear.

Tourne la tête.	*Turn your head.*
Il a mal au pied.	*His foot hurts.*

d. With days of the week in a plural sense.

Le dimanche je m'amuse.	*On Sunday(s) I have fun.*
L'école est fermée le samedi.	*School is closed on Saturday(s).*

e. With names of seasons except after the preposition *en*.

J'adore l'été.	*I love (the) summer.*
En été et au printemps il fait beau.	*In the summer and spring the weather is nice.*

f. In certain common expressions.

à l'école	*to (in) school*	le week-end	*on the weekend*
à l'église	*to (in) church*	le mois prochain	*next month*
à la maison	*at home, home*	la semaine dernière	*last week.*
le matin	*in the morning*	l'année passée	*last year*
l'après-midi	*in the afternoon*	l'été prochain	*next summer*
le soir	*in the evening*		

g. With dates.

C'est aujourd'hui dimanche, le onze juillet.	*Today is Sunday, July 11.*
On est le trois mai.	*It's May 3.*

h. With names of most countries, except after the preposition *en*.

La France et l'Italie sont en Europe.	*France and Italy are in Europe.*
Je vais en France cet été.	*I go to France this summer.*

EXERCICE B

Complétez le dialogue suivant avec la forme correcte de l'article défini s'il est nécessaire.

PIERRE: Que fais-tu _____ week-end?

1.

CLAUDE: Généralement _____ samedi matin, à _____ dix heures, je vais

2. 3.

à _____ Maison des Jeunes faire du karaté et apprendre à parler

4.

_____ japonais. _____ après-midi je reste à _____

5. 6. 7.

maison faire _____ devoirs. Que fais-tu?

8.

PIERRE: _____ natation me passionne. Je vais à _____ piscine couverte

9. 10.

en ville et je nage pendant toute _____ matinée. _____

11. 12.

samedi après-midi je vais travailler à _____ bibliothèque. Que fais-tu

13.

_____ dimanche ?

14.

CLAUDE: Je me lève tôt. Je vais à _____ église; je déjeune en famille et je lis des livres
                                              15.

de _____ science-fiction.
              16.

PIERRE: Je me réveille à 7 heures mais je referme tout de suite _____ yeux et je ne me
                                                                        17.

lève pas avant midi. En _____ été je passe _____ après-midi à
                          18.   19.

_____ plage. En _____ hiver, je vais faire du patin à glace. Si tu
        20.   21.

veux, tu peux venir avec moi _____ dimanche prochain. Nous passerons
                                22.

_____ journée ensemble.
        23.

CLAUDE: Quelle est _____ date ?
                        24.

PIERRE: C'est _____ douze juin.
                   25.

CLAUDE: Quelle bonne idée ! Ça me fera plaisir.

EXERCICE C

Répondez aux questions d'un(e) ami(e).

1. Quelle langue parles-tu?

_____

2. Quand vas-tu au cinéma généralement?

_____

3. Quelle est la date d'aujourd'hui?

_____

4. Quelle saison aimes-tu?

_____

5. Quel cours aimes-tu à l'école?

_____

6. Que fais-tu l'après-midi?

_____

7. Quelles fleurs aimes-tu?

_____

8. Quel animal aimes-tu?

_____

[3] GENDER OF NOUNS

French nouns are either masculine or feminine. There are no general rules to determine the gender of all nouns, but the gender of many nouns can be determined by their meaning or their ending. The gender of other nouns must be learned individually.

a. Nouns that refer to male beings are masculine. Nouns that refer to female beings are feminine.

MASCULINE		FEMININE	
l'homme	*man*	la femme	*woman*
le fils	*son*	la fille	*daughter*
le prince	*prince*	la princesse	*princess*
le dentiste	*dentist*	la dentiste	*dentist*

b. The gender of some nouns may be determined by their ending.

MASCULINE		FEMININE	
-acle	spect*acle*	**-ade**	limon*ade*
-age★	gar*age*	**-ale**	cathédr*ale*
-al	anim*al*	**-ance**	dist*ance*
-eau★	bat*eau*	**-ence**	ess*ence*
-et	livr*et*	**-ette**	cass*ette*
-ier	coll*ier*	**-ie**	compagn*ie*
-isme	journal*isme*	**-ique**	gymnast*ique*
-ment	gouverne*ment*	**-oire**	hist*oire*
		-sion	expres*sion*
		-tion	nata*tion*
		-ure	fig*ure*

c. Some feminine nouns are formed by adding *e* to the masculine.

MASCULINE	FEMININE	
l'ami	l'amie	*friend*
l'avocat	l'avocate	*lawyer*
le client	la cliente	*client*
le cousin	la cousine	*cousin*
l'employé	l'employée	*employee*
l'étudiant	l'étudiante	*student*
le voisin	la voisine	*neighbor*

★ Note these exceptions, which are all feminine: *la page, la plage; l'eau, la peau.*

d. Some feminine nouns are formed by changing the masculine ending to a feminine ending.

MASCULINE		FEMININE		
-an	pays*an*	**-anne**	paysanne	*peasant*
-ien	Parisi*en*	**-ienne**	Parisienne	*Parisian*
-on	patr*on*	**-onne**	patronne	*boss*
-er	boulang*er*	**-ère**	boulangère	*baker*
-ier	épici*er*	**-ière**	épicière	*grocer*
-eur	programm*eur*	**-euse**	programmeuse	*programmer*
-teur	ac*teur*	**-trice**	actrice	*actor/actress.*

e. Other masculine nouns and their feminine counterparts:

MASCULINE		FEMININE	
le chat	*cat*	la chatte	*cat*
le chien	*dog*	la chienne	*dog*
l'hôte	*host*	l'hôtesse	*hostess*
le neveu	*nephew*	la nièce	*niece*
l'oncle	*uncle*	la tante	*aunt*
le roi	*king*	la reine	*queen*

f. Some nouns have the same form in the masculine and the feminine.

l'artiste	*artist*	l'enfant	*child*
le (la) camarade	*friend*	le (la) secrétaire	*secretary*
l'élève	*student*	le (la) touriste	*tourist*

g. Some nouns are always masculine or feminine regardless of the gender of the person referred to.

ALWAYS MASCULINE

l'agent de police	*police officer*
le bébé	*baby*
le chef	*chef, cook, chief, head*
le médecin	*doctor*
le professeur	*teacher, professeur*

ALWAYS FEMININE

la personne	*person*
la victime	*victim*

EXERCICE D

Give the male or female counterpart. *Donnez l'équivalent de l'autre genre pour chacun des mots suivants.*

EXEMPLE: la mère: **c'est le père**

1. la femme: _____

2. l'oncle: _____

3. le neveu: _____

4. la fille: _____

5. le grand-père: _____

6. le cousin: _____

7. l'enfant: _____

8. la camarade: _____

EXERCICE E

Both parents in each family work together. What is the job of the other parent? *Suivez l'exemple.*

EXEMPLE: M. Dumas est l'épicier de la ville.
        Mme Dumas est l'épicière de la ville.

1. Mme Billet est la secrétaire du patron.

_____.

2. M. Cavin est l'avocat de l'accusé.

_____.

3. Mme Paillot est la pâtissière du restaurant.

_____.

4. M. Lignon est le patron de la société.

_____.

5. Mme Silvain est la mécanicienne du garage.

_____.

EXERCICE F

Janine has to match the following words to the definitions below. *Exprimez les mots qu'elle trouve avec l'article défini approprié.*

natation	garage	oncle	boucher
pâtisserie	livret	bateau	cathédrale
gymnastique	mère	serviette	

EXEMPLE: le mari de la tante: **l'oncle**

1. le petit livre: _____

2. le sport où l'on nage: _____

3. ce qui permet de voyager sur l'eau: _____

4. la femme du père: _____

5. le magasin où l'on achète des gâteaux: _____

6. l'homme qui vend la viande: _____

7. le lieu où l'on garde la voiture: _____

8. le sport où l'on fait des exercices: _____

9. le linge pour la table: _____

10. une grande église: _____

[4] PLURAL OF NOUNS

a. The plural of most French nouns is formed by adding *s* to the singular.

SINGULAR	PLURAL
le garçon *boy*	les garçons *boys*
l'arbre *(m.) tree*	les arbres *trees*
la voiture *car*	les voitures *cars*

b. Nouns ending in *-s*, *-x*, or *-z* remain unchanged in the plural.

SINGULAR	PLURAL
le fils *son*	les fils *sons*
le prix *price, prize*	les prix *prices, prizes*
le nez *nose*	les nez *noses*

Other nouns ending in *-s*

l'autobus *bus*	la fois *time*	le pays *country*
le bras *arm*	le mois *month*	le repas *meal*

Other nouns ending in *-x*

la croix *cross*	la voix *voice*

c. Nouns ending in *-eau* and *-eu* add *x* in the plural.

SINGULAR	PLURAL
le bateau *boat*	les bateaux *boats*
le neveu *nephew*	les neveux *nephews*

Other nouns ending in -*eau*

le bureau *desk*	le couteau *knife*	le manteau *coat*
le cadeau *gift*	l'eau *(f.)* *water*	l'oiseau *(m.)* *bird*
le chapeau *hat*	le gâteau *cake*	le tableau *painting; board*
le château *castle*		

Other nouns ending in -*eu*

le cheveu★   *hair*   le feu   *fire*

d. Nouns ending in -*al* change -*al* to -*aux* in the plural.

SINGULAR	PLURAL
l'animal *(m.)* *animal*	les animaux *animals*
le cheval *horse*	les chevaux *horses*
le journal *newspaper*	les journaux *newspapers*
l'hôpital *hospital*	les hôpitaux *hospitals*

e. Some nouns have irregular plurals.

SINGULAR	PLURAL
l'œil *(m.)* *eye*	les yeux *eyes*
madame *Madam, Mrs.*	mesdames *ladies*
mademoiselle *Miss*	mesdemoiselles *Misses*
monsieur *gentleman, Mr.*	messieurs *gentlemen,*

f. A few nouns are used mainly in the plural.

les gens *(m. or f.)* *people*	les mathématiques *(f.)* *mathematics*
les lunettes *(f.)* *eyeglasses*	les vacances *(f.)* *vacation*

g. Family names do not add **s** in the plural.

les Bertrand   les Dupont

EXERCICE G

The students in M. Chaumont's art class are drawing pictures of mirror images. *Exprimez ce que vous voyez dans chaque illustration.*

EXEMPLE:

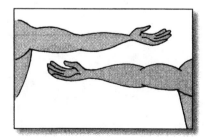

Je vois deux bras.

★Since *cheveu* refers to a single hair, the plural *les cheveux* is more common.

1.

_____

2.

_____

3.

_____

4.

_____

5.

_____

6.

_____

7.

_____

8.

_____

9.

_____

10.

_____

11.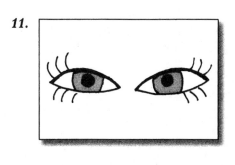

12.

_____

_____

13.

14.

_____

_____

EXERCICE H

Fill in the words missing in this picture story. *Complétez l'histoire.*

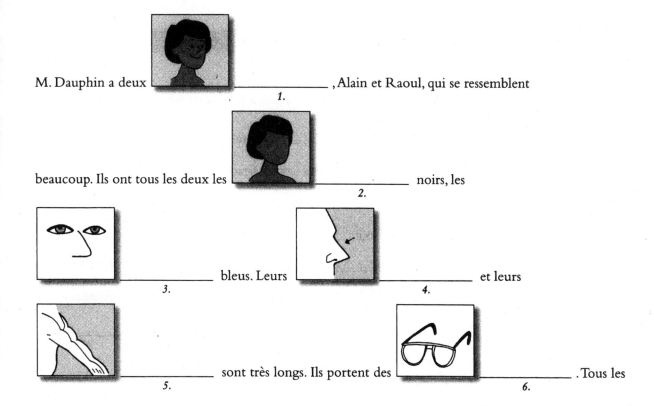

M. Dauphin a deux _____ , Alain et Raoul, qui se ressemblent
  1.

beaucoup. Ils ont tous les deux les _____ noirs, les
  2.

_____ bleus. Leurs _____ et leurs
  3.   **4.**

_____ sont très longs. Ils portent des _____ . Tous les
  5.   **6.**

deux aiment les _____ , surtout les _____
                          7.   *8.*

et les _____ . Alain et Raoul lisent les mêmes
              9.

_____ et mangent les mêmes _____
        10.   *11.*

et les mêmes _____ . Pourquoi? Ils sont jumeaux.
                    12.

M A S T E R Y   E X E R C I S E S

EXERCICE I

Complétez cette composition en ajoutant l'article défini s'il y a lieu (if appropriate).

C'est aujourd'hui _____ mercredi _____ quatorze octobre. Nous sommes à
                              1.   *2.*

_____ école. _____ mercredi nous avons beaucoup de cours: _____
        3.   *4.*   *5.*

anglais, _____ français, _____ histoire, _____ biologie, _____
                    6.   *7.*   *8.*   *9.*

maths et _____ gymnastique sont _____ cours _____ mercredi.
                    10.   *11.*   *12.*

_____ français est mon cours préféré. M. Lenoir est _____ prof de français. Il est
        13.   *14.*

français et formidable. _____ classe de _____ français est toujours si amusante et in-
                                15.   *16.*

téressante que je lève _____ main mille fois par jour. Avant les vacances en _____
                                17.   *18.*

été, M. Lenoir va donner une grande fête et nous inviter. Quelle chance pour nous !

EXERCICE J

Demandez à un(e) ami(e) de vous aider. Employez le pluriel des mots indiqués.

EXEMPLE: arranger / tableau
Arrange les tableaux, s'il te plaît.

1. acheter / cadeau

_____

2. chercher / couteau

_____

3. accepter / paquet

_____

4. fermer / rideau

_____

5. ramasser / journal

_____

6. allumer / feu

_____

7. contacter / hôpital

_____

8. couper / gâteau

_____

9. ranger / chambre

_____

10. préparer / repas

_____

EXERCICE K

Write a note to a friend telling about a gift you bought for someone you love. You may want to include:

• for whom you bought the gift
• for what occasion
• what you bought
• a description of the item
• where you bought the gift
• how much you paid for it

_____

_____

_____

_____

Chapter 15
Indefinite and Partitive Articles

[1] FORMS

a. The indefinite singular article in French has two forms *un* and *une*, corresponding to English *a (an)*. It refers to beings and things not specifically identified (a cake, *any* cake, not the chocolate cake on the table).

ARTICLE	USED BEFORE	EXAMPLE	MEANING
un	masculine singular nouns	un livre	a book
une	feminine singular nouns	une règle	a ruler

Les Dupont ont une jolie maison
dans un grand jardin.

*The Duponts have a pretty house
in a large garden.*

EXERCICE A

M. Delatre is taking a walk in the country. *Dites ce qu'il voit.*

EXEMPLE: **Il voit un lac.**

1. _____

2. _____

3. _____

4. _____

5. _____

6. _____

7. _____

8. _____

9. _____

10. _____

   b. The partitive article expresses an indefinite quantity or part of a whole (*some, any*). It is expressed in French by *de* + definite article.

ARTICLE	USED BEFORE	EXAMPLE	MEANING
du	masculine singular nouns beginning with a consonant	**du pain**	*some (any) bread*
de la	feminine singular nouns beginning with a consonant	**de la viande**	*some (any) meat*
de l'	singular nouns beginning with a vowel	**de l'argent** **de l'eau**	*some (any) money* *some (any) water*

Je vais mettre du parfum.   *I'm going to put on some perfume.*
Il a envie de manger de la glace. *He feels like eating some ice cream.*
As-tu de l'argent?   *Do you have any money?*

NOTE: Unlike English, where *some* or *any* may be omitted, the partitive may not be omitted in French and is repeated before each noun.

Veux-tu du poisson et de la salade?   *Do you want fish and salad?*

EXERCICE B

Richard is packing a picnic basket. *Exprimez ce qu'il met dedans.*

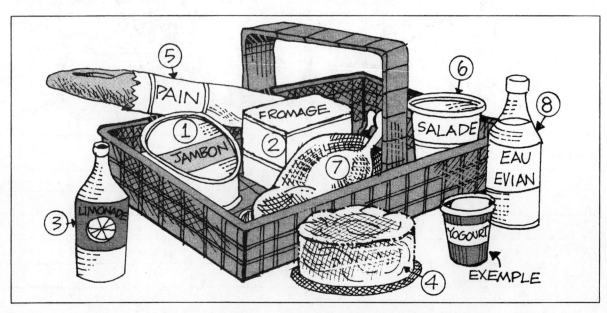

EXEMPLE: Il met **du yogourt.**

1. _____

2. _____

3. _____

4. _____

5. _____

6. _____

7. _____

8. _____

EXERCICE C

What subjects are you taking in school? *Dites-le en français.*

EXEMPLE: physique *(f.)*
  Je fais **de la physique.**

1. algèbre *(f.)*

_____

2. biologie *(f.)*

_____

3. français *(m.)*

_____

4. science naturelle *(f.)*

_____

5. italien *(m.)*

_____

6. chimie *(f.)*

_____

7. histoire *(f.)*

_____

8. latin *(m.)*

_____

9. gymnastique *(f.)*

_____

c. The plural form is *des* (*some*) for both the indefinite and the partitive articles; it expresses an unspecified amount or quantity, more than one item. It has no direct English equivalent.

ARTICLE	USED BEFORE	EXAMPLE	MEANING
des	all plural nouns, masculine or feminine	**des légumes** **des confitures** **des hommes** **des idées**	(some) vegetables (some) preserves (some) men (some) ideas

Elle a des problèmes.	*She has (some) problems.*
Les élèves ont des devoirs.	*The students have homework.*
Donnez-lui des crayons.	*Give him some pencils.*
Vois-tu des fautes ?	*Do you see any mistakes?*

EXERCICE D

The Quentins are taking a tour of the new home their friends have just moved into. *Exprimez ce qu'ils voient.*

EXEMPLES: garage *(m.)* Ils voient **un garage.**
 balcons *(m.pl.)* Ils voient **des balcons.**

1. jardin *(m.)* _____

2. cuisine *(f.)* _____

3. fenêtres *(f.pl.)* _____

4. terrasse *(f.)* _____

5. lampes *(f.pl.)* _____

6. escaliers *(m.pl.)* _____

7. piano *(m.)* _____

8. piscine *(f.)* _____

9. tableaux *(m.pl.)* _____

10. portes *(f.pl.)* _____

11. grenier *(m.)* _____

12. meubles *(m.pl.)* _____

13. chaises *(f.pl.)* _____

14. arbres *(m.pl.)* _____

EXERCICE E

What is sold in each of these stores in France? *Suivez l'exemple.*

crème	légumes	parfum	saucisson	viande
essence	médicaments	poisson	vêtements	

EXEMPLE: Dans une charcuterie **on vend du saucisson.**

1. Dans une poissonnerie _____

2. Dans une pharmacie _____

3. Dans une station-service _____

4. Dans une épicerie _____

5. Dans une boutique _____

6. Dans une boucherie _____

7. Dans une parfumerie _____

8. Dans une crémerie _____

EXERCICE F

What does one need to buy in the following situations? *Choisissez les mots appropriés.*

bâton *(m.)*	chocolat *(m.)*	film *(m.)*	jambon *(m.)*	pain *(m.)*	skis *(m.pl.)*
beurre *(m.)*	crayon *(m.)*	fromage *(m.)*	laitue *(f.)*	papier *(m.)*	stylo *(m.)*
bottes *(f.pl.)*	crème *(f.)*	gomme *(f.)*	œuf *(m.)*	parfum *(m.)*	sucre *(m.)*

EXEMPLE: Lisette veut faire une omelette.
Elle achètera **des œufs et du jambon.**

1. Les Morin veulent faire du ski.

_____

2. Mme Laurin veut préparer une mousse au chocolat.

_____

3. Je veux faire un sandwich.

_____

4. Nous voulons prendre des photos.

_____

5. Vous voulez offrir un cadeau à une amie qui adore se parfumer.

_____

6. Tu veux te préparer pour la rentrée scolaire.

_____

NOTES:

1. **When an adjective precedes a plural noun, *des* is usually replaced by *de* (*de* becomes *d'* before a vowel or silent *h*).**

Je vois de jolies fleurs.	*I see pretty flowers.*
Elle met de vieux gants.	*She puts on old gloves.*
Il fait de bonnes crêpes.	*He makes good crepes.*

2. **When a plural adjective is part of a noun compound, the form *des* is used.**

des grands-mères	*grandmothers*
des petits pois	*peas*
des jeunes filles	*girls*

EXERCICE G

Isabelle goes to the flea market with the Chabrols. *Dites ce que chaque personne achète.*

EXEMPLE: Mme Chabrol / bons chocolats
Mme Chabrol achète **de bons chocolats**.

1. Catherine / nouveaux CD

_____

2. François / bons livres

_____

3. M. Chabrol / vieux vases

_____

4. Isabelle / jolies affiches

_____

5. François / excellents articles de sport

_____

6. Mme Chabrol / belles assiettes

_____

d. **In a negative sentence all forms of the indefinite article and of the partitive become *de* without the article (*de* becomes *d'* before a vowel or a silent *h*).**

J'ai un chat et j'ai des chiens.	*I have a cat and dogs.*
Je n'ai pas de chat et je n'ai pas de chiens.	*I don't have a cat and I don't have dogs.*
Je n'ai pas de stylo.	*I don't have a pen.*
Il n'a plus d'argent.	*He doesn't have any money left.*
Je n'achète pas de vêtements.	*I am not buying clothes.*

EXERCICE H

What's in the Duvals' refrigerator? What's not there? *Employez la forme correcte du partitif.*

EXEMPLE: glace / viande
               Il y a **de la glace** mais il n'y a **pas de viande**.

1. beurre / pain

_____

2. café / crème

_____

3. légumes / fruits

_____

4. soupe / biscuits

_____

5. poisson / fromage

_____

6. œufs / saucisses

_____

EXERCICE I

Mme Legros talks with her friends about ways to stay thin. Using the negative word provided, write what they say they don't do.

EXEMPLE: Elles suivent un régime. (pas)
               Elles ne suivent pas de régime.

1. Elle mange de la viande. (jamais)

_____

2. Vous choisissez des gâteaux à la crème. (plus)

_____

3. Je fais des exercices. (pas)

_____

4. Elles mangent du chocolat. (plus)

_____

5. Nous prenons des médicaments. (jamais)

_____

6. Tu bois de l'eau? (pas)

_____

EXERCICE J

Exprimez ce que ces personnes font (et ne font pas) dans les situations suivantes.

EXEMPLE: Georges veut s'amuser. lire: bandes dessinées, roman, livre d'école
                Il lit **des bandes** dessinées.
                Il lit **un roman.**
                Il ne lit **pas de livre d'école.**

1. Alain veut jouer au golf. employer: raquette, balles, club

_____

_____

_____

2. Les filles veulent préparer un dessert. acheter: glace, bœuf, fruits

_____

_____

_____

3. Je veux aller à la plage. mettre: sandales, manteau, maillot de bain

_____

_____

_____

4. Nous avons mal à l'estomac. prendre: médicaments, thé, bonbons

_____

_____

_____

5. Tu offres un cadeau à un(e) ami(e). donner: argent, disque, livres

_____

_____

_____

6. Vous voulez impressionner votre professeur. apporter: bandes dessinées, gâteau, affiches

_____

_____

_____

[2] OMISSION OF THE INDEFINITE ARTICLE

a. The indefinite article is omitted after *être* and *devenir* with unmodified names of nationalities, occupations, or professions.

Je suis Américain.   I'm an American.

Son frère veut devenir médecin.   His brother wants to become a doctor.

NOTE: The article is used if the noun is modified or when *c'est* is used.

M. Legrand est un bon professeur.   *Mr. Legrand is a good teacher.*

C'est un ingénieur.   *He is an engineer.*

b. The indefinite article is omitted after the exclamatory adjectives *quel, quelle, quels, quelles.*

Quel bon film!   *What a good movie!*

c. The indefinite article is omitted before the numbers *cent* and *mille.*

cent hommes   *one hundred men*

mille dollars   *a thousand dollars*

EXERCICE K

A friend writes you a note about a friend of hers. *Complétez la lettre avec les articles définis ou indéfinis qui sont nécessaires.*

Chère Gisèle,

Je voudrais te présenter mon ami Pierre. C'est _____ professeur célèbre. Il est
                                                                1.

_____ Anglais. Il a publié _____ articles dans des revues péda-
    2.   **3.**

gogiques. Quel _____ homme intéressant! Il a beaucoup voyagé en Europe.
                    4.

_____ langues étrangères le passionnent. Il parle bien _____
    5.   **6.**

français, _____ anglais et _____ japonais. Quand il a du temps
        7.   **8.**

libre il est _____ entraîneur pour _____ équipe de football
          9.   **10.**

au lycée du quartier. J'espère que tu peux faire la connaissance de mon ami.

Ton amie Françoise

EXERCICE L

Both parents in each family have the same job. *Décrivez en français la profession de l'autre parent.*

EXEMPLE: Mme Bagot est artiste.
           M. Bagot : C'est un artiste.

1. M. Seguin est vendeur.

_____

2. Mme Guérin est médecin.

_____

3. M. Hervé est infirmier.

_____

4. M. Ribet est professeur.

_____

5. Mme Joubert est programmeuse.

_____

6. M. Destombes est acteur.

_____

[3] ADVERBS AND NOUNS OF QUANTITY

Nouns and adverbs that express quantity or measure are followed by *de* alone before another noun. Some common nouns of quantity are:

une boîte *a box*	**un paquet** *a package*
une bouteille *a bottle*	**un sac** *a bag*
une douzaine *a dozen*	**une tasse** *a cup*
une paire *a pair*	**un verre** *a glass*

Donnez-moi une douzaine **d'**œufs.	*Give me a dozen eggs.*
Elle ouvre un sac **de** chips.	*She opens a bag of chips.*
Je voudrais une bouteille **d'**eau.	*I would like a bottle of water.*

Some common adverbs of quantity are:

assez de *enough*	**peu de** *little, few*
beaucoup de *much, many*	**plus de** *more*
combien de *how much, how many*	**trop de** *too much, too many*
moins de *less, fewer*	

J'ai beaucoup **d'**amis.	*I have many friends.*
Avez-vous assez **de** pain?	*Do you have enough bread?*

NOTE: With some expressions constructed with *de*, *de* is used alone.

avoir besoin de *to need* **avoir envie de** *to desire*

J'ai besoin d'argent. *I need money.*

J'ai envie de chocolats. *I desire some chocolates.*

EXERCICE M

What do you need to bake a cake? Exprimez la réponse en français.

EXEMPLE: **J'ai besoin d'un verre d'eau**.

1. _____

2. _____

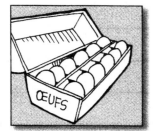

3. _____

4. _____

5. _____

6. _____

EXERCICE N

Décrivez votre personnalité en employant les suggestions données.

assez	ambition	imagination
beaucoup	charme	intelligence
besoin	courage	patience
peu	énergie	prudence
trop	enthousiasme	talent
	force	

EXEMPLE: **J'ai beaucoup de force.**

1. _____

2. _____

3. _____

4. _____

5. _____

6. _____

7. _____

8. _____

9. _____

10. _____

[4] THE PARTITIVE AND THE DEFINITE ARTICLE

While the partitive is used to express *some* or *part of* something, the definite article is used with nouns in a general sense.

Les Anglais aiment le thé.	*The British like tea* (in general).
Je bois du thé pendant les repas.	*I drink tea during meals.*

EXERCICE O

You are in a restaurant with a friend who says what he/she likes to eat. Suggest that you order some.

EXEMPLE: jambon *(m.)*.   —**J'aime le jambon.**
                                         — Alors, **commandons du jambon.**

1. salade *(f.)*

   — _____

   — _____

2. eau minérale *(f.)*

   — _____

   — _____

3. poisson *(m.)*

   — _____

   — _____

4. fromage *(m.)*

   — _____

   — _____

5. frites *(f.pl.)*

   — _____

   — _____

6. mousse au chocolat *(f.)*

   — _____

   — _____

EXERCICE P

Exprimez ce que vous aimez ou n'aimez pas manger.

1. Mon plat préféré est _____ .

2. Je déteste _____ .

3. Quand j'ai soif je prends _____ .

4. Le matin je mange _____ .

5. Au déjeuner à la cantine à l'école je choisis _____ .

6. Quand ma mère prépare de la soupe pour moi j'aime _____ .

7. Comme dessert je choisis _____ .

8. Mon légume préféré est _____ .

9. Mon fruit préféré est _____ .

10. Quand je veux maigrir je ne prends pas _____ .

11. Je mange toujours _____ .

12. Je ne mange jamais _____ .

MASTERY EXERCISES

EXERCICE Q

You and a friend are preparing a chocolate mousse. Complete what you say to each other.
Employez les articles définis ou partitifs qui conviennent.

EXEMPLE: Ma spécialité est **la** mousse au chocolat.

1. J'ai acheté beaucoup _____ chocolat.

2. Tu dois allumer _____ four.

3. Est-ce qu'on utilise _____ crème et _____ beurre?

4. Oui, et il faut ajouter _____ œufs.

5. On met une douzaine _____ œufs.

6. Il est nécessaire de séparer _____ œufs, n'est-ce pas ?

7. Oui, tu mets _____ jaunes dans le bol et tu fouettes (*whip*) _____ blancs.

8. Il faut que tu ajoutes _____ café.

9. Tu as acheté _____ sucre?

10. On ne met pas _____ sucre dans _____ recette.

EXERCICE R

Nicole is having a party. Complete the description of how she prepares for it. *Ajoutez les articles définis, indéfinis ou partitifs qui conviennent.*

_____ semaine dernière Nicole a envoyé _____ invitations à beaucoup _____ amis. Elle a
    1.   **2.**   **3.**

indiqué _____ date et _____ heure de la boum. _____ boum est aujourd'hui. Nicole et ses
         4.   **5.**   **6.**

sœurs mettent _____ décorations partout. Puisqu'elle adore _____ ballons, elle met
                   7.   **8.**

_____ ballons de toutes _____ couleurs sur _____ murs du salon. Elle a aussi préparé
    9.   **10.**   **11.**

_____ douzaines _____ sandwiches et _____ gâteaux au chocolat et à la vanille. Sa mère a
   12.   **13.**   **14.**

déjà acheté _____ bouteilles _____ soda, _____ sacs _____ chips et _____ pa-
         15.   **16.**   **17.**   **18.**   **19.**

quets _____ bonbons et _____ glace. Elle n'a pas trouvé _____ biscuits. Tant pis. Elle
     20.   ·**21.**   **22.**

trouve qu'elle a acheté assez _____ choses et puis, les jeunes d'aujourd'hui n'aiment pas tellement
                          23.

_____ biscuits. Ils préfèrent _____ gâteau. Maintenant Nicole cherche _____ vieilles cas-
   24.   **25.**   **26.**

settes et aussi _____ CD populaires. Elle est très nerveuse parce que _____ boum va com-
         27.   **28.**

mencer dans une heure.

EXERCICE S

You are going to attend a barbecue. Write a note to a friend telling about it. You may want to include:

- where you are going for the barbecue
- the date of the barbecue

- how you will get there
- what you will bring
- who else will be going
- what you will eat

_____

_____

_____

_____

_____

_____

_____

Chapter 16
Subject Pronouns

A pronoun is a word used in place of a noun. A subject pronoun is used in place of a subject noun.

[1] FORMS

SINGULAR	PLURAL
je (j') *I* **tu** *you* (familiar) **il** *he* **elle** *she* **on** *one, you, we, they*	**nous** *we* **vous** *you* (also formal singular) **ils** *they* (masculine) **elles** *they* (feminine)

NOTES:

1. A subject pronoun normally precedes the verb.

   Tu travailles bien.   *You work well.*

2. In an inverted question, a subject pronoun follows the verb in simple tenses and follows the auxiliary verb in compound tenses.

   Travailles-tu à la maison?   *Do you work at home?*
   Est-elle allée à la bibliothèque?   *Has she gone to the library?*

   When the question is formed with *est-ce que,* there is no inversion of the verb and pronoun.

   Est-ce que tu travailles à la maison?   *Do you work at home?*
   Est-ce qu'elle est allée à la bibliothèque?   *Has she gone to the library?*

   Inversion with *je* is generally avoided and occurs only with a few verbs: *avoir, être, pouvoir, savoir.*

   Puis-je venir?   *May I come?*

3. Subject pronouns are omitted in the imperative.

   Écoute les informations!   *Listen to the news!*
   Regardez cet article!   *Look at this article!*
   Allons au cinéma!   *Let's go to the movies!*

4. The familiar singular subject pronoun *tu* is used to address a friend, a relative, a child, or a pet, and the formal *vous* is used in the singular to show respect, or to address an older person or someone one does not know well.

5. The third-person pronoun *on* means *one* or *someone.* It may also refer to an indefinite *you, we, they,* or *people* in general.

   On a besoin d'amitié.   *One needs (People need / We need) friendship.*

On dit que le français est la langue de l'amour.	*They say that French is the language of love.*
On a pris mon stylo.	*Someone took my pen.*

In spoken French, *on* is often used in place of *nous*.

On va au parc ?	*Are we going to the park?*

EXERCICE A

Write who did what yesterday. *Employez le pronom sujet approprié.*

EXEMPLE: **Elle est revenue** tard.

1. _____ t'es amusé.

2. _____ avons joué avec l'ordinateur.

3. _____ est allée à une fête.

4. _____ ai joué au tennis.

5. _____ sont restés à la maison.

6. _____ avez travaillé dur.

7. _____ se sont promenées.

8. _____ est venu chez Roger.

EXERCICE B

Complete the description of the guests at Janine's party. *Employez le pronom sujet approprié.*

1. Marie et Sylvie sont sœurs. _____ travaillent dans le même bureau.

2. Êtes-_____ professeur de biologie? _____ suis experte en physique.

3. Henri étudie les maths. _____ veut devenir ingénieur.

4. Claire et moi, _____ suivons un cours de latin.

5. Pierre et Jean réparent les voitures. _____ sont mécaniciens.

6. _____ es le meilleur élève de la classe.

7. La mère de Berthe va à l'université. _____ étudie l'histoire.

EXERCICE C

State the rules observed in the office of Entreprises Laurent. *Employez on.*

EXEMPLES: écouter le directeur / ne pas faire de bruit
    On écoute le directeur. / **On ne fait pas** de bruit.

1. arriver à l'heure

_____

2. ne pas téléphoner à ses amis

_____

3. travailler consciencieusement

_____

4. ne pas parler trop fort

_____

5. respecter les autres

_____

6. ne jamais oublier ses responsabilités

_____

[2] CE + ÊTRE

The pronoun *ce (c')* (*it, he, she, this, that, they, these, those*) is used with the verb *être* to describe someone or something. *Ce* can replace *il, elle, ils,* and *elles* in the following constructions.

a. **Before a modified noun.**

C'est une erreur.	*It's a mistake.*
C'est un bon film.	*That's a good film.*
Ce sont de vieux amis.	*They're old friends.*
BUT	
Il est docteur.	*He's a doctor.*

b. **Before a proper noun.**

Qui est là? — C'est Marc.	*Who is it? — It's Marc.*
Quelle est la capitale de la France?	*What is the capital of France?*
— C'est Paris.	*— It's Paris.*

c. **In dates.**

C'est aujourd'hui lundi.	*Today is Monday.*
Demain ce sera le 6 juin.	*Tomorrow will be June 6.*

NOTE: Use *Il est* to express the hour of the day.

Il est neuf heures.	*It is nine o'clock.*

d. Before a pronoun.

Qui frappe à la porte? C'est vous?   *Who's knocking at the door? Is it you?*

EXERCICE D

Explain what everyone thinks Joseph's abstract painting represents. *Employez C'est ou ce sont.*

EXEMPLES:

C'est un arbre.

Ce sont des arbres.

1.

_____

2.

_____

3.

_____

4.

_____

5.

_____

6.

_____

EXERCICE E

Answer your Social Studies teacher's questions. *Employez* **c'est** *or* **ce sont.**

1. Qui est le premier président des États-Unis?

_____

2. Quelle est la capitale des États-Unis?

_____

3. Quels sont deux sites touristiques intéressants aux États-Unis?

_____

4. Qui est le maire (*mayor*) de votre ville?

_____

EXERCICE F

What are the dates of the following holidays? *Utilisez* **c'est.**

1. Noël, _____

2. Le Nouvel An, _____

3. La Fête de l'Indépendance américaine, _____

4. la Fête nationale française, _____

5. La Saint-Valentin _____

EXERCICE G

Richard is talking about people and things with his new friend Christophe. *Complétez ce qu'il dit en employant* **ce (c'), il, elle, ils,** *ou* **elles.**

1. Regarde cette fille. _____ est Janine, ma sœur. _____ est très jolie.

2. Qui sonne à la porte? _____ sont Paul et Luc. _____ sont en retard.

3. Quelle est la date? _____ le premier mai. Anne célèbre son anniversaire aujourd'hui. _____ a quatorze ans.

4. Qui sont les filles là-bas? _____ sont Odette et Danielle. _____ sont dans ma classe d'anglais.

5. Qu'est-ce que c'est? _____ est mon scooter. Jean le répare. _____ est mécanicien.

M A S T E R Y   E X E R C I S E S

EXERCICE H

Complétez l'histoire suivante en employant ce (c') *ou le pronom sujet correct.*

_____ est mercredi après-midi. _____ est 4 heures précises. Quelqu'un sonne à
    1.   *2.*

la porte. Qui est-_____ ? Je pense que _____ est Jacques, mon frère. _____ ai
           3.   *4.*   *5.*

tort. Imagine ma surprise. _____ est M. Mercier. _____ est bibliothécaire. Que
          6.   *7.*

fait-_____ ici? Il dit: "_____ est une affaire sérieuse. Ma petite fille, _____ as
    8.   *9.*   *10.*

beaucoup de problèmes. Ton frère et toi, _____ avez négligé de rendre vos livres à la
                  11.

bibliothèque." _____ réponds que c'est impossible puisque _____ allons à la
         12.   *13.*

bibliothèque chaque semaine. M. Mercier pense que _____ avons vingt livres à la
                      14.

maison! _____ veut parler à mes parents, mais _____ ne sont pas à la maison.
      15.   *16.*

Finalement Annick, ma sœur aînée, arrive. _____ est elle qui est responsable de tous
                    17.

ces livres. _____ est vraiment très embarrassée.
      18.

EXERCICE I

Répondez aux questions des parents d'un(e) ami(e). Employez ce (c') *ou un pronom sujet.*

1. Quelle est la date de ton anniversaire?

   _____

2. Que fais-tu après l'école?

   _____

3. Où est-ce que ta famille habite?

   _____

4. À quelle heure est-ce que tu rentres de classe?

   _____

5. Qui est ton (ta) meilleur(e) ami(e)?

   _____

6. Est-ce que tes parents travaillent tous les deux?

   _____

EXERCICE J

Write a note to a friend about a movie you saw. You may want to include:

- the title of the movie
- when you went
- with whom you went
- why you went with this person
- what the movie was about
- your opinion of the movie

_____

_____

_____

_____

_____

_____

_____

Chapter 17
Object Pronouns

[1] DIRECT OBJECT PRONOUNS

a. Forms

SINGULAR		PLURAL	
me (m')	me	nous	us
te (t')	you (familiar)	vous	you (also formal singular)
le (l')	him, it (masculine)	les	them
la (l')	her, it (feminine)		
se (s')	himself, herself, oneself, itself	se (s')	themselves

NOTE: *Me, te, se, nous,* and *vous* are reflexive pronouns that may be used as a direct object. See chapter 12, page 128.

Pierre se lave.	*Pierre washes himself.*
Nous nous levons.	*We get up.*

b. Uses of direct object pronouns

A direct object pronoun replaces a direct object noun and answers the question *whom?* or *what?*

Je vois **Richard**.	*I see Richard.*
Je **le** vois.	*I see him.*
Nous regardons **la télévision**.	*We watch television.*
Nous **la** regardons.	*We watch it.*
Il cherche **ses amis**.	*He looks for his friends.*
Il **les** cherche.	*He looks for them.*

NOTE: Verbs like *attendre (to wait for), écouter (to listen to), chercher (to look for), demander (to ask for), payer (to pay for),* and *regarder (to look at)* take a direct object in French.

Je **l'**écoute.	*I am listening to him (her, it).*
Il **les** regarde.	*He looks at them.*

c. Position of direct object pronouns

(1) The direct object pronoun precedes the words *voici (here is, here are)* and *voilà (there is, there are).*

Me voici.	*Here I am.*
Le voilà.	*There he (it) is.*

EXERCICE A

Danielle is packing a bag to go away for the weekend. She is late and her sister is helping her. *Exprimez comment sa sœur répond à ses questions.*

EXEMPLE:

Où est mon _____ ?
Le voilà.

1.

Où sont mes _____ ?

_____

2.

Où est mon _____ ?

_____

3.

Où est ma _____ ?

_____

4.

Où est mon _____ ?

_____

5.

Où sont mes _____ ?

_____

6.

Où est ma _____ ?

_____

7.

Où est ma _____ ?

_____

8.

Où est mon _____ ?

_____

(2) The direct object pronoun normally precedes the verb of which it is the object.

Il **le** prend.	*He takes it.*
Te cherche-t-il?	*Is he looking for you?*
S'amusent-ils?	*Are they having fun?*
Il **l'a** fait.	*He did it.*
Je ne **vous** attendrai pas.	*I will not wait for you.*

EXERCICE B

You and a friend are discussing your likes and dislikes. *Exprimez votre conversation.*

EXEMPLE: écouter la musique classique
        AMI(E):   **L'écoutes-tu?**
        VOUS: Oui, **je l'écoute.**
        AMI(E):   Moi, **je ne l'écoute pas.**

1. collectionner les bandes dessinées

    AMI(E): _____

    VOUS: _____

    AMI(E): _____

2. aimer la natation

    AMI(E): _____

    VOUS: _____

    AMI(E): _____

3. préférer le rock

    AMI(E): _____

    VOUS: _____

    AMI(E): _____

4. adorer la poésie moderne

    AMI(E): _____

    VOUS: _____

    AMI(E): _____

5. lire le journal tous les jours

AMI(E): _____

VOUS: _____

AMI(E): _____

6. regarder souvent les films vidéo

AMI(E): _____

VOUS: _____

AMI(E): _____

EXERCICE C

What were these people doing in the Galeries Lafayette department store? *Suivez l'exemple.*

EXEMPLE: chercher ses amis
           Pierre *les* cherchait.

1. acheter les vêtements

Je _____ .

2. regarder les mannequins

Janine _____ .

3. chercher leur fille

Les Pompon _____ .

4. trouver la vendeuse

Nous _____ .

5. attendre ton amie

Tu _____ .

6. payer le caissier

Vous _____ .

(3) **When a pronoun is the direct object of a verb in the infinitive, the pronoun precedes the infinitive.**

Il voulait voir **Pauline**.	*He wanted to see Pauline.*
Il voulait **la** voir.	*He wanted to see her.*
Sais-tu réparer **la radio**?	*Do you know how to repair the radio?*
Sais-tu **la** réparer?	*Do you know how to repair it?*
Je ne vais pas **le** faire.	*I'm not going to do it.*

EXERCICE D

Your mother has asked you to help in the kitchen and would like to know what you want to do. *Écrivez ses questions et vos réponses basées sur les indications données.*

EXEMPLE: goûter la soupe (oui) / (non)
> **Veux-tu la goûter?**
> **Oui, je veux la goûter.**
> **Non, je ne veux pas la goûter.**

1. faire la vaisselle (non)

_____

_____

2. arranger les fruits (oui)

_____

_____

3. préparer la salade (oui)

_____

_____

4. mettre le couvert (non)

_____

_____

5. laver les légumes (non)

_____

_____

6. allumer le four (oui)

_____

_____

(4) In an affirmative command, the object pronoun follows the verb and is attached to it by a hyphen. The pronouns *me* and *te* change to *moi* and *toi* after the verb. In a negative command, the object pronoun retains its usual position before the verb.

AFFIRMATIVE COMMAND		NEGATIVE COMMAND	
Ouvre-le.	*Open it.*	**Ne l'ouvre pas.**	*Don't open it*
Regardez-moi.	*Look at me.*	**Ne me regardez pas.**	*Don't look at me.*
Lève-toi.	*Get up.*	**Ne te lève pas.**	*Don't get up.*

EXERCICE E

Paul can never make a decision about anything. He sees things he wants to buy but he's not sure, and his two friends don't help. *Exprimez ce qu'ils disent.*

EXEMPLE: Quel bel imperméable!
          Achète-le!
          Ne l'achète pas!

1. Quel beau portefeuille!

_____

_____

2. Quelle belle montre!

_____

_____

3. Quels beaux vêtements!

_____

_____

4. Quelle belle chemise!

_____

_____

5. Quel beau pantalon!

_____

_____

6. Quelles belles baskets *(basketball sneakers)*!

_____

_____

EXERCICE F

Nicole is driving her boyfriend crazy. One day she's wild about him and the next day she's not. *Exprimez ce qu'elle lui dit.*

EXEMPLE: pardonner
          Pardonne-moi!
          Ne me pardonne pas!

1. regarder

_____

_____

2. embrasser

_____

_____

3. oublier

_____

_____

4. attendre

_____

_____

5. aimer

_____

_____

6. écouter

_____

_____

EXERCICE G

A friend gives you advice on getting ready for school in the morning. *Exprimez ce que votre ami(e) dit.*

EXEMPLE: se lever à 7 h, pas à 8 h
          Lève-toi à 7 h.
          Ne te lève pas à 8 h.

1. se réveiller à 7 h, pas à 7 h 15

_____

_____

2. se laver avant le petit déjeuner, pas après

_____

_____

3. s'habiller dans ta chambre, pas dans la salle de bains

_____

_____

4. choisir tes vêtements le soir, pas le matin

_____

_____

5. se préparer pour l'école le soir, pas le matin

_____

_____

6. se coucher à 11 h, pas à minuit

_____

_____

EXERCICE H

Your parents ask you about your friends. *Écrivez leurs questions et vos réponses.*

EXEMPLE: aimer
      Tes amis *t*'aiment?
      Mes amis *m*'aiment.

1. écouter

_____

_____

2. respecter

_____

_____

3. aider

_____

_____

4. trouver sympathique

_____

_____

EXERCICE I

Now your friends ask you and your brother about your parents. *Écrivez leurs questions et vos réponses.*

EXEMPLE: menacer
      Vos parents ***vous* menacent?**
      Nos parents ***ne nous* menacent *jamais*.**

1. gâter

_____

_____

2. punir

_____

_____

3. ennuyer

_____

_____

4. gronder

_____

_____

[2] INDIRECT OBJECT PRONOUNS

a. Forms

SINGULAR	PLURAL
me (m') _(to) me_	**nous** _(to) us_
te (t') _(to) you_ (familiar)	**vous** _(to) you_ (also formal singular)
lui (l') _(to) him, (to) her_	**leur** _(to) them_
se (s') _(to) himself, (to) herself, (to) itself_	**se** (s') _(to) themselves_

NOTE: _Me, te, se, nous,_ and _vous_ are reflexive pronouns that may be used as an indirect object. See chapter 12, page 129.

Je **me** lave les mains.	_I wash my hands._
Il **se** brosse les dents.	_He brushes his teeth._

b. Uses of indirect object pronouns

An indirect object pronoun replaces an indirect object noun and answers the questions _to whom? for whom?_

Je parle **à** Georges.	_I speak to Georges._
Je **lui** parle.	_I speak to him._
Elle donne des pommes **aux** enfants.	_She gives apples to the children._
Elle **leur** donne des pommes.	_She gives them apples._

NOTE: **The verbs** _obéir (to obey),_ _désobéir (to disobey),_ _répondre (to answer),_ _ressembler (to resemble),_ **and** _téléphoner (to telephone)_ **take an indirect object in French.**

Je **leur** obéis.	_I obey them._
Elle **lui** téléphone.	_She calls him (her)._

c. Position of indirect object pronouns

(1) Indirect object pronouns, including reflexives, normally precede the verb.

Il **lui** parle.	*He speaks to him (her).*
Leur obéis–tu?	*Do you obey them?*
Se brossent–ils les dents?	*Do they brush their teeth?*
Les enfants **leur** ont écrit.	*The children wrote to them.*
Je ne **vous** parlerai pas.	*I will not speak to you.*

EXERCICE J

You are talking with a teacher about yourself and your family. *Racontez votre conversation en suivant l'exemple.*

EXEMPLE: obéir à vos parents (oui) / désobéir à vos parents (non)
　　　　　Leur obéissez–vous?　　Oui, **je leur obéis.**
　　　　　Leur désobéissez–vous?　Non, **je ne leur désobéis pas**.

1. parler à vos parents de vos problèmes (oui)

_____

_____

2. prêter de l'argent à vos frères (non)

_____

_____

3. écrire à vos grands-parents (oui)

_____

_____

4. dire la vérité à votre père (oui)

_____

_____

5. défendre à votre frère cadet de sortir (non)

_____

_____

6. répondre à vos parents avec respect (oui)

_____

_____

7. téléphoner à vos parents quand vous allez être en retard (oui)

_____

_____

8. raconter tout à votre mère (non)

_____

_____

(2) **When a pronoun is the indirect object of a verb in the infinitive, the pronoun precedes the infinitive.**

Il voulait parler **à Pauline**.	_He wanted to speak to Pauline._
Il voulait **lui** parler.	_He wanted to speak to her._
Peux-tu téléphoner **aux filles**?	_Can you call the girls?_
Peux-tu **leur** téléphoner?	_Can you call them?_
Je ne vais pas **leur** écrire.	_I'm not going to write to them._

EXERCICE K

You are working in a store. _Exprimez vos conversations avec les autres employés en suivant l'exemple._

EXEMPLE: donner les commandes à Jacques (oui) / (non)
Peux-tu lui donner les commandes **?**
Oui, je peux lui donner les commandes.
Non, je ne peux pas lui donner les commandes.

1. prêter ton stylo à Lucie (oui)

_____

_____

2. répondre aux clients (oui)

_____

_____

3. montrer la marchandise à M. Legrand (oui)

_____

_____

4. demander les renseignements au directeur (non)

_____

_____

5. lire le journal à Thomas et à Renée (non)

_____

_____

6. écrire aujourd'hui à Mme Bonnet (oui)

_____

_____

7. offrir le café au propriétaire (non)

_____

_____

8. apprendre le travail aux nouveaux employés (oui)

_____

_____

> (3) In an affirmative command, the object pronoun follows the verb and is attached to it by a hyphen. The pronouns *me* and *te* change to *moi* and *toi*. In a negative command, the object pronoun retains its usual position before the verb.

AFFIRMATIVE COMMAND		NEGATIVE COMMAND	
Téléphone-moi!	*Call me.*	**Ne me téléphone pas!**	*Don't call me.*
Dépêche-toi!	*Hurry up.*	**Ne te dépêche pas!**	*Don't hurry!*
Écrivez-leur!	*Write to them.*	**Ne leur écrivez pas!**	*Don't write to them.*

EXERCICE L

What would you tell a friend to do in the following situations? *Exprimez vos conseils en employant les indications données.*

EXEMPLES: Il a eu une dispute avec son meilleur ami. (téléphoner)
Téléphone-lui.

Son ami est parti en vacances. (ne pas téléphoner)
Ne lui téléphone pas.

1. Ses grands-parents sont allés en Floride. (écrire)

_____

2. Son frère a envie d'emprunter son nouveau pull. (ne pas prêter le pull)

_____

3. Sa petite amie est triste. (donner des fleurs)

_____

4. Il fait la connaissance d'un nouvel élève. (demander son numéro de téléphone)

_____

5. Des étudiants l'ennuient. (ne pas parler)

_____

6. Un homme veut acheter sa voiture. (ne pas vendre ta voiture)

_____

7. C'est l'anniversaire de ses parents. (acheter un cadeau)

_____

8. Des élèves essaient de copier ses réponses à un examen. (ne pas montrer les réponses)

_____

EXERCICE M

Your friend asks you what your boyfriend does for you. *Exprimez ses questions et vos réponses.*

EXEMPLE: prêter sa voiture
      — **Il *te* prête** sa voiture?
      — Oui, **il *me* prête** sa voiture.

1. écrire des lettres d'amour

_____

_____

2. dire: "Je t'aime"

_____

_____

3. donner des bonbons

_____

_____

4. acheter des fleurs

_____

_____

EXERCICE N

A friend asks what your parents tell you and your sister to do. *Exprimez ses questions et vos réponses.*

EXEMPLE: conseiller d'étudier tout le temps
      — **Vous conseillent-ils** d'étudier tout le temps ?
      — **Ils ne nous conseillent pas** d'étudier tout le temps.

1. défendre de sortir

_____

_____

2. dire de rester toujours à la maison

_____

_____

3. ordonner de faire le ménage

_____

_____

4. demander souvent d'aller faire les courses

_____

_____

[3] PRONOUN *Y*

The adverbial pronoun *y* always refers to previously mentioned things or places. It generally replaces *à (au, aux)* + noun but may also replace other prepositions of position or location such as *chez, dans, en, sous,* or *sur* + noun. The pronoun *y* most commonly means *to it/them, in it/them, on it/them* and *there*.

Je vais **à Paris**.	*I am going to Paris.*
J'**y** vais.	*I am going there.*
Elle répond **à la lettre**.	*She answers the letter.*
Elle **y** répond.	*She answers it.*
Ils sont **dans le bureau**?	*Are they in the office?*
Ils **y** sont.	*They are there.*

Sometimes the meaning of *y* is not expressed in English.

Le chat est **sous la chaise**?	*Is the cat under the chair?*
Oui, il **y** est.	*Yes, he is.*

NOTES:

1. The pronoun *y* follows the same rules of position in the sentence as direct and indirect object pronouns.

Il voulait y aller.	*He wanted to go there.*
Tu y vas?	*Are you going there?*
Je n'y vais pas.	*I am not going there.*
Je ne vais pas y rester.	*I'm not going to stay there.*

2. Affirmative familiar commands (*tu* form) of *-er* verbs and *aller* retain the final *s* before *y*.

Restes–y!	*Stay there!*
N'y reste pas!	*Don't stay there!*
Vas–y!	*Go there!*
N'y va pas!	*Don't go there!*

EXERCICE O

Your younger sister wants to know about you and your friend's plans for your senior prom.
Répondez à ses questions selon le modèle suivant.

EXEMPLES: Vous allez à un bal élégant ? (oui) / (non)
      Oui, **nous y allons**.
      Non, **nous n'y allons pas**.

1. Le bal est dans les salons de l'hôtel Prince ? (non)

2. Vous dînez à l'hôtel ? (oui)

_____

3. Vous pensez à la fête ? (oui)

_____

4. La limousine arrive chez nous à 7 heures ? (non)

_____

5. Vous restez longtemps au bal ? (oui)

_____

6. Vous dansez sur la terrasse ? (oui)

_____

7. Vous allez au parc après ? (non)

_____

8. Vous descendez en ville prendre le petit déjeuner ? (non)

_____

EXERCICE P

Your friend suggests how you can spend your vacation. *Sometimes you agree and other times you disagree. Exprimez votre conversation.*

EXEMPLE: aller au Canada (oui) / (non)
— **Veux-tu y aller?**
— **Oui, je veux y aller. / — Non, je ne veux pas y aller.**

1. dormir à la belle étoile (non)

_____

_____

2. voyager en Italie (oui)

_____

_____

3. dîner dans des restaurants élégants (non)

_____

_____

4. rester chez ta grand-mère (non)

_____

_____

5. aller aux îles Caraïbes (oui)

_____

_____

6. jouer au golf (oui)

_____

_____

7. assister à un cours de vacances (non)

_____

_____

8. travailler dans une disco (oui)

_____

_____

EXERCICE Q

You have schoolwork to do but your mind really isn't on it. Your conscience is wavering as contradictory ideas pop into your head. *Exprimez ces idées.*

EXEMPLE: aller à la bibliothèque
          Vas-y. / N'y va pas.

1. penser au travail scolaire

_____

2. jouer au tennis

_____

3. dîner dans un restaurant

_____

4. aller chez des amis

_____

5. rester dans ta chambre

_____

[4] PRONOUN *EN*

a. The adverbial pronoun *en* refers to previously mentioned nouns introduced by *de*. It means *about it/them*, *from it/them*, *of it/them* or *from there* when it replaces a noun referring to places or things and introduced by the preposition *de*.

Nous venons **de Paris.**	*We come from Paris.*
Nous **en** venons.	*We come from there.*
Je parle **de ma voiture**.	*I'm talking about my car.*
J'**en** parle.	*I'm talking about (of) it.*

b. *En* means *some* or *any* (*of it/of them*) when it replaces a noun introduced by the partitive article. In this case it may refer to persons as well as things.

Elle veut **de la glace**?	*Does she want some ice cream?*
Oui, elle **en** veut.	*Yes, she wants some.*
Il ne prend **pas de légumes**.	*He doesn't take any vegetables.*
Il **n'en** prend pas.	*He doesn't take any.*
As-tu **des amis**?	*Do you have friends?*
J'**en** ai.	*I have some.*

c. *En* is also used when the noun is omitted after a number or an expression of quantity.

J'ai **vingt dollars**.	*I have twenty dollars.*
J'en ai vingt.	*I have twenty (of them).*
As-tu **de l'argent**?	*Do you have any money?*
Oui, **j'en** ai **beaucoup**.	*Yes, I have a lot (of money).*

d. *En* is always expressed in French even though it may have no English equivalent.

Avez-vous **du sucre**?	*Do you have any sugar?*
Oui, j'**en** ai.	*Yes, I do (have some).*
Tu joues bien du piano.	*You play the piano well.*
Tu **en** joues bien.	*You play (it) well.*

NOTES:

1. *En* follows the same rules of position in the sentence as other personal pronouns.

Il voulait **en** acheter.	*He wanted to buy some.*
Je **n'en** veux pas.	*I don't want any.*
Tu **n'en** veux pas?	*Don't you want some (any)?*
Peux-tu **en** trouver ?	*Can you find any?*
Je ne peux pas **en** trouver.	*I can't find any.*

2. Affirmative familiar commands (*tu* form) of *-er* verbs retain the *s* before *en*.

Manges-en!	*Eat some!*
N'**en** mange pas!	*Don't eat any!*

3. *En* precedes *voici* and *voilà*.

En voici deux.   *Here are two of them.*
En voilà.   *Here are some.*

EXERCICE R

Exprimez ce qui arrive aux personnes suivantes après l'école.

EXEMPLE: Jean a des problèmes.
            Jean *en* a.

1. Je sors du lycée.

_____

2. Claude et moi prenons de la glace.

_____

3. Vous parlez de vos classes.

_____

4. Tu achètes des bonbons.

_____

5. Janine et Lise trouvent de l'argent.

_____

6. Antoine prépare des sandwiches.

_____

EXERCICE S

The Dubois have decided to lose weight. *Exprimez ce qu'ils vont faire.*

EXEMPLE: Maman va acheter du poisson.
            Maman **va *en* acheter**.

1. Papa ne va pas manger de viande.

_____

2. Je vais faire des exercices.

_____

3. Julien va préparer des recettes amaigrissantes.

_____

4. Les filles ne vont pas choisir de dessert.

_____

5. Claude et moi, nous allons prendre des vitamines.

_____

6. Tu ne vas pas acheter de gâteau.

_____

7. Mariane ne va pas parler de son régime.

_____

8. Les garçons vont avoir de la salade.

_____

EXERCICE T

You want to have a good time on your vacation. *Dites ce que vos amis vous conseillent de faire. Suivez l'exemple.*

EXEMPLE: chercher de l'amusement, pas d'ennuis.
Cherches-en. N'en cherche pas.

1. faire du sport, pas de travail

_____

_____

2. acheter des souvenirs, pas de vêtements

_____

_____

3. manger des spécialités, pas de plats ordinaires

_____

_____

4. parler de tes aventures, pas de tes problèmes

_____

_____

5. raconter des histoires drôles, pas d'histoires ennuyeuses

_____

_____

6. porter des vêtements sport, pas de vêtements élégants

_____

_____

MASTERY EXERCISES

EXERCICE U

A friend asks you questions about an upcoming trip. *Répondez en employant un pronom d'objet direct ou indirect ou un pronom adverbial.*

EXEMPLES: L'avion va-t-il partir de Chicago?   Vas-tu téléphoner à tes parents?
Oui, **il va en partir.**   Non, **je ne vais pas leur téléphoner.**

1. Vas-tu voyager en Europe ?

_____

2. Penses-tu visiter la France ?

_____

3. Vas-tu écrire à tes amis ?

_____

4. Est-ce que tu vas passer plusieurs jours à Paris ?

_____

5. Descends-tu dans des hôtels de luxe ?

_____

6. Aimes-tu visiter les musées importants ?

_____

7. Achètes-tu souvent des souvenirs ?

_____

8. Offres-tu un cadeau à ta mère ?

_____

9. Vas-tu revenir d'Europe avant septembre ?

_____

10. Vas-tu rentrer à Chicago tout de suite après le voyage?

_____

EXERCICE V

Express your feelings about the following people and things. *Employez les pronoms appropriés.*

EXEMPLE: ta tante (écrire de temps en temps, aimer beaucoup)
Je lui écris de temps en temps.
Je l'aime beaucoup.

1. ta meilleure amie (embrasser souvent, téléphoner tous les jours)

_____

_____

2. le cinéma (aller le samedi soir, aimer beaucoup)

_____

_____

3. tes parents (parler souvent, respecter)

_____

_____

4. des bonbons (manger deux fois par jour, acheter pour une fête)

_____

_____

5. le tennis (jouer tous les jours, aimer beaucoup)

_____

_____

6. la France (vouloir visiter, compter rester deux semaines)

_____

_____

EXERCICE W

Write a note to a friend about a concert you attended. You may want to include:

- what concert you saw
- when you went
- with whom you went
- the type of music played
- why you liked or disliked the concert
- to whom you are going to describe it

_____

_____

_____

_____

_____

_____

Chapter 18
Stress Pronouns

[1] FORMS

SINGULAR			PLURAL		
(je)	moi	*I, me*	(nous)	nous	*we*
(tu)	toi	*you* (familiar)	(vous)	vous	*you* (also formal singular)
(il)	lui	*he, him*	(ils)	eux	*they, them*
(elle)	elle	*she, her*	(elles)	elles	*they, them*

[2] USES OF STRESS PRONOUNS

A stress pronoun can function either as subject or as object. It can either replace another word or reinforce it for added emphasis.

a. Stress pronouns are used in a compound subject or object.

Lui et Marie arrivent.	*He and Marie are arriving.*
J'ai invité Jean **et lui**.	*I invited Jean and him.*

NOTE

1. If one of the stress pronouns is *moi*, the verb is put in the first person plural (*nous* form) and the pronoun *nous* (which may or may not be expressed) is used to summarize the compound.

   Paul et moi sommes contents.
   Paul et moi, nous sommes contents. } *Paul and I are happy.*

2. If *toi* is one of the stress pronouns, the verb is put in the second person plural (*vous* form) and the pronoun *vous* (which may or may not be expressed) is used to summarize the compound.

   Luc et toi, vous êtes en retard.   *Luc and you are late.*

EXERCICE A

A friend of yours is sick and you want to cheer him/her up. *Dites ce que les personnes suivantes ont décidé de faire.*

lui acheter un livre amusant
lui apporter quelque chose à manger
lui donner des bandes dessinées
lui écrire une lettre

lui envoyer des cartes
lui offrir un nouveau disque
lui parler au téléphone

EXEMPLE: **Claire et vous, vous allez** lui écrire une lettre.

1. Toi et moi _____ .

2. Janine et eux _____ .

3. Denise et toi _____ .

4. Paul et lui _____ .

5. Les filles Dupont et elle _____ .

6. André et nous _____ .

    b. Stress pronouns are used when there is no verb expressed.

        Qui est là? — **Moi**.   *Who's there? — Me. (I am)*

        J'aime le golf. **Lui aussi**.   *I like golf. He (does) too.*

        Il est plus grand que **toi**.   *He is taller than you.*

EXERCICE B

Your youth group had tryouts for a play it plans to present. Your friend asks who got picked.
Exprimez vos réponses.

EXEMPLE: Claude et toi ?   **Oui, nous aussi.**

1. Toi ?

_____

2. Lise ?

_____

3. Cécile et toi?

_____

4. Jacques et Patrick?

_____

5. Catherine et Claire?

_____

6. Charles?

_____

7. Moi?

_____

8. Éric et moi?

_____

c. Stress pronouns are used to add emphasis to a noun or another pronoun.

Moi, je vais étudier.	*I'm going to study.*
Paul, **lui**, est très intelligent.	*Paul is very intelligent.*
Je l'aime bien, **elle**.	*I do like her.*

EXERCICE C

Dites de quel sport les personnes suivantes sont passionnées.

EXEMPLE: Marc/football
Lui, il est passionné de football.

1. vous/golf

_____

2. Antoine et Serge/baseball

_____

3. Janine/tennis

_____

4. tu/ski

_____

5. nous/rugby

_____

6. Brigitte et Nicole/volleyball

_____

d. Stress pronouns are used after *ce* + *être*.

Qui est-ce ? — **C'est moi.**	*Who is it? — It's I.*
C'est lui qui est parti.	*He's the one who left.*

NOTE: Before the stress pronouns *eux* and *elles*, the verb *être* may be used either in the singular (*C'est eux, c'est elles*) or in the plural (*Ce sont elles, ce sont eux*) although the singular is more commonly used.

EXERCICE D

The principal wants to know who does what in your class. *Exprimez vos réponses à ses questions selon l'exemple.*

EXEMPLE: Qui est très gentille? (Suzanne)
C'est elle.

1. Qui efface le tableau tout le temps? (André)

_____

2. Qui aide les élèves après l'école? (je)

_____

3. Qui écrit les devoirs au tableau? (Nicole et moi)

_____

4. Qui étudie la leçon? (tu)

_____

5. Qui travaille sérieusement? (les garçons)

_____

6. Qui corrige les fautes au tableau? (Antoine et vous)

_____

    e. Stress pronouns are used after a preposition to refer to people.

Elle va **chez toi.**	_She is going to your house._
Je parle **d'eux.**	_I'm speaking about them._
Je pense souvent **à lui**.	_I am often thinking of him._
Ce livre est **à moi.**	_This book belongs to me._

EXERCICE E

Your younger brother is curious about you and your friends. _Répondez à ses questions en suivant l'exemple._

EXEMPLE: Tu danses **avec Jacques**?
                  Oui, je danse **avec lui**.

1. Tu joues au tennis avec Antoinette et Patricia ?

_____

2. Tu vas souvent chez Lucien ?

_____

3. Nous habitons près de Lucie ?

_____

4. Raoul est assis à côté de toi dans la classe de français ?

_____

5. Tu travailles quelquefois pour les Moreau ?

_____

6. Est-ce que tu parles de mes amis et de moi ?

_____

7. Tu veux aller au parc sans moi?

_____

8. Anne et toi, vous parlez entre vous?

_____

> **f.** Stress pronouns *moi* and *toi* are used in affirmative commands instead of the pronouns *me* and *te*.
>
> | | |
> |---|---|
> | **Écoutez-moi.** | *Listen to me.* |
> | **Donne-moi** un journal. | *Give me a newspaper.* |
> | **Repose-toi** demain. | *Take a rest tomorrow.* |

MASTERY EXERCISES

EXERCICE F

Complete Isabelle's story about life with her two sisters. *Utilisez le pronom accentué approprié.*

_____ , je m'appelle Isabelle. D'habitude, mes sœurs et _____ , nous sommes
   1.   *2.*

bonnes amies. Ma sœur Nicole est plus grande que _____ . J'aime parler avec
                                                3.

_____ . C'est avec _____ que je discute de tous mes problèmes. Chantal a neuf ans
   4.   *5.*

et elle n'est pas toujours sage. Hier, elle a pris mon bracelet et elle a dit : «Il est à _____ .»
                                                           6.

«Il n'est pas à _____ !» j'ai répondu. Elle a pleuré et appelé maman. «Donne-_____
        7.   *8.*

mon bracelet!» j'ai crié. Maman nous a dit: « _____ , les filles, vous n'êtes pas sages.
                                                9.

Qui a commencé cette querelle? Répondez _____ » J'ai dit: «Ce n'est pas _____ .
                                        10.   *11.*

C'est _____ !» Chantal a dit: «C'est _____ qui a commencé! » et elle a pleuré.
     12.   *13.*

Heureusement maman a emmené Chantal faire des courses avec _____ , et Nicole et
                                                          14.

_____ avons fait une promenade ensemble. Je lui ai dit: « _____ , Nicole, tu es ma
   15.   *16.*

meilleure amie.» Nous avons rencontré nos amis Pierre et Claude et nous avons parlé avec

_____ un moment. Ensuite nous sommes rentrées chez _____ . La journée a bien fini.
   17.   *18.*

EXERCICE G

Your father is a little angry and wants to know what is going on. Use stress pronouns in your answers.

EXEMPLE: Est-ce que Paul travaille avec Michel?
Paul travaille avec lui.

1. Vous êtes sortis sans vos sœurs ?

   Nous sommes sortis _____

2. Est-ce que tu es allé chez tes amis après l'école ?

   Je suis allé _____

3. Est-ce vous qui faites tout ce bruit?

   Ce n'est pas _____

4. Anne a cassé le vase bleu?

   Ce n'est pas _____

5. Est-ce que ce livre est à toi ou à ton frère?

   Ce livre est _____

6. Venez-vous au cinéma avec votre mère et moi?

   Nous allons _____

EXERCICE H

Your week-end picnic was rained out. Write a note to a friend explaining what you and the others did instead. Use as many stress pronouns as possible. You may want to include:

- what you wanted to do instead
- the suggestions of your other friends
- where you finally decided to go
- what you did there
- how everyone felt about the activity

_____

_____

_____

_____

_____

_____

Chapter 19
Relative Pronouns

A relative pronoun introduces a clause that describes someone or something mentioned in the main clause. The person or thing the pronoun refers to is called the *antecedent* because it precedes the relative pronoun. The most common relative pronouns are *qui* and *que*.

[1] QUI

Qui (*who, which, that*) serves as the subject of the verb in the relative clause which it introduces. It is used for both persons and things.

[relative clause]
Où est *la fille* **qui parle** si bien?   *Where is the girl who speaks so well?*
[antecedent] [subject] [verb]

[relative clause]
Voilà *une voiture* **qui coûte** cher.   *There is a car that is expensive.*
[antecedent]   [subject] [verb]

NOTE: The verb of a relative clause introduced by *qui* agrees with its antecedent.

[relative clause]
C'est *toi* **qui** en **es** responsable.   *You are the one who is responsible for it*
[antecedent][subject] [verb]

[relative clause]
C'est *nous* **qui sommes restés.**   *We are the ones who stayed.*
[antecedent] [subject] [verb]

EXERCICE A

You are looking through binoculars from the top of the Eiffel Tower. Describe what you see below. *Employez le pronom relatif* qui .

EXEMPLE: Je vois des voitures. Elles roulent vite.
                Je vois des voitures **qui** roulent vite.

1. Il y a un homme. Il consulte un plan de la ville.

_____

2. Regarde ces enfants. Ils jouent dans la rue.

_____

3. Voilà une église. Elle est magnifique.

_____

4. Une femme entre dans un musée. Il n'est pas loin.

_____

5. J'observe des dames. Elles prennent des photos.

_____

6. Une famille marche dans une rue. La rue est très animée.

_____

7. Un monsieur rencontre une femme. Elle a l'air très belle.

_____

8. Cette fille prend un bus. Il va sur les quais de la Seine.

_____

EXERCICE B

Use a stress pronoun and a relative clause in the *passé composé. Exprimez ce que les personnes suivantes ont fait.*

EXEMPLE: je/écrire cette lettre
           C'est moi qui ai écrit cette lettre.

1. nous/manger tout le gâteau

_____

2. tu/oublier de vider les ordures

_____

3. il/jeter le journal d'aujourd'hui

_____

4. elles/laver le chien

_____

5. je/déranger les autres

_____

6. vous/couper les fleurs

_____

7. elle/crier à haute voix

_____

8. ils/téléphoner toute la soirée

_____

EXERCICE C

Donnez votre opinion en utilisant le pronom relatif qui.

EXEMPLE: Le président est un homme **qui travaille dur.**

1. Paris est une ville _____ .

2. La Porsche est une voiture _____ .

3. Mon professeur de français est une personne _____ .

4. Le base-ball est un sport _____ .

5. Eddie Murphy est un acteur _____ .

6. Le français est une langue _____ .

7. La glace est un dessert _____ .

8. Le cheval est un animal _____ .

[2] QUE

Que (*whom, which, that*) serves as the direct object of the verb in a relative clause and is usually followed by a subject noun or pronoun. It is used for both persons and things.

[relative clause]
C'est l'ami que nous aimons.
[antecedent] [object] [subject] [verb]

It's the friend (that) we like.

[relative clause]
Voilà le sac que Lucie veut.
[antecedent] [object] [subject] [verb]

Here is the bag (that) Lucie wants.

NOTES:

1. The relative pronoun is always expressed in French although it is frequently omitted in English.

   C'est la chanson **que j'adore.**   *That's the song (that) I love.*

2. *Que* becomes *qu'* before a vowel.

   Je vais acheter le livre **qu'il recommande.**   *I am going to buy the book (that) he recommends.*

EXERCICE D

Combine the sentences with the relative pronoun que. *Exprimez ce que les personnes suivantes sont en train de faire (are doing).*

EXEMPLE: Elle sort une cassette. Elle va écouter la cassette.
Elle sort une cassette **qu'elle** va écouter.

1. Je cherche un CD. Je veux acheter le CD.

_____

2. Elles achètent des livres. Elles vont lire ces livres.

_____

3. Vous préparez un plat. Vous allez manger ce plat.

_____

4. Nous écoutons une chanson. Nous aimons cette chanson.

_____

5. Tu regardes un film. Tu trouves le film intéressant.

_____

6. Ils réparent une bicyclette. Ils vont utiliser cette bicyclette.

_____

7. Elle présente l'homme. Elle va épouser cet homme.

_____

8. Il écrit une lettre. Il va envoyer cette lettre à une amie.

_____

EXERCICE E

Explain how people feel about the following persons. *Employez* que. *Suivez l'exemple.*

EXEMPLE: Mon père est le parent / mon frère / trouver indulgent
            Mon père est le parent *que* **mon frère trouve indulgent.**

1. Un(e) ami(e) est une personne / nous / respecter

_____

2. Nos professeurs sont des gens / les étudiants / trouver sympathique

_____

3. Le président est un homme / on / adorer

_____

4. Ma mère est une femme / tu / estimer

_____

5. Sean Penn est un acteur / les gens / aimer

_____

6. Isaac Asimov est un auteur / tout le monde / trouver intéressant

_____

7. Mick Jagger est un musicien / je / admirer

_____

8. Tiger Woods est un athlète / vous / vouloir rencontrer

_____

EXERCICE F

Donnez votre opinion sur les personnes et les choses suivantes en employant que.

EXEMPLE: Le président est un homme **que j'écoute.**

1. Paris est une ville _____ .

2. La Porsche est une voiture _____ .

3. Mon prof de français est une personne _____ .

4. Le base-ball est un sport _____ .

5. Eddie Murphy est un acteur _____ .

6. Le français est une langue _____ .

7. La glace est un dessert _____ .

8. Le chien est un animal _____ .

M A S T E R Y   E X E R C I S E S

EXERCICE G

Write a description of a person, place, or thing using *qui* and *que*. Then see if your classmates can guess what you've described. *Suivez l'exemple.*

EXEMPLE: C'est un homme **que** tout le monde admire. C'est un homme **qui** travaille dans un restaurant. C'est l'homme **qui** prépare les repas.
(Réponse: **C'est le chef.**)

_____

_____

_____

_____

_____

_____

EXERCICE H

What is your opinion? *Complétez les phrases suivantes en employant* qui *ou* que.

1. Je respecte les gens _____ tout le monde admire.

Je respecte les gens _____ travaillent dur.

2. J'ai des professeurs _____ j'admire.

J'ai des professeurs _____ sont très sympathiques.

3. J'ai un ami _____ parle tout le temps au téléphone.

   J'ai un ami _____ j'aime beaucoup.

4. J'ai vu un film _____ est trop violent.

   J'ai vu un film _____ mes ami(e)s n'aiment pas.

5. Je vais acheter un disque compact _____ mon ami(e) recommande.

   Je vais acheter un disque laser _____ coûte trop cher.

6. Je veux une voiture _____ est très sport.

   Je veux une voiture _____ mes ami(e)s trouvent chic.

7. J'ai un chien _____ est très fidèle.

   J'ai un chien _____ tout le monde adore.

8. Je vais voir une pièce _____ les critiques trouvent excellente.

   Je vais voir une pièce _____ se joue dans notre ville.

EXERCICE I

Write a short paragraph describing someone you admire. You may want to include:

- the name of the person
- his/her relationship to you
- what the person does for a living
- why you admire this person
- an accomplishment of this person
- how others feel about this person

_____

_____

_____

_____

_____

_____

_____

Chapter 20
Prepositions

Prepositions relate two elements of a sentence (noun to noun; verb to noun, pronoun, or another verb).

Regarde la maison **de** mon ami.	*Look at my friend's house. (the house of my friend)*
Paul parle **à** ses parents.	*Paul speaks to his parents.*
Elle sort **avec** lui.	*She is going out with him.*

The most frequently used prepositions in French are *à* and *de*.

[1] PREPOSITION *À*: AT, IN, TO

a. It often indicates a location or a moment in time.

J'habite **à** la campagne.	*I live in the country.*
Elle viendra **à** midi.	*She will come at noon.*
Ils vont **au** cinéma.	*They are going to the movies.*

b. A number of verbs require the preposition *à*.

aller à	*to go to*	penser à	*to think of*
demander à	*to ask*	répondre à	*to answer*
donner à	*to give*	ressembler à	*to resemble*
obéir à	*to obey*	téléphoner à	*to telephone*

NOTE: The preposition *à* contracts with the articles *le* and *les* to become *au* and *aux*. There is no contraction with *la* or *l'*.

Allons **au** cinéma.	*Let's go to the movies.*
Elle va parler **aux** garçons.	*She is going to speak to the boys.*
Il donne des fleurs **à** la fille.	*He gives flowers to the girl.*

EXERCICE A

Exprimez où vont les personnes suivantes.

EXEMPLE:

Nous allons à la bibliothèque.

1.

Je _____ .

2.

Les filles _____ .

3.

Roger _____ .

4.

Nous _____ .

5.

Tu _____ .

6.

Claire et moi _____ .

[2] PREPOSITION *DE* : ABOUT, FROM, OF

a. It indicates possession, relationship, or a specific characteristic of a noun.

C'est la maison **de** mon oncle.	*It is my uncle's house.*
Bruno est le frère **de** mon amie.	*Bruno is my friend's brother.*
C'est la couleur **du** ciel.	*It is the color of the sky.*
Elle veut un collier **de** perles.	*She wants a pearl necklace.*

NOTE: The preposition *de* contracts with the articles *le* and *les* to become *du* and *des*. There is no contraction with *l'* or *la*.

Ouvre la porte **du** jardin.	*Open the door of the garden.*
Voici les livres **des** étudiants.	*Here are the books of the students.*
Où est l'arrêt **de** l'autobus?	*Where is the bus stop?*

b. A number of verbs require the preposition *de*.

parler de	*to speak of*	rêver de	*to dream of*
partir de	*to leave from*	venir de	*to come from*

Nous parlons **du** docteur.   *We speak about the doctor.*
Nous venons **de la** ville.   *We come from the town.*

EXERCICE B

What are we talking about? *De quoi parle-t-on?*

EXEMPLE: je/voyage (*m.*)
               Je parle *du* voyage.

1. Jean et Henri/professeur (*m.*)

_____

2. tu/examens (*m.pl.*)

_____

3. nous/film (*m.*)

_____

4. M. Arnoux/classe (*f.*)

_____

5. les filles/garçons (*m.pl.*)

_____

6. je/école (*f.*)

_____

[3] OTHER COMMON PREPOSITIONS

après *after*
Il te verra après la classe   *He'll see you after class.*

autour de *around*
Luc marche autour de la salle.   *Luc walks around the room.*

avant (de) *before*
Je partirai avant toi.   *I shall leave before you.*
Avant de partir, je rangerai   *Before I leave, I'll tidy up my room.*
ma chambre

avec *with*
Viens avec moi.   *Come with me.*

chez (+ person) *to (at) (the house/place of (a person)*
Vas-tu chez le docteur?   *Are you going to the doctor's?*
Je vais chez moi.   *I'm going home.*

contre *against*

C'est une course contre la montre.   *It's a race against time.*

dans *in, into,*

Ne va pas dans la cuisine.   *Don't go into the kitchen.*

Je reviendrai dans cinq minutes.   *I'll be back in five minutes.*

derrière *behind*

Jean est derrière le garage.   *Jean is behind the garage.*

devant *in front of*

La voiture est devant la maison.   *The car is in front of the house.*

en *in, within*

Elle a fait le dîner en une heure.   *She made dinner in one hour.*

Je voudrais un sac en cuir.   *I would like a leather bag.*

entre *between, among*

Ils parlent entre eux.   *They speak among themselves.*

loin de *far from*

J'habite loin d'ici.   *I live far from here.*

par *by, through*

Ils sont entrés par la fenêtre.   *They entered through the window.*

près de *near*

Le théâtre est près d'ici.   *The theater is near here.*

sans *without*

Ne pars pas sans moi.   *Don't leave without me.*

sous *under*

Cherche sous le lit.   *Look under the bed.*

sur *on, upon*

Le livre est sur la table.   *The book is on the table.*

vers *towards*

Il marche vers le train.   *He's walking toward the train.*

EXERCICE C

Décrivez la journée de Jacques en complétant les phrases avec la préposition qui convient.

1. Jean est allé _____ son ami Paul.

2. Paul habite à cinq minutes de Jean. Ce n'est pas _____ sa maison.

3. Il a joué au basket _____ Paul.

4. _____ le match, ils avaient faim et soif.

5. Ils sont entrés _____ la cuisine.

6. Ils ont vu des biscuits et du soda _____ la table.

7. _____ leur goûter ils sont allés se laver les mains.

8. Ils ont mangé en silence _____ un mot.

[4] PREPOSITIONS USED BEFORE AN INFINITIVE

In French, the infinitive is the verb form that normally follows a preposition.

Il commence **à** applaudir.	*He begins to applaud.*
Elle a oublié **de** me téléphoner.	*She forgot to call me.*
Elle est partie **sans** parler.	*She left without speaking.*

a. Some verbs require *à* before an infinitive.

s'amuser à *to have fun*	se mettre à *to begin to*
commencer à *to begin to*	penser à *to think about*
continuer à *to continue to*	se préparer à *to prepare to*
demander à *to ask to*	renoncer à *to give up*
encourager à *to encourage to*	réussir à *to succeed in*

Jean **s'amuse *à* jouer** au football.	*John has fun playing soccer.*
Nous **demandons *à* sortir**.	*We ask to go out.*

b. Some verbs require *de* before an infinitive.

s'arrêter de *to stop*	oublier de *to forget to*
choisir de *to choose to*	parler de *to speak about*
décider de *to decide to*	refuser de *to refuse to*
se dépêcher de *to hurry to*	regretter de *to regret to*
essayer de *to try to*	rêver de *to dream about*

J'ai décidé de partir.	*I decided to leave.*
Tu essaies de patiner.	*You try to skate.*

EXERCICE D

The following persons are trying to improve themselves. *Exprimez comment.*

EXEMPLE: Lise/commencer/travailler sérieusement
            Lise **commence *à* travailler** sérieusement.

1. Paul/essayer/trouver un bon travail

_____

2. Régine et Lise/décider/étudier une autre langue étrangère

_____

3. Luc et moi/se préparer/passer le bac

_____

4. vous/parler/travailler davantage *(more)*

_____

5. je/se mettre/tout prendre au sérieux

_____

6. tu/encourager tes amis/respecter les autres

_____

EXERCICE E

Complétez l'histoire de Raoul avec les prépositions nécessaires.

    Mon ami Raoul rêve _____ devenir docteur. Il commence _____ remplir les

                         1.   *2.*

papiers nécessaires pour aller à l'université. Naturellement il parle _____ ses résultats

                                                    3.

scolaires. Ses professeurs l'encouragent _____ mentionner ses accomplissements sportifs. Il

                                   4.

décide _____ écrire un paragraphe sur son talent musical. Aussi, il n'oublie pas _____

            5.   *6.*

raconter une anecdote amusante. Enfin, Raoul finit son essai et il s'arrête _____ écrire. Je suis sûr

                                                   7.

qu'il réussira _____ devenir docteur. C'est un garçon qui ne renonce jamais _____ ses

              8.   *9.*

ambitions. Il choisit _____ envoyer sa demande d'inscription à toutes les universités renommées.

                        10.

EXERCICE F

Your friend is offering you tips on how to succeed. Use the command form of the verbs in parentheses and the appropriate preposition. _Exprimez ce qu'il/elle dit._

EXEMPLE: copier tes amis (renoncer)

                    Renonce _à_ copier tes amis.

1. saisir chaque occasion (choisir)

_____

2. étudier (continuer)

_____

3. gagner le respect des autres (penser)

_____

4. travailler dur (commencer)

_____

5. parler toujours correctement (essayer)

_____

6. trouver de bons amis (réussir)

_____

7. perdre ton temps (refuser)

_____

8. faire de ton mieux (décider)

_____

EXERCICE G

Complete these sentences about yourself using a preposition and an infinitive.

1. Je me prépare _____ .

2. Je choisis _____ .

3. Je commence _____ .

4. Je continue _____ .

5. J'oublie _____ .

6. Je regrette _____ .

c. **Some other prepositions are commonly followed by an infinitive.**

au lieu de *instead of*	pour *in order to, for the purpose of*
avant de *before*	sans *without*

Elle écoute des disques **au lieu d'**étudier. *She listens to records instead of studying.*

Il se peigne **avant** de sortir. *He combs his hair before going out.*

Nous travaillons **pour** gagner de l'argent. *We work to earn money.*

Tu parles **sans** penser. *You speak without thinking.*

EXERCICE H

Say what these people do. *Combinez les phrases avec la préposition indiquée entre parenthèses.*

EXEMPLE: Jeanne quitte la maison. Elle ne fait pas ses devoirs. (sans)
Jeanne quitte la maison **sans faire** ses devoirs.

1. Pierre regarde la télévision. Il ne lave pas la voiture de son père. (*au lieu de*)

_____

2. Roger se rase. Il sort avec Gisèle. (*avant de*)

_____

3. Lise garde les enfants. Elle gagne de l'argent. (*pour*)

_____

4. Marie prend la voiture. Elle ne demande pas la permission à ses parents. (*sans*)

_____

5. Paul met de l'argent de côté (*saves money*). Il se marie avec Georgette. (*avant de*)

_____

6. Janine va à un grand magasin. Elle ne prend pas son portefeuille. (*sans*)

_____

7. Joseph s'amuse. Il ne travaille pas. (*au lieu de*)

_____

8. Liliane dîne au restaurant. Elle célèbre son anniversaire. (*pour*)

_____

EXERCICE I

Complétez les phrases suivantes avec un verbe à l'infinitif.

1. Je regarde ma montre avant de _____ .

2. Je vais en ville pour _____ .

3. Je quitte la maison sans _____ .

4. Je fais mes devoirs au lieu de _____ .

d. Some verbs take an infinitive object without a preposition.

aimer	*to like, love*	penser	*to intend*
aller	*to go*	pouvoir	*to be able*
compter	*to intend*	préférer	*to prefer*
désirer	*to wish, want*	savoir	*to know how to*
espérer	*to hope*	vouloir	*to wish, want*

Il va sortir.	*He is going to go out.*
Nous ne savons pas cuisiner.	*We don't know how to cook.*
Peux-tu venir?	*Can you come?*

EXERCICE J

Express the following people's hopes and dreams. *Combinez un élément de chaque colonne.*

aimer	acheter une villa en France
aller	changer le monde
compter	devenir un athlète célèbre
désirer	écrire un livre
espérer	être bien connu(e)(s)
penser	explorer l'espace
pouvoir	faire fortune
préférer	gagner beaucoup d'argent
savoir	travailler en France
vouloir	voyager autour du monde

1. Je _____

2. Charles _____

3. Ces garçons _____

4. Danielle _____

5. Vous _____

6. Cette fille _____

7. Ma sœur et moi _____

8. Marie et Anne _____

9. Tu _____

10. Nous _____

EXERCICE K

Complete the sentences in French. *Exprimez vos idées.*

1. Je sais _____ .

2. Je veux _____ .

3. Je préfère _____ .

4. Je compte _____ .

5. Je peux _____ .

6. J'espère _____ .

[5] PREPOSITIONS WITH GEOGRAPHICAL EXPRESSIONS

a. To express *to* or *in* with names of places

en	feminine countries continents provinces islands masculine countries beginning with vowel or silent h	**en France** *to (in) France* **en Amérique** *to (in) America* **en Bretagne** *to (in) Brittany* **en Corse** *to (in) Corsica* **en Israël** *to (in) Israel* **en Iran** *in Iran*
au	masculine countries	**au Canada** *(to) in Canada*
aux	plural countries	**aux États-Unis** *(to) in the United States*
à	cities	**à Paris** *to (in) Paris*

Elle habite **en** France.	*She lives in France.*
Je vais aller **en** Espagne cet été.	*I'm going to Spain this summer.*
J'ai de la famille **au** Canada.	*I have relatives in Canada.*
As-tu jamais été **à** New York?	*Have you ever been to New York?*

b. To express *from* with names of places

de	feminine countries continents provinces islands masculine countries beginning with vowel or silent h cities	**de France** *from France* **d'Amérique** *from America* **de Bretagne** *from Brittany* **de Corse** *from Corsica* **d'Israël** *from Israel* **d'Iran** *from Iran* **de Paris** *from Paris*
du	masculine countries	**du Canada** *from Canada*
des	plural countries	**des États-Unis** *from the United States*

Il va venir **d'**Italie.	*He is going to come from Italy.*
Elle part **du** Canada.	*She is leaving from Canada.*
Le vol arrive **de** Paris.	*The flight is arriving from Paris.*

NOTES:

1. Generally, geographical names are feminine if they end in -*e*, with the exception of *le Mexique* and *le Cambodge (Cambodia)*.

2. The definite article is not used with *Israël* and *Haïti*.

c. Feminine countries, continents, provinces:

l'Allemagne	*Germany*	l'Écosse	*Scotland*
l'Angleterre	*England*	l'Égypte	*Egypt*
l'Autriche	*Austria*	l'Espagne	*Spain*
la Belgique	*Belgium*	la France	*France*
la Chine	*China*	la Grèce	*Greece*

Haïti   *Haiti*

la Hongrie   *Hungary*

l'Irlande   *Ireland*

l'Italie   *Italy*

la Norvège   *Norway*

la Pologne   *Poland*

la Roumanie   *Romania*

la Russie   *Russia*

la Suède   *Sweden*

la Suisse   *Switzerland*

l'Afrique   *Africa*

l'Amérique du Nord   *North America*

l'Amérique du Sud   *South America*

l'Asie   *Asia*

l'Australie   *Australia*

l'Europe   *Europe*

l'Alsace   *Alsace*

la Bourgogne   *Burgundy*

la Bretagne   *Brittany*

la Champagne   *Champagne*

la Flandre   *Flanders*

la Lorraine   *Lorraine*

la Normandie   *Normandy*

la Provence   *Provence*

d. Masculine countries:

le Brésil   *Brazil*

le Canada   *Canada*

le Cambodge   *Cambodia*

le Congo   *Congo*

le Danemark   *Denmark*

les États-Unis   *the United States*

Israël   *Israel*

le Japon   *Japan*

le Maroc   *Morocco*

le Mexique   *Mexico*

les Pays-Bas   *the Netherlands, Holland*

le Portugal   *Portugal*

NOTE: *Antarctica* is a masculine continent: l'Antarctique

e. Mountains and waterways follow the rules for countries; they are usually feminine if they end in -e.

les Alpes (*f.*)   *the Alps*

le Jura   *the Jura Mountains*

les Pyrénées (*f.*)   *the Pyrenees*

les Vosges (*f.*)   *the Vosges*

la Manche   *the English Channel*

la mer Méditerranée   *the Mediterranean Sea*

la Loire   *the Loire*

le Rhin   *the Rhine*

la Seine   *the Seine*

le Rhône   *the Rhone*

la Garonne   *the Garonne*

EXERCICE L

You are taking a trip around the world and you send postcards with pictures of the following sites. *Dites où vous êtes.*

EXEMPLE:

Je suis en France.

1.

_____

2.

_____

3.

_____

4.

_____

5.

_____

6.

_____

7.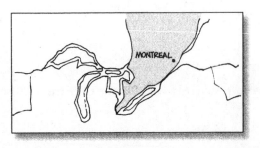

_____

8.

_____

9.

10.

EXERCICE M

People from far and wide attend your school. *Dites d'où les élèves suivants viennent.*

EXEMPLE: Luis/Mexique
       Luis vient du Mexique.

1. Nathalie/Haïti

_____

2. Stavros/Grèce

_____

3. Juan/Espagne

_____

4. Hiro/Japon

_____

5. Maria/Italie

_____

6. Rabiat/Afrique

_____

7. Antonio/Portugal

_____

8. Jean-Paul/France

_____

9. Mark/Canada

_____

10. Ilya/Russie

_____

[6] EXPRESSIONS INTRODUCED BY À

The preposition *à* is used in the following expressions.

(1) Mode of travel (*on, by*)

à bicyclette   *on a bicycle, by bicycle*
à cheval   *on horseback*
à pied   *on foot*

Il va à l'école **à pied.**   *He goes to school on foot. (He walks to school.)*

(2) Time

à bientôt	*see you soon, so long*
à demain	*see you tomorrow*
à samedi	*see you Saturday*
à ce soir	*see you tonight*
à l'heure	*on time; per hour*
à tout à l'heure	*see you later*
au revoir	*good-bye, see you again*

Je pars. **À demain.**   *I'm leaving. See you tomorrow.*

(3) Position and direction

à côté (de) *next to, beside*
J'habite à côté de Marie.   *I live next door to Marie.*

à droite (de) *on (to) the right (of)*
La banque est à droite.   *The bank is on the right.*

à gauche (de) *on (to) the left (of)*
Tourne à gauche.   *Turn to the left.*

au bas de *at the bottom of*
Le livre est au bas de l'escalier.   *The book is at the bottom of the staircase.*

au fond (de) *in (at) the bottom (of)*
Il a trouvé de l'argent au fond   *He found some money at the bottom of*
du lac.   *the lake.*

au haut (de) *at the top (of)*
Écris ton nom au haut de la page.   *Write your name at the top of the page.*

au milieu (de) *in the middle (of)*
Il danse au milieu de la rue.   *He is dancing in the middle of the street.*

(4) Other expressions

à la campagne *in (to) the country*
Nous sommes allés à la campagne.   *We went to the country.*

à la maison *at home, home*

Il est resté à la maison.   *He stayed home.*

à l'école *in (to) school*

J'aime aller à l'école.   *I like to go to school.*

à peu près *nearly, about, approximately*

J'ai à peu près vingt dollars.   *I have about $20.*

à voix haute, à haute voix *aloud, out loud, in a loud voice*

Il parle à voix haute.   *He speaks out loud.*

à voix basse *in a low voice*

Parle à voix basse.   *Speak in a low voice.*

au contraire *on the contrary*

Ne sait-il pas jouer au football?   *He doesn't know how to play soccer?*
— Au contraire, il joue bien.   *— On the contrary, he plays well.*

au moins *at least*

Ça coûte au moins dix dollars.   *That costs at least $10.*

EXERCICE N

Your friend Nicolas wants to come to your house. Write to tell him how to get there. *Employez les expressions appropriées.*

Si tu veux, tu peux venir _____ ou bien tu peux venir
                          1. (by bicycle)

_____ .Va _____ .Tourne _____ .
   2. (on foot)   *3. (to school)*   *4. (to the left)*

Continue tout droit pour trois rues. Tu es à l'Avenue Vernon. Tourne _____
                                                              5. (to the right)

Continue pour _____ quatre rues encore. Descends la petite colline.
              6. (at least)

Ma maison est juste là. C'est la maison grise _____ cette colline, _____
                                              7. (at the bottom)   *8. (next to)*

la pharmacie. Je t'attendrai _____ .Viens _____ .
                             9. (at home)   *10. (on time)*

Il te faut _____ une demi-heure pour venir chez moi.
           11. (about)

_____ .
12. (See you later)

Daniel

EXERCICE O

Décrivez la soirée de Justine en complétant chaque phrase avec l'expression appropriée.

à bicyclette	à la maison	au contraire
à bientôt	à l'heure	au milieu de
à la campagne	à peu près	à voix haute

1. Paul est arrivé en retard. Il n'est jamais _____ .

2. Rose a pris son vélo. Elle est venue _____ .

3. La maison de Justine n'est pas petite, _____ elle est grande.

4. Il y a un grand arbre _____ du jardin.

5. Justine n'habite pas en ville. Elle habite _____ .

6. Ses parents sont sortis. Ils n'étaient pas _____ .

7. Claude crie toujours. Il parle _____ .

8. Il y avait _____ cinquante personnes à la fête.

9. Après la fête tout le monde a dit: « _____ .»

[7]   EXPRESSIONS INTRODUCED BY *DE, EN,* AND *PAR*

d'abord *first, at first*

D'abord, écris ton nom.   *First, write your name.*

d'accord *agreed, O.K.*

Tu veux aller au parc?   *Do you want to go to the park?*
— D'accord.   — *O.K.*

de l'autre côté (de) *on the other side (of)*

Le magasin est de l'autre côté du parc.   *The store is on the other side of the park.*

de bonne heure *early*

Lève-toi de bonne heure.   *Get up early.*

de quelle couleur . . .? *What color . . .?*

De quelle couleur est la robe?   *What color is the dress?*

De rien.
Il n'y a pas de quoi.
Pas de quoi.   *You're welcome. Don't mention it.*
Je vous en prie.

Merci de ton aide. — De rien.   *Thanks for your help. —You're welcome*

de temps en temps *from time to time*

Je vais au cinéma de temps en temps.   *I go to the movies from time to time.*

en (when one is inside the means of transportation) *by*

en automobile (auto) *by automobile*

en avion *by plane*

en train *by train*

en voiture *by car*

Je vais à Paris en voiture. *I'm going to Paris by car.*

en (with the name of a language) *in*

Le livre est écrit en espagnol. *The book is written in Spanish.*

en bas *downstairs,* (**en bas de** *at the bottom of*)

Cette famille habite en bas. *That family lives downstairs.*

en haut *upstairs,* (**en haut de** *at the top of*)

Tes clefs sont en haut. *Your keys are upstairs.*

en face (de) *opposite*

Le café est en face du parc. *The café is opposite the park.*

en retard *late, not on time*

Le train est arrivé en retard. *The train arrived late.*

en ville *downtown, in (to, into) town*

Je suis allé(e) en ville avec papa. *I went downtown with Dad.*

par exemple *for example*

Je veux lire un bon livre, une *I want to read a good book, a love*
histoire d'amour, par exemple. *story, for example.*

par jour (semaine, mois, etc.) *a/per day (week, month, etc.)*

Je gagne cinquante dollars *I earn $50 per day.*
par jour.

Je vais au cinéma une fois *I go to the movies once a week.*
par semaine.

EXERCICE P

Répondez aux questions qu'un(e) ami(e) vous pose.

1. Tu vas comment à l'école ?

   _____

2. De quelle couleur est ton manteau ?

   _____

3. Tu vas au cinéma combien de fois par mois ?

   _____

4. Que fais-tu de bonne heure ?

   _____

5. Quand tu rentres après l'école, que fais-tu d'abord ?

   _____

6. Qu'est-ce que tu réponds quand un(e) ami(e) te dit merci ?

   _____

MASTERY EXERCISES

EXERCICE Q

Say what the following people are going to do. *Complétez les phrases avec la préposition ou l'expression qui convient.*

1. Victor va passer ses vacances _____ la campagne

2. Lucien a perdu son chapeau. Il l'a cherché pendant une heure _____ succès.

3. L'équipe des jaunes va jouer _____ l'équipe des rouges.

4. Marie n'est pas très studieuse. Elle finit ses devoirs _____ cinq minutes.

5. Claire va sortir _____ Roger. Elle est allée _____ le coiffeur ce matin.

6. Le garçon met le plat de spaghetti _____ la table _____ moi.

7. Je veux gagner mille dollars _____ semaine.

8. Si tu ne trouves pas ton CD sur ton lit, cherche _____ ton lit.

EXERCICE R

Michel always sees both sides of things. *Complétez ses pensées avec l'expression opposée qui convient.*

1. Si ce n'est pas à droite, c'est _____ .

2. Si je dis bonjour quand j'entre, je dis _____ quand je sors.

3. Si je me lève de bonne heure, je ne suis jamais _____ .

4. Si je parle à haute voix, je ne parle pas _____ .

5. Si je reste à la maison, je ne vais pas _____ .

6. Si je monte en haut, je ne descends pas _____ .

EXERCICE S

Complétez cette histoire en ajoutant les prépositions nécessaires.

Jean a quitté sa maison _____ 8h ce matin. Il ne s'est pas levé _____ bonne
                                    1.   *2.*

heure parce qu'il a oublié _____ régler son réveil hier soir. Aujourd'hui il a peur d'arriver
                              3.

_____ sa première classe _____ retard. Le problème est que ça lui arrive
        4.   *5.*

_____ moins deux fois _____ semaine et naturellement, le professeur encourage les
        6.   *7.*

élèves _____ arriver _____ l'heure. Malgré son retard, Jean s'amuse
            8.   *9.*

_____ jouer _____ son chien. Puis il choisit _____ parler
    10.   *11.*   *12.*

_____ ses voisins. Il continue _____ parler pendant dix minutes. Il oublie
    13.   *14.*

_____ regarder sa montre. Finalement, il décide d'aller _____ l'école
    15.   *16.*

_____ bicyclette. Il ne peut pas aller _____ voiture parce que ses parents sont déjà
    17.   *18.*

partis. _____ il commence _____ pédaler lentement. Puis il se met _____
        19.   *20.*   *21.*

pédaler plus vite parce qu'il espère _____ arriver _____ l'heure. La classe va
                              22.   *23.*

_____ commencer _____ cinq minutes. Jean se dépêche _____ ne pas
    24.   *25.*   *26.*

arriver en retard. Il compte _____ réussir _____ gagner cette course
                         27.   *28.*

_____ la montre. Il peut _____ faire cela facilement. Il va _____ doute
    29.   *30.*   *31.*

être à sa place _____ le commencement de la leçon, n'est-ce pas?
        32.

EXERCICE T

Write a note to a friend giving directions to your house. You may want to include:

- your address
- mode of transportation to take
- how long it will take
- where to get off
- what to do next
- how to recognize your house

_____

_____

_____

_____

_____

_____

_____

_____

Part Three

Adjective/Adverb and Related Structures

Chapter 21
Adjectives

An adjective is a word that describes a noun or a pronoun.

La fleur **rouge** est **jolie**.	*The red flower is pretty.*
Il est très **intelligent**.	*He's very intelligent.*

[1] AGREEMENT OF ADJECTIVES

French adjectives agree in gender (masculine or feminine) and in number (singular or plural) with the nouns or pronouns they modify. Adjectives are masculine or feminine, singular or plural in the same way as the noun or pronoun they modify.

le sable **blanc** (masculine singular)	*the white sand*
les sables **blancs** (masculine plural)	*the white sands*
la rose **blanche** (feminine singular)	*the white rose*
les roses **blanches** (feminine plural)	*the white roses*

a. Gender of adjectives

(1) Most adjectives form the feminine by adding *e*.

MASCULINE	FEMININE	
américain	américaine	*American*
bleu	bleue	*blue*
brun	brune	*brown*
content	contente	*glad*
court	courte	*short*
espagnol	espagnole	*Spanish*
fort	forte	*strong*
français	française	*French*
grand	grande	*large, tall, big*
haut	haute	*high*
intelligent	intelligente	*intelligent*
intéressant	intéressante	*interesting*
joli	jolie	*pretty*
laid	laide	*ugly*
lourd	lourde	*heavy*
mauvais	mauvaise	*bad*
méchant	méchante	*naughty, wicked*
noir	noire	*black*
petit	petite	*small, little*
poli	polie	*polite*
prochain	prochaine	*next*
vert	verte	*green*
vrai	vraie	*true*

NOTE: Adjectives ending in -*é* also form the feminine by adding *e*.

MASCULINE	FEMININE	
âgé	âgé*e*	*old*
fatigué	fatigué*e*	*tired*
passé	passé*e*	*past*

EXERCICE A

The two people named in each question share the characteristic mentioned. *Décrivez ces personnes.*

EXEMPLE: Jean est grand. Et Marie ?
Marie est grand*e* aussi.

1. Béatrice est polie. Et Lucien ?

_____

2. Christophe est fort. Et Berthe?

_____

3. Grégoire est brun. Et Marianne ?

_____

4. Lise est contente. Et Luc ?

_____

5. Joseph est fatigué. Et Lisette ?

_____

6. Claudine est intelligente. Et Hubert ?

_____

7. Patrick est amusant. Et Claire ?

_____

8. Mme Augier est âgée. Et M. Caron ?

_____

9. Richard est français. Et Marie-Claire ?

_____

10. Marc est espagnol. Et Marie ?

_____

(2) Adjectives ending in silent *-e* do not change in the feminine.

MASCULINE	FEMININE	
aimable	aimable	*kind*
célèbre	célèbre	*famous*
confortable	confortable	*comfortable*
difficile	difficile	*difficult*
drôle	drôle	*funny, strange*
égoïste	égoïste	*selfish*
facile	facile	*easy*
faible	faible	*weak*
formidable	formidable	*great*
honnête	honnête	*honest*
jaune	jaune	*yellow*
jeune	jeune	*young*
magnifique	magnifique	*magnificent*
malade	malade	*sick*
moderne	moderne	*modern*
pauvre	pauvre	*poor*
populaire	populaire	*popular*
riche	riche	*rich*
rouge	rouge	*red*
splendide	splendide	*splendid*
sympathique	sympathique	*nice, likable*
triste	triste	*sad*
vide	vide	*empty*

EXERCICE B

Describe the following people. *Employez l'adjectif qui convient.*

1. M. Leroux a beaucoup d'argent. Il est _____ .

2. Odette n'aime pas prêter ses affaires. Elle est _____ .

3. Claude a mal à l'estomac. Il est _____ .

4. Mme Dupont n'est pas contente. Elle est _____ .

5. Jacques n'est pas fort. Il est _____ .

6. Josette dit toujours la vérité. Elle est _____ .

7. Claudine a seulement cinq ans. Elle est très _____ .

8. Robert fait rire tout le monde. Il est _____ .

(3) **Adjectives ending in -*x* form the feminine by changing -*x* to -*se*.**

MASCULINE	FEMININE	
ambitieux	ambitieuse	*ambitious*
consciencieux	consciencieuse	*conscientious*
courageux	courageuse	*courageous*
curieux	curieuse	*curious*
dangereux	dangereuse	*dangerous*
délicieux	délicieuse	*delicious*
furieux	furieuse	*furious*
généreux	généreuse	*generous*
heureux	heureuse	*happy*
malheureux	malheureuse	*unhappy*
paresseux	paresseuse	*lazy*
sérieux	sérieuse	*serious*
superstitieux	superstitieuse	*superstitious*

EXERCICE C

Décrivez les personnes ou les choses (things) que vous voyez (see) dans les illustrations.

EXEMPLE:

Il est curieux.

1.

2.

_____ . _____ .

3.

_____ .

4.

_____ .

5.

_____ .

6.

_____ .

7.

_____ .

8.

_____ .

(4) Adjectives ending in -*f* form the feminine by changing -*f* to -*ve*.

MASCULINE	FEMININE	
actif	active	*active*
attentif	attentive	*attentive*
imaginatif	imaginative	*imaginative*
impulsif	impulsive	*impulsive*
naïf	naïve	*naive*
neuf	neuve	*new*
sportif	sportive	*sporty*
vif	vive	*lively*

EXERCICE D

Décrivez les personnes suivantes en employant les adjectifs indiqués.

actif	impulsif	naïf
attentif	imaginatif	sportif

1. Ma mère est _____ .

2. Mon père est _____ .

3. Je suis _____ .

4. Ma sœur est _____ .

5. Mon frère est _____ .

6. Mon professeur de français est _____ .

(5) Adjectives ending in *-er* form the feminine by changing *-er* to *-ère*.

MASCULINE	FEMININE	
cher	chère	*dear, expensive*
dernier	dernière	*last*
entier	entière	*entire, whole*
étranger	étrangère	*foreign*
fier	fière	*proud*
léger	légère	*light* (weight)
premier	première	*first*

(6) Some adjectives double the final consonant before adding *-e* in the feminine.

MASCULINE	FEMININE	
ancien	ancienne	*old, ancient, former*
bas	basse	*low*
bon	bonne	*good*
cruel	cruelle	*cruel*
européen	européenne	*European*
gentil	gentille	*nice, kind*
gros	grosse	*fat*

(7) Some adjectives have irregular feminine forms.

MASCULINE	FEMININE	
blanc	blanche	*white*
complet	complète	*complete*
doux	douce	*sweet, mild, gentle*
faux	fausse	*false*
favori	favorite	*favorite*
frais	fraîche	*fresh, cool*

franc	franche	*frank*
long	longue	*long*
secret	secrète	*secret*
beau (bel)	belle	*beautiful*
nouveau (nouvel)	nouvelle	*new*
vieux (vieil)	vieille	*old*

NOTE: **The adjectives *beau, nouveau,* and *vieux* change to *bel, nouvel,* and *vieil* before a masculine singular noun beginning with a vowel or silent *h*.**

Cet homme est beau.	*This man is handsome.*
Regarde ce **bel homme**.	*Look at this handsome man.*
Cet avion est nouveau.	*This plane is new.*
Regarde ce **nouvel avion**.	*Look at this new plane.*
Cet immeuble est vieux.	*This building is old.*
Regarde ce **vieil immeuble**.	*Look at this old building.*

EXERCICE E

Complétez chaque paragraphe avec la forme correcte des adjectifs entre parenthèses.

1. (*beau*) Nous sommes allés à un très _____ hôtel. Cet hôtel est _____ à

cause de sa _____ vue panoramique de la ville.

2. (*vieux*) Que cet appartement est _____ ! Un _____ homme en est le

propriétaire et une _____ femme en est la concierge.

3. (*nouveau*) Une _____ pièce va être présentée dans un _____ théâtre.

Un _____ acteur joue le rôle principal.

EXERCICE F

Your sister always contradicts you. *Écrivez ce qu'elle vous dit.*

EXEMPLE: Le monument est grand.
Mais non. **Il est petit.**

1. La pièce est mauvaise.

_____

2. Elle est la première chanteuse de ce groupe.

_____

3. Le livre est lourd.

_____

4. La montagne est haute.

_____

5. La dame est gentille.

_____

6. La blouse est jolie.

_____

7. Sa voix est dure.

_____

8. L'émission est courte.

_____

9. La réponse est vraie.

_____

10. La robe est noire.

_____

11. Cette fille est laide.

_____

12. Cette chanson est ancienne.

_____

b. **Plural of Adjectives**

(1) **The plural of most adjectives is formed by adding -s to the singular whether masculine or feminine.**

SINGULAR	PLURAL	
âgé (_m._)	âgés	_old_
blond (_m._)	blonds	_blond_
bonne (_f._)	bonnes	_good_
blanche (_f._)	blanches	_white_
active (_f._)	actives	_active_

(2) **Adjectives ending in -s or -x do not change in the masculine plural.**

MASCULINE SINGULAR	MASCULINE PLURAL	
anglais	anglais	_English_
frais	frais	_fresh, cool_
français	français	_French_

gris	gris	*gray*
heureux	heureux	*happy*
mauvais	mauvais	*bad*

(3) **Most adjectives ending in *-al* change *-al* to *-aux* in the masculine plural.**

MASCULINE	MASCULINE	
SINGULAR	PLURAL	
égal	égaux	*equal*
général	généraux	*general*
loyal	loyaux	*loyal*
national	nationaux	*national*
principal	principaux	*principal*
social	sociaux	*social*
spécial	spéciaux	*special*

(4) **The adjective *tout* is irregular in the masculine plural.**

tout	tous	*all*

(5) **Both masculine forms of *beau (bel)*, *nouveau (nouvel)*, and *vieux (vieil)* have the same plural forms.**

MASCULINE	MASCULINE	
SINGULAR	PLURAL	
un **bel** homme	de **beaux** hommes	*handsome men*
un **beau** garçon	de **beaux** garçons	*handsome guys*
un **nouvel** immeuble	de **nouveaux** immeubles	*new buildings*
un **nouveau** disque	de **nouveaux** disques	*new records*
un **vieil** appartément	de **vieux** appartements	*old apartments*
un **vieux** bateau	de **vieux** bateaux	*old boats*

NOTES:

1. When an adjective precedes a plural noun, *des* becomes *de*.

    de **nouveaux** magazines   *new magazines*

2. An adjective modifying two or more nouns of different genders is masculine plural.

    Le garçon et la fille sont intelligents.   *The boy and the girl are intelligent.*

EXERCICE G

Décrivez les garçons et les filles de votre classe. **Use the plural of the adjectives provided below.**

intelligent	optimiste	fier	généreux	sympathique
bon	intéressant	ambitieux	gentil	fort
franc	sérieux	sportif	heureux	beau

1. Les garçons sont _____ , _____ ,

_____ , _____ , _____ ,

_____ , _____ , _____ .

2. Les filles sont _____ , _____ , _____ ,

_____ , _____ ,

_____ , _____ .

3. Les garçons et les filles sont _____ , _____ ,

_____ , _____ ,

_____ , _____ .

EXERCICE H

Décrivez vos amis et leurs familles.

EXEMPLE: André est brun. **Ses frères sont bruns aussi.**

1. Marie est sportive. Ses parents sont _____ aussi.

2. Louis est franc. Ses sœurs sont _____ aussi.

3. Janine est belle. Ses frères sont _____ aussi.

4. M. Chenet est vieux. Ses cousines sont _____ aussi.

5. Lucien est ambitieux. Ses sœurs sont _____ aussi.

6. Claudine est intellectuelle. Ses neveux sont _____ aussi.

7. Laurent est loyal. Ses oncles sont _____ aussi.

8. Paul est fier. Ses tantes sont _____ aussi.

9. Mme Legrand est gentille. Ses enfants sont _____ aussi.

10. M. Costeau est riche. Ses nièces sont _____ aussi.

EXERCICE I

The following people are getting rid of their old belongings and buying themselves some new things. *Décrivez ce qu'ils achètent.*

EXEMPLES: M. Dupont / une radio
M. Dupont a **une vieille radio.**
Il s'achète **une nouvelle radio.**
Quelle belle radio!

Mlle Colin / des assiettes (*f.*)
Mlle Colin a **de vieilles assiettes.**
Elle s'achète **de nouvelles assiettes.**
Quelles belles assiettes!

1. Mlle Perrier/un appareil photo

_____

_____

_____

2. M. Richard/des meubles (*m.*)

_____

_____

_____

3. Mme Doucet/un ordinateur

_____

_____

_____

4. Mlle Charton/des casseroles (*f.*)

_____

_____

_____

5. Mme Ginet/une machine à laver

_____

_____

_____

6. M. Janic/des verres (*m.*)

_____

_____

_____

[2] POSITION OF ADJECTIVES

a. Descriptive adjectives normally follow the noun they modify.

une blouse blanche	*a white blouse*
un garçon actif	*an active boy*

b. Some short descriptive adjectives usually precede the noun.

beau	gentil	joli
bon / mauvais	gros	nouveau
court / long	jeune / vieux	petit / grand

une **courte** histoire   *a short story*
une **belle** femme   *a beautiful woman*

NOTE: *Des* becomes *de* when a plural adjective precedes a plural noun.

de belles femmes   *beautiful women*

c. Some other common adjectives precede the noun.

autre *other*	plusieurs *several*	quelques *a few*
chaque *each*	premier *first*	tel *such*
dernier *last*	quelque *some*	

un autre livre	*another book*
d'autres livres	*other books*
plusieurs articles	*several articles*

d. The adjective **tout** (*all, whole, every*) precedes both the noun and the definite article.

tout le monde	*everybody*	toutes les filles	*every girl*
toute la journée	*all day*	tous les jours	*every day*

EXERCICE J

You are very hungry. *Exprimez ce que vous mangez.*

EXEMPLE: **Je mange tout le gâteau.**

1. _____

2. _____

3. _____

4. _____

5. _____

6. _____

EXERCICE K

You recently went to a friend's new house. *Décrivez la maison avec les adjectifs entre parenthèses.*

EXEMPLE:　une maison (*grand*)
　　　　　　Ils ont une **grande** maison.

1. un balcon (*magnifique*)

　_____

2. une chaîne stéréo (*bon*)

　_____

3. deux salles de bains (*bleu*)

　_____

4. une piscine (*splendide*)

　_____

5. une table (*long*)

　_____

6. un arbre (*vieux*)

　_____

7. un grenier (*charmant*)

　_____

8. deux garages (*nouveau*)

_____

9. trois chambres (*joli*)

_____

10. un salon (*énorme*)

_____

[3] COMPARISON OF ADJECTIVES

Things or people can be compared with each other by using the comparative or superlative of the adjectives that modify them. Comparisons are formed as follows.

$$\left.\begin{array}{l}\text{plus } (more)\\ \text{moins } (less)\\ \text{aussi } \ (as)\end{array}\right\} \quad + \quad \text{adjective} \quad + \quad \text{que}$$

Le livre est **plus amusant que** le film.	*The book is more amusing than the movie.*
Anne est **moins gentille que** son frère.	*Anne is less nice than her brother.*
Les filles sont **aussi intelligentes que** les garçons.	*Girls are as intelligent as boys.*

The superlative is formed as follows.

$$\left.\begin{array}{ll}\text{le (la, les)} & \text{plus } (the\ most)\\ \text{le (la, les)} & \text{moins } (the\ least)\end{array}\right\} \quad + \quad \text{adjective} \quad + \quad \text{de}$$

Le printemps est la saison **la plus agréable.**	*Spring is the most pleasant season.*
Paul est **le plus beau** des garçons.	*Paul is the most handsome boy.*
Les pommes sont les fruits **les moins chers** (**de** tous).	*Apples are the least expensive fruit (of all).*

POSITIVE	amusant (-e, -s, -es) *amusing*
COMPARATIVE	**plus amusant (e, s, es) que** *more amusing than* **moins amusant (-e, -s, -es) que** *less amusing than* **aussi amusant (-e, -s, -es) que** *as amusing as*
SUPERLATIVE	**le, la, les plus amusant (-e, -s, -es) de** *the most amusing in, of* **le, la, les moins amusant (-e, -s, -es) de** *the least amusing in, of*

NOTE: The adjective *bon (good)* has an irregular comparative *meilleur (better)* and superlative *le meilleur (the best).*

Le pain est bon, mais le gâteau est meilleur.	*Bread is good, but cake is better.*

EXERCICE L

Exprimez les opinions de vos amis en suivant l'exemple.

EXEMPLES: la physique / + / intéressant / la chimie
La physique est **plus intéressante que** la chimie.

les Américains/=/sportif/les Français
Les Américains sont **aussi sportifs que** les Français.

1. la viande /−/ délicieux / le poisson

_____

2. les joueurs de football / = / fort / les joueurs de volley-ball

_____

3. un film comique / + / amusant / un film policier

_____

4. les voitures de sport / + / rapide / les bicyclettes

_____

5. la musique classique /−/ agréable / le jazz

_____

6. le français / = / utile / l'espagnol

_____

EXERCICE M

What is written in the school yearbook about each of these students? *Suivez l'exemple.*

EXEMPLES: Delphine /−−−/ optimiste
Delphine est **la moins optimiste de** la classe.

Jean et Henri /+++/ grand
Jean et Henri sont **les plus grands de** la classe.

1. Janine /+++/ intelligent

_____

2. Lucien et Michel /−−−/ sympathiques

_____

3. Monique et Sylvie /−−−/ sérieux

_____

4. Patrick /+++/ drôle

_____

5. Marie /+++/ franc

_____

6. Richard et Julie /−−−/ sportif

_____

M A S T E R Y   E X E R C I S E S

EXERCICE N

Describe the following people and things. *Employez autant d'adjectifs que possible.*

1. Mes parents sont _____ .

2. Ma mère est _____ .

3. Mon père est _____ .

4. Notre voiture est _____ .

5. Notre maison est _____ .

6. Mon école est _____ .

7. Mon professeur préféré est _____ .

8. Mes amis sont _____ .

9. Mes notes scolaires sont _____ .

10. Mes idées sont _____ .

EXERCICE O

You are writing a report about France. Describe the following people, places, and things that are typically French. *Employez différents adjectifs.*

EXEMPLE: Paris (*une ville*)
              Paris est **une grande ville.**

1. La Normandie et la Bretagne (*des provinces*)

_____

2. L'Arc de Triomphe (*un monument*)

_____

3. Le Louvre (*un musée*)

_____

4. Le Sacré-Cœur (*une église*)

_____

5. Nice et Cannes (*des villes*)

_____

6. La bouillabaisse (*une soupe*)

_____

7. Euro Disney (*un parc d'attractions*)

_____

8. Les Galeries Lafayette et le Printemps (*des magasins*)

_____

9. La tour Eiffel (*une tour*)

_____

10. Gérard Depardieu (*un acteur*)

_____

EXERCICE P

Write a note to a prospective employer explaining why you should get a job with a French company. You may want to include:

- a description of yourself
- your qualifications
- what your teachers say about you
- what you excel at doing
- your familiarity with French
- when you are available to work

_____

_____

_____

_____

_____

_____

_____

Chapter 22
Adverbs

An adverb is a word that modifies a verb, an adjective, or another adverb.

La fleur est **très** jolie.	*The flower is **very** pretty.*
Il court **vite**.	*He runs **fast**.*
Elle court **très vite**.	*She runs **very fast**.*

[1] FORMATION OF ADVERBS

Most French adverbs are formed by adding *-ment* to adjectives while most English adverbs are formed by adding *-ly* to adjectives.

a. When the masculine singular adjective ends in a vowel, *-ment* is added to the masculine singular form.

ADJECTIVE		ADVERB	
facile	*easy*	**facilement**	*easily*
poli	*polite*	**poliment**	*politely*
possible	*possible*	**possiblement**	*possibly*
probable	*probable*	**probablement**	*probably*
rapide	*quick*	**rapidement**	*quickly*
triste	*sad*	**tristement**	*sadly*
vrai	*true*	**vraiment**	*truly*

EXERCICE A

Describe Joseph's behavior. *Combinez les phrases ci-dessous (below).*

EXEMPLE: Il parle. Il est sévère.
            Il parle **sévèrement**.

1. Il joue. Il est timide.

_____

2. Il répond. Il est brave.

_____

3. Il demande. Il est poli.

_____

4. Il sort. Il est brusque.

_____

5. Il mange. Il est rapide.

_____

6. Il écrit. Il est sincère.

_____

7. Il travaille. Il est calme.

_____

8. Il nage. Il est remarquable.

_____

> **b.** When the masculine singular adjective ends in a consonant, -*ment* is added to the feminine singular form.

ADJECTIVE			ADVERB	
MASCULINE	FEMININE			
actif	active	active	activement	actively
certain	certaine	certain	certainement	certainly
correct	correcte	correct	correctement	correctly
cruel	cruelle	cruel	cruellement	cruelly
doux	douce	soft, gentle	doucement	softly, gently
fier	fière	proud	fièrement	proudly
franc	franche	frank	franchement	frankly
heureux	heureuse	happy	heureusement	fortunately
léger	légère	light	légèrement	lightly
secret	secrète	secret	secrètement	secretly
seul	seule	only	seulement	only

EXERCICE B

Michel is learning how to swim. Describe his lesson. *Remplacez l'adjectif par un adverbe.*

EXEMPLE: Michel arrive. (immédiat)

    Michel arrive **immédiatement**.

1. Le maître-nageur lui parle. (franc)

_____.

2. Michel écoute. (attentif)

_____.

3. Michel commence à nager. (nerveux)

_____.

4. Le maître-nageur le rassure. (doux)

_____.

5. D'abord il nage. (lent)

_____ .

6. Il s'applique. (sérieux)

_____ .

7. Enfin il nage. (fier)

_____ .

8. La maître-nageur applaudit. (vif)

_____ .

c. Some adverbs have forms distinct from the adjective forms.

ADJECTIVE		ADVERB	
bon	_good_	**bien**	_well_
mauvais	_bad_	**mal**	_badly_
petit	_little_	**peu**	_little_

Jean est un **bon** élève   _Jean is a good student because he_
   parce qu'il **écoute bien**.   _listens well._
Louise est une **petite** fille   _Louise is a little girl who eats_
   qui mange très **peu**.   _very little._

EXERCICE C

Lucie is babysitting. Describe the children she watches. _Employez la forme correcte des mots entre parenthèses._

1. (_mauvais, mal_) Janine joue _____ avec ce _____ garçon.

2. (_bon, bien_) Carine est une _____ enfant qui m'écoute _____ .

3. (_petit, peu_) Le _____ Guy mange _____ .

4. (_bon, bien_) Je traite _____ ces _____ enfants.

5. (_petit, peu_) Elle regarde très _____ la télévision, cette _____ fille.

6. (_mauvais, mal_) Ces filles sont _____ parce qu'elles parlent _____ .

[2] OTHER COMMON ADVERBS AND ADVERBIAL EXPRESSIONS

alors	*then*	hier	*yesterday*	souvent	*often*
après	*afterward*	ici	*here*	surtout	*especially*
assez	*enough, quite*	là	*there*	tard	*late*
aujourd'hui	*today*	loin	*far*	tôt	*soon*
aussi	*also, too*	longtemps	*a long time*	toujours	*always, still*
beaucoup	*much*	maintenant	*now*	tout	*quite, entirely*
bientôt	*soon*	même	*even*	tout à coup	*suddenly*
déjà	*already*	moins	*less*	tout à fait	*entirely*
demain	*tomorrow*	partout	*everywhere*	tout de suite	*immediately*
encore	*still, yet, again*	peut-être	*perhaps, maybe*	très	*very*
enfin	*at last*	plus	*more*	trop	*too much*
ensemble	*together*	près	*near*	vite	*quickly*
ensuite	*then*	quelquefois	*sometimes*		

EXERCICE D

Read the following sentences about Guy. *Remplacez l'adverbe donné par l'adverbe contraire.*

1. Guy parle **beaucoup** au téléphone. _____ .

2. Il chante **bien**. _____

3. Voici ma maison. Il habite tout **près**. _____

4. Il va arriver **tard**, comme d'habitude. _____

5. Guy travaille **ici**. _____

6. Il va **certainement** obtenir son diplôme. _____

7. Il gagne **moins** d'argent que moi. _____

8. Il marche **lentement**. _____

9. Il prépare **rarement** ses repas. _____

10. Guy s'amuse **quelquefois**. _____ .

[3] ADVERBS OF QUANTITY

Certain adverbs expressing quantity are followed by *de*, without an article, when they precede a noun.

assez de	*enough*	peu de	*little, few*
beaucoup de	*much, many*	plus de	*more*
combien de	*how much, how many*	trop de	*too much, too many*
moins de	*less, fewer*		

As-tu **assez d'argent**?   *Do you have enough money?*

J'ai **beaucoup de devoirs**.   *I have a lot of homework.*

EXERCICE E

You are in a restaurant. *Exprimez ce que le serveur vous apporte.*

beaucoup

EXEMPLE: **Il apporte beaucoup de soda.**

beaucoup

1. _____

beaucoup trop

2. _____

assez

3. _____

peu

4. _____

trop

5. _____

[4] POSITION OF ADVERBS

a. When modifying a verb in a simple tense, an adverb is usually placed directly after the verb it modifies.

Il **mange rarement** des fruits.   *He rarely eats fruits.*
Elle va **parler sérieusement**.   *She is going to speak seriously.*

EXERCICE F

What happens in M. Moreau's French class? *Mettez l'adverbe à la place qui convient.*

EXEMPLE: Les élèves arrivent en classe. (tôt)
                      Les élèves **arrivent tôt** en classe.

1. Les élèves écoutent le professeur. (attentivement)

_____

2. On écrit les devoirs sur le tableau. (généralement)

_____

3. M. Moreau parle aux élèves. (sérieusement)

_____

4. Les élèves aiment parler français. (beaucoup)

_____

5. On s'amuse en classe. (quelquefois)

_____

6. Les leçons sont intéressantes. (souvent)

_____

7. Les élèves participent à la leçon. (activement)

_____

8. M. Moreau explique la grammaire. (clairement)

_____

b. When modifying a verb in the *passé composé*, the adverb generally follows the past participle. However, a few common adverbs, such as *bien, mal, souvent, toujours, déjà* and *encore*, as well as adverbs of quantity, usually precede the past participle.

Hier, Jean **est arrivé tard**.   *Yesterday, Jean arrived late.*

Tu **as beaucoup mangé** à la fête.   *You ate a lot at the party.*

EXERCICE G

Odette had an argument with her friend. *Exprimez ce qu'elle a fait en mettant l'adverbe à la place qui convient.*

EXEMPLE: Elle a présenté son point de vue. (bien)
            Elle a *bien* présenté son point de vue.

1. Elle a crié à voix haute. (souvent)

_____

2. Elle a parlé. (impulsivement)

_____

3. Elle lui a répondu. (furieusement)

_____

4. Elle a blâmé son ami(e). (toujours)

_____

5. Elle a expliqué le problème. (mal)

_____

6. Elle a écouté son ami(e). (attentivement)

_____

7. Elle a quitté son ami(e). (brusquement)

_____

8. Ensuite, elle a regretté sa mauvaise humeur. (beaucoup)

_____

c. When modifying an adjective or another adverb, the adverb usually precedes the word it modifies.

une **très grande** maison   *a very large house*

lire **assez lentement**   *to read rather slowly*

EXERCICE H

Unscramble the words and form sentences to find out Paul's opinions of his classmates. *Suivez l'exemple.*

EXEMPLE: correct Pierre tout à fait est.
Pierre est tout à fait correct.

1. doucement Christophe trop parle

_____

2. jolie bien est Madeleine

_____

3. veut plus Marie être optimiste

_____

4. très Fabienne franche est

_____

5. Lucien lentement assez lit

_____

6. curieuses sont trop les filles

_____

7. peut attentivement Jean écouter plus

_____

8. répond sérieusement Annick très

_____

9. assez les garçons intelligents sont

_____

10. vraiment gentil Charles est

_____

MASTERY EXERCISES

EXERCICE I

Answer these questions. *Employez un adverbe dans vos réponses.*

1. Avec qui parles-tu sincèrement ?

_____

2. Quand écoutes-tu attentivement ?

_____

3. Pourquoi travailles-tu sérieusement ?

_____

4. Comment traites-tu tes amis ?

_____

5. Que fais-tu facilement ?

_____

6. Où vas-tu souvent ?

_____

7. Comment as-tu joué au tennis?

_____

8. Es-tu déjà allé(e) en France ?

_____

EXERCICE J

Complete the descriptions of the following people. *Employez un adverbe qui convient.*

EXEMPLE: Richard passe deux heures à parler au téléphone.
             Il parle *longtemps* **au téléphone.**

1. Grégoire ne range jamais sa chambre. Il laisse ses vêtements, ses livres et ses disques

   _____ .

2. Michelle dit toujours la vérité. Elle parle toujours _____ .

3. Suzanne a de bonnes manières. Elle dit toujours «merci», «s'il vous plaît» et «de rien». Elle parle

   _____ .

4. Christophe va arriver dans dix minutes. Il va arriver _____ .

5. Claire joue au tennis avec beaucoup d'énergie et de force. Elle joue _____ .

6. Paul achète une motocyclette sans la permission de ses parents. Il l'achète _____ .

7. Janine ne sait pas si elle va aller au cinéma cet après-midi. À un moment elle dit «oui», puis elle dit

   «non». Elle va _____ y aller.

8. Claude va chez le docteur à cet instant. Il y va _____ .

9. Annette reçoit un coup de téléphone urgent. Elle part _____ .

10. Olivier va au match de football avec Robert. Les deux garçons vont _____ .

EXERCICE K

Write a note to a friend explaining how to succeed in your French class. You may want to include:

- a description of your French class
- how your teacher teaches
- the things you need to do to succeed
- how often you speak French in class
- when the teacher assigns a lot of homework
- one thing you always do in class

_____

_____

_____

_____

_____

_____

_____

_____

Chapter 23
Numbers

[1] CARDINAL NUMBERS

0	zéro	20	vingt	88	quatre-vingt-huit
1	un(e)	21	vingt et un	90	quatre-vingt-dix
2	deux	22	vingt-deux	95	quatre-vingt-quinze
3	trois	30	trente	100	cent
4	quatre	31	trente et un	101	cent un
5	cinq	33	trente-trois	200	deux cents
6	six	40	quarante	316	trois cent seize
7	sept	45	quarante-cinq	500	cinq cents
8	huit	48	quarante-huit	527	cinq cent vingt-sept
9	neuf	50	cinquante	580	cinq cent quatre-vingts
10	dix	51	cinquante et un	1.000	mille
11	onze	57	cinquante-sept	1.001	mille un
12	douze	60	soixante	1.100	mille cent / onze cents
13	treize	61	soixante et un	1.200	mille deux cents / douze cents
14	quatorze	70	soixante-dix	3.000	trois mille
15	quinze	71	soixante et onze	3.210	trois mille deux cent dix
16	seize	75	soixante-quinze	10.000	dix mille
17	dix-sept	77	soixante-dix-sept	100.000	cent mille
18	dix-huit	80	quatre-vingts	1.000.000	un million
19	dix-neuf	81	quatre-vingt-un	one billion	un milliard

NOTES:

1. The conjunction *et* is used in 21, 31, 41, 51, 61, and 71. In all other compound numbers through 99, the hyphen is used. *Un* becomes *une* before a feminine noun.

vingt et **un** étudiants	*twenty-one students*
trente et **une** étudiantes	*thirty-one students*

2. *Quatre-vingts* and multiples of *cent* drop the *s* before another number.

quatre-vingts livres	*eighty books*
quatre-vingt-deux livres	*eighty-two books*
quatre cents livres	*four hundred books*
quatre cent cinquante livres	*four hundred fifty books*

3. *Cent* and *mille* are not preceded by the indefinite article.

cent hommes	*a (one) hundred men*
mille dollars	*a (one) thousand dollars*

4. *Mille* does not change in the plural.

sept mille personnes	*seven thousand people*

5. *Mille* often becomes *mil* in dates.

Il est né en mil neuf cent trente.   *He was born in 1930.*

6. *Million* and *milliard* are nouns and must be followed by *de* if another noun follows.

un million d'étoiles   *a (one) million stars*
deux milliards de dollars   *two billion dollars*

7. In numerals and decimals, where English uses periods, French uses commas and vice versa. The period marking thousands is often replaced by a space.

4.000 *or* 4 000 quatre mille   *4,000 four thousand*
0,05 zéro virgule zéro cinq   *.05 point zero five*
$4,60 quatre dollars soixante   *$4.60 four dollars and sixty cents*

EXERCICE A

Exprimez le prix des articles suivants.

EXEMPLE:

un dollar

1.

_____ .

2.

_____ .

3.

_____ .

4.

_____ .

5.

_____ .

6.

_____ .

7.

_____ .

8.

_____ .

EXERCICE B

How much will the following items cost? *Additionez les prix indiqués.*

EXEMPLE:

cinquante-six dollars

1.

_____ .

2.

_____ .

3.

_____ .

4.

_____ .

5.

_____ .

6.

_____ .

7.

_____ .

8.

_____ .

9.

_____ .

10.

_____ .

EXERCICE C

Exprimez l'âge des cousins Delon.

EXEMPLE: Marc / 6
            Marc a six ans.

1. Lucie / 12

_____

2. Raoul / 15

_____

3. Jean / 20

_____

4. Patrick / 14

_____

5. Odette / 11

_____

6. Robert / 3

_____

7. Nathalie / 18

_____

8. Jeanne / 13

_____

9. Roger / 16

_____

10. Berthe / 9

_____

EXERCICE D

A new student in your class has asked for some of your friends' phone numbers. *Exprimez ces numéros en français.*

EXEMPLE: Suzanne Baillot 01.45.58.17.86
            zéro un, quarante-cinq, cinquante-huit, dix-sept, quatre-vingt-six

1. Pierre Boyer 02.46.51.71.81

_____

2. Antoine Roselle 06.42.36.97.89

_____

3. Henri Machet 03.48.63.55.94

_____

4. Florence Belaud 01.45.77.85.92

_____

5. Isabelle Chambon 04.43.73.16.68

_____

EXERCICE E

What number does each player wear on his/her jersey? *Suivez l'exemple.*

EXEMPLE:

Il porte le trente-deux.

1.

_____ .

2.

_____ .

3.

_____ .

4.

_____ .

5.

_____ .

6.

_____ .

7.

_____ .

8.

_____ .

9.

_____ .

10.

_____ .

EXERCICE F

How many phone calls did each member of the Cordier family make last month? *Suivez l'exemple.*

EXEMPLE: Gisèle / 18
Gisèle **a fait dix-huit coups de téléphone.**

1. maman / 24

_____

2. Oncle Henri / 32

_____

3. Jacques / 61

_____

4. Tante Lise / 58

_____

5. Nadine / 87

_____

6. papa / 75

_____

7. Sylvie / 66

_____

8. Robert / 44

_____

EXERCICE G

What are the license plate numbers of the following cars? *Suivez l'exemple.*

EXEMPLE: **neuf cent trente-sept – huit cent soixante-deux**

1. _____

2. _____

3. _____

4. _____

5. _____

6. _____

EXERCICE H

On which page is your homework? *Suivez l'exemple.*

EXEMPLE: les maths/138
Les maths sont **à la page cent trente-huit.**

1. le français / 315

_____

2. la biologie/488

_____

3. l'anglais/295

_____

4. l'histoire/554

_____

5. le latin/226

_____

6. l'algèbre/165

_____

7. l'informatique/211

_____

8. la géographie/322

_____

EXERCICE I

You see an ad for a travel agency in the paper. *Exprimez le prix d'un voyage aux destinations suivantes.*

1. Londres / $699 _____

2. Portugal / $1,019 _____

3. Grèce / $1,339 _____

4. Paris / $855 _____

5. Espagne / $1,229 _____

6. Irlande / $969 _____

7. Allemagne / $1,119 _____

8. Canaries / $1,065 _____

EXERCICE J

You want to buy your first car. How expensive are the cars below? *Exprimez le prix en français.*

EXEMPLE:

cinq mille quatre cent vingt-six dollars.

1.

2.

_____ .   _____ .

3.

_____ .

4.

_____ .

5.

_____ .

6.

_____ .

7.

_____ .

8.

_____ .

[2] ARITHMETIC EXPRESSIONS

The following expressions are used in arithmetic problems in French.

et _plus_		**multiplié par** _multiplied by_	
fois _multiplied by, times_		**moins** _minus_	
font _equals_		**divisé par** _divided by_	

huit et trois font onze	$8 + 3 = 11$
deux fois sept font quatorze	$2 \times 7 = 14$
dix moins quatre font six	$10 - 4 = 6$
quinze divisé par cinq font trois	$15 : 5 = 3$
sept cent multiplié par six	$700 \times 6 = 4.200$

EXERCICE K

You are working in a French bank. Express the operations you must perform by doing the math in French. *Suivez l'exemple.*

EXEMPLE: $80 \times 2 = 160$
Quatre-vingts fois deux font cent soixante.

1. $96 \times 13 = 1.248$

_____

2. $12.000 : 100 = 120$

_____

3. $828 + 633 = 1.461$

_____

4. $1947 - 179 = 1.768$

_____

5. $1.800 : 9 = 200$

_____

6. $33 \times 49 = 1.617$

_____

7. $16.500 - 886 = 15.614$

_____

8. $496 + 384 = 880$

_____

[3] ORDINAL NUMBERS

1st **premier (première)**	*7th* **septième**	*17th* **dix-septième**
2nd **deuxième, second(e)**	*8th* **huitième**	*20th* **vingtième**
3rd **troisième**	*9th* **neuvième**	*21st* **vingt et unième**
4th **quatrième**	*10th* **dixième**	*34th* **trente-quatrième**
5th **cinquième**	*11th* **onzième**	*100th* **centième**
6th **sixième**	*16th* **seizième**	*103rd* **cent-troisième**

NOTES:

1. Ordinal numbers are adjectives and agree in gender and number with the noun they modify. *Premier* and *second* are the only ordinal numbers to have a feminine form different from the masculine form.

Elle est **la première** à gagner.   *She is the first one to win.*
Les **dix-huitièmes** anniversaires   *Eighteenth birthdays are very important.*
sont très importants.

2. Except for *premier* and *second*, ordinal numbers are formed by adding *-ième* to the cardinal numbers. Silent *e* is dropped before *-ième*.

3. Note the *u* in *cinquième* and the *v* in *neuvième*.

4. *Second(e)* generally replaces *deuxième* in a series which does not go beyond two.

   sa seconde fille   *his/her second daughter*

5. The final *a* or *e* of the preceding article is not dropped before *huit, huitième, onze,* and *onzième*.

   le huit mai   *the eighth of May*
   la onzième course   *the eleventh race*

6. Ordinal numbers are abbreviated as follows in French.

   premier 1er (première 1re)   seizième 16e
   deuxième 2e   cinquantième 50e
   dixième 10e   centième 100e

EXERCICE L

Paris is divided into twenty *arrondissements* (districts). *Exprimez les numéros et les arrondissements indiqués dans ces adresses parisiennes.*

EXEMPLE: 24, rue Niger, 12e
           vingt-quatre, rue Niger, douzième (arrondissement)

1. 92, boulevard Barbès, 18e

_____

2. 12, rue Émile-Duclaux, 15e

_____

3. 5, rue Delambre, 14e

_____

4. 13, rue du Docteur-Lamaze, 19e

_____

5. 224, rue de Belleville, 20e

_____

6. 80, rue du Bac, 7e

_____

7. 67, boulevard Suchet, 16e

_____

8. 96, avenue des Ternes, 17e

_____

EXERCICE M

Where are the following students seated in the classroom? Look at the seating plan below. *Suivez l'exemple.*

Rang 3	Robert	Richard	André	Nadine	Suzanne	Grégoire
Rang 2	Odette	Raoul	Pierre	Joseph	Annick	Marie
Rang 1	Lise	Paul	Georges	Anne	Luc	Sylvie

EXEMPLE: Joseph
Joseph **est au deuxième rang, à la quatrième place.**

1. Sylvie

_____

2. Pierre

_____

3. Richard

_____

4. Annick

_____

5. Nadine

_____

6. Lise

_____

EXERCICE N

Which birthday are the following people celebrating? *Suivez l'exemple.*

EXAMPLE: Georgette / 46ᵉ
Georgette **célèbre son quarante-sixième anniversaire.**

1. M. Duclos / 54ᵉ

_____

2. Mme Renard / 79ᵉ

_____

3. Claude / 28ᵉ

_____

4. Joseph / 11ᵉ

_____

5. Janine / 36e

_____

6. Mlle Boyer / 102e

_____

7. Le professeur Arnaud / 63e

_____

8. Marie-Laure / 5e

_____

EXERCICE O

You are applying for a job. *Répondez aux questions ci-dessous.*

1. En quelle année êtes-vous né(e)?

_____

2. Quel âge avez-vous?

_____

3. Quelle est votre adresse?

_____

4. Quel est votre numéro de téléphone?

_____

5. Combien d'années d'expérience avez-vous?

_____

6. Quel salaire désirez-vous?

_____

MASTERY EXERCISES

EXERCICE P

You are refurnishing your room. *Écrivez combien coûtent les objets suivants.*

EXEMPLE:

Le tapis coûte cinq cent trente-cinq dollars.

1. _____

2. _____

3. _____

4. _____

5. _____

6. _____

7. _____

8. _____

EXERCICE Q

Find all the numbers in the ads below. *Écrivez-les en toutes lettres.*

1.

LES ACACIAS

retraite privée – valides – semi-valides
28 chambres, 1 et 2 personnes
cadre agréable, jardin
19, rue des Acacias
94254 Sainte-Maure
400 m. R.E.R. La Défense
Autobus 103
01 48 55 52 40

2.

LOCATION LARCOR

Chapiteaux 300 à 800 places
Gradins 5 à 17 rangs - Tentes 40 à 150 mètres
Chauffage air pulsé 50.000 à 1.000.000 calories

65229 Longueau
01 62 24 56 77

1. _____

_____

_____

_____

_____

2. _____

_____

_____

_____

_____

_____

EXERCICE R

Write a note to a friend describing the new apartment your parents just rented in Paris for the summer. You may want to include the following:

- the arrondissement you will live in
- how many stories the building has
- the floor on which your apartment is located
- how many rooms the apartment has
- how much rent your parents will have to pay
- how many days you will stay in Paris for the summer

_____

_____

_____

_____

_____

_____

_____

_____

Chapter 24

Time and Dates

[1] TIME

Quelle heure est-il?	What time is it?
Il est une heure.	It is one o'clock.
Il est une heure cinq.	It is 1:05.
Il est une heure et quart.	It is 1:15.
Il est une heure vingt-cinq.	It is 1:25.
Il est une heure et demie.	It is 1:30.
Il est deux heures moins vingt-cinq.	It is 1:35.
Il est deux heures moins vingt.	It is 1:40.
Il est deux heures moins le quart.	It is 1:45.
Il est deux heures moins dix.	It is 1:50.
Il est deux heures moins cinq.	It is 1:55.
Il est midi.	It is twelve o'clock (noon).
Il est minuit.	It is twelve o'clock (midnight)
Il est midi (minuit) et demi.	It is half past twelve.

NOTES:

1. To express time after the hour, the number of minutes is placed directly after the hour; *et* is used only with *quart* and *demi(e)*. To express time before the hour, *moins* is used.

2. *Midi* and *minuit* are masculine.

[2] TIME EXPRESSIONS

à quelle heure?	at what time?
à une heure	at one o'clock
à deux heures précises	at two o'clock sharp
deux heures du matin	2:00 a.m.
cinq heures de l'après-midi	5:00 p.m.
sept heures du soir	7:00 p.m.
vers onze heures	about eleven o'clock
un quart d'heure	a quarter of an hour
une demi-heure	a half hour
midi et quart	12:15 p.m.
minuit dix	12:10 a.m.

NOTES:

1. To express the time of day, *du matin* expresses *a.m.*, *de l'après-midi* expresses early *p.m.* and *du soir* expresses late *p.m.*

2. In public announcements such as timetables, the "official" twenty-four-hour system is commonly used, with midnight as the zero hour. The words *minuit, midi, quart,* and *demi* are not used and the number of minutes is expressed by a full number.

0h20	zéro heure vingt	*12:20 a.m.*
11h10	onze heures dix	*11:10 a.m.*
15h30	quinze heures trente	*3:30 p.m.*
22h40	vingt-deux heures quarante	*10:40 p.m.*
21h15	vingt et une heures quinze	*9:15 p.m.*

EXERCICE A

You are learning how to tell time in French. *Exprimez les heures indiquées.*

EXEMPLE: 2:30
Il est deux heures et demie.

1. 11:00

_____

2. 3:50

_____

3. 9:05

_____

4. 6:35

_____

5. 10:20

_____

6. 1:30

_____

7. 2:45

_____

8. 2:10

_____

9. 10:55

_____

10. 5:15

_____

11. 8:25

_____

12. 9:40

_____

EXERCICE B

Each person in the Duval family has set his/her digital alarm for a different time. At what time does each wake up? *Dites-le en français.*

EXEMPLE:

Jacques se réveille à huit heures quatorze.

1.   Jean _____ .

2.   Mme Duval _____ .

3.   Claude et moi _____ .

4.   Lise et Anne _____ .

5.   M. Duval _____ .

6.   La mère de Mme Duval _____ .

EXERCICE C

At what time do you do the following? *Suivez le modèle.*

EXEMPLE: **Je me réveille à sept heures du matin.**

1. _____

2. _____

3. _____

4. _____

5. _____

6. _____

7. _____

8. _____

EXERCICE D

You are looking at the television section of a French newspaper. Tell your parents at what time the following shows can be seen. Suivez le modèle.

6h58	Météo		15h45	_Les Simpson_
8h25	Télé-Shopping		18h05	_FBI—Opérations secrètes_
10h30	Disney classique		19h30	_Les défis de l'océan —_
11h35	_Le scooby-gang_			documentaire
12h30	_Questions pour un champion_		23h45	_Desperate Housewives_
13h35	_Will & Grace_		0h40	Journal—Informations

EXEMPLE: *Le scooby-gang*
Le scooby-gang **commence à onze heures trente-cinq.**

1. *Les Simpson*

_____

2. *Questions pour un champion*

_____

3. *FBI – Opérations secrètes*

_____

4. *Le Journal—Informations*

_____

5. *Le Disney Classique*

_____

6. *Desperate Housewives*

_____

7. *Will & Grace*

_____

8. *Le Télé-Shopping*

_____

9. *La météo*

_____

10. *Les défis de l'océan*

_____

EXERCICE E

You want to go to the movies and you call several theaters to learn at what time films start.
Dites à quelle heure les films suivants commencent.

EXEMPLE: Ciné Georges V—*Batman*: 14h15, 17h20, 20h25
Batman **commence à deux heures et quart, cinq heures vingt et huit heures vingt-cinq.**

1. Forum Orient Express—*La maison du bonheur*: 14h10, 16h35, 19h, 21h25.

_____

_____

_____

_____

2. Gaumont Opéra—*Pirates des Caraïbes: le secret du coffre maudit*: 13h50, 15h35, 17h20, 19h05.

_____

_____

_____

_____

3. Ciné Beaubourg—*Miami Vice – Deux flics à Miami*: 13h30, 16h05, 18h40, 21h15.

_____

_____

_____

_____

[3] DAYS, MONTHS, SEASONS

LES JOURS DE LA SEMAINE	LES MOIS DE L'ANNÉE	LES SAISONS DE L'ANNÉE
lundi *Monday* **mardi** *Tuesday* **mercredi** *Wednesday* **jeudi** *Thursday* **vendredi** *Friday* **samedi** *Saturday* **dimanche** *Sunday*	**janvier** *January* **février** *February* **mars** *March* **avril** *April* **mai** *May* **juin** *June* **juillet** *July* **août** *August* **septembre** *September* **octobre** *October* **novembre** *November* **décembre** *December*	**le printemps** *spring* **l'été** *summer* **l'automne** *autumn* **l'hiver** *winter*

NOTES:

1. Days, months, and seasons are all masculine and are not capitalized in French.

2. To express *in* with months and seasons, *en* is used, except with *printemps*.

    en janvier *in January*   **en été** *in (the) summer*
    en août *in August*   **en automne** *in (the) autumn*
    en novembre *in November*   **en hiver** *in (the) winter*
                                     But:
                                     au printemps *in (the) spring*

3. The definite article is used with days of the week in a plural sense. If the day mentioned is a specific day, the article is omitted.

    Le dimanche je me lève tard.   *On Sunday(s) I get up late.*
    Appelez-moi **mardi**.   *Call me (on) Tuesday.*

EXERCICE F

Everybody's leaving for summer vacation. *Regardez le calendrier (calendar) et dites quel jour chacun va partir.*

L	M	M	J	V	S	D
		1	2	3	4	5
6	7	8	9	10	11	12
13	14	15	16	17	18	19
20	21	22	23	24	25	26
27	28	29	30	31		

EXEMPLE: Jean—le 6
Il va partir le lundi 6.

1. Christophe—le 9

_____

2. Odette et Claire—le 28

_____

3. Paul et toi—le 11

_____

4. Lucien et Georges—le 20

_____

5. Suzanne et moi—le 3

_____

6. Toi—le 12

_____

EXERCICE G

You have just received your new schedule for the term. *Dites quels jours vous avez les classes suivantes.*

	lundi	mardi	mercredi	jeudi	vendredi
8–9	latin	français	maths	français	maths
9–10	biologie	anglais	musique	gym	français
10–11	histoire	histoire	anglais	anglais	gym
11–12	français	maths	histoire	musique	biologie
12–1					
1–2	maths	biologie	art	maths	histoire
2–3	gym	art	latin	biologie	anglais

EXEMPLE: gym
J'ai gym lundi, jeudi et vendredi.

1. art

_____

2. maths

_____

3. musique

_____

4. français

_____

5. histoire

_____

6. biologie

_____

EXERCICE H

En quel mois sommes-nous? Regardez l'illustration.

EXEMPLE:

Nous sommes en février.

1.

_____

2.

_____

3.

_____

4.

_____

5.

_____

6.

_____

7.

_____

8.

_____

9.

_____

10.

_____

11.

_____

12.

_____

EXERCICE I

Écrivez le nom des mois de chaque saison.

au printemps	en été	en automne	en hiver
_____	_____	_____	_____
_____	_____	_____	_____
_____	_____	_____	_____
_____	_____	_____	_____

[4] DATES

Quelle est la date d'aujourd'hui ?	_What is today's date?_
Quel jour (de la semaine) est-ce aujourd'hui ? **Quel jour sommes-nous aujourd'hui ?**	_What day of the week is today?_
C'est aujourd'hui samedi. **Nous sommes samedi.**	_Today is Saturday._
C'est aujourd'hui le premier mai. **Aujourd'hui nous sommes le premier mai.**	_Today is May 1st (the first of May)._
en dix-neuf cent quatre-vingt-quinze **en mil(le) neuf cent quatre-vingt-quinze**	_in 1995_
le trente juillet dix-neuf cent quatre-vingt-douze **le 30 juillet 1992**	_July 30, 1992_
lundi 10 décembre 2007 **le lundi 10 décembre 2007** **lundi, le 10 décembre 2007**	_Monday, December 10, 2007_

NOTES:

1. In dates, *le premier* is used for the first day of the month. For all other days, cardinal numbers are used.

2. Years are commonly expressed in hundreds, as in English. The word for one thousand in dates, if used, is often written *mil*.

3. The date in numbers follows the sequence *day, month, year*.

> le 22 avril 2007 (22.4.07)   *April 22, 2007 (4/22/2007)*
> le 3 mai 1992 (3.5.92)   *May 3, 1992 (5/3/1992)*

EXERCICE J

On which dates will you write the following information in your new calendar? *Suivez le modèle.*

EXEMPLE: L'anniversaire de mon frère
           le onze juillet

1. mon anniversaire

_____

2. l'anniversaire de mon (ma) meilleur(e) ami(e)

_____

3. les classes finissent

_____

4. les examens commencent

_____

5. je vais en vacances

_____

6. je rentre à l'école

_____

7. je vais à une fête

_____

8. Je vais à un concert

_____

EXERCICE K

You have recorded the birthdays of all the French exchange students who are visiting your school. *Écrivez les dates en français.*

EXEMPLE: Janine 5/8
           Elle célèbre son anniversaire le huit mai.

1. Hubert 12/9

_____

2. Lisette 11/7

_____

3. Roland 9/1

_____

4. Nadine 5/11

_____

5. Sylvie 1/6

_____

6. Michel 2/4

_____

7. Robert 6/2

_____

8. Denis 9/12

_____

9. Mireille 7/8

_____

10. Mathieu 4/5

_____

11. Christophe 10/26

_____

12. Anne 3/14

_____

EXERCICE L

Écrivez en français la date des anniversaires des membres de la famille Raspail.

EXEMPLE: Caroline / April 20, 1981
           Caroline, le vingt avril dix-neuf / mil(le) neuf cent quatre-vingt-un.

1. Mme Raspail, September 21, 1954

_____

2. M. Raspail, July 11, 1945

_____

3. Nicole, April 22, 1977

_____

4. Philippe, October 24, 1984

_____

5. la mère de Mme Raspail, April 15, 1922

_____

6. Cousin Jacques, February 1, 1992

_____

7. Oncle Paul, January 9, 1963

_____

8. le père de M. Raspail, June 30, 1918

_____

MASTERY EXERCISES

EXERCICE M

You are showing pictures of some past holidays to your pen pal who is visiting from France. *Pour chaque fête, donnez la date, le jour et l'heure. Suivez l'exemple.*

EXEMPLE:  C'était le vingt-cinq décembre deux mille. Il était minuit dix.

1. _____

_____

2. _____

_____

3.

_____

_____

4.

_____

_____

EXERCICE N

You are studying French history. *Écrivez la date des événements suivants en utilisant le mot mil(le) une fois seulement.*

1. (1412) Jeanne d'Arc est née en

_____

2. (1598) Henri IV a proclamé l'Édit de Nantes en

_____

3. (1634) Le cardinal de Richelieu a fondé l'Académie française en

_____

4. (July 14, 1789) Les habitants de Paris ont attaqué la Bastille le

_____

5. (1848) Napoléon III a été élu président de la Seconde République en

_____

EXERCICE O

Write a note to a friend about your new nephew. You may want to include the following:

- his name
- his birth date (including the year)
- the time he was born

- his weight
- his length
- how many brothers and sisters he has

_____

_____

_____

_____

_____

_____

_____

Chapter 25
Interrogatives and Exclamations

[1] INTERROGATIVE ADVERBS

combien?	*how much? how many*	**d'où?**	*from where?*
comment?	*how?*	**pourquoi?**	*why?*
où?	*where (to)?*	**quand?**	*when?*

a. Questions beginning with an interrogative adverb are frequently formed with *est-ce que* following the adverb.

Quand est-ce que tu sors?	*When do you go out?*
Comment est-ce qu'il va?	*How is he?*
Où est-ce que vous allez?	*Where are you going?*
Combien est-ce que ce livre coûte?	*How much does this book cost?*

b. A question beginning with an interrogative adverb can also be formed by inversion of the verb and the subject pronoun.

Quand sors-tu?	*When do you go out?*
Comment va-t-il?	*How is he?*
Où allez-vous?	*Where are you going?*

NOTES:

1. With *combien, comment, où, d'où,* and *quand*, when the subject is a noun, if the verb has no object, a question may be formed by inverting the order of subject and verb.

Combien **coûte ce livre**?	*How much does this book cost?*
Comment **s'appelle ce café**?	*What's the name of this café?*

2. In colloquial spoken French, questions are often formed by placing an interrogative adverb after the verb.

Tu vas où?	*Where are you going?*
Il s'appelle comment?	*What's his name?*
Ce livre coûte combien?	*How much does this book cost?*

EXERCICE A

Your French pen pal is coming to visit you. Use two ways to express each of the questions your friends are asking you about her, based on the answers below. *Suivez l'exemple.*

EXEMPLE: Elle est jolie. (*comment*)
   Comment est-elle ?
   Comment est-ce qu'elle est ?

1. Elle est de Toulouse. (*d'où*)

_____

_____

2. Elle vient aux États-Unis en avion. (*comment*)

_____

_____

3. Elle paie son billet $250. (*combien*)

_____

_____

4. Elle habitera chez moi. (*où*)

_____

_____

5. Elle arrivera dans une semaine. (*quand*)

_____

_____

6. Elle vient aux États-Unis pour perfectionner son anglais. (*pourquoi*)

_____

_____

EXERCICE B

Write as many questions as you can about the following people. *Suivez l'exemple.*

EXEMPLE:　Jeudi, à cinq heures, Lise, qui vient du Canada, marche
　　　　　lentement en ville parce qu'elle a mal aux pieds.
　　　　　Quand est-ce que Lise marche en ville ?
　　　　　D'où vient–elle ?
　　　　　Lise marche comment ?
　　　　　Où est-ce que Lise marche ?
　　　　　Pourquoi marche–t–elle lentement ?

1. À trois heures de l'après-midi, Marie Legros danse parfaitement bien trois nouvelles danses modernes devant le miroir du studio parce qu'elle fait partie du club de danse.

_____

_____

_____

_____

_____

2. Marc sort rapidement de sa chambre à quatre heures de l'après-midi parce qu'il voit deux jolies filles marcher devant sa maison.

_____

_____

_____

_____

_____

_____

[2] INTERROGATIVE ADJECTIVES

The interrogative adjective *quel (which? what?)* agrees with the noun it modifies.

	MASCULINE	FEMININE
SINGULAR	quel	quelle
PLURAL	quels	quelles

Quelle heure est-il?
 Quelle heure est-ce qu'il est?
 Il est quelle heure?   *What time is it?*

Quelles chansons préfères-tu?
 Quelles chansons est-ce que tu préfères?
 Tu préfères quelles chansons?   *Which songs do you prefer?*

NOTES:

1. The only verb that may follow *quel* directly is *être*.

Quel est ton nom?	*What is your name?*
Quelle est ton adresse?	*What is your address?*
Quels sont tes cours favoris?	*What are your favorite classes?*

2. *Quel* may be preceded by a preposition.

   | Pour quelle raison êtes-vous ici? | *For what reason are you here?* |
   | À quelle heure est-ce que Paul vient? | *At what time is Paul coming?* |

EXERCICE C

You've made a new friend. Ask this friend some personal questions using *quel + être*.

EXEMPLE: nom
 Quel est ton nom ?

1. adresse

_____

2. numéro de téléphone

_____

3. date de naissance

_____

4. sports préférés

_____

5. plat favori

_____

6. classes préférées

_____

EXERCICE D

Your friend's room is a mess. *Demandez-lui ce qu'il/elle cherche.*

EXEMPLE:

Quel livre cherches-tu ?

1.

_____.

2.

_____.

3.

_____.

4.

_____.

5.

_____ .

6.

_____ .

7.

_____ .

8.

_____ .

[3] INTERROGATIVE PRONOUNS

	PEOPLE	THINGS
SUBJECT OF A VERB	**qui?** *who?*	**qu'est-ce qui?** *what?*
DIRECT OBJECT OF A VERB	**qui?** **qui est-ce que?** } *whom?*	**que?** **qu'est-ce que?** } *what?*

NOTE: The *e* of *que* is dropped before a word beginning with a vowel; the *i* of *qui* is never dropped.

Qu'as-tu vu?   *What did you see?*

Qui as-tu vu?   *Whom did you see?*

a. Interrogative pronouns as subjects

Qui? (*who?*) is used for people. *Qu'est-ce qui?* (*what?*) is used for things. The verb that follows is in the third person singular *il*.

Qui va arriver en retard?   *Who is going to arrive late?*

Qu'est-ce qui arrive?   *What is happening?*

EXERCICE E

M. et Mme Léger are back from vacation and they ask their children how they managed. Use *qui* to write their questions based on the answers given. *Suivez l'exemple.*

EXEMPLE: Jean a lavé la voiture.
          Qui a lavé la voiture ?

1. Lucien a promené le chien.

_____

2. J'ai fait le lavage.

_____

3. Berthe et Robert ont préparé les repas.

_____

4. Nous avons passé l'aspirateur.

_____

5. Richard et Claudine ont vidé les ordures.

_____

6. Tout le monde a nettoyé la maison.

_____

EXERCICE F

M. Leduc wants to spend a relaxing day in his garden. Ask why this is impossible. *Suivez l'exemple.*

EXEMPLE: Un coup de tonnerre réveille M. Leduc.
             Qu'est-ce qui réveille M. Leduc?

1. Le téléphone ne cesse pas de sonner.

_____

2. Trois paquets arrivent.

_____

3. Le mauvais temps continue toute la journée.

_____

4. Un arbre tombe dans son jardin.

_____

5. Un accident de voiture dérange sa paix.

_____

6. Le bruit l'empêche de rester calme.

_____

EXERCICE G

You have been absent from school for a week. Your friends come by to visit. *Complétez les questions que vous posez avec* **qui** *ou* **qu'est-ce qui.**

1. _____ est arrivé à Jean-François?

2. _____ a gagné le championnat de tennis?

3. _____ va aider Marie avec ses devoirs?

4. _____ se passe dans la classe de français?

5. _____ empêche Nathalie de me rendre visite?

6. _____ va me téléphoner ce soir?

7. _____ est dans cette jolie boîte?

8. _____ m'a envoyé ces cartes?

b. Interrogative pronouns as direct objects.

Qui? and *qui est-ce que?* *(whom?)* are used for people. *Que?* and *qu'est-ce que?* *(what?)* are used for things.

Qui aimes-tu?	
Qui est-ce que tu aimes?	*Whom do you love?*
Que fait-elle?	
Qu'est-ce qu'elle fait?	*What is she doing?*
Qu'est-ce que cet enfant raconte?	*What is this child saying?*

NOTES:

1. After the short forms *qui?* and *que?* the word order is inverted; after the long form with *est-ce que* the word order is regular.

2. *Qui?* can be preceded by a preposition.

   À qui parles-tu?   *To whom do you speak?*

3. *Qu'est-ce que c'est ?* means: *What is it?* and is used for things.

   Qu'est-ce que c'est?   *What is it?*

   —C'est un livre.   *It's a book.*

EXERCICE H

Michelle is Éric's new girlfriend. *Posez des questions sur eux.*

EXEMPLE: Éric adore Michelle.
        Qui est-ce qu'Éric adore ?
        Qui adore-t-il ?

1. Éric accompagne Michelle au cinéma.

   _____

   _____

2. Éric ignore les autres filles.

_____

_____

3. Éric aide Michelle à faire ses devoirs.

_____

_____

4. Éric amène Michelle aux matches de foot.

_____

_____

5. Michelle écoute les amis d'Éric.

_____

_____

6. Michelle embrasse Éric tout le temps.

_____

_____

EXERCICE I

You are going to take a trip to France. *Exprimez les questions que vos amis vous posent en employant* **que** *ou* **qu'est-ce que.**

EXEMPLE: Je mangerai des spécialités françaises.
            Qu'est-ce que tu mangeras?
            Que mangeras-tu?

1. J'achèterai de jolis souvenirs.

_____

_____

2. Je verrai des monuments importants.

_____

_____

3. Je lirai les journaux français..

_____

_____

4. Je ferai de longues promenades en ville.

_____

_____

5. Je photographierai le paysage.

_____

_____

6. J'aimerai tout.

_____

_____

EXERCICE J

Votre classe va faire un pique-nique. Posez des questions avec **qui** *ou* **que.**

1. _____ apporteras-tu?

2. _____ amènera-t-elle?

3. _____ mangerons-nous?

4. _____ ferons-nous s'il fait mauvais?

5. Avec _____ irons-nous?

6. _____ remercierez-vous?

7. _____ boirons-nous?

8. _____ aideras-tu?

EXERCICE K

Your friend is in a grumpy mood. Ask why and what you can do. *Complétez les questions avec* **qu'est-ce qui** *ou* **qu'est-ce que.**

1. _____ te dérange ?

2. _____ tu veux faire ?

3. _____ je peux te donner ?

4. _____ arrive ?

5. _____ est si terrible ?

6. _____ tu trouves si ennuyeux ?

[4] EXCLAMATIONS

The forms of *quel* are used in exclamations to express *what a...!* or *what...!*

Quel beau château!   *What a beautiful castle!*
Quels livres intéressants!   *What interesting books!*
Quelle jolie fille!   *What a pretty girl!*
Quelles histoires!   *What stories!*

EXERCICE L

What would you say if you received the following gifts for Valentine's Day?

EXEMPLE: livre intéressant
        Quel livre intéressant!

1. belles fleurs

_____

2. chocolats délicieux

_____

3. carte magnifique

_____

4. photos splendides

_____

5. joli bracelet

_____

6. montre formidable

_____

MASTERY EXERCISES

EXERCICE M

A little boy is lost in a department store. Write the questions that he was asked, based on the answers below. *Suivez l'exemple.*

EXEMPLE: Ma mère **est** Jeanne Duval.
        Qui est ta mère?

1. Je suis Paul Duval.

_____

2. Je pleure parce que je suis perdu.

_____

3. Je cherche ma mère.

_____

4. Elle était ici.

_____

5. Nous sommes arrivés au magasin à deux heures.

_____

6. Ma mère est grande.

_____

7. Elle porte une robe verte.

_____

8. Ma mère regardait les pulls.

_____

9. Ma tante est avec ma mère.

_____

10. J'ai deux dollars.

_____

11. Mon adresse est 57 rue Monique.

_____

12. Mon numéro de téléphone est 01.45.67.78.89.

_____

EXERCICE N

Ask as many questions as you can about the following situations, based on the words in bold letters. *Suivez l'exemple.*

EXEMPLE: Janine accompagne **Nadine** en ville. Elles décident d'aller **à une discothèque. Cette nouvelle disco** est vraiment amusante. **Les filles** rentrent très tard.

Qui est-ce que Janine accompagne en ville ? Où décident-elles d'aller ? Qu'est-ce qui est vraiment amusant ? Qui rentre très tard ?

1. Roger ouvre **une magnifique boîte de chocolat**. **Un bonbon** tombe par terre. Il appelle **son chien, Champ**. **Champ** trouve le bonbon délicieux.

_____

_____

_____

_____

2. **Le téléphone** ne marche pas. **Pierre** veut parler à son amie Alice. Il aime beaucoup **cette fille**. Pierre décide d'aller **chez elle en vélo**.

_____

_____

_____

_____

3. **Georgette** accompagne son ami Marc au cinéma. **Marc** adore les films. **Ce film** est intéressant. Ils ont envie de voir **ce film**.

_____

_____

_____

_____

EXERCICE O

Write a note to a French penpal in which you tell him/her about life in the United States. You may want to include:

• what you do for fun
• when you go to school
• who your friends are
• what you do after school
• how life is different in America

_____

_____

_____

_____

_____

_____

_____

Chapter 26
Possession

[1] EXPRESSING POSSESSION

a. In French the preposition *de* expresses possession and relationship (English *'s* or *s'*, *of*).

les crayons **de** Michel	*Michel's pencils*
le livre **du** professeur	*the teacher's book*
le tableau **de** l'artiste	*the artist's painting*
la mère **des** enfants	*the children's mother*

NOTE: *De* is repeated before each noun.
le frère **de** Paul et **de** Luc   *Paul and Luc's brother*

EXERCICE A

It is the end of the school year and the items in the Lost and Found have to be returned.
Déterminez le propriétaire (owner) de chaque objet.

EXEMPLES: l'écharpe / Madeleine
C'est l'écharpe de Madeleine.

les gants/Jean
Ce sont les gants de Jean.

1. le livre/instituteur

_____

2. les lunettes/directeur

_____

3. le tee-shirt/Henri

_____

4. le stylo/maîtresse

_____

5. les bandes dessinées/Michel et Luc

_____

6. la brosse/Nadine

_____

7. la carte/professeur Lamont

_____

8. les cahiers/Marie et Lise

_____

b. The idiom **être à** *(to belong to)* also expresses possession.

Ces cahiers **sont au** garçon.   *These notebooks belong to the boy.*

Ce livre **est à** moi.   *This book belongs to me.*

Est-ce que ce stylo **est à** Éric?   *Does this pen belong to Éric?*

NOTE: À is repeated before each noun.

Ces cassettes sont **à** Marc et **à** Guy.   *These cassettes belong to Marc and Guy.*

EXERCICE B

You are cleaning out the attic. Your mother asks to whom each of the things you find belongs. *Exprimez ses questions et vos réponses.*

EXEMPLE:

François
La bicyclette *est à* François?
Oui, **elle** *est à* **lui.**

Pierre

1. _____

_____

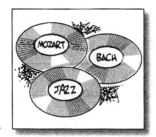

Henri et Joseph

2. _____

_____

moi

3. _____

_____

ta sœur et toi

4. _____

toi

5. _____

Charline et Odette

6. _____

ton père et moi

7. _____

Claire

8. _____

[2] POSSESSIVE ADJECTIVES

SINGULAR		PLURAL	
MASCULINE	**FEMININE**		
mon	ma	mes	*my*
ton	ta	tes	*your* (familiar)
son	sa	ses	*his, her, its*
notre	notre	nos	*our*
votre	votre	vos	*your* (formal or plural)
leur	leur	leurs	*their*

NOTES:

1. Possessive adjectives, like other adjectives, agree with the nouns they modify. They are repeated before each noun.

sa sœur et son frère	*his / her sister and brother*
mes chiens et mon chat	*my dogs and my cat*
ton livre et leurs cahiers	*your book and their notebooks*

2. The forms *mon, ton,* and *son* are used instead of *ma, ta,* and *sa* before a feminine singular noun beginning with a vowel or silent *h.*

mon amie	*my friend*
ton écharpe	*your scarf*
son école	*his / her school*

3. With parts of the body, the possessive adjective is usually replaced by the definite article if the possessor is clear.

Elle se lave les mains.	*She washes her hands.*
Il a un chapeau sur la tête.	*He has a hat on his head.*

EXERCICE C

You are very hungry and your friend is preparing your lunch rather slowly. Exprimez ce que vous lui dites et ses réponses.

EXEMPLE: sandwich
Où est *mon* sandwich?
Ton sandwich? Un moment.

1. hamburger

_____

_____

2. salade

_____

_____

3. fromages

_____

_____

4. légumes

_____

_____

5. omelette

_____

_____

6. soupe

_____

_____

EXERCICE D

You and a friend are getting off a plane in Europe. The stewardess approaches and asks if you've left something behind. _Exprimez ses questions et vos réponses._

EXEMPLE:

Ce sont *vos* chapeaux?
Ce ne sont pas *nos* chapeaux.

1. _____

_____

2. _____

3. _____

4. _____

5. _____

6. _____

EXERCICE E

Jacques is curious about his friends' families. *Répondez à ses questions.*

EXEMPLE: Le père d'Henri est mécanicien? (ingénieur)
  Mais non. Son père est ingénieur.

1. La mère de Georgette est avocate? (docteur)

_____

2. Les parents de Marie sont docteurs? (professeurs)

_____

3. L'oncle de Jules est ingénieur? (électricien)

_____

4. La cousine de Nadine est programmeuse? (secrétaire)

_____

5. Les filles de M. Dupont sont infirmières? (coiffeuses)

_____

6. Le fils de Mme Nalet est artiste? (vendeur)

_____

7. La fille cadette de Mme Lenoir est peintre? (décoratrice)

_____

8. Les grands-parents d'Yves sont professeurs? (dentistes)

_____

EXERCICE F

You are on a tour bus in Europe. *Exprimez ce que les personnes suivantes ont avec elles.*

EXEMPLE: Les Dupont / enfants
           Les Dupont **ont leurs enfants.**

1. Jean et Richard / lunettes de soleil

_____

2. Les Duchamp / crème solaire

_____

3. M. et Mme Soland / parapluie

_____

4. Nathalie et Robert / argent

_____

5. Les parents de Luc / chèques de voyage

_____

6. Les Pierrot / chapeaux

_____

7. Claudine et Mireille / appareil photo

_____

8. tous les voyageurs / guides touristiques

_____

EXERCICE G

You get paid to do chores in your neighborhood. Someone asks what you've done. *Répondez-lui.*

EXEMPLE: Tu as promené le chien des Chénier?
   Oui, j'ai promené *leur* chien.

1. Tu as lavé la voiture de M. Sultan?

_____

2. Tu as réparé la bicyclette de Nicole?

_____

3. Tu as fait les courses des Verdon?

_____

4. Tu as envoyé les paquets de Paul et de Robert Picot?

_____

5. Tu as rangé le garage de Mlle Blanchet?

_____

6. Tu as nettoyé la maison de Mme Mamet?

_____

7. Tu as installé l'ordinateur de Claire et de Richard?

_____

8. Tu as gardé les enfants des Raynaud?

_____

EXERCICE H

Say what the following people are wearing to Lise's party.

EXEMPLES: Raoul porte **son** pantalon bleu.
   Sylvie a **ses** bracelets en argent sur le bras droit.

1. Marie porte _____ pull rouge.

2. Nous portons _____ nouveaux vêtements.

3. Je porte _____ écharpe blanche sur _____ cou.

4. Marie et Louise portent _____ chapeaux verts.

5. Luc porte _____ nouvelles baskets.

6. Tu portes _____ grande chemise jaune.

7. Vous portez _____ jupe noire.

8. Lucien porte _____ chemise brune.

9. Claude a _____ mains dans les poches de _____ robe longue.

10. Henri s'est couvert _____ tête avec _____ casquette rouge.

MASTERY EXERCISES

EXERCICE I

Jean and the members of his family like to share their belongings. His friend Paul is surprised. *Complétez leur conversation avec l'adjectif possessif correct.*

JEAN: Mes frères, mes sœurs et moi, nous partageons toutes _____ affaires.
1.

PAUL: Par exemple?

JEAN: Maintenant je porte le pantalon de _____ frère Jacques et le pull de _____ sœur
2. 3.

Christine.

PAUL: Tu aimes porter _____ vêtements?
4.

JEAN: Pourquoi pas? De cette façon, nous avons tous des vêtements très divers et _____ amis
5.

pensent que nous sommes très bien vêtus.

PAUL: Quelles autres choses empruntes-tu à _____ frères et à _____ sœurs ?
6. 7.

JEAN: À _____ frères, j'emprunte toujours de l'équipement sportif et à _____ sœurs, des
8. 9.

disques et des cassettes.

PAUL: Est-ce que tu leur prêtes _____ scooter?
10.

JEAN: Bien sûr!

PAUL: _____ frères, _____ sœurs et toi, qu'est-ce que vous empruntez à _____
11. 12. 13.

parents

JEAN: _____ nouvelle voiture!
14.

EXERCICE J

A new classmate is talking to you. *Répondez à ses questions.*

1. Quel est ton nom ?

_____

2. Tu es l'ami de qui ?

_____

3. Ta famille habite ici maintenant ?

_____

4. Où est votre maison ?

_____

5. À qui est la voiture devant ta maison ?

_____

6. Quels sont tes sports préférés ?

_____

7. Tu veux savoir mon numéro de téléphone ?

_____

8. Peux-tu me présenter à tes amis ?

_____

EXERCICE K

Write a note in French to your friend about your new pet. Once you've mentioned the name of your pet, use possessive adjectives to describe him / her. You may want to include:

- the type of pet you chose
- where you bought your pet
- your pet's name
- the age of your pet
- a description of your pet
- why you love your pet

_____

_____

_____

_____

_____

_____

_____

_____

Chapter 27
Demonstrative Adjectives

Demonstrative adjectives point out the object or person referred to (*this, that, these, those*).

ce	before a masculine singular noun beginning with a consonant	ce garçon	*this (that) boy*
cet	before a masculine singular noun beginning with a vowel or silent **h**	cet avion cet homme	*this (that) plane* *this (that) man*
cette	before a feminine singular noun	cette femme	*this (that) woman*
ces	before all plural nouns	ces garçons ces avions ces hommes ces femmes	*these (those) boys* *these (those) planes* *these (those) men* *these (those) women*

Ce garçon est très gentil.	*This boy is very nice.*
Cet appartement est joli.	*This apartment is pretty.*
J'aime **cette musique**.	*I like this music.*
As-tu lu **ces livres** ?	*Have you read those books?*

NOTES:

1. Demonstrative adjectives precede and agree with the nouns they modify.

2. The demonstrative adjective is repeated before each noun.

   ce garçon et **cette** fille   *that boy and that girl*
   ces légumes et **ces** fruits   *these vegetables and fruits*

3. To distinguish between *this* and *that* or between *these* and *those*, -ci and -là are placed, with hyphens, after the nouns being contrasted. For *this* or *these*, -ci is added; for *that* or *those*, -là is added.

   ce livre-**ci** ou ce livre-**là**   *this book or that book*
   ces disques-**ci** et ces disques-**là**   *these records and those records*

EXERCICE A

You are in a grocery store. *Demandez le prix des articles suivants.*

EXEMPLE:

C'est combien ce café?

1.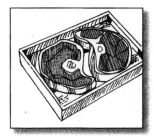

_____

2.

_____

3.

_____

4.

_____

5.

_____

6.

_____

7.

_____

8.

_____

9.

10.

EXERCICE B

You are vacationing on a tropical island. *Exprimez ce que vous dites à vos parents de regarder.*

EXEMPLE: lac tranquille
            Regardez **ce** lac tranquille.

1. ciel bleu

   _____

2. forêt magnifique

   _____

3. herbe verte

   _____

4. arbre gracieux

   _____

5. hautes montagnes

   _____

6. immense océan

   _____

7. jolies fleurs

   _____

8. mer calme

   _____

EXERCICE C

You are looking at a map and you ask people for directions to various places. *Exprimez vos questions.*

EXEMPLE: tour (*f.*) (ici)
Où est **cette tour-ci?**

1. musée (*m.*) (ici)

_____

2. avenue (*f.*) (là)

_____

3. parc (*m.*) (là)

_____

4. magasins (*m.pl.*) (ici)

_____

5. monument (*m.*) (là)

_____

6. boutiques (*f. pl.*) (ici)

_____

7. hôtel (*m.*) (là)

_____

8. cathédrale (*f.*) (là)

_____

EXERCICE D

You received gifts for your birthday. *Est-ce que vous les aimez ?*

EXEMPLE: chemise (*f.*) / joli
Cette chemise est jolie.

1. posters (*m. pl.*) / imaginatif

_____

2. pull (*m.*) / élégant

_____

3. montre (*f.*) / moderne

_____

4. écharpes (*f. pl.*) / formidable

_____

5. chapeau (*m.*) / beau

_____

6. caméscope numérique (*m.*) / perfectionné

_____

7. équipement sportif (*m.*) / pratique

_____

8. livres (*m. pl.*) / intéressant

_____

MASTERY EXERCISES

EXERCICE E

Exprimez vos opinions sur les sujets suivants.

EXEMPLE: Kennedy: président
           Ce président est renommé.

1. Tom Cruise: acteur

_____

2. le français: langue

_____

3. *Gone With the Wind*: livre

_____

4. *American Idol*: émission

_____

5. le tennis et le foot: sports

_____

6. *Star Wars*: film

_____

7. *Time* et *Newsweek*: magazines

_____

8. Porsche: voiture

_____

EXERCICE F

Describe the following. *Suivez l'exemple.*

EXEMPLE:

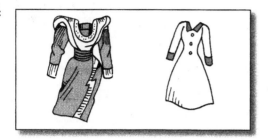

Cette robe-ci est élégante.
Cette robe-là est ordinaire.

1.

_____

_____

2.

_____

_____

3.

_____

_____

4.

_____

_____

5.

_____

_____

6.

_____

_____

7.

_____

_____

8.

_____

_____

EXERCICE G

You went shopping for new school clothes. Write a note to a friend in which you compare two of each item you saw. You may want to include:

- 2 pairs of pants
- 2 pairs of shoes
- 2 shirts
- 2 tee shirts
- 2 raincoats
- 2 hats

_____

_____

_____

_____

_____

_____

_____

_____

Part Four

Word Study

Chapter 28
Antonyms and Synonyms

[1] *CONTRAIRES* / ANTONYMS (OPPOSITES)

Adjectives

absent *absent*	présent *present*
bas *low*	haut *high*
beau *beautiful*	laid *ugly*
blanc *white*	noir *black*
bon *good*	mauvais *bad*
chaud *hot*	froid *cold*
cher *expensive*	bon marché *inexpensive*
court *short*	long *long*
droit *right*	gauche *left*
facile *easy*	difficile *difficult*
fort *strong*	faible *weak*
grand *big*	petit *little*
heureux *happy*	malheureux *unhappy*
léger *light*	lourd *heavy*
né *born*	mort *dead*
paresseux *lazy*	diligent *diligent*
pauvre *poor*	riche *rich*
plein *full*	vide *empty*
possible *possible*	impossible *impossible*
premier *first*	dernier *last*
utile *useful*	inutile *useless*
vieux *old*	⎰ jeune *young* ⎱ neuf, nouveau *new*
vrai *true*	faux *false*

Adverbs

aujourd'hui *today*	⎰ hier *yesterday* ⎱ demain *tomorrow*
beaucoup *a lot, much, many*	peu *a little, few*
bien *well*	mal *badly*
enfin *finally*	d'abord *first, at first*
ici *here*	là *there*
oui *yes*	non *no*
plus *more*	moins *less*
souvent *often*	rarement *rarely*
vite *quickly*	lentement *slowly*

Nouns

l'ami *(m.)*	*friend*	l'ennemi *(m.)*	*enemy*
l'automne *(m.)*	*autumn*	le printemps	*spring*
le bruit	*noise*	le silence	*silence*
le commencement	*beginning*	la fin	*end*
l'été *(m.)*	*summer*	l'hiver *(m.)*	*winter*
le fils	*son*	la fille	*daughter*
le frère	*brother*	la sœur	*sister*
le garçon	*boy*	la fille	*girl*
le grand-père	*grandfather*	la grand-mère	*grandmother*
la guerre	*war*	la paix	*peace*
l'homme *(m.)*	*man*	la femme	*woman*
le jour	*day*	la nuit	*night*
le mari	*husband*	la femme	*wife*
le matin	*morning*	{ le soir *evening,* l'après-midi *(m.)* *afternoon*	
la mère	*mother*	le père	*father*
midi	*noon*	minuit	*midnight*
monsieur	*sir, Mr.*	{ madame *madam, Mrs.* mademoiselle *Miss*	
le neveu	*nephew*	la nièce	*niece*
le nord	*north*	le sud	*south*
l'oncle *(m.)*	*uncle*	la tante	*aunt*
l'ouest *(m.)*	*west*	l'est *(m.)*	*east*
le plancher	*floor*	le plafond	*ceiling*
quelque chose	*something*	rien	*nothing*
quelqu'un	*someone*	personne	*no one, nobody*
la question	*question*	la réponse	*answer*
le roi	*king*	la reine	*queen*
le soleil	*sun*	la lune	*moon*
la terre	*earth, land*	{ la mer *sea* le ciel *heaven, sky*	
la vie	*life*	la mort	*death*
la ville	*city*	la campagne	*country*

Prepositions

avant	*before*	après	*after*
avec	*with*	sans	*without*
devant	*in front of*	derrière	*behind, in back of*
près de	*near*	loin de	*far from*
sur	*on (top of)*	sous	*under*
voici	*here is*	voilà	*there is*

Verbs

accepter *to accept*	refuser *to refuse*
aller *to go*	venir *to come*
arriver *to arrive*	partir *to leave*
commencer *to begin*	finir *to finish* / terminer *to end*
demander *to ask*	répondre *to answer*
donner *to give*	prendre *to take* / recevoir *to receive*
emprunter *to borrow*	prêter *to lend*
fermer *to close*	ouvrir *to open*
jouer *to play*	travailler *to work*
monter *to go up*	descendre *to go down*
obéir *to obey*	désobéir *to disobey*
ôter *to remove*	mettre *to put on*
perdre *to lose*	trouver *to find* / gagner *to win*
pleurer *to cry*	rire *to laugh*
vivre *to live*	mourir *to die*

EXERCICE A

Write the female counterpart of each of the following masculine terms.

1. le neveu _____
2. le père _____
3. le mari _____
4. le fils _____
5. l'oncle _____
6. le grand-père _____
7. le frère _____
8. le garçon _____
9. l'homme _____
10. le roi _____

EXERCICE B

You disagree with a friend's descriptions of people and things. *Dites le contraire de ce qu'il/elle dit.*

EXEMPLE: Jean est grand.
Jean est **petit.**

1. Lucie est diligente.

_____

2. Un ordinateur est inutile.

_____

3. M. Lenoir est vieux.

_____

4. Cet article est vrai.

_____

5. Janine est absente.

_____

6. Le latin est facile.

_____

7. Cette réponse est possible.

_____

8. Nos livres sont légers.

_____

9. Ce CD est cher.

_____

10. Il fait chaud.

_____

11. Pierre est laid.

_____

12. Ce sac est vide.

_____

13. Claude est fort.

_____

14. Cette soupe est bonne.

_____

15. Nos devoirs sont longs.

_____

EXERCICE C

Change this story about Mme Boyer. *Donnez le contraire du mot en caractères gras.*

1. Aime-t-elle bavarder avec ses amis ? **Oui.** _____

2. Elle parle **vite.** _____

3. Elle habite **près** de Mme Chenier. _____

4. Elle travaille **moins** que ses amies. _____

5. Elle va **rarement** au cinéma. _____

6. Elle sort **avant** midi. _____

7. Elle parle **mal** de Mme Blanchet. _____

8. Elle s'amuse **peu**. _____

9. Elle attend son amie **devant** sa maison. _____

10. Elle quitte sa maison **avec** son argent. _____

EXERCICE D

Jules and Jim are twins who try to be different: each does the exact opposite of what the other does. *Exprimez leurs actions en français.*

EXEMPLE: Jules **obéit**.
            Jim désobéit.

1. Jules **emprunte** des disques.

    _____

2. Jules **commence** ses devoirs.

    _____

3. Jules **arrive**.

    _____

4. Jules **joue** toute la journée.

    _____

5. Jules **accepte** tout.

    _____

6. Jules **rit** souvent.

    _____

7. Jules **ôte** son chapeau.

    _____

8. Jules **monte**.

    _____

9. Jules **ferme** la fenêtre.

_____

10. Jules **perd** le match.

_____

EXERCICE E

Change the boldface words to make the following sentences true. *Suivez l'exemple.*

EXEMPLE: La neige est **noire**.
          La neige est **blanche**.

1. On met un tapis sur **le plafond**.

_____.

2. La nuit, on voit **le soleil** dans le ciel.

_____.

3. Je me réveille **le soir**.

_____.

4. Décembre est le **premier** mois de l'année.

_____.

5. La Floride est au **nord** des États-Unis.

_____.

6. Quand tout le monde parle, il y a du **silence**.

_____.

7. Il est généreux. Il **prend** des cadeaux.

_____.

8. Je déjeune à **minuit**.

_____.

9. On met une lampe **sous** une table.

_____.

10. Septembre marque **la fin** de l'année scolaire.

_____.

11. Les fleurs poussent **en automne**.

_____.

12. Quand Lucie est triste, elle **rit**.

_____.

[2] SYNONYMES / SYNONYMS

Adjectives

certain, sûr	*certain, sure*
heureux, content	*happy, pleased*
triste, malheureux	*sad, unhappy*

Adverbs

immédiatement, tout de suite	*immediately, at once*
puis, ensuite, après	*then, afterwards*
quelquefois, parfois	*sometimes*
vite, rapidement	*quickly*

Conjunctions

car, parce que	*because*

Nouns

le château, le palais	*castle, palace*
le chemin, la route	*road*
la faute, l'erreur (*f.*)	*mistake*
la figure, le visage	*face*
l'image (*f.*), l'illustration (*f.*)	*picture*
le maître, le professeur	*teacher*
le médecin, le docteur	*doctor*
le milieu, le centre	*middle*
le sud, le midi	*south*
les vêtements (*m.*), les habits (*m.*)	*clothes*

Verbs

finir, terminer, achever	*to finish*
habiter, demeurer	*to live, stay*
préférer, aimer mieux	*to prefer*
rompre, casser	*to break*
vouloir, désirer	*to wish, want*

EXERCICE F

Describe Dr. Gaumont's trip to work by using a synonym for each boldface word.

1. Le **docteur** quitte sa maison pour aller travailler.

   _____

2. **Quelquefois** il arrive en retard.

   _____

3. Le docteur habite le **midi** de la France.

_____

4. Il **habite** loin de son bureau.

_____

5. Il **préfère** prendre le bus.

_____

6. Aujourd'hui le bus prend **une route** étrange.

_____

7. Le docteur est **certain** qu'il arrivera à l'heure.

_____

8. Il est **heureux**.

_____

9. En route, il **finit** un article.

_____

10. Il **veut** arriver à l'heure.

_____

11. Après une demi-heure, il comprend qu'il a fait une **faute**.

_____

12. Regarde **sa figure**.

_____

13. Il est **triste**.

_____

14. Il descend vite du bus **car** il est en retard.

_____

15. Il marche **vite**.

_____

16. **Puis** il commence à courir.

_____

17. Malheureusement, il tombe au **milieu** de la rue.

_____

18. Ses **vêtements** ne sont plus propres. Quel problème!

_____

MASTERY EXERCISES

EXERCICE G

Each of the following items consists of a pair of related words followed by the first word of a second pair which is related in the same way. *Complétez la deuxième paire avec le mot approprié.*

EXEMPLE: petit / grand — bon / **mauvais**

1. court / long — droit / _____

2. médecin / docteur — illustration / _____

3. faute / erreur — professeur / _____

4. plein / vide — riche / _____

5. habiter / demeurer — rompre / _____

6. sous / sur — bas / _____

7. vrai / faux — ici / _____

8. nord / sud — est / _____

9. possible / impossible — quelque chose / _____

10. frère / sœur — guerre / _____

11. automne / printemps — hiver / _____

12. jour / nuit — matin / _____

13. accepter / refuser — donner / _____

14. présent / absent — blanc / _____

15. obéir / désobéir — demander / _____

16. soleil / lune — ville / _____

17. jeune / vieux — vivre / _____

18. bruit / silence — quelqu'un / _____

19. facile / difficile — utile / _____

20. premier / dernier — question / _____

EXERCICE H

Write the antonyms or synonyms that describe each pair you see in the illustrations below.
Suivez les exemples.

EXEMPLES:

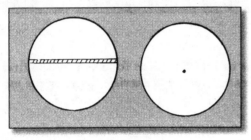

le milieu / le centre   **grand / petit**

1.

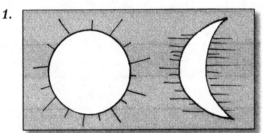

2.

_____

3.

4.

_____

5.

6.

_____

7.

_____

8.

_____

9.

_____

10.

_____

11.

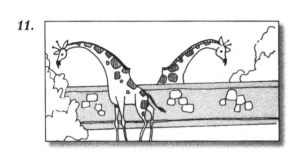

_____

12.

_____

13.

_____

14.

_____

15.

_____

16.

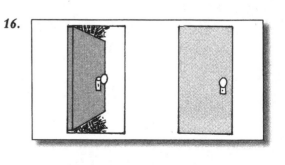

_____

EXERCICE 1

Write a paragraph comparing and contrasting two of your friends who are completely different. You may want to include:

- a physical description
- their nationalities
- a description of their personalities
- how they act
- their attitudes

_____

_____

_____

_____

_____

_____

_____

_____

Chapter 29
Topical Vocabulary

[1] PERSONAL IDENTIFICATION

a. Biographical information

   (1) **La nationalité** / *Nationality*

africain *African*	étranger(-ère) *foreign*
allemand *German*	européen(ne) *European*
américain *American*	français *French*
anglais *English*	grec(que) *Greek*
asiatique *Asian*	haïtien(ne) *Haitian*
belge *Belgian*	indien(ne) *Indian*
canadien(ne) *Canadian*	italien(ne) *Italian*
chinois *Chinese*	japonais *Japanese*
espagnol · *Spanish*	sud-américain *South American*

   (2) **L'adresse (f.)** / *Address*

l'avenue (f.) *avenue*	la rue *street*
le boulevard *boulevard*	le village *village*
la place *square*	la ville *city*

   (3) **La famille** / *Family*

le cousin *cousin*	la grand-mère *grandmother*	la nièce *niece*
la cousine *cousin*	le grand-père *grandfather*	l'oncle *uncle*
l'enfant (*m.* or *f.*) *child*	les grands-parents *grandparents*	les parents *parents*
la femme *wife, woman*	l'homme *man*	le père *father*
la fille *daughter, girl*	le mari *husband*	la personne *person*
le fils *son*	la mère *mother*	la sœur *sister*
le frère *brother*	le neveu *nephew*	la tante *aunt*
le garcon *boy*		

b. Physical characteristics

âgé *old*	grand *big*	mince *skinny*
ancien(ne) *old*	gros(se) *fat*	pauvre *poor*
beau (belle) *beautiful*	jeune *young*	petit *small*
court *short*	joli *pretty*	riche *rich*
faible *weak*	laid *ugly*	vieux (vieille) *old*
fatigué *tired*	maigre *thin*	
fort *strong*	malade *sick*	

avoir . . . ans   *to be . . . years old*

avoir les cheveux blonds   *to have blond hair*

avoir les cheveux châtains   *to have light brown hair*

avoir les cheveux noirs   *to have black hair*

avoir les cheveux roux   *to have red hair*

avoir les yeux bleus   *to have blue eyes*

avoir les yeux marron   *to have brown eyes*

avoir les yeux noirs   *to have black eyes*

avoir les yeux verts   *to have green eyes*

c. **Psychological characteristics**

actif (-ve) *active*	heureux (-se) *happy*
aimable *friendly*	honnête *honest*
ambitieux (-se) *ambitious*	imaginatif (-ve) *imaginative*
amusant *funny*	impulsif (-ve) *impulsive*
attentif (-ve) *attentive*	intelligent *intelligent*
bon(ne) *good*	intéressant *interesting*
conscientieux (-se) *conscientious*	intuitif (-ve) *intuitive*
content *happy*	malheureux (-se) *unhappy*
courageux (-se) *courageous*	méchant *nasty*
cruel(le) *cruel*	naïf (-ve) *naive*
curieux (-se) *curious*	paresseux (-se) *lazy*
drôle *funny, strange*	poli *polite*
dynamique *dynamic*	populaire *popular*
égoïste *selfish*	sérieux (-se) *serious*
fier (fière) *proud*	sociable *sociable*
franc(he) *frank*	sportif (-ve) *athletic*
furieux (-se) *furious*	superstitieux (-se) *superstitious*
généreux (-se) *generous*	sympathique *nice*
gentil(le) *nice*	triste *sad*

EXERCICE A

Répondez aux questions que votre nouveau / nouvelle correspondant(e) français(e) vous pose dans sa première lettre.

1. Quelle est ta nationalité?

_____

2. Comment est ta ville/ton village?

_____

3. Combien de personnes y a-t-il dans ta famille?

_____

4. Combien de frères et de sœurs as-tu?

_____

5. De quelle couleur sont tes yeux?

_____

6. De quelle couleur sont tes cheveux?

_____

7. Comment es-tu physiquement?

_____

8. Quelles sont tes bonnes qualités?

_____

[2] HOUSE AND HOME

a. La maison / *House*

l'appartement (*m.*) *apartment*	le living *living room*
l'ascenseur (*m.*) *elevator*	le mur *wall*
le balcon *balcony*	la pelouse *lawn*
la chambre (à coucher) *bedroom*	la penderie *closet*
la cheminée *fireplace*	la pièce *room*
la clef *key*	le placard *cabinet, closet*
le coin *corner*	le plafond *ceiling*
le couloir *hallway*	le plancher *floor*
la cour *courtyard*	la porte *door*
la cuisine *kitchen*	le rez-de chaussée *ground floor*
la douche *shower*	la salle à manger *dining room*
l'entrée (*f.*) *entrance*	la salle de bains *bathroom*
l'escalier (*m.*) *stairs*	la salle de séjour, *family room*
l'étage (*m.*) *floor, story*	le séjour *family room*
la fenêtre *window*	le salon *living room*
le garage *garage*	le sous-sol *basement*
le grenier *attic*	la terrasse *terrace*
l'immeuble (*m.*) *apartment building*	les toilettes (*f.*) *toilet*
le jardin *garden*	le toit *roof*

b. Les meubles / *Furniture*

l'armoire (*f.*) *wardrobe*	la cuisinière *stove*	le magnétoscope *VCR*
le bureau *desk*	le fauteuil *armchair*	le meuble *piece of furniture*
le canapé *sofa*	le four *oven*	le miroir *mirror*
la chaîne stéréo *stereo*	la glace *mirror*	l'ordinateur (*m.*) *computer*
la chaise *chair*	la lampe *lamp*	la pendule *clock*
le congélateur *freezer*	le lit *bed*	le piano *piano*

le réfrigérateur   *refrigerator*   la table de nuit   *night table*   le tapis   *rug*
le rideau   *curtain*   le tableau   *picture*   la télévision   *television*
la table   *table*   le tiroir   *drawer*

EXERCICE B

Identifiez les parties de la maison dans l'illustration ci-dessous.

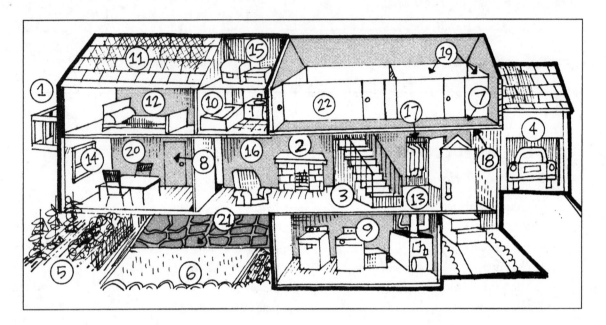

1. _____   12. _____

2. _____   13. _____

3. _____   14. _____

4. _____   15. _____

5. _____   16. _____

6. _____   17. _____

7. _____   18. _____

8. _____   19. _____

9. _____   20. _____

10. _____   21. _____

11. _____   22. _____

EXERCICE C

Tell what furniture or appliances you would expect to find in the following rooms.

la cuisine	le salon	la chambre à coucher	la salle à manger
_____	_____	_____	_____
_____	_____	_____	_____
_____	_____	_____	_____
_____	_____	_____	_____
_____	_____	_____	_____
_____	_____	_____	_____
_____	_____	_____	_____

c. Les travaux domestiques / *Household chores*

cuisiner, faire la cuisine	*to cook*	mettre le couvert	*to set the table*
débarrasser la table	*to clear the table*	nettoyer la maison	*to clean the house*
faire la vaisselle	*to do the dishes*	passer l'aspirateur	*to vacuum*
faire le ménage	*to do the housework*	ranger le salon	*to tidy the living room*
faire les courses	*to go shopping*	vider les ordures	*to take out the garbage*
garder les enfants	*to watch the children*		

EXERCICE D

Exprimez ce que Jacques fait pour aider sa mère.

EXEMPLE: **Il nettoie la maison.**

1. _____

2. _____

3. _____

4. _____

5. _____

6. _____

7. _____

8.

[3] COMMUNITY, NEIGHBORHOOD, PHYSICAL ENVIRONMENT

a. La ville / *The city*

l'avenue (f.)   *avenue*

la banque   *bank*

le bâtiment   *building*

la bibliothèque   *library*

la boucherie   *butcher shop*

la boulangerie   *bakery*

le boulevard   *boulevard*

la boutique   *shop*

le bureau de poste   *post office*

le café   *cafe*

le carrefour   *intersection*

la cathédrale   *cathedral*

le centre commercial   *mall, shopping center*

le cinéma   *movies*

l'école (f.)   *school*

l'église (f.)   *church*

l'épicerie (f.)   *grocery*

la fruiterie   *fruit store*

la gare   *station*

l'hôpital (m.)   *hospital*

l'hôtel (m.)   *hotel*

l'hypermarché (m.)   *large supermarket*

la librairie   *book store*

le lycée   *high school*

le magasin   *store*

la mairie   *town hall*

la maison des jeunes et de la culture

(M.J.C.)   *youth center*

le marché   *market*

la maroquinerie   *leather store*

le musée   *museum*

le parc   *park*

la parfumerie   *perfume store*

la pâtisserie   *pastry shop*

la pharmacie   *drugstore*

la piscine   *swimming pool*

la place   *square*

le pont   *bridge*

la poste   *post office*

le quartier   *neighborhood*

le restaurant   *restaurant*

la rue   *street*

le stade   *stadium*

la station-service   *gas station*

le supermarché   *supermarket*

le théâtre   *theater*

le trottoir   *sidewalk*

le village   *village*

la ville   *city*

b. La nature / *Nature*

l'arbre (m.)   *tree*

le(s) bois (m.)   *woods*

la campagne   *country*

le champ   *field*

le ciel   *sky*

le désert   *desert*

l'étoile (*f.*) *star*	le lac *lake*	la plage *beach*
la feuille *leaf*	la lune *moon*	la plante *plant*
la fleur *flower*	la mer *sea*	la pluie *rain*
le fleuve *river*	le monde *world*	la rivière *stream*
la forêt *forest*	la montagne *mountain*	le soleil *sun*
l'herbe (*f.*) *grass*	la neige *snow*	le temps *weather, time*
la glace *ice*	l'océan (*m.*) *ocean*	la terre *earth*
l'île (*f.*) *island*	le paysage *landscape*	le vent *wind*

c. **Les animaux** / *Animals*

l'âne (*m.*) *donkey*	le cochon *pig*	l'oiseau (*m.*) *bird*
l'animal (*m.*) *animal*	l'éléphant (*m.*) *elephant*	l'ours (*m.*) *bear*
le chat *cat*	le lapin (*m.*) *rabbit*	le poisson (*m.*) *fish*
le cheval *horse*	le lion *lion*	le tigre *tiger*
le chien *dog*	le mouton *sheep*	la vache *cow*

EXERCICE E

Where does one go for the following items?

EXEMPLE:

On va **à la pâtisserie**.

1.

_____

2.

_____

3.

_____

4.

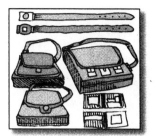

_____

5.

_____

6.

_____

7.

_____

8.

_____

9.

_____

10.

_____

11.

_____

12.

_____

EXERCICE F

Exprimez ce que vous voyez dans cette peinture.

EXEMPLE: **Il y a le soleil.**

1. _____

2. _____

3. _____

4. _____

5. _____

6. _____

7. _____

8. _____

9. _____

10. _____

EXERCICE G

Exprimez quel animal est décrit ci-dessous.

1. _____ donne du lait.

2. _____ protège la maison.

3. _____ vole dans le ciel.

4. _____ est le roi de la jungle.

5. _____ est très stupide.

6. _____ donne de la laine.

7. _____ donne du jambon et des saucisses.

8. _____ trotte dans les champs.

[4] MEALS—FOOD AND DRINK

a. Les repas / *Meals*

l'assiette (f.) *plate*	le dîner *dinner*	le plat *dish*
la bouteille *bottle*	la fourchette *fork*	la serviette *napkin*
le couteau *knife*	le goûter *snack*	la tasse *cup*
la cuiller *spoon*	le petit déjeuner *breakfast*	le verre *glass*
le déjeuner *lunch*		

b. Les aliments / *Foods*

l'artichaut (*m.*) *artichoke*	la carotte *carrot*
l'asperge (*f.*) *asparagus*	les céréales *cereal*
la banane *banana*	la cerise *cherry*
le beurre *butter*	le chocolat *chocolate*
le bifteck *steak*	le cidre *cider*
le biscuit *cookie*	le citron *lemon*
le bœuf *beef*	la citronnade *lemonade*
les bonbons (*m.*) *candies*	la confiture *jelly*
la brioche *sweet roll*	la crème *cream*
le café *coffee*	le croissant *crescent roll*

le dessert *dessert*	le pain grillé *toast*
l'eau (*f.*) *water*	le pâté *meat appetizer*
l'eau minérale *mineral water*	la pêche *peach*
la fraise *strawberry*	les petits pois (*m.*) *peas*
les frites (*f.*) *French fries*	la poire *pear*
le fromage *cheese*	le poisson *fish*
le fruit *fruit*	le poivre *pepper*
les fruits de mer *seafood*	la pomme *apple*
le gâteau *cake*	la pomme de terre *potato*
le gâteau au chocolat *chocolate cake*	le potage *soup*
la glace *ice cream*	le poulet *chicken*
la glace à la vanille *vanilla ice cream*	la prune *plum*
le hamburger *hamburger*	le rafraîchissement *refreshment*
les haricots verts (*m.*) *string beans*	le raisin *grape*
le hors-d'œuvre *appetizer*	la salade *salad*
le jambon *ham*	le sandwich *sandwich*
le jus *juice*	la saucisse *sausage*
le lait *milk*	le saucisson *hard sausage*
la laitue *lettuce*	le sel *salt*
le légume *vegetable*	la soupe *soup*
la limonade *lemon soda*	le sucre *sugar*
l'œuf (*m.*) *egg*	le thé *tea*
l'omelette (*f.*) *omelet*	la tomate *tomato*
l'orange (*f.*) *orange*	le veau *veal*
l'orangeade (*f.*) *orange soda*	la viande *meat*
le pain *bread*	le vin *wine*

EXERCICE H

Exprimez ce que vous mangez à chacun de ces repas.

au petit déjeuner	au déjeuner	au dîner
_____	_____	_____
_____	_____	_____
_____	_____	_____
_____	_____	_____
_____	_____	_____
_____	_____	_____
_____	_____	_____

EXERCICE I

Exprimez les objets que vous mettez sur la table à chaque repas.

_____   _____   _____

_____   _____   _____

_____   _____   _____

_____   _____   _____

_____   _____   _____

[5] HEALTH AND WELFARE

a. Les parties du corps / *Parts of the body*

la bouche *mouth*	l'épaule (f.) *shoulder*	l'ongle (m.) *nail*
le bras *arm*	l'estomac (m.) *stomach*	l'oreille (f.) *ear*
les cheveux (m.) *hair*	la figure *face*	l'orteil (m.) *toe*
le cœur *heart*	la gorge *throat*	le pied *foot*
le corps *body*	la jambe *leg*	la poitrine *chest*
le cou *neck*	la langue *tongue*	la tête *head*
le coude *elbow*	la main *hand*	le ventre *stomach*
la dent *tooth*	le nez *nose*	le visage *face*
le doigt *finger*	l'œil (m.) *eye*	les yeux (m.) *eyes*
le dos *back*		

b. Les maladies (f.) / *Illnesses*

avoir mal à l'estomac *to have a stomachache*	avoir mal aux dents *to have a toothache*
avoir mal à la gorge *to have a sore throat*	la grippe *flu*
avoir mal à la tête *to have a headache*	un rhume *a cold*
avoir mal au pied *to have a sore foot*	la température *temperature*
avoir mal au ventre *to have a stomachache*	la toux *cough*

EXERCICE J

Richard played basketball today for the first time in months. Express what aches he suffers as a result. *Suivez l'exemple.*

EXEMPLE:

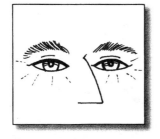

Il a mal aux yeux.

1.

2.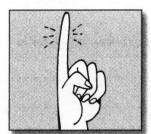

3.

4.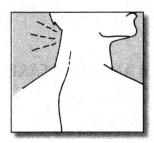

5.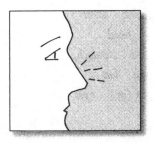

6.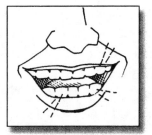

7.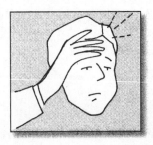

8.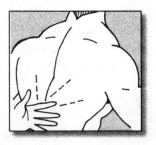

[6] EDUCATION

a. L'école (f.) / *School*

le banc *seat, bench*	la calculette *calculator*
le bureau *desk*	le calendrier *calendar*
le cahier *notebook*	le cartable *schoolbag*

la carte   *map*

les ciseaux (*m.*)   *scissors*

la classe   *class*

le classeur   *loose-leaf notebook*

la cloche   *bell*

la corbeille à papier   *wastebasket*

la cour   *courtyard*

la craie   *chalk*

le crayon   *pencil*

les devoirs (*m.*)   *homework*

le dictionnaire   *dictionary*

l'élève (*m.* or *f.*)   *student*

l'emploi du temps (*m.*)   *schedule*

l'encre (*f.*)   *ink*

l'étudiant (*m.*)   *student*

l'examen (*m.*)   *test*

l'exemple (*m.*)   *example*

l'exercice (*m.*)   *exercise*

la gomme   *eraser*

l'histoire (*f.*)   *story*

l'horloge (*f.*)   *clock*

la leçon   *lesson*

la lecture   *reading*

le livre   *book*

la lumière   *light*

le lycée   *high school*

le matériel scolaire   *school supplies*

la matière (school)   *subject*

le mot   *word*

la note   *grade, note*

la page   *page*

le papier   *paper*

la permission   *pass*

la phrase   *sentence*

la plume   *pen; feather*

le pupitre   *pupil's desk*

la question   *question*

la règle   *ruler*

la réponse   *answer*

le sac à dos   *backpack*

la salle de classe   *classroom*

le scotch   *scotch tape*

le store   *shade, blind*

le stylo   *pen*

le sujet   *subject*

le tableau   *(chalk)board*

le travail   *work*

la trousse   *pencil case*

le vocabulaire   *vocabulary*

b. **Les matières** (*f.*) / *Subjects*

l'anglais (*m.*)   *English*

la biologie   *biology*

la chimie   *chemistry*

l'éducation physique (*f.*)   *gym*

l'espagnol   *Spanish*

le français   *French*

la géographie   *geography*

la gymnastique   *gym*

l'histoire (*f.*)   *history*

l'informatique (*f.*)   *computer science*

le latin   *Latin*

les mathématiques (*f.pl.*)   *math*

la physique   *physics*

la science   *science*

la technologie   *technology*

c. **Les activités scolaires** (*f.*) / *School activities*

le cercle   *club*

le cercle dramatique   *drama club*

le cercle français   *French club*

le cercle international   *international club*

le cercle de maths   *math club*

le ciné-club   *film club*

le club d'échecs   *chess club*

la distribution des prix   *award ceremony*

l'équipe (*f.*) de base-ball   *baseball team*

l'équipe de football   *soccer team*

la fanfare   *band*

les jeunesses musicales   *music association*

l'orchestre (*m.*)   *orchestra*

le prix (*m.*) d'excellence   *prize given to best student*

le tableau (*m.*) d'honneur   *honor roll*

EXERCICE K

Identifiez toutes les choses que vous voyez dans la classe de Mme Rousseau.

1. _____
2. _____
3. _____
4. _____
5. _____
6. _____
7. _____

8. _____
9. _____
10. _____
11. _____
12. _____
13. _____
14. _____

15. _____
16. _____
17. _____
18. _____
19. _____
20. _____
21. _____

EXERCICE L

Identifiez les matières que vous étudiez et les activités auxquelles (in which) vous participez.

les matières	les matières	les activités
_____	_____	_____
_____	_____	_____
_____	_____	_____
_____	_____	_____

[7] PROFESSIONS

agent (*m.*) de police *police officer*	le garçon *waiter*
artiste (*m.* or *f.*) *artist*	infirmier (–ière) *nurse*
avocat(e) *lawyer*	ingénieur (*m.*) *engineer*
boucher (–ère) *butcher*	le médecin *doctor*
boulanger (–ère) *baker*	le métier *job, profession*
le chef *chef*	ouvrier (–ière) *factory worker*
coiffeur (–euse) *hair stylist*	le peintre *painter*
commerçant(e) *merchant*	président(e) *president*
cuisinier (–ière) *cook*	le professeur *teacher*
dentiste (*m.* or *f.*) *dentist*	programmeur (–euse) *programmer*
directeur (–trice) *director, principal*	secrétaire (*m.* or *f.*) *secretary*
le docteur *doctor*	serveur (–euse) *waiter, waitress*
épicier (–ière) *grocer*	vendeur (–euse) *salesperson*
fermier(–ière) *farmer*	

EXERCICE M

Identifiez les personnes suivantes et leurs professions.

EXEMPLE: Il dessine.
C'est un artiste.

1. Il enseigne les élèves.

_____

2. Elle travaille dans un restaurant.

_____

3. Il arrête les criminels.

_____

4. Il prépare les repas dans un restaurant.

_____

5. Il guérit les malades.

_____

6. Il vend de la viande.

_____

7. Il est expert en informatique.

_____

8. Il prépare des gâteaux.

_____

9. Elle protège les innocents au tribunal.

_____

10. Il guérit un mal de dents.

_____

11. Il travaille dans une ferme.

_____

12. Elle vous coiffe les cheveux.

_____

[8] LEISURE

a. Les loisirs (*m.*) / *Leisure activities*

le bal *ball*	le jour de congé *day off*	la plage *beach*
le ballet *ballet*	le jour férié *legal holiday*	la promenade *walk*
la campagne *country*	la montagne *mountain*	la radio *radio*
les cartes (*f.*) *cards*	le musée *museum*	le site pittoresque
le centre commercial *mall*	l'opéra (*m.*) *opera*	*picturesque site*
le cinéma *movies*	le parc *park*	la télévision *television*
le concert *concert*	le parc national *national*	le théâtre *theater*
la fête *holiday, party*	*park*	les vacances (*f.*) *vacation*
l'île tropicale *tropical island*	le (parc) zoo(logique) *zoo*	

b. Les sports (*m.*) / *Sports*

le base-ball *baseball*	le golf *golf*	le rugby *rugby*
le bowling *bowling*	le match *match*	le stade *stadium*
le football *soccer*	la natation *swimming*	le tennis *tennis*
le football américain *football*	la pêche *fishing*	le volley-ball *volleyball*

EXERCICE N

Where do these persons go to have a good time? *Suivez l'exemple.*

EXEMPLE: **Elles vont à la montagne.**

1. Je _____

2. Nous _____

3. Ils _____

4. Vous _____

5. Tu _____

6. Il _____

7. Elles _____

8. Nous _____

9. Je _____

10. Vous _____

EXERCICE O

Dites dans quel sport on utilise l'équipement suivant.

EXEMPLE:

le bowling

1.

_____

2.

_____

3.

_____

4.

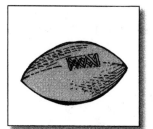

_____

5.

_____

6.

_____

7.

_____

8.

_____

[9] PUBLIC AND PRIVATE SERVICES

a. Le téléphone / _Telephone_

l'annuaire (_m._) _phone book_   la cabine _phone booth_   l'opératrice (_f._) _operator_

l'appel (_m._) _call_   le numéro _number_   le téléphone _telephone_

b. La poste / _Post Office_

l'adresse (_f._) _address_   le courrier _mail_   la lettre _letter_

la boîte aux lettres _mail box_   l'enveloppe (_f._) _envelope_   le nom _name_

la carte postale _post card_   le facteur _mailman_   par avion _air mail_

le code postal _zip code_   le guichet _window_   le timbre _stamp_

EXERCICE P

Replace the pictures with the correct French words.

Un jour, tout d'un coup, j'ai envie de parler à mon ami Georges. Je vais dans une

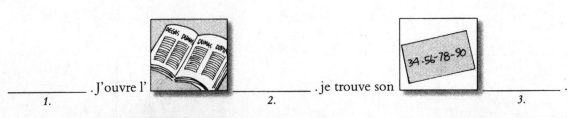

_____ . J'ouvre l' _____ . je trouve son _____ .
   1.   **2.**   **3.**

Malheureusement, le _____ ne marche pas. J'appelle l'
                                    4.

_____ . Elle dit: «Je regrette, mais la ligne est en dérangement.» Tant pis! Je vais chez moi lui
  5.

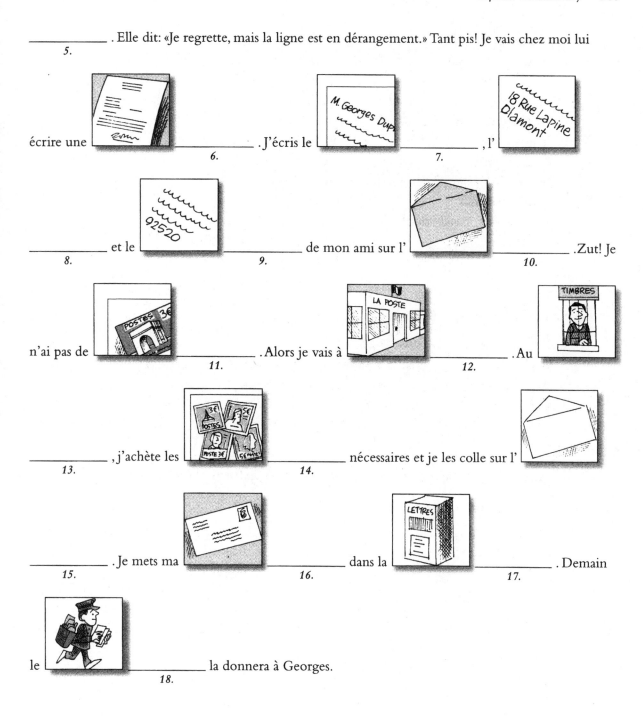

écrire une _____ . J'écris le _____ , l'

_____ et le _____ de mon ami sur l' _____ .Zut! Je
  8.   9.   10.

n'ai pas de _____ .Alors je vais à _____ .Au
                11.   12.

_____ , j'achète les _____ nécessaires et je les colle sur l'
   13.   14.

_____ . Je mets ma _____ dans la _____ . Demain
   15.   16.   17.

le _____ la donnera à Georges.
     18.

[10] CLOTHING

a. Les vêtements (*m.*) / *Clothing*

les bas (*m.*)   *stockings*

les baskets (*f.*)   *high-top sneakers*

la blouse   *blouse*

les bottes (*f.*)   *boots*

le chapeau   *hat*

les chaussettes (*f.*)   *socks*

les chaussures (*f.*)   *shoes*

la chemise   *shirt*

le chemisier   *woman's shirt*

le complet   *man's suit*

le costume   *suit*

la cravate   *tie*

l'écharpe (*f.*)   *scarf*

les gants (*m.*)   *gloves*

les habits (*m.*)   *clothing*

l'imperméable (*m.*)   *raincoat*

la jaquette   *jacket*

le jean   *jeans*

la jupe   *skirt*

le maillot de bain   *bathing suit*

le manteau   *coat*

le mouchoir   *handkerchief*

le pantalon   *pants*

le parapluie   *umbrella*

le pardessus   *overcoat*

la poche   *pocket*

le pull   *pullover*

la robe   *dress*

le sac   *handbag*

les sandales (*f.*)   *sandals*

le short   *shorts*

les souliers (*m.*)   *shoes*

le tailleur   *woman's suit*

le tee-shirt   *T-shirt*

les tennis (*f.*)   *tennis sneakers*

la veste   *jacket*

b. **Les couleurs (*f.*) / *Colors***

blanc(he)   *white*

bleu   *blue*

brun   *brown*

gris   *gray*

jaune   *yellow*

mauve   *purple*

noir   *black*

orange   *orange*

rose   *pink*

rouge   *red*

vert   *green*

EXERCICE Q

You're going on a trip. *Indiquez les vêtements que vous allez emporter et leur couleur.*

EXEMPLE: **mes chaussettes vertes**

_____   _____

_____   _____

_____   _____

_____   _____

_____   _____

[*11*] TRAVEL

l'aéroport (*m.*)   *airport*

l'arrêt (*m.*)   *stop*

l'autobus (*m.*)   *bus*

l'auto(mobile) (*f.*)   *car*

l'avion (*m.*)   *airplane*

le bateau   *boat*

la bicyclette   *bicycle*

le billet   *ticket*

le car   *tour bus*

le chemin   *road*

le chemin de fer   *railroad*

la gare   *train station*

le guichet   *ticket window*

l'horaire (*m.*)   *schedule*

le métro   *subway*

la mobylette   *moped*

la motocyclette   *motorcycle*

le moyen de transport   *means of transportation*

la porte   *gate*

la promenade   *walk*

la route   *route, road*

le scooter   *motorscooter*

la station   *station*

le taxi   *taxi*

le ticket   *ticket*

le train   *train*

le tramway   *streetcar*

le vélo   *bicycle*

la voie   *track*

la voiture   *car*

le vol   *flight*

le voyage   *trip, travel*

EXERCICE R

Exprimez comment les personnes suivantes vont à leur travail.

EXEMPLE:    **Jean prend le tramway.**

1.    Je _____

2.    Nous _____

3. M. Dupont _____

4. Vous _____

5. Nadine et Raoul _____

6. Tu _____

7. Marie _____

8. Les filles _____

9. M. Rameau _____

10. Mme Lefarge _____

MASTERY EXERCISES

EXERCICE S

Choisissez le mot qui n'est pas de la même classe que les autres.

EXEMPLE: l'immeuble, le grenier, l'escalier, la rivière
   la rivière

1. belge, rue, grec, chinois _____ .

2. neveu, sœur, fils, joli _____ .

3. le grenier, le balcon, le séjour, le village _____ .

4. la gare, la chaise, le fauteuil, le tiroir _____ .

5. l'épicerie, le magasin, le tapis, la banque _____ .

6. naïf, violet, poli, fier _____ .

7. le ciel, la lune, le soleil, le cochon _____ .

8. le cheval, le mouton, le musée, l'oiseau _____ .

9. le couteau, la fourchette, le pont, la cuiller _____ .

10. le chat, le fromage, le poisson, le jambon _____ .

11. les cheveux, les meubles, les orteils, les yeux _____ .

12. le crayon, le visage, la trousse, le stylo _____ .

13. le médecin, le garçon, la fille, l'avocat _____ .

14. la fête, le stade, le jour férié, le jour de congé _____ .

15. le timbre, l'enveloppe, le facteur, le tableau _____ .

16. le bureau, l'imperméable, le pardessus, le manteau _____ .

17. gris, brun, jeune, noir _____ .

18. le vélo, le métro, le bateau, la douche _____ .

EXERCICE T

Complétez les phrases avec les mots qui conviennent.

1. _____ est un énorme animal gris.

2. Dans la classe de géographie on regarde _____ du monde.

3. On va au _____ pour voir un match de football.

4. Après les repas on vide _____ .

5. La Seine est _____ qui traverse Paris.

6. _____ apporte le courrier tous les jours.

7. La sœur de ma mère est ma _____ .

8. Si j'ai envie d'emprunter des livres, je vais à _____ .

9. Pour chercher un numéro de téléphone, regardez dans _____ .

10. Pour envoyer une lettre je vais à _____ .

11. Si on a mal aux dents, on va chez _____ .

12. On voit avec _____ .

13. On va à _____ si on aime nager.

14. Pour ouvrir la porte, il faut utiliser _____ .

15. Pour savoir l'heure, on regarde une _____ .

16. Un Airbus est un _____ .

17. Le premier repas du jour est _____ .

18. Le président des États-Unis habite la Maison _____ .

19. On prépare les repas dans _____ .

20. On coupe la viande avec _____ .

EXERCICE U

Write a note to a friend about one of your classes. You may want to include:

- why you are writing about this class
- the name of the teacher
- when you go to this class
- the school supplies you need for this class
- what you do in this class
- your opinion of the class

_____

_____

_____

_____

_____

_____

_____

Part Five
Civilization

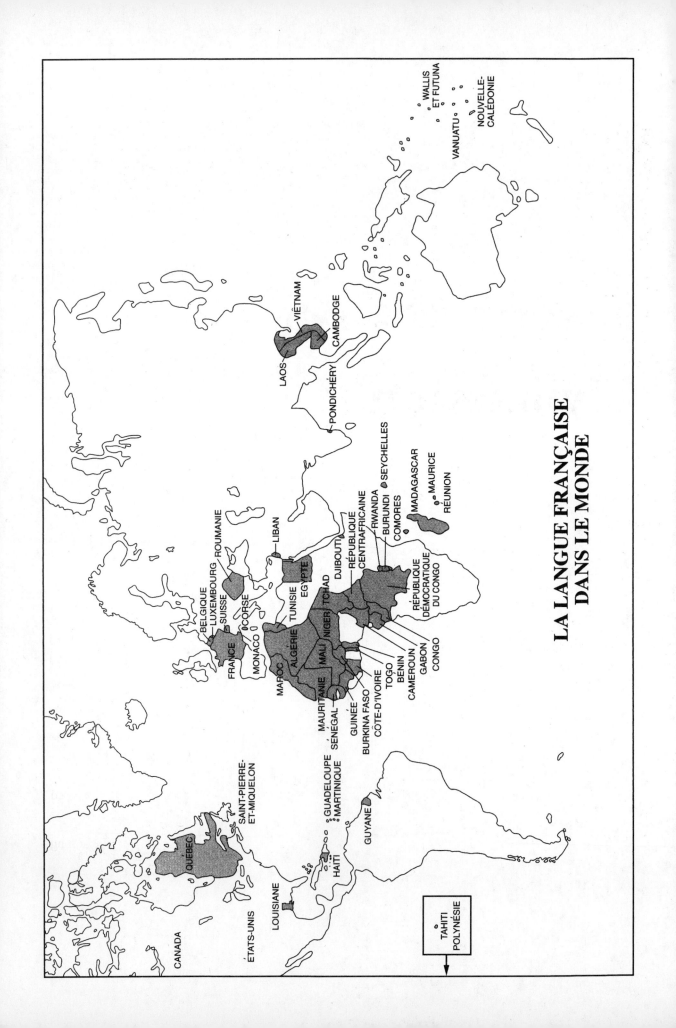

LA LANGUE FRANÇAISE
DANS LE MONDE

CANADA

ÉTATS-UNIS

LOUISIANE

SAINT-PIERRE-
ET-MIQUELON

QUÉBEC

GUADELOUPE
MARTINIQUE

HAÏTI

GUYANE

TAHITI
POLYNÉSIE

BELGIQUE
LUXEMBOURG
SUISSE
FRANCE
CORSE
MONACO
MAROC
ALGÉRIE
TUNISIE
ÉGYPTE
LIBAN
ROUMANIE

MAURITANIE
SÉNÉGAL
GUINÉE
BURKINA FASO
CÔTE-D'IVOIRE
MALI
NIGER
TCHAD
TOGO
BÉNIN
CAMEROUN
GABON
CONGO

DJIBOUTI
RÉPUBLIQUE
CENTRAFRICAINE
RWANDA
BURUNDI
COMORES
RÉPUBLIQUE
DÉMOCRATIQUE
DU CONGO

SEYCHELLES
MADAGASCAR
MAURICE
RÉUNION

LAOS
VIÊTNAM
CAMBODGE
PONDICHÉRY

WALLIS
ET FUTUNA
VANUATU
NOUVELLE-
CALÉDONIE

Chapter 30
The French Language and the French-Speaking World

THE FRENCH LANGUAGE

French is a Romance language, derived principally from the popular spoken Latin of the Romans. Over 2,000 years ago, a Roman army led by Julius Caesar invaded the country then known as Gaul, and the Gauls adopted the language of their conquerors. Their own languages, which included Celtic and Germanic languages, have made contributions to French.

Different dialects developed in the various regions of France. The one spoken in Île-de-France, where the kings held court, became the official language of the nation.

In 1635, Cardinal Richelieu founded the French Academy (**l'Académie française**), whose forty members were to study, preserve, and perfect the French language.

Outside of France, French is spoken in many countries and territories, which include Belgium, Switzerland, Luxembourg, eastern Canada, and several countries in Africa. In the United States, French is still spoken in parts of Louisiana. French is also one of the official languages of the United Nations (**l'Organisation des Nations Unies**).

Other Romance languages are Italian, Spanish, Portuguese, and Romanian.

French has exerted a strong influence on the English language as a result of the invasion of England in 1066 by William, Duke of Normandy, known as William the Conqueror (**Guillaume le Conquérant**). After the conquest, French became the official language of the English royal court, the educated classes, and the law courts. Thus, a vast number of French words became part of the English language. Constant cultural exchange between France and the English-speaking countries has strengthened the bond between the two languages.

Cognates are words in different languages that originate from the same source. In the case of English and French, the common root is often a Latin one. Some examples of cognates in French and English are:

FRENCH	ENGLISH	FRENCH	ENGLISH
appeler	*appeal*	**femme**	*feminine*
blanc	*blank*	**maison**	*mansion*
chien	*canine*	**mouton**	*mutton*
doigt	*digit*	**pauvre**	*pauper*
enfant	*infant*	**petit**	*petty*
état	*state*	**pied**	*pedal*
faim	*famine*	**sœur**	*sorority*

English has borrowed and incorporated a number of French words and expressions, some examples of which are listed below. In English, the accents may in some cases be omitted.

à la carte, term used in dining when foods are ordered individually from the menu

blasé, bored as a result of frequent exposure or overindulgence; too sophisticated

bon voyage, *have a good trip*

boulevard, broad avenue or thoroughfare

bourgeoisie, the middle class of society

camouflage, *disguise*, particularly in warfare

chaise longue, chair with extended seat supporting a person's outstretched legs

coup d'état, sudden illegal overthrow of a government by force

cuisine, style and preparation of cooking

débris, rubbish, especially resulting from destruction

début, entrance into society or a career; first appearance on the stage

déjà vu, when you're seeing something, and sense that you've already seen that same thing before

demi-tasse, *small cup of black coffee*

élite, group treated or considered as superior

en route, *on the way*

esprit de corps, devotion to a group

faux pas, social blunder

fiancé(e), man or woman engaged to be married

gourmet, person who understands and appreciates fine food

hors-d'œuvre, appetizer served at the beginning of a meal

Mardi gras, Shrove Tuesday (last day before Lent), a day of carnival and festivity

matinée, daytime entertainment, usually in the afternoon

naïve, simple and ingenuous in manner

née, term applied to the maiden name of a married woman

nom de plume, *pen name* assumed by an author

nonchalant, appearing to be indifferent

objet d'art, article of artistic worth

rendez-vous, *appointment, meeting place*

R.S.V.P. (répondez, s'il vous plaît), *please answer*

sabotage, malicious destruction of property

tête-à-tête, private conversation between two persons

Many geographical names in the United States are of French origin for instance, Bayonne, Champlain, Detroit, Joliet, Louisiana, New Orleans, New Rochelle, St. Louis, Terrre Haute, Vermont.

French has likewise borrowed many terms from the English language, for example: **club, détective, match, steak, jazz, parking, tunnel, interview, week-end.**

THE FRENCH-SPEAKING WORLD

French is spoken in over forty countries and territories throughout the world by about 200 million people as their native language or as a second official language.

NORTH AMERICA

In the United States French is spoken by over 2 million people in areas of Maine, New Hampshire, Vermont, Massachussetts, and Louisiana.

As early as 1604, French settlers lived in Acadie, a French colony that included what is now Nova Scotia and that extended from Quebec to Maine. When the British took possession of this territory in the 18th century, they expelled most of the French inhabitants, who moved to Louisiana. Cajuns are the descendents of those French-speaking Acadians.

In 1682, the French explorer, Robert Cavalier de la Salle claimed the territory along the Mississippi River that he named Louisiane, in honor of the French King Louis XIV. French pioneers were attracted to this land by prospects of fur trading and gold mining. Creoles are the descendents of the French settlers who lived around New Orleans.

In Canada, about one third of the population speaks French. Most live in Canada's largest province, Quebec, founded in 1534 by Jacques Cartier. Montreal is the second largest French-speaking

city in the world. French and English are official languages of Canada.

THE FRENCH WEST INDIES

Martinique and Guadeloupe are overseas departments (there are 96 *départements*, administrative subdivisions, within France), which means that the people who live there are French citizens. Martinique was discovered in 1502 by Christopher Columbus and has been French since 1635. Fort-de-France is its capital and Trois Ilets is the birthplace of Josephine de Beauharnais, the wife of Emperor Napoleon Bonaparte.

Guadeloupe was discovered in 1493 by Christopher Columbus. Although the island has changed hands several times, it has remained French since 1816. Guadeloupe is comprised of two islands (Basse-Terre and Grande-Terre) which form the shape of a butterfly.

Les Saintes, Marie Galante, La Désirade, St. Barthélemy, and St. Martin are small islands near Guadeloupe that are part of the same administrative subdivision.

French Guiana, located in South America and bordering Brazil and Suriname, is also a French overseas department. This is the only country in South America where French is the official language.

Haiti was discovered in 1492 by Christopher Columbus. Haiti is an independent country in which French influence plays an important role. Although French is the official language of this country, most people speak creole, a French dialect with African elements.

EUROPE

In Europe, French is the major language not only in France, but in Belgium, the seat of NATO (North Atlantic Treaty Organization); in Luxembourg, one of Europe's smallest and oldest independent countries; in Switzerland, the European seat of the United Nations; in Monaco, an independent state within France; and on the French Mediterranean island of Corsica, Napoleon Bonaparte's birthplace.

AFRICA

France had built a very large colonial empire in Africa starting with the conquest of Algeria in 1830. Between 1956 and 1962 all of its former African colonies became independent, with the exception of Réunion, still an overseas department, and Mayotte, one of the Comoro islands. Many of these nations, however, continue to have very close cultural and economic ties with France and have chosen to retain French as their official language. French is spoken in 24 countries in Africa with a combined population of about 150 million. France gives them financial and technical assistance, especially in the areas of health and education.

Algeria, Morocco, and Tunisia belong to a region referred to by Arabs as the Maghreb (the setting sun). Arabic is the official language of these three countries, but they have maintained wide use of the French language which is taught in schools, and they have kept institutions and school systems based on the systems originally established by the French. Other countries in Africa are inhabited by varied ethnic groups who use French as a common language.

In **ASIA**, French is still taught and spoken to a certain extent in Vietnam, Laos and Cambodia as well as in French territories in the Pacific ocean, such as Tahiti.

EXERCICE

Complete the sentences.

1. French is called a Romance language because it is derived chiefly from _____ ,

    the language of the _____ .

2. Two other languages that have contributed vocabulary to French are Celtic and

    _____ .

3. The dialect of the province of _____ became the official language of France.

4. The forty members of the _____ are entrusted with maintaining the

    purity of the French language.

5. In addition to French and Spanish, _____ and _____ are

    Romance languages.

6. A large number of French words came into the English language after the Norman invasion of

    England under the leadership of _____ .

7. Words in different languages derived from the same original source are called

    _____ .

8. In the United States you can expect to hear French spoken in the state of _____ .

9. Most Canadian speakers of French live in the province of _____ .

10. The only country in South America where French is spoken is _____ .

11. Three countries in Europe where French is spoken are _____ ,

    _____ and _____ .

12. About _____ people speak French in Africa.

EXERCICE CRÉATIF

Choisissez une des activités suivantes.

1. Write a short report explaining the importance and function of the *Académie Française.*

2. Draw a map of the United States indicating names of states and cities with French names.

3. Select a country where French is spoken. Write an ad trying to convince people to visit this country.

Chapter 31
Geography of France

SIZE, POPULATION, BOUNDARIES

France is a country of great natural beauty and diversity. It has been called "**la belle France**" and "**la douce France**". It is located on a latitude about halfway between the equator and the North Pole.

With an area of 213,000 square miles including the island of Corsica (**la Corse**), France is smaller than the state of Texas but is geographically the largest country in the European Union (**l'Union européenne**). In 2004 its metropolitan population was over 60 million.

Shaped like a hexagon, hence its nickname (**l'hexagone**), France has water on three sides: on the north, the English Channel (**la Manche**); on the west, the Atlantic Ocean (**l'océan Atlantique**); on the south, the Mediterranean Sea (**la mer Méditerranée**). This geographical position gives the country an extensive coastline. The surrounding waters, and the Gulf Stream make the climate essentially temperate. In most of France, there is abundant rainfall.

France borders on Belgium (**la Belgique**) and Luxembourg (**le Luxembourg**) to the northeast; on Germany (**l'Allemagne**), Switzerland (**la Suisse**), and Italy (**l'Italie**) to the east; and on Spain (**l'Espagne**) to the south.

Corsica, in the Mediterranean Sea southeast of continental France, is a mountainous island with a rugged coast. It is here, in the city of Ajaccio, that Napoléon Bonaparte was born.

PRINCIPAL MOUNTAIN RANGES

1. The Alps (**les Alpes**) form the frontier with Italy. This highest French range includes **Mont Blanc** (15,780 feet, or 4,807 meters), the tallest peak in western Europe.

2. The Pyrenees (**les Pyrénées**) are a natural barrier separating France from Spain. This second-highest range in France has numerous steep, jagged peaks.

3. The Vosges (**les Vosges**) are located in the northeast in Alsace and Lorraine, near Germany. Erosion has given their summits a gently rounded shape.

4. The Jura (**le Jura**), in the east, forms the principal frontier with Switzerland. Rich in fossils, this mountain range gave its name to the Jurassic period of geologic time.

5. The Central Plateau (**le Massif Central**), in the south-central part of the country, comprises the oldest French mountains, formed of extinct volcanoes. The **Cévennes** are part of this range.

PRINCIPAL RIVERS

1. The Seine (**la Seine**) is the most navigable and most important river. It flows through Paris and Normandy and empties into the English Channel (**la Manche**) near Le Havre.

2. The Loire (**la Loire**) is the longest river, but the least navigable. It rises in the Massif Central and flows into the Atlantic at the port city of Saint-Nazaire. The Loire is famous for the magnificent châteaux along its banks.

3. The Garonne (**la Garonne**) rises in the Pyrenees and flows through Bordeaux to the Atlantic, where it forms a long, wide tidal inlet named **la Gironde**.

4. The Rhone (**le Rhône**) is a swift-flowing source of waterpower exploited by many hydroelectric dams. Rising in Switzerland, it joins the Saone River (**la Saône**) at Lyon. Then it flows south and empties into the Mediterranean near Marseille, forming a large delta, **la Camargue**.

5. The Rhine (**le Rhin**), the river which defines part of the border between France and Germany, is Europe's main artery for navigation. The Rhine is famous for its spectacular beauty.

France possesses an elaborate system of canals, several of them linking the rivers. The best known is the **Canal du Midi**, built around 1670, which connects the Mediterranean with the Garonne River and thus with the Atlantic.

> NOTE: This book uses the French spelling of the names of towns. English often has a different spelling, for instance, Lyons, Marseilles, Rheims.

EXERCICE A

Match the mountains and the rivers with the correct numbers on the map.

1. _____ la Seine

2. _____ la Loire

3. _____ la Garonne

4. _____ le Rhône

5. _____ le Rhin

6. _____ les Alpes

7. _____ les Pyrénées

8. _____ les Vosges

9. _____ le Jura

10. _____ le Massif Central

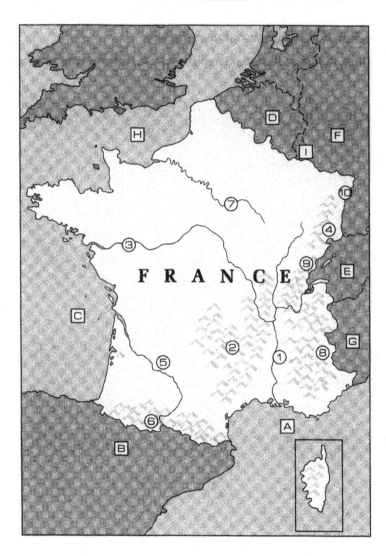

EXERCICE B

Match the boundaries of France with the correct letters on the map.

1. _____ l'océan Atlantique

2. _____ la Belgique

3. _____ la Manche

4. _____ l'Allemagne

5. _____ l'Italie   8. _____ la Suisse

6. _____ la mer Méditerranée   9. _____ le Luxembourg

7. _____ l'Espagne

EXERCICE CRÉATIF

Choisissez une des activités suivantes.

1. Make a map of France that shows its location in Europe with respect to the other countries on the continent.

2. Prepare a travel brochure for a winter vacation in the Alps.

3. Pick one château along the Loire River and explain why it attracts many tourists.

Chapter 32
Provinces

Until the French Revolution of 1789, France was divided into 32 **provinces**, each with its own customs and cultural traditions. Each province had a regional costume which is still worn today on festive occasions. The distinctive headdress, the **coiffe,** and the wooden shoes, the **sabots,** are still seen in parts of France.

Today, although the old French provinces are no longer separate political divisions, their original names are still used to refer to one part of France or another. In 1982, France was divided into 22 new administrative units, the **régions,** which were given names and boundaries recalling the old provinces.

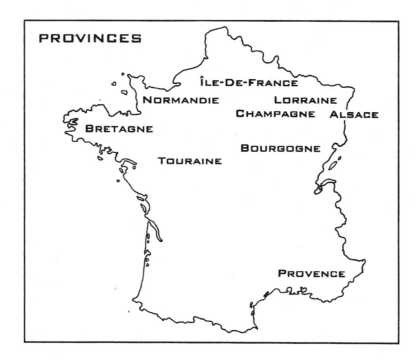

1. **La Bretagne** (*Brittany*), the peninsula jutting out into the Atlantic in northwestern France, is known for its sturdy stock of peasants, fishermen, and sailors. Numerous fishing villages dot the rugged coastline of Brittany. In addition to French, a Celtic dialect, **le breton,** is still spoken. The Bretons hold religious festivals known as **"pardons"**. Cider and **crêpes** are foods associated with Brittany.

2. **La Normandie** (*Normandy*), in northwestern France, bordering on the English Channel, is a region of fertile farms and rich pastureland. The Seine flows through Normandy. In addition to producing large quantities of milk, butter, and cheese, Normandy is also an industrial center. Along the coast there are several busy ports and fashionable beaches. In 1066, William the Conqueror (**Guillaume le Con-** quérant) set out from here to invade England. During the Second World War, the Allies landed on the beaches of Normandy to liberate the Continent from the armed forces of Nazi Germany.

3. **L'Île-de-France,** with Paris as its capital, was the administrative heart of France. It was there that the kings lived and held their court. The dialect spoken in Île-de-France became the official language of France.

4. **L'Alsace** and **la Lorraine,** two provinces in northeastern France, were for many years the subject of a bitter territorial dispute between France and Germany. Alsace is chiefly an agricultural area, while Lorraine, an industrial region, is valuable especially for its iron-ore deposits.

5. **La Provence,** in southeastern France, borders on the Mediterranean. The best-preserved Roman monuments in France may be seen here. **Provençal,** the old dialect of Provence, is still spoken by some of the inhabitants. The stretch of coast running east of Marseille to the Italian frontier — the **Riviera,** or **Côte d'Azur** — is one of the most famous resort areas of Europe.

6. **La Touraine,** in the valley of the Loire River, is often called the "Garden of France" because it produces large quantities of fruits and vegetables. Several of the famous **châteaux de la Loire** are located here: **Blois, Chambord, Chenonceaux.**

7. **La Bourgogne** *(Burgundy)* and **la Champagne** are two important grape-producing regions of France. Their wines are world famous.

EXERCICE

For each description in the first column, write the letter of the matching item in the second column:

1. region of iron-ore mines	*a.* Bretagne
2. "garden of France"	*b.* Normandie
3. peninsula in northwestern France	*c.* Lorraine
4. province known for its Burgundy wines	*d.* Alsace
5. where the kings had their court	*e.* Touraine
6. landing place of Allies during Second World War	*f.* Champagne
7. province in southeastern France	*g.* Île de France
8. province known for its bubbly wine	*h.* Bourgogne
9. an agricultural region near Germany	*i.* Provence

EXERCICE CRÉATIF

Choisissez une des activités suivantes.

1. Make a map of France showing where all the provinces are located.

2. Find the names of 5 other French provinces and say why they are important.

3. Make a poster advertising one of the French provinces.

Chapter 33
Paris

Paris (in ancient times, **Lutèce**) received its name from the **Parisii**, the Gallic tribe that founded the city over 2000 years ago on the present **Île de la Cité**, "the cradle of Paris." The city has a population of over two million, and it forms, with its suburbs, a complex of about ten million inhabitants. Paris is not only the political and economic capital of France but also the center of French cultural life. That is one reason it has been called **La Ville Lumière**, the city of light. For administrative purposes, the city is divided into twenty **arrondissements**, each one headed by a mayor.

The Seine River divides Paris into two parts: **la rive droite** and **la rive gauche,** the right bank and the left bank. The rive droite on the north is somewhat larger and includes business and commercial areas, department stores, and theaters. **Montmartre**, a colorful neighborhood long associated with artists and other free spirits, is also located on the right bank. On the left bank is the **Quartier latin,** the old student quarter. (In the Middle Ages all university students spoke Latin.) Many of the well-known institutes of higher learning are located here: **la Sorbonne, le Collège de France, l'École de Médecine, l'École Normale Supérieure**. Several bridges connect the two banks. The oldest is the **Pont-Neuf**, which was built in the sixteenth century and crosses the Seine at the **Île de la Cité**. The most recent, the Pont Charles-de-Gaulle, was built in the 1990s in eastern Paris.

Paris is a city of wide boulevards, magnificent monuments, museums, churches, and parks.

MUSEUMS

There are more than thirty museums in Paris. The following attract a great number of visitors.

1. The **Musée du Louvre**, a former palace of the kings, is one of the richest art museums in the world, housing such treasures as Leonardo Da Vinci's *la Joconde* (portrait of Monna Lisa) and the Greek statues known as *la Vénus de Milo* and *la Victoire de Samothrace*. A huge glass pyramid designed by the American architect J. M. Pei now serves as an entrance to the Louvre.

2. The **Hôtel des Invalides**, built by Louis XIV, contains the red marble tomb of Napoleon and a military museum.

3. The **Panthéon**, in the **Quartier latin**, was originally built as a church in honor of **Sainte Geneviève**, the patron saint of Paris. It is now used as a burial place for illustrious Frenchmen: Voltaire, Rousseau, Hugo, and Zola, among others. Over the entrance are inscribed the words: « *Aux grands hommes la patrie reconnaissante* » *(The homeland expresses gratitude to its great men)*.

4. The **Centre national d'art et de culture Georges-Pompidou**, also known as the **Centre Beaubourg**, opened in 1977. This architecturally imaginative modern-art museum draws more visitors each year than any other museum or monument in France. It features a variety of artistic, musical, and other cultural activities.

5. The **Musée d'Orsay**, installed in the restored train station called the **gare d'Orsay**, contains a notable collection of late nineteenth and early twentieth century art, with an emphasis on Impressionist paintings.

6. The **Cité des sciences et de l'industrie** is a new science and technology museum. In its spectacular theater, **la Géode**, three-dimensional films are shown.

7. The Museum of Natural History, created in the 18th century, was renovated in 1994 with a spectacular Great Gallery of Evolution.

8. The **Musée Picasso**, containing Picasso's own private art collection, is located in an 18th century mansion.

9. The **Musée du Quai Branly**, built in 2006 by Jean Nouvel, is an exotic and fascinating museum. It is located in an extraordinary building near the Eiffel tower.

CHURCHES

1. **Notre-Dame de Paris**, on the Île de la Cité, is a majestic Gothic cathedral begun in the twelfth century. From its roof one has a splendid view of Paris.

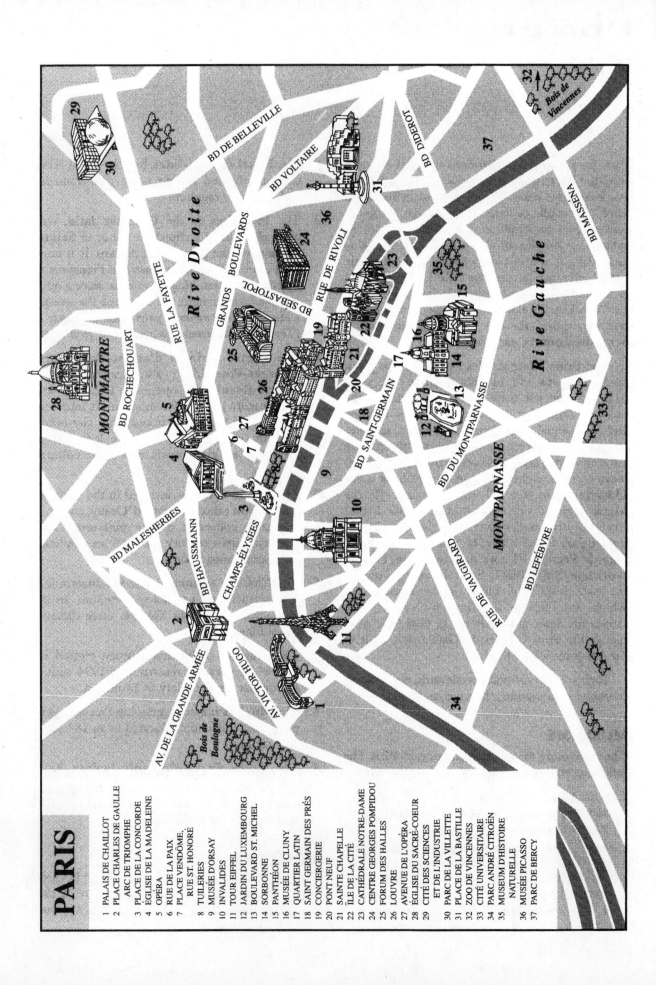

PARIS

2. The **Madeleine** is an elegant church built in the form of a Greek temple.

3. The imposing white **Sacré-Cœur**, in Montmartre, overlooks the whole city.

4. The **Sainte-Chapelle**, the jewel of Gothic architecture, is famed for its beautiful stained-glass windows. It was built by Saint Louis (Louis IX) in the thirteenth century.

PARKS

1. The **Bois de Boulogne**, formerly a forest, is the city's largest park. It has quiet lakes, several restaurants, two racetracks, and even a baseball diamond. It is situated at the western end of Paris.

2. The **Jardin des Tuileries**, containing numerous statues, was once the private garden of the kings of France. It is located between the Louvre and the Place de la Concorde.

3. The **Jardin du Luxembourg**, on the left bank, is a favorite meeting place for students and has many activities for children.

4. Several new parks were built in the 1990s: the **parc André Citroën** (located on the site of the former Citroën car factories); the **parc de Bercy** (located on the site of the former central wine market); the **parc de la Villette** with its *follies* (small pavilions); and the **Promenade plantée (**located on top of a former elevated railway). Each has a different, imaginative, modern design.

SQUARES

1. The **Place de la Concorde** is the largest and most beautiful square in Paris, with its fountains, Egyptian obelisk, and statues representing important cities of France. It was originally called the **Place Louis XV.** In the most violent phase of the French Revolution it was renamed the **Place de la Revolution,** and a guillotine was set up where there had once been a statue of the King. More than a thousand people, including Louis XVI and Marie-Antoinette, were executed here. A few years later, in a gesture of hope by a more moderate government, it was given its present name.

2. The **Place Charles de Gaulle** was formerly called the **Place de l'Étoile** because twelve avenues form a star as they radiate in all directions from the **Arc de Triomphe.** Under this arch, ordered by Napoleon to commemorate his victories, is the *Tomb of the Unknown Soldier of World War I,* illuminated by the eternal flame.

3. The **Place de l'Opéra** is named for the building that dominates the square. The **Opéra**, designed by Charles Garnier in 1875, is noted for its sculptured façade, grand marble staircase, and sumptuous foyer or gallery.

4. On the **Place de la Bastille** stood the old prison that was captured and destroyed by the Parisians in 1789. On the square today is the **Colonne de Juillet**, erected in memory of those killed in the revolution of 1830. Nearby is the modern **Opéra de la Bastille.**

OTHER LANDMARKS

1. The steel **Tour Eiffel** was constructed by the engineer Gustave Eiffel for the Paris Exposition of 1889. Over 1000 feet high, it is now used for the transmission of radio and television broadcasts. There are two restaurants on the tower and a great view of Paris.

2. The **Sorbonne**, the oldest part of the University of Paris, was founded about 1253 by Robert de Sorbon, chaplain of Louis IX.

3. The **Palais de Chaillot**, across the Seine from the Eiffel Tower, houses several museums and a theater.

4. The central market (**les Halles**) was relocated to Rungis, near Orly Airport, in 1969. In its place, a large shopping center and entertainment complex called **le Forum des Halles**, has been built.

5. Two celebrated palaces are in the vicinity of Paris: **Versailles**, the tremendous palace built for Louis XIV, and **Fontainebleau,** the favorite retreat of Napoleon.

STREETS

1. The wide, tree-lined **Avenue des Champs-Élysées** extends from the Place de la Concorde to the Place Charles de Gaulle. It is an avenue of many shops, boutiques, hotels, theaters, cafés, and restaurants.

2. The arcaded **Rue de Rivoli** runs parallel to the Seine. Its many boutiques are popular.

3. Other streets known for their elegant boutiques are the **Avenue de l'Opéra**, the **Rue de la Paix,** and the **Rue St-Honoré.**

4. The beautiful **Grands Boulevards** were built on the site of old fortifications. They are wide, tree-lined streets with many theaters, cinemas, cafés, and restaurants.

5. The **Quais** are the streets that border the two banks of the Seine. They are a favorite place for Parisians to stroll and to shop for second-hand books in the stalls along the river.

TRANSPORTATION

Paris enjoys a superb location for commerce. The city is the principal river port of France and the center of its highway system. All the major railroad lines pass through Paris, where there are five stations. The high-speed TGV trains link Paris to all cities throughout France.

Two airports serve the city: **Charles de Gaulle**, the vast international airport, and **Orly** just south of Paris. Thus the city is linked to the rest of the country, the European continent, and the most distant parts of the world.

To travel within Paris itself, there are three public systems:

1. The **métro (métropolitain)** is the subway. The multiple lines extend throughout the city and intersect at many points.

2. The **R.E.R. (Réseau Express Régional)** is a network of rail lines that cross the city and its suburbs. This "super-métro" is uniquely automated.

3. Numerous bus lines serve the city and its suburbs. Taxis are generally available.

There are also excursion boats (**bateaux-mouches, batobus**) that go up and down the Seine.

EXERCICE

Read carefully the paragraph below; then answer the questions that follow.

> There we stood in what some consider the most beautiful square in the world. It certainly looked like the largest! We could not help noticing the Egyptian obelisk flanked by sparkling fountains. Gazing in one direction, we could see a magnificent arch at the end of a wide tree-lined avenue. In the opposite direction, there was a park that looked as though it might have belonged to a king. When we reached the end of the park, we arrived in front of an imposing structure, an immense palace, now one of the richest art museums in the world.

1. What Parisian square were we in? _____ .

2. What is the name of the arch mentioned? _____ .

3. Who had it built and why? _____ . _____ .

4. Who is buried under this arch? _____ .

5. On what square is this arch located? _____ .

6. What was its former name, and why did the French give the square that name?

_____

_____

7. Which "wide tree-lined avenue" were we looking at? _____

8. What park did we walk through? _____ .

9.   What is the name of the art museum at the end of the park? _____

10.   Name two art masterpieces found in this museum. _____ .

EXERCICE CRÉATIF

Choisissez une des activités suivantes.

1.   You spent the day sightseeing in Paris. Write an e-mail to your friend explaining where you went and what you saw.

2.   Write a paragraph describing the Pompidou Center and describe what there is to do there.

3.   Notre-Dame is a gothic cathedral. Explain what distinguishes the architecture of this type of cathedral from that of others.

Chapter 34
Other Cities

After Paris, the most populous cities in France are Marseille, Lyon, Toulouse, Nice, Lille, Bordeaux, and Nantes.

PORTS

1. **Marseille,** on the Mediterranean near the mouth of the Rhône River, is the largest seaport in France. It is the port for extensive trade with Africa and the Orient. It is also a very active industrial center.

2. **Le Havre,** at the mouth of the Seine, is the largest seaport on the English Channel.

3. **Bordeaux,** on the Atlantic at the mouth of the Garonne, is the great wine port in France.

4. **Nantes,** at the mouth of the Loire, is a center of shipbuilding, farm equipment and food industries.

5. Other ports are:
   on the Atlantic: **Brest, La Rochelle, Saint-Nazaire**
   on the English Channel: **Boulogne, Calais, Cherbourg, Dunkerque**

INDUSTRIAL CITIES

1. **Clermont-Ferrand,** in the center of France, manufactures rubber. It is the center of the tire industry.

2. **Grenoble,** on the main road leading to the Alps, is a center for tourism and numerous industries, including the manufacture of gloves.

3. **Lille,** in northeastern France, is known for the manufacture of textiles and machinery.

4. **Lyon,** at the junction of the Rhône and Saône Rivers, is a business center and the traditional home of the silk industry.

5. **Metz** and **Nancy,** in Lorraine, are important industrial centers (iron and steel, manufacture of machinery and automobiles).

6. **Reims,** the center of the champagne industry, is the site of a beautiful Gothic cathedral where the kings of France were crowned.

Other towns renowned for their Gothic cathedral are **Chartres** and **Amiens.**

7. **Rouen,** in Normandy on the Seine River, is an industrial city and river port. Jeanne d'Arc was burned at the stake in this city in 1431.

8. **Strasbourg,** on the Rhine River in Alsace, across from Germany, is an industrial city and an important river port. It is famous for its Gothic cathedral which contains an astronomical clock. Strasbourg is the seat of the European Parliament.

9. **Toulouse,** on the Garonne River where it connects with the Canal du Midi, is a manufacturing city and an important market for the region. **Airbus-Industrie** builds its planes here.

RESORTS

1. **Biarritz** is an elegant beach resort on the Atlantic near the Spanish border.

2. **Chamonix,** located at the foot of Mont Blanc in the Alps, is a celebrated winter resort and ski center.

3. **Deauville** is a popular beach resort on the English Channel.

4. **Nice,** the largest city on the French Riviera, and the neighboring town of **Cannes** are fashionable resorts. An important international film festival is held each May in Cannes.

5. **Vichy,** a health and pleasure resort in the Massif Central, is the best known French spa. Its mineral water is shipped all over the world. For a time during World War II, Vichy was the seat of the French government.

HISTORICAL CITIES

1. **Avignon,** on the Rhône in Provence, is known for its **Palais des Papes,** where the popes lived in the fourteenth century. The bridge of Avignon is celebrated in the song *"Sur le pont d'Avignon, on y danse."*

2. **Arles** and **Nîmes,** in Provence, contain some of the best-preserved Roman monuments in France. The famous Roman aqueduct, the **Pont du Gard,** is near Nîmes.

3. **Carcassonne,** in the south, is the best-preserved medieval fortified town in Europe, distinguished by its double ramparts and numerous towers.

4. **Lourdes,** in the Pyrenees, is the most famous shrine in France and a world-renowned Catholic pilgrimage center.

5. **Mont-Saint-Michel** is a medieval fortress and Benedictine abbey built on a rocky island in the English Channel, off the coast where Normandy and Brittany meet.

EXERCICE

Identify the city.

1. The best-preserved medieval fortified town in Europe. _____ .

2. The seaport at the mouth of the Seine. _____ .

3. The largest city on the Riviera. _____ .

4. A center of the glove industry, near the Alps. _____ .

5. The site of the Gothic cathedral where the Kings of France were crowned.

   _____

6. A ski center in the Alps at the foot of Mont Blanc. _____

7. The largest Mediterranean port. _____ .

8. A noted beach resort in the Atlantic near Spain. _____ .

9. The town noted for its Palace of the Popes _____ .

10. A great wine port on the Atlantic. _____ .

11. The city where an International Film Festival is held each May. _____

12. The industrial city located at a point where the Rhône and Saône Rivers meet.

    _____

13. The fortified abbey on an island in the English Channel. _____ .

14. The most famous pilgrimage center in France. _____

15. The important river port in Alsace, across from Germany. _____

EXERCICE CRÉATIF

Choisissez une des activités suivantes.

1. Draw a picture of Mont-Saint-Michel. Explain why going there could be dangerous.

2. Write a radio announcement convincing tourists that they should go to see Carcassonne. Explain how the city got its name and what there is to see there.

3. Learn the words to the song, "Sur le pont d'Avignon . . ."

Chapter 35
History of France

PREHISTORY

Prehistoric civilizations flourished in the land that is now France. Primitive paintings depicting animals have been found on the walls of caves at **Lascaux** and **Les Eyzies** in southwestern France. These were the work of Cro-Magnon Man during the last ice-age. Near **Carnac**, in Brittany, long rows of huge, unhewn stones called **menhirs** and **dolmens** can be seen. These constructions date from about 2000 B.C. Almost nothing is known about the civilization that produced them.

In the first century B.C., France was known as Gaul (**la Gaule**). It was the land of the Celts, or Gauls (**les Gaulois**), who had a primitive civilization. The Gauls were divided into numerous tribes, who often waged war on one another. Their priests, called Druids, served also as doctors and judges and exerted social, political, and religious influence. They taught the immortality of the soul and worshipped the forces of nature, encouraging a special reverence for the evergreen mistletoe (**le gui**).

THE ROMANS

Julius Caesar, the Roman general, took advantage of conflicts among the Gauls to undertake the conquest of their country.

Vercingétorix was the courageous chieftain and brilliant general who succeeded in uniting all the Gauls against Caesar in the last decisive battle of the Gallic War (52 B.C.). After his defeat, he was taken to Rome in Caesar's triumphal procession, imprisoned, and finally executed. Vercingétorix is considered the first national hero of France.

The Romans gave Gaul more than 400 years of peace and prosperity. The Gauls adopted the advanced culture of the Romans, their customs, their language, and their code of justice. The Romans developed agriculture and commerce. They constructed roads, aqueducts, amphitheaters, temples, and other beautiful monuments.

THE FRANKS

The Roman Empire was vast and difficult to defend. Barbaric tribes began to invade Gaul in the third century A.D. In the fifth century, a Germanic tribe called the Franks (**les Francs**) conquered the country and settled there. They gave their name to France.

Clovis, chief of the Franks in the fifth century, succeeded in ending Roman domination and extended his authority to all Gaul. He founded a dynasty and converted to Christianity, which became the official religion of the country.

Sainte Geneviève is the patron saint of Paris. During the fifth century A.D., the Huns (a nomadic and warlike people from north central Asia) seized control of large parts of Europe for a time. When they invaded France, the shepherd girl Geneviève gave courage to the people of Paris. The Huns never attacked the city.

THE MIDDLE AGES

Charlemagne, or Charles the Great, was one of the most powerful figures in European history. Originally king of the Franks, he was crowned in A.D. 800 as the first emperor of the vast Holy Roman Empire, which consisted of most of western Europe. A lover of learning, he encouraged education by founding numerous schools. As a statesman, he administered his empire with wisdom and justice. His military exploits are celebrated in the *Chanson de Roland*, the first masterpiece of French literature. Unfortunately, within a generation after his death, his empire had been divided among warring princes.

Towards the end of the ninth century, the Normans (**les Normands**) invaded the country. These Scandinavian pirates from the north came by sea and traveled up the rivers, looting along the way. They finally settled in the region subsequently known as Normandy.

In 1066, William the Conqueror (**Guillaume le Conquérant**), duke of Normandy, crossed the English Channel, conquered England, and became king of that country.

Saint Louis (1214–1270), or **Louis IX**, was considered a brave and just king, interested in the welfare of all, and a friend of the poor. For religious reasons, he took an active part in the Crusades. He did much to strenghten the royal power.

THE HUNDRED YEARS' WAR

The Hundred Years' War was a dynastic struggle between the royal houses of England and France, interrupted by several truces and lasting from 1337 to 1453. **Jeanne d'Arc**, known as "the Maid of Orléans" (**la Pucelle d'Orléans**), is honored as a national heroine because of the role she played in that war. She was born of peasant stock in 1412, in Domrémy, Lorraine, at a time when French fortunes were at their lowest.

Convinced that she had received from God the task of liberating France, she succeeded in reuniting the scattered French forces against the invading English. After winning the battle of Orléans, she had the king crowned in the cathedral of Reims. Later she fell into the hands of the English, was accused of being a witch, and in 1431 was burned at the stake in Rouen. After her death, the French rallied their forces and drove the English from France.

FROM THE SIXTEENTH TO THE EIGHTEENTH CENTURY

François 1er was king of France during the first half of the sixteenth century, the period of the Renaissance. A brilliant administrator and patron of the arts, he invited Italian artists, men of letters, and other scholars to his court. He founded the **Collège de France**, had splendid castles built along the Loire, and encouraged exploration of the New World.

Henri IV, the first monarch of the Bourbon family line, was the best-loved and most democratic king of France. He is often called "**le bon roi Henri**" because he had the welfare of his people at heart. Born Protestant, he became Catholic to end the religious wars and bring peace to France. In 1598, he issued the Edict of Nantes, granting freedom of worship to the Protestant minority. He was a skillful statesman who established an efficient and stable government, fostered commerce, industry, and agriculture, reduced taxes, and ensured prosperity.

Cardinal de Richelieu, the talented and energetic Prime Minister of Louis XIII, increased the power and prestige of France. He made the king supreme by curtailing the power of the feudal nobles. During his ministry, France became a

world power. An excellent administrator and military strategist, he was also a patron of the arts and literature. It was he who founded the French Academy (**l'Académie française**) in 1635.

Louis XIV, the "Sun King," ruled as an absolute monarch. He is famous for having said, **"L'État, c'est moi."** His long reign of 72 years was marked by the brilliance of his court and his patronage of arts and sciences. His lavish palace at Versailles became the political, social, and cultural center of the nation. Through his encouragement, art and literature reached splendid heights. But his egotism and ambition drove him to spend money and men's lives freely. He waged numerous wars that were disastrous for France. In 1685, he revoked the Edict of Nantes, thus destroying the religious freedom granted by Henry IV and causing many French Protestants (called **Huguenots**) to leave the country.

Louis XV, who reigned from 1715 to 1774, spent his time amusing himself instead of tending to affairs of State. The discontent stirred up during his reign was one of the principal causes of the French Revolution.

THE REVOLUTION OF 1789

Louis XVI was well-meaning but weak, and he proved unequal to the responsibilities of being a king. The country was financially bankrupt. The queen, Marie-Antoinette, was unpopular with the people. On July 14, 1789, mobs of Parisians stormed the dreaded prison of the Bastille. This marked the beginning of the French Revolution, in which the king and queen were executed along with thousands of nobles.

In 1789, the *Déclaration des droits de l'homme et du citoyen* was passed, proclaiming the fundamental rights of the individual. **La Première République**, established in 1792 as a society based on the equality of all citizens, began with a period of crises and violence. This was the time of **la Terreur**, masterminded by **Robespierre.**

Napoléon Bonaparte, who had become prominent during the early years of the Revolution, made himself First Consul by a coup d'état, and in 1804 had himself crowned Emperor. An ambitious military genius and diplomat, he succeeded in conquering most of western Europe but was defeated by a coalition of his enemies at Waterloo in 1815. He died in exile on the island of St. Helena. His tomb is in the Hôtel des Invalides in Paris.

Although he was responsible for many people being killed in war, Napoleon established law and order and brought about many reforms. He systematized the laws with the **Code Napoléon** — a civil code that has become the foundation of much modern legislation; he established a central system of education; he improved finances and founded the Bank of France; he set up a program of public works; he encouraged arts and sciences and created the Legion of Honor (**la légion d'honneur**).

NINETEENTH AND TWENTIETH CENTURIES

La Deuxième République was proclaimed in 1848, and **Louis-Napoléon**, the nephew of Napoléon Bonaparte, was elected President. In 1852, he made himself emperor and set up **le Second Empire.** After the defeat of France in the Franco-Prussian War of 1870–1871, **la Troisième République** was established.

In 1914, Germany declared war on Russia and France. Other nations were drawn in on both sides and World War I lasted until the defeat of Germany in 1918. The year 1940, when France was again invaded by Germany, saw the beginning of the German occupation. In June 1944, the Allies landed on the beaches of Normandy and France was liberated soon after. World War II ended in 1945. **La Quatrième République** dates from 1947.

General **Charles de Gaulle**, who headed the French Resistance movement and later the French troops, became a national hero. In 1958, he was elected to the presidency of **la Cinquième République** and held that office until 1969.

Since then, there have been five other presidents: **Georges Pompidou** (1969–1974), **Valéry Giscard d'Estaing** (1974–1981), and **François Mitterrand** (1981–1995). **Jacques Chirac** was elected president in 1995 and reelected in 2002. After the elections of 2007, the new president is **Nicolas Sarkozy.**

Since the end of World War II, the concept of Europe as a political and economic entity has slowly become a reality under the early leadership of French statesmen. The European Economic Community (**Communauté économique européenne, CEE**), was established in 1957. It created a common market and removed trade barriers between the six constituent member countries (Belgium, France, West Germany, Italy, Luxembourg, and the Netherlands). In 1958 a European Parliament was created.

In 1992, the treaty of Maastricht established the European Union (**Union européenne, UE**), which succeeded the **CEE.** It created a single currency, the **euro**, which replaced the national currencies of the member countries in 2002. It abolished internal fontiers between member countries and provided for free movement of people, goods, and capital; it established a common foreign policy and promoted cooperation between the member countries in the areas of justice and education. There are currently 27 member countries in the European Union and Europe is a strong and forceful partner in the affairs of the world.

POLITICAL INSTITUTIONS

The constitution of the Fifth Republic guarantees public liberties and grants to all citizens who have reached the age of 18, regardless of origin, race, or religion, the right to vote by secret ballot.

1. *Executive power* is vested in the president of the Republic and in the cabinet of ministers led by a prime minister.
   Le président de la République represents the highest authority of the nation. He is currently elected for five years by direct popular vote. (Until 2002 the president was elected for seven years.) The president is expected to insure the stability of the nation's institutions. He appoints the prime minister (based on the results of parliamentary elections) as well as the cabinet ministers, who are proposed by the prime minister. The president may turn directly to the people by dissolving the Parliament (thus bringing about new elections) or by calling for a direct popular vote (**un référendum**) on specific issues. He is Commander-in-Chief of the armed forces and may assume exceptional powers in an emergency. His official residence is the **Palais de l'Élysée**, in Paris.

   The prime minister (**le Premier ministre**) is appointed by the president and heads the government. The prime minister and his cabinet (**le Conseil des ministres**) formulate national policies and carry out the laws. They are responsible to the National Assembly and can be removed from office by a vote of an absolute majority of that body. The cabinet ministers, who are not permitted to be members of Parliament, are free from the pressures of seeking reelection.

2. *Legislative power* is held by the Parliament (**le Parlement**) which consists of two houses:

 (*a*) The National Assembly (**l'Assemblée Nationale**), elected by direct popular vote for five years, is the larger and more influential of the two.

 (*b*) The Senate (**le Sénat**), elected indirectly for nine years by certain elected local officials, represents the departments as well as French citizens residing abroad.

The Parliament passes the laws, votes the budget, and ratifies treaties. It acts as a check on the actions of the Prime Minister and his Cabinet and can force them to resign. War cannot be declared without the consent of Parliament.

3. *Judicial power* is held by the courts. Its independence is guaranteed by the constitution. The highest court is **la Cour de Cassation**, based in Paris.

For administrative purposes, France, including Corsica, is divided into 96 **départements**. There are also four overseas departments. Each department is headed by an appointed **préfet.** In 1982, in an effort to decentralize the government, 22 **régions** were created. They are, to some extent, based on the old provinces and are headed by an elected regional council whose president has executive power in the region.

The national emblem is the tricolor flag consisting of blue, white, and red vertical stripes. The motto (**la devise**) of the Republic is **Liberté, Égalité, Fraternité** — the slogan of the French Revolution. *La Marseillaise,* written in 1792 by **Rouget de Lisle**, is the national anthem (**l'hymne national**).

The national holiday is **le quatorze juillet**, the anniversary of the storming of **la Bastille** by the people of Paris in 1789. The Bastille was a prison that had become a symbol of tyranny. The day is celebrated in Paris by parades, ceremonies at the Tomb of the Unknown Soldier, free performances at many theaters, fireworks, and dancing in the streets. Similar celebrations take place all over France.

FRENCH INFLUENCE IN AMERICA

French explorers played an important part in opening up the North American continent.

Jacques Cartier discovered the St. Lawrence River in 1535 and took possession of Canada in the name of the king of France. Later he sailed up the river to the mountain that he named **Montréal**.

Samuel de Champlain founded the city of **Québec** in 1608 and discovered Lake Champlain.

Father Jacques Marquette explored the region of the Great Lakes and discovered the Mississippi. He and **Louis Joliet** sailed down the river in 1673.

In 1682 **Robert Cavelier de la Salle** explored the Mississippi as far as the Gulf of Mexico. He took possession of the immense valley of the river, naming it "**Louisiane**" in honor of Louis XIV. In 1803, Napoleon sold the territory to the United States.

Three French nobles took an active part in the War of Independence of the American colonies.

The young **Marquis de La Fayette** became a personal friend of General Washington. After the American Revolution, La Fayette returned to France to defend liberal causes in his native land. The key to the Bastille can be seen in Washington's home in Mount Vernon, Virginia. It was La Fayette who gave it to the first President of the United States.

Le Comte de Rochambeau was the head of the French army sent to defend the cause of the colonies.

L'Amiral de Grasse commanded the French naval forces.

All three helped defeat the British at the battle of Yorktown.

EXERCICE

Rewrite the following in their correct chronological order, placing the earliest figure first.

Napoléon Bonaparte	Henri IV	Marie-Antoinette	Saint Louis
Charlemagne	Jeanne d'Arc	Georges Pompidou	Sainte Geneviève
Charles de Gaulle	Louis XIV	Richelieu	Vercingétorix

1. _____   *2.* _____

3. _____   *4.* _____

5. _____   *6.* _____

7. _____   *8.* _____

9. _____   *10.* _____

11. _____   *12.* _____

EXERCICE CRÉATIF

Choisissez une des activités suivantes.

1. Write a short biography of an historic French person who interests you.

2. Write a time line showing the most important dates in French history.

3. Write the text for a TV ad promoting the activities for Bastille Day in Paris.

Chapter 36
Agriculture, Industry, and Commerce

AGRICULTURE

Agriculture, industry, and commerce sustain the well-balanced economy of France. The fertile soil makes the country almost self-sufficient agriculturally. The richest farm regions are the plains and river basins. Of the countries of the European Union, France is the principal agricultural producer. The French continue to develop an intensive agriculture based on modern techniques. The excellence and variety of the soil and climate have helped make France a country famous for its gastronomy.

Wheat (**le blé**), the principal ingredient of bread — a staple of the French diet — is an important agricultural product. An abundance of other cereals is cultivated, as well as a variety of fruits and vegetables.

Sugar beets are cultivated extensively, especially in the north.

Dense forests supply lumber and play an essential role in protecting the environment.

The grapes of French vineyards are used principally in the production of wines. They tend to be named after their place of origin, such as Burgundy (**le bourgogne**), Champagne (**le champagne**), and Bordeaux (**le bordeaux**). **Cognac**, a grape brandy, is distilled from wine. Drinks offered before the meal (to stimulate the appetite) are called **apéritifs**; those served after it are called **liqueurs**. Other popular beverages produced in France are mineral water from spas, such as Vichy, Évian, and Vittel, and cider from Normandy and Brittany.

In addition to agriculture, there is considerable cattle raising. France is noted for the excellence of its animal breeds: cows, sheep, goats, pigs, poultry, and horses. Normandy, in particular, is a rich dairy region. The French are skilled in the making of cheeses, of which there are about 400 different kinds. The best known are **le brie, le camembert, le roquefort,** and many kinds of **chèvre** which are made with goat's milk.

The French diet is enriched by seafood. Along the coast, and especially in Brittany, fishing is an important industry. There are many canneries in the ports.

Thanks to these riches of both land and sea, the food industries flourish in France.

INDUSTRY

French industry is varied, ranging from the production of heavy machinery to the making of delicate precision instruments, and from the huge modern factory to the small craft shop. In general, the French are craftsmen who take pride in their work, prefer quality to quantity, and combine originality with artistic skill. To maintain its competitive position in international trade, France has intensified its scientific research and its efforts to develop commercial applications.

As a result, France remains on the leading edge of nuclear power, electrical and electronic equipment, aeronautics, aerospace, and railroad technology. The principal industrial areas are centered around Paris, Lille, Lyon, Toulouse, Marseille, and the region of Lorraine. Metallurgy is a very important industry. France is also a major producer of industrial machinery.

The production of automobiles helps the balance of trade because a large number are exported abroad. France is the fourth-largest producer of automobiles in the world. The principal makes are **Renault** and **Peugeot-Citroën**.

The aeronautics industry produces airplanes, helicopters, and aerospace equipment. Planes manufactured by the international company, **Airbus-Industrie,** fly throughout the entire world. The supersonic Franco-British **Concorde** was a great technological success. The European space rocket **Ariane** has proven a reliable and low-cost means of launching satellites into orbit.

Shipbuilding is an important industry in ports on the Atlantic coast and the Channel.

A flourishing chemical industry includes the processing of bauxite (an ore used in making aluminum) and potash, both found in France. The production of pharmaceutical products, glass, rubber, and plastics continues to increase.

The textile industry, though less important than it used to be, still produces cotton, silk, and synthethic fabrics. Lyon is still the center of silk production. Fashions (**haute couture**) for the whole world are created in Paris.

Porcelain and chinaware are manufactured in **Sèvres**, near Paris, and in **Limoges** in central France, among other places. Rugs and tapestries are created by skilled artists.

Luxury articles including gloves, leather goods, jewelry, watches, crystal, perfumes, and cosmetics are also manufactured in France.

The fertile soil and sunny climate of the French Riviera supply the enormous quantities of flowers needed at the perfume center of Grasse, near Nice. Much of the final processing of perfumes is done in Paris, the home of the cosmetics industry.

Because of its lack of natural energy resources, France has developed an ambitious nuclear program, which has been the country's principal source of energy for years. A limited amount of energy is also supplied by hydroelectric power produced by the fast-flowing rivers, by natural gas, by solar energy, and even by the winds and the tides. The last important coal mines closed in 2004.

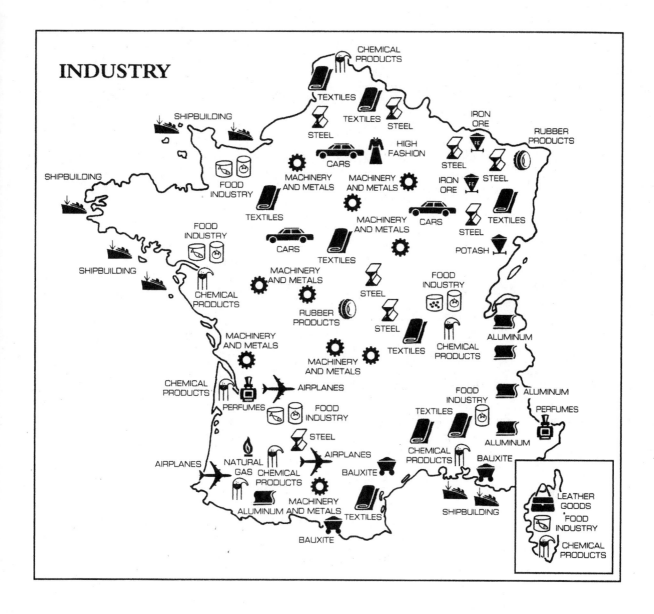

COMMERCE

France exports automobiles, railroad cars, airplanes, machinery, and chemical and pharmaceutical products. It also exports agricultural and food products as well as luxury items. France imports oil, coal, natural gas, and some raw materials for its industries.

Economic activities are closely linked to both interior and exterior transportation systems: the road network, maritime and river navigation, railroad and air transport.

1. The main national highways radiate out of Paris toward the frontiers. Superhighways (**au-** **toroutes**) help the flow of traffic in many areas.

2. The **S.N.C.F.** (**Société nationale des chemins de fer**), an agency of the government, administers the railroad system. All the important lines form a web with Paris at its center. The network links the capital with the other important cities of France and Europe. French trains travel at great speed. The **TGV** (**Train à grande vitesse**) has set a world record.

3. Heavy merchandise is easily and economically transported by river and on the excellent canal

system. The main river ports are: Paris, Rouen, Strasbourg, and Lyon.

4. **Air France** is the French national airline. There are, in addition, several small private airlines.

5. Other means of communication are also the responsibility of the government. Postal, telephone, and telegraph services are administered by the State.

6. A direct link for trains and automobile traffic between France and Great Britain was established in 1994 when a tunnel, the '*chunnel*', was opened under the English Channel (**la Manche**).

France, an influential member first of the European Economic Community and since 1992 of the European Union, plays an important role in the economic life of Europe.

EXERCICE

Complétez les phrases.

1. An important crop in France is _____ .

2. Grasse is the center for making _____ .

3. French grapes are used mainly for producing _____ .

4. The haute couture is centered in the city of _____ .

5. Roquefort is a famous French _____ .

6. The city of _____ ,on the Garonne, is known as a wine center.

7. Bauxite is used in the production of _____ .

8. _____ water from the spas is a popular beverage.

9. The French national airline is _____ .

10. The production of silk is centered in the city of _____ .

11. Much French cider comes from the provinces of _____ .

12. Nuclear energy is France's _____ source of energy.

13. The ports of the English Channel and the Atlantic coast are centers for the

    _____ industry.

14. Beautiful chinaware is made in the town of _____ in central France.

15. Fishing is an important industry along the _____ , especially in the

    province of _____ .

EXERCICE CRÉATIF

Choisissez une des activités suivantes.

1. Research the Chunnel and explain how a tourist would use it.

2. Write a paragraph discussing the products that the United States imports from France.

3. Draw a map of France showing its principal cities and their important industries.

Chapter 37
Daily Living

RELIGION

All religions are respected by the French Republic. The large majority of French people belong to the Roman Catholic faith. The government and public schools, however, are totally independent from any religion and make no reference to any god.

EDUCATION

Education is compulsory from the ages of six to sixteen. All education, both public and private, is controlled by the national government, with similar requirements nationwide. Public education, which is free, includes elementary and secondary schools as well as a number of universities and institutions of higher learning. The numerous private schools are often run by religious groups.

There are no classes on Wednesdays in the lower grades, but there are classes on Saturday morning.

The five years of elementary school (**école primaire**) are followed by four years of secondary education in the **collège**. After this, students may continue their secondary education in the **lycée** or may choose a program of technical courses. The lycée ends in a difficult examination called the **baccalauréat (le bachot, le bac)** which is required for entrance into a university. There are numerous universities and professional schools known as **les grandes écoles.**

LEISURE ACTIVITIES

1. Virtually all sports are practiced in France. Some of the favorite ones are: **le football** (*soccer*), **le cyclisme** (*bicycling*), **l'alpinisme** (*mountain climbing*), **le ski, la natation** (*swimming*), **la pêche** (*fishing*), and **le tennis.** Camping and all water sports are very popular. **Le Tour de France**, an international bicycle race which lasts for several weeks each year in July, is one of the top sporting events in France. Soccer is a favorite spectator sport. An 80,000 seat modern stadium was built on the north side of Paris for the World Cup of 1998.

2. Although the **café** plays an important rôle in French social life, it is said to have lost some of its importance since the advent of new technologies such as the Internet and DVD players for films. The café provides a meeting place for both serious discussion and light conversation. In cafés people can also read the daily newspapers, write letters, and play cards. Most cafés have tables outside on the sidewalk as well as tables indoors.

3. The French enjoy the theater, the movies, opera, ballet, and concerts. National theaters such as **l'Opéra, la Comédie-Française, l'Odéon Théâtre de l'Europe,** and **le Théâtre National Populaire** are subsidized by the government. In theaters and moviehouses, it is customary to tip the usher.

4. The numerous museums and art exhibits attract many people. **"Son et Lumière"** shows take place at night near historic monuments. The **Son** is the recorded narration, accompanied by music; the **Lumière** is the dramatic lighting effects.

HOLIDAYS

The French celebrate many holidays, most of which are religious in origin. French legal holidays are:

1. New Year's Day, January 1st, (**le jour de l'an**) is a day when the French give and receive New Year's presents and wish a Happy New Year to family and friends alike.

2. Easter (**Pâques**) is a religious holiday celebrated on a Sunday and Monday in March or April.

3. Labor Day, May 1st, (**la fête du Travail**) is a day when lillies of the valley, which are thought to bring good luck, are sold on every street corner.

4. Ascension Thursday (**l'Ascension**) is a religious holiday celebrated 40 days after Easter.

5. On May 8th, the Fête of Joan of Arc and Victory Day (**le jour V**) commemorate the end of World War II.

6. Pentecost (**la Pentecôte**) is a religious holiday that takes place the 7th Sunday after Easter. It is celebrated on a Sunday and on a Monday.

7. Bastille Day, July 14th, (**la Fête nationale**) marks the anniversary of the storming of the Bastille at the beginning of the French Revolution.

8. The Assumption, August 15th, (**l'Assomption**) is a religious holiday marking Mary's ascent into heaven.

9. All Saints' Day, November 1st, (**la Toussaint**) is a religious holiday honoring all of the saints and the dead.

10. Victory Day, November 11th, (**la Fête de la Victoire**) commemorates the end of World War I.

11. Christmas, December 25th, (**Noël**) is a holiday when children (not adults) receive gifts. Instead of hanging stockings, French children leave their shoes in front of the fireplace or near the Christmas tree in anticipation of Père Noël's visit. On Christmas Eve, after midnight mass, a festive meal, "*le réveillon*," is served.

UNITS OF MEASURE

1. The metric system, based on the number 10, originated in France and is now used almost universally.

   The meter (**le mètre**), the unit of length, is slightly longer than the yard.

   1 meter = 100 centimeters = 39.37 inches

   1 kilometer (**kilomètre**) = 1,000 meters = 5/8 mile (approximately)

   The gram (**le gramme**) is the unit of weight.

   1 kilogram (**kilogramme**) = 1,000 grams = 2.2 lbs. (approximately)

   The liter (**le litre**), the liquid measure, is a little more than the American quart.

2. Temperature is measured on the *centigrade* scale: 0 (freezing point) to 100 degrees (boiling water). It is now known as the Celsius scale.

3. The monetary unit of France, and of almost all countries belonging to the European Union, is now the **euro** (**€**) (more or less equivalent to the American dollar). There are 100 **centimes,** or **cents,** in an **euro.** Before January 2002, the **franc** was the monetary unit in France.

CUISINE

Although American influence has contributed to the introduction of "fast-food" restaurants in France, cooking is still considered a fine art by most French people. French cuisine has achieved an international reputation. Its chefs are known particularly for their sauces, fine dishes, and pastries. Each region of France has its own delicious specialties. Some typical French foods are:

croissant and **brioche**, two types of flaky rolls served as part of a French breakfast

hors-d'œuvre, appetizer(s) served at the beginning of the meal

soupe à l'oignon, onion soup

bouillabaisse, a stew made with a variety of fish; a specialty of Provence

escargots, snails

pâtés and **foie gras**, rich and tasty dishes with a goose liver base

pot-au-feu, a kind of stew, consisting of boiled beef and vegetables

crêpes Suzette, thin dessert pancakes with a liquor sauce

Outside each restaurant, the menu is posted. Meals may be ordered **à la carte,** each dish individually priced, or **à prix fixe,** at one price for the complete meal. The **bistro,** a small establishment that combines a simple restaurant with a bar, is very popular in France.

EXERCICE

Complete the sentence.

1. The predominant religion in France is _____ .

2. In French schools, in the lower grades, there are no classes on _____ and on Sunday.

3. Bouillabaisse is made with _____ .

4. The French celebrate their National Holiday on _____ .

5. The metric system originated in _____ .

6. The yard is a little shorter than the _____ .

7. A favorite sport in France is _____ .

8. 1 kilometer equals _____ mile.

9. French people often eat **brioches** for _____

10. A **bistro** is _____ .

EXERCICE CRÉATIF

Choisissez une des activités suivantes.

1. Write a composition in which you compare the schools in France with the schools in the United States.

2. Make a diorama showing a French café scene.

3. Pick one French holiday and explain how it is celebrated.

Chapter 38
Literature

The literature of France is one of the great literatures of the world.

MIDDLE AGES

The first literary works in France, the **chansons de geste,** date from the Middle Ages. These legendary epic poems recount the patriotic and religious exploits of the knights of feudal society. The most famous is *La Chanson de Roland,* composed at the beginning of the twelfth century by an unknown author. It deals with Charlemagne's wars against the Moors of Spain.

François Villon, the eloquent poet of the fifteenth century, was considered the first of the great lyric poets of France. One of his verses, bemoaning the passage of time, is often cited: *"Mais où sont les neiges d'antan?"* ("But where are the snows of yesteryear?")

SIXTEENTH CENTURY

During the sixteenth century, writers turned to the classical era of ancient Greece and Rome for their inspiration. This was the period of the Renaissance.

François Rabelais expressed the enthusiasm of the Renaissance and the love of life. He was the author of amusing satires on the evils of society.

Pierre de Ronsard, the greatest poet of the sixteenth century, found inspiration in the poets of antiquity as he searched for new poetic styles.

Michel de Montaigne, the skeptical philosopher and moralist, recommended moderation in daily living, common sense, and a spirit of tolerance.

SEVENTEENTH CENTURY

The seventeenth century, especially the reign of Louis XIV, was the golden age of French literature. It was the period of classicism, a movement of order and discipline. The writers sought perfection in form, expression, and style.

The two great dramatic authors were **Pierre Corneille** and **Jean Racine.** Their classical tragedies are masterpieces of French drama.

Molière, who is often called "the Shakespeare of France", was the greatest French writer of classical comedies. In his plays he ridiculed human vices.

Jean de la Fontaine was the famous writer of fables. Using the animal kingdom, he painted in verse a picture of human society.

EIGHTEENTH CENTURY

The literature of the eighteenth century, mostly in prose, set human reason and individualism against tradition and authority. It was the period of liberal thinkers and of great philosophers who had a profound influence on political thought. By stressing the need for reform and the rights of the individual, they prepared the way for the French Revolution.

Charles de Secondat de Montesquieu criticized French institutions and proposed the separation of governmental powers. He pioneered the comparative study of social institutions, and in his classic *De l'Esprit des Lois* strongly influenced the framing of the constitution of the United States.

Voltaire dominated the eighteenth century. He attacked social injustice and became the defender of humanity and liberty in all forms. His immense work, which displays his ironic wit and skeptical philosophy, included many genres.

Jean-Jacques Rousseau was the theoretician of democracy. In attacking the social order, he inspired an intellectual revolt. He defended individual liberty and upheld the sovereignty of the people.

Denis Diderot directed the publication of an Encyclopedia that included the ideas of all the great writers and philosophers of the period. He attacked tradition and expressed faith in the progress of humanity.

NINETEENTH CENTURY

The first half of the nineteenth century produced a reaction to classical tradition. It was the period of romanticism, which prized freedom of expression, and stemmed from the theories of Rousseau.

In romantic literature, each writer expressed his own personality and individualism. The essential elements were imagination, feeling, and the love of nature.

Victor Hugo was the head of the romantic school and its greatest poet. He was also known for his plays and his novels (*Les Misérables, Notre-Dame de Paris*), which remain popular today.

Other romantic poets were **Alphonse de Lamartine, Alfred de Vigny**, and **Alfred de Musset.**

Honoré de Balzac painted a picture of the customs of his time in *La Comédie humaine,* a series of twenty-four admirable novels and numerous novelettes. With Balzac, who depicted all classes of society with precision, the novel evolved from romanticism toward realism.

Alexandre Dumas père wrote a large number of historical novels which became popular worldwide (*Les Trois Mousquetaires, Le Comte de Monte-Cristo*).

In the middle of the nineteenth century, new movements arose in opposition to romanticism, which stressed truth, materialism, and the reality of life. This movement of realism evolved into naturalism, which sought to analyze and portray life and nature as they were. Writers became impersonal, intellectual, and scientific.

Gustave Flaubert is most well-known for his novel, *Madame Bovary*. His works are generally characterized by minute observation and careful documentation.

Jules Verne, the author of fantastic novels of adventure, was the creator of science fiction. He wrote *Le Tour du monde en 80 jours.*

Alphonse Daudet wrote sensitive works that described life in the south of France during his time.

Émile Zola was the head of the naturalist school. He scientifically observed and analyzed the masses of human society.

Guy de Maupassant was the greatest French writer of short stories.

The poets of this time included **Baudelaire** and **Verlaine**, who used symbols to represent or to suggest ideas. For example: a flag suggests freedom or patriotism; rain suggests tears or sadness.

TWENTIETH CENTURY AND AFTER

There were numerous gifted writers working in France during the twentieth century. Several were awarded the Nobel Prize in Literature. The following are some who have achieved world fame.

Novelists

Anatole France was a novelist, a satirist, and a philosopher.

André Gide received the Nobel Prize in 1947 for his vast and varied work as a humanist.

Marcel Proust, in his famous work, *À la recherche du temps perdu,* treated unconscious memory as a work of art that is indestructible and eternal. Proust described in great detail the beauty and happiness awakened by memory and contrasts them with the sadness and disappointments of real life.

André Maurois wrote biographies, historical studies, and essays as well as novels.

François Mauriac wrote novels, plays, and essays which were often influenced by his religious beliefs.

Antoine de Saint-Exupéry, a pilot in peace and in war, described the adventures and heroic acts of aviators in his novels. In 1942 he wrote *Le Petit Prince*, a story of love, loneliness, and friendship.

André Malraux wrote novels celebrating human fraternity and heroism and books of art criticism.

Marguerite Yourcenar was the first woman elected to the Académie Française en 1980.

Claude Simon was one of the authors who attempted to renew the novel by changing its style. His novels did not depend on a traditional story. He was awarded the Nobel Prize of Literature in 1985.

Other novelists who have written in this new style are **Marguerite Duras**, **Alain Robbe-Grillet, Jean-Marie Le Clézio,** and **Patrick Modiano.**

Playwrights

Edmond Rostand was a brilliant dramatic author who wrote *Cyrano de Bergerac.*

Paul Claudel was a powerful dramatist and mystical poet.

Eugène Ionesco was a representative of the theater of the Absurd. His plays show the ridiculous tragedy of mankind.

Samuel Beckett was a pessimistic playwright who denounced the absurdity of the human condition. He wrote "*Waiting for Godot.*"

Philosophers

Jean-Paul Sartre was the brilliant theoretician of atheistic existentialism. He affirmed that the existence of man excludes the existence of God. Sartre spoke of the absurdity of life and developed his theses in novels, dramas, and essays. His greatest success was in the theater.

Albert Camus, a philosopher and moralist, was the author of essays, novels, and dramas. As a representative of the "philosophy of the Absurd," he wrote of the mechanical character of human existence without a goal. He received the Nobel Prize for Literature in 1957.

Poets

Paul Valéry created poetry with subtle and mysterious symbolism.

Paul Éluard and **Louis Aragon** are important poets of the twentieth century.

Jacques Prévert wrote satirical poems and poems about love and human kindness that served as the text for many songs.

FRANCOPHONE LITERATURE

French literature is not limited to works written in France by French writers. There are many writers throughout the world who have chosen to write in French. For some, French is their native language. For others, it is a language learned in school, used in place of a local dialect in order to reach a wider audience, or simply it is a language they love.

Among the many excellent francophone writers, who have often won the great literary prizes awarded in France every year, are:

Gabrielle Roy, born in Manitoba, Canada, was the author of psychological novels about life in Montreal or in her native province.

Georges Simenon, born in Belgium, wrote many detective novels featuring his well-known character, Maigret. More than 500 million copies of his novels have been published in over 50 different languages.

Tahar Ben Jalloun is the most famous Moroccan poet and novelist. He writes about the loneliness and difficulties of foreign immigrants in France. He received the coveted Prix Goncourt in 1987 for his novel *La Nuit sacrée* and the Prix du Mahgreb in 1994.

Assia Djebar writes about the women of Algeria and, in 2005, became the first non-French writer elected to the Académie française.

Léopold Sédar Senghor was the president of Sénégal and one of the country's most important poets. With Aimé Césaire he was a co-founder of the cultural movement known as "la négritude," which fought against colonialism and tyranny and which sought to affirm the importance of the black identity. His poems contrast the greatness of Africa in the past with the alienation that has resulted from the assimilation with European cultures.

Ousmane Sembène is a well-known Senegalese novelist and filmmaker. He criticizes the social injustices in Africa after colonialization and the problems that exist as a result of independence.

David Diop, a West African, criticized in his poems the values of the West and colonialism and he praised African women for their courage and strength.

Mariama Bâ described the problems of Senegalese women in her remarkable novel, *Une si longue lettre.*

Aimé Césaire and Frantz Fanon, born in Martinique, attacked colonial racism and promoted black pride.

EXERCICE

Identify the famous writer.

1. the famous author of classical comedies, "the Shakespeare of France"   _____

2. the greatest writer of short stories   _____

3. the famous writer of fables   _____

4. the greatest poet of the romantic school   _____

5. the creator of science fiction   _____

6. the 18th century writer who attacked social injustice and defended humanity and liberty   _____

7. the existentialist philosopher and moralist   _____

8. the 20th century poet who wrote poems used as songs   _____

9. the Belgian author of detective stories   _____

10. a Senegalese writer who also creates important films   _____

EXERCICE CRÉATIF

Choisissez une des activités suivantes.

1. Memorize one of La Fontaine's fables. Write it out in French and illustrate it.

2. Write a short biography of a francophone author.

3. Explain the purpose of the cultural movement known as *la négritude*.

Chapter 39
The Arts

Throughout the centuries, the French have distinguished themselves in the arts. Many French artists have achieved fame and worldwide influence.

PAINTING

In prehistoric times there were artists in France who created extraordinary paintings of animals on the walls of caves. These works of art can still be seen nowadays.

In the sixteenth century, **Jean** et **François Clouet** painted beautiful small portraits.

In the seventeenth century, **Nicolas Poussin** and **Claude Lorrain** painted great landscapes with antique elements.

Antoine Watteau, the great classical painter of the eighteenth century, created beautiful pastoral scenes. His pictures reflect the elegant society of his time.

Louis David, head of the *neoclassical* school, was the painter of the French Revolution. He painted portraits and scenes from Greek and Roman history.

In the nineteenth century, Paris became the world center of painting where artists with similar tendencies grouped themselves in a variety of schools.

Romanticism attempted to break away from the discipline and rules of classicism. **Eugène Delacroix**, the best-known of this school, created paintings showing vitality and dramatic movement.

Realism was the reaction against both romanticism and classicism. **Honoré Daumier**, a realist lithographer and painter, is known especially for his political and social caricatures.

Several landscape painters formed a group known as *l'École de Barbizon*, after a small village outside Paris where they liked to go. **Jean-Baptiste Corot** painted with poetic charm. **Jean-François Millet** liked to paint scenes of peasant life and **Théodore Rousseau** painted mostly landscapes.

In the second half of the nineteenth century, *impressionism* evolved from realism. The impressionists tried to translate into painting the feelings evoked by their visual perceptions. They chose modern subjects, ignored details, and made light the essential element of their paintings.

Édouard Manet, one of the founders of impressionism, is famous for his dazzling texture and color.

Edgar Degas, an expert at expressing form and movement, painted many ballet scenes.

Claude Monet, the greatest landscape painter, often painted the same subject in varying light at different times of day.

Auguste Renoir was a great painter of women and landscapes.

Georges Seurat developed *pointillism*, a technique using many points of pure colors to create an effect of depth and light.

Pierre Puvis de Chavannes painted the murals that decorate the Panthéon and the Sorbonne in a classical style.

Post-impressionism, a modern movement at the end of the nineteenth century, was a reaction against the excesses of impressionism and realism. The modernists of this school did not hesitate to distort the appearance of nature and the human body. They were individualists who painted in their own personal styles.

Paul Cézanne is considered the father of modern French painting. His works, mainly landscapes and still lifes, give the impression of a third dimension.

Paul Gauguin is known especially for his Breton landscapes and scenes of Tahiti painted in vivid colors with moving simplicity and spiritual depth.

Vincent Van Gogh, born in Holland, found his inspiration in Provence. His canvasses, — still lifes, landscapes, portraits — are filled with brilliant colors and sunlight.

Henri de Toulouse-Lautrec painted music-hall and circus scenes, many of which were reproduced and distributed as posters in his time.

At the start of the twentieth century, a group of artists reacted against impressionist analyses and decided to paint as they pleased, simplifying forms and using pure strong colors. They called themselves *les Fauves* (wild beasts).

Henri Matisse, the head of *fauvism*, is considered one of the greatest painters of his time. His masterpiece of decorative art is the chapel of Vence, in southern France.

Georges Braque founded the school of *cubism,* which represents objects in geometric form, often from different angles at the same time.

Pablo Picasso, the most versatile painter of the twentieth century, tried a variety of techniques, attaining a synthesis between cubism and surrealism. He had a profound influence on the evolution of modern art. He was born in Spain but lived most of his life in France.

Surrealism, in the 1920s, was opposed to every kind of convention and sought an instinctive and dreamlike expression. **André Masson** and **René Magritte** were surrealists.

Other important painters of the twentieth century are **Fernand Léger**, who painted monumental works inspired by modern life and machinery; and Russian born **Marc Chagall**, whose paintings are imbued with poetical fantasy.

SCULPTURE

In the eighteenth century, **Jean-Antoine Houdon** produced realistic busts of several famous men: Voltaire, Rousseau, Washington, La Fayette, Franklin, and Jefferson among others.

In the nineteenth century, **François Rude**, a sculptor of the Romantic school, created the famous bas-relief *La Marseillaise* that decorates the Arc de Triomphe in Paris.

Frédéric-Auguste Bartholdi is best known as the sculptor of the Statue of Liberty (*La Liberté éclairant le monde.*)

Auguste Rodin is usually considered the greatest of modern sculptors. He used the human figure to express the emotions and the power of life in such works as *Le Penseur* (The Thinker) and *Le Baiser* (The Kiss).

In the twentieth century, **Aristide Maillol** is known particularly for his simple and graceful statues of nude women.

Jacques Lipchitz, who was associated with cubism in his early years, brought imaginative and lyrical energy to his powerful sculptures.

ARCHITECTURE

In the Gallo-Roman period, remarkable structures were built: temples, arenas, amphitheaters, aqueducts. The best surviving examples are found in southern France, in Provence.

In the Middle Ages the arts were mostly in the service of religion. The thick-walled *Romanesque* churches of the tenth through the mid-twelfth centuries were dark inside. Later, the French created a new style of architecture, *Gothic*, brightened up by large stained-glass windows that let in plenty of light, and ornamented with sculpture, statues, and gargoyles. Outstanding examples of gothic architecture are the cathedrals of Notre-Dame de Paris, Amiens, Chartres, and Reims.

Many splendid castles were built all over France, particularly along the Loire river and around Paris, by the kings and nobles, especially during the sixteenth and seventeenth centuries.

Jules Hardouin Mansart (seventeenth century), the chief architect of Louis XIV, built most of the palace of Versailles as well as the dome of the Invalides and the place Vendôme in Paris.

Eugène Viollet-le-Duc (nineteenth century) restored numerous historic monuments of the Middle Ages, such as Notre-Dame de Paris, the cathedral of Amiens, and the Cité de Carcassonne.

Le Corbusier (twentieth century) exerted a wide influence through his theorical writings, his daring use of reinforced concrete, and his innovative design of urban housing developments.

At the present time, many important architectural projects are in progress in France, especially in Paris. Several French architects, like **Jean Nouvel,** have become known throughout the world.

MUSIC

Jean-Baptiste Lully, who served at the court of Louis XIV, created the French opera. He wrote music for several of Molière's comedies.

Hector Berlioz, the greatest composer of the Romantic school, which flourished in the first half of the nineteenth century, wrote beautifully orchestrated and powerful dramatic works. *La Damnation de Faust* is now considered his masterpiece.

In the second half of that century, French music attained international prominence. **César Franck**, an organist of great renown, wrote music which combined classical forms with romantic harmonies.

Camille Saint-Saëns, a virtuoso of the piano and organ, wrote symphonic poems (*La Danse macabre*), piano concertos, and operas. His masterpiece is *Samson et Dalila*.

Claude Debussy, whose career extended into the early part of the 20ᵗʰ century, was influenced by the symbolists and the impressionists. His music is dreamy, delicate, and highly original. Among his principal works are: *Prélude à l'après-midi d'un faune; la Mer; Clair de lune;* and the opera, *Pelléas et Mélisande*.

Maurice Ravel composed pieces for the piano and for the orchestra: *Daphnis et Chloé, Boléro, Ma mère l'Oye (Mother Goose Suite)*.

Other composers of famous operas are:

Georges Bizet: *Carmen, Les Pêcheurs de perles*

Charles Gounod: *Faust, Roméo et Juliette*

Jules Massenet: *Manon, Thaïs*

Jacques Offenbach: *Les Contes d'Hoffmann*

The twentieth century has witnessed the rise of a number of talented composers including: **Darius Milhaud, Francis Poulenc, Olivier Messiaen,** and **Pierre Boulez.**

SONGS

French songs began with the love songs of the wandering minstrels (*troubadours*) during the Middle Ages. During the seventeenth century, romantic, satirical or heroic songs became popular. The eighteenth century saw the appearance of Revolutionary songs. In the nineteenth century, poets created songs of a political nature. Twentieth century songs were influenced by jazz.

The following traditional singers are renowned.

Édith Piaf (1915–1963), nicknamed "the little sparrow," was well-known for her love songs, the most popular being "*La vie en rose*."

Yves Montand (1921–1991) was not only a popular singer, but an accomplished actor.

Charles Aznavour 1924-) composed more than 600 songs and sold more than 100 million records and CDs.

Gilbert Bécaud (1927–2001) was a dynamic and vital star during the 1950s and 1960s.

Georges Brassens (1921–1981) sang the poems of Villon and Aragon, as well as his own.

Jacques Brel (1929–1978), born in Belgium, was the author and composer of poetic songs.

Joe Dassin (1938–1980) was famous for his rendition of *Autumn Leaves*.

During the 60s, **Johnny Hallyday** (who sang American rock songs translated into French), **Françoise Hardy**, **Michel Polnareff**, and **Sylvie Vartan** were quite popular.

Today in France and in francophone countries throughout the world all genres of music are popular.

Well known alternative rock groups are **Noir Désir** and **Mano Negra**.

M.C. Solaar, born in Sénégal, is a famous French rapper.

World Music singers and groups include: **Papa Wemba** (Congo), **Baaba Maal** (Sénégal), **Angélique Kidjo** (Bénin), **Alpha Blondy** (Ivory Coast), **Oumou Sengaré** (Mali), **Youssou N'-Dour** (Sénégal), and **Lo'Jo Triban** (France).

Pop musicians include: **Céline Dion** (Canada), **Patrick Bruel** (Tunisia), **Étienne Daho** (France), **Jean-Jacques Goldman** (France), and **Véronique** and **Patricia Kaas** (France).

FILM

The cinema was born in France. **Louis Lumière** showed the first animated images in 1895 in Paris. In 1897, **Georges Méliès** built the first studio near Paris and made short, imaginative science-fiction films filled with special effects.

Émile and **Charles Pathé** opened a studio, manufactured films, and started a newsreel program to be shown before a main film (1909).

Among the many recent movie directors who have become internationally renowned, one should mention the following.

Louis Malle is famous for many films, including two that deal with World War II: *Lacombe Lucien* and *Au revoir les enfants*.

Éric Rohmer is known for his series of films such as *les Comédies et Proverbes* and *les Contes moraux*.

Alain Resnais explored the relationship between literature and cinema in works such as *Hiroshima mon amour*, *L'Année dernière à Marienbad* and *Mon Oncle d'Amérique*.

Jean-Luc Godard had a great influence on filmmaking by questioning artistic creation and ideologies. Among his famous films are *À bout de souffle*, *Passion*, and *Prénom Carmen*.

François Truffaut expressed the fragility of man in his romantic affairs and daily life. He is known for *Les Quatre cents coups, Tirez sur le pianiste, Jules et Jim, Farenheit 451, Le Dernier métro,* and *La Femme d'à côté*.

Jacques Tati is known for his comic films that mock the pretentions of some of his contemporaries. His films *Jour de Fête, Les Vacances de M. Hulot* and *Mon Oncle* have had great success.

Ousmane Sembène, Senegalese writer and filmmaker, is considered the real founder of African cinema. In his movies, such as *la Noire de...* , *Xala,* and *Camp de Thiaroye,* he hopes to reach a wider audience than with his books.

EXERCICE

Identify the artists.

1. the painter of scenes of peasant life _____

2. the painter of murals for the Panthéon _____

3. the "father" of modern art _____

4. the painter of scenes of Tahiti _____

5. a realist painter known for his political and social caricatures _____

6. the painter of ballet scenes _____

7. the inventor of *pointillism* _____

8. head of the neoclassic school during the French Revolution, who painted scenes from Greek history _____

9. the most inventive painter of the 20th century, who used many different techniques _____

10. the architect of Louis XIV _____

11. the sculptor of busts of Voltaire and Washington _____

12. a famous French architect of the 20th century _____

13. the sculptor of *Le Penseur* _____

14. the sculptor of the Statue of Liberty in New York _____

15. the director of two movies taking place during World War II. _____

16. a well-known African filmmaker _____

EXERCICE CRÉATIF

Choisissez une des activités suivantes.

1. Find a picture of one of Rodin's sculptures. Explain what it looks like and give your opinion of it.

2. Listen to a modern French song. Compare it to a popular American song of the same genre.

3. Watch a French film and write a review of it.

4. Look at a painting by Pablo Picasso. Give its title and describe it.

Chapter 40
The Sciences

The French have made significant contributions in many fields of sciences. Among French scientists, the following men and women should be mentioned.

MATHEMATICS

René Descartes (1596–1650), philosopher and mathematician, founded the scientific method, based on reasoning from the simple to the complex. Applied to philosophy, this rational method lead him to prove his own existence first — *"Je pense, donc je suis"* (I think, therefore I am) — and then the existence of the exterior world.

Blaise Pascal (1623–1662), mathematician, physicist, and philosopher, formulated the laws of atmospheric pressure and of hydraulics. At the age of nineteen he invented the mechanical adding machine.

Pierre-Simon de Laplace (1749–1827) made important contributions to the understanding of the dynamics of the solar system and to the theory of probability.

Henri Poincaré (1854–1912) is called the last mathematical universalist because he contributed important work to all branches of mathematics as well as to the philosophy of sciences.

PHYSICS

Charles-Augustin de Coulomb (1736–1806) studied the mathematical laws of electricity and magnetism. The *coulomb* is the unit of electrical charges.

André Ampère (1775–1836) developed electromagnetic theory. An *ampere* is the unit used to measure the intensity of electrical currents.

Henri Becquerel (1852–1908) discovered natural radioactivity in 1896.

Pierre Curie (1859–1906) and his wife **Marie Curie** (1867–1934) discovered radium in 1899, thus effecting great changes in the fields of chemistry and physics. They received the Nobel Prize in Physics in 1903 and the Nobel Prize in Chemistry in 1911. Their daughter and her hus-

band, **Irène** and **Pierre Joliot-Curie**, discovered artificial radioactivity in 1934. They received the Nobel Prize in Physics in 1935.

CHEMISTRY

Antoine-Laurent de Lavoisier (1743–1794), one of the founders of modern chemistry, ascertained the composition of air and made many important discoveries. One of his sayings is often quoted, *"Rien ne se perd, rien ne se crée; dans la nature tout se transforme."* (Nothing is lost, nothing is created; in nature everything is transformed.)

NATURAL SCIENCE

Georges Louis de Buffon (1707–1788), an important naturalist and writer, was the author of the much admired *L'Histoire naturelle* in 40 volumes.

Jean-Baptiste de Lamarck (1744—1829) developed a theory about the evolution of animals and plants which predates Darwin's work.

BIOLOGY AND MEDICINE

Claude Bernard (1813–1878) was the founder of modern physiology and experimental medicine.

Louis Pasteur (1822–1895), chemist and biologist, was one of the great benefactors of mankind. He formulated the germ theory of infection, found a cure for rabies and anthrax, and invented the process of pasteurization. His work revolutionized medicine.

L'institut Pasteur, founded in 1888 under his direction in Paris, remains a leading research center in the fields of biochemistry and infectious diseases.

Émile Roux (1853–1933) discovered that the diphteria bacillus produces a toxin. This was the first step in the development of effective medicines for what was once a dreaded childhood disease.

In other fields as well, French scientists have made important contributions.

Jean-François Champollion (1790–1832), an archaeologist, deciphered the Egyptian hieroglyphics on the Rosetta stone.

Louis-Jacques Daguerre (1789–1851) developed a way to record images on metal plates and deserves to be called one of the inventors of photography.

Louis Braille (1809–1852) invented a system of reading and writing for the blind.

Jacques Cousteau (1910–1997) explored the marine world and made extraordinary films such as *Le Monde du silence.*

Since 1911 many French scientists have been awarded the Nobel Prize for their contributions to research and science. Much of the scientific research in France is done at the **CNRS (Centre national de la Recherche scientifique)** which has more than 1000 laboratories throughout France.

EXERCICE

Complete the sentences.

1. _____ is one of the founders of modern chemistry.

2. _____ contributed to the discovery of a serum to cure diphtheria.

3. _____ founded modern physiology and experimental medicine.

4. Henri Becquerel won the Nobel Prize for his discovery of _____ .

5. _____ founded a scientific method based on reason.

6. _____ is a famous mathematician of the 18th century.

EXERCICE CRÉATIF

Choisissez une des activités suivantes.

1. Write a detailed description of the scientific contributions of the Curie family.

2. Write a biography of Louis Pasteur.

3. Write a report for your French club in which you explain the contributions of René Descartes.

Appendix

[1] VERBS WITH REGULAR FORMS

INFINITIVE

parler	finir	vendre	s'amuser

PAST PARTICIPLE

parlé	fini	vendu	amusé

PRESENT

parle	finis	vends	m' amuse
parles	finis	vends	t' amuses
parle	finit	vend	s' amuse
parlons	finissons	vendons	nous amusons
parlez	finissez	vendez	vous amusez
parlent	finissent	vendent	s' amusent

IMPERATIVE

parle	finis	vends	amuse-toi
parlons	finissons	vendons	amusons-nous
parlez	finissez	vendez	amusez-vous

IMPERFECT

parlais	finissais	vendais	m' amusais
parlais	finissais	vendais	t' amusais
parlait	finissait	vendait	s' amusait
parlions	finissions	vendions	nous amusions
parliez	finissiez	vendiez	vous amusiez
parlaient	finissaient	vendaient	s' amusaient

FUTURE

parlerai	finirai	vendrai	m' amuserai
parleras	finiras	vendras	t' amuseras
parlera	finira	vendra	s' amusera
parlerons	finirons	vendrons	nous amuserons
parlerez	finirez	vendrez	vous amuserons
parleront	finiront	vendront	s' amuseront

PASSÉ COMPOSÉ

ai parlé	ai fini	ai vendu	me suis amus**é(e)**
as parlé	as fini	as vendu	t'es amus**é(e)**
a parlé	a fini	a vendu	s'est amus**é(e)**
avons parlé	avons fini	avons vendu	nous sommes amus**é(e)s**
avez parlé	avez fini	avez vendu	vous êtes amus**é(e)(s)**
ont parlé	ont fini	ont vendu	se sont amus**é(e)s**

[2] -ER VERBS WITH SPELLING CHANGES

	-cer VERBS	*-ger* VERBS	*-yer* VERBS*	*-eler* / *-eter* VERBS		e + CONSONANT + *-er* VERBS	é + CONSONANT(S) + *-er* VERBS
INFINITIVE	pla**cer**	man**ger**	emplo**yer**	app**eler**	**jeter**	m**ener**	esp**érer**
PRESENT	place	mange	emplo**ie**	app**elle**	j**ette**	m**è**ne	esp**è**re
	places	manges	emplo**ies**	app**elles**	j**ettes**	m**è**nes	esp**è**res
	place	mange	emplo**ie**	app**elle**	j**ette**	m**è**ne	esp**è**re
	pla**çons**	man**geons**	employons	appelons	jetons	menons	espérons
	placez	mangez	eniployez	appelez	jetez	menez	espérez
	placent	mangent	emplo**ient**	app**ellent**	j**ettent**	m**è**nent	esp**è**rent
IMPERFECT	pla**çais**	man**geais**					
	pla**çais**	man**geais**					
	pla**çait**	man**geait**					
	placions	mangions					
	placiez	mangiez					
	pla**çaient**	man**geaient**					
FUTURE			emplo**ierai**	app**ellerai**	j**etterai**	m**è**nerai	
			emplo**ieras**	app**elleras**	j**etteras**	m**è**neras	
			emplo**iera**	app**ellera**	j**ettera**	m**è**nera	
			emplo**ierons**	app**ellerons**	j**etterons**	m**è**nerons	
			emplo**ierez**	app**ellerez**	j**etterez**	m**è**nerez	
			emplo**ieront**	app**elleront**	j**etteront**	m**è**neront	
IMPERATIVE	place	mange	emplo**ie**	app**elle**	j**ette**	m**è**ne	esp**è**re
	pla**çons**	man**geons**	employons	appelons	jetons	menons	espérons
	placez	mangez	employez	appelons	jetons	menez	espérez

*Verbs ending in *-ayer*, like *payer* and *balayer*, may be conjugated like *employer* or retain the *y* in all conjugations: *je paye* or *je paie*.

[3] VERBS WITH IRREGULAR FORMS

NOTES:
1. Irregular forms are printed in bold type.
2. Verbs conjugated with *être* in compound tenses are indicated with an asterisk (*)

INFINITIVE, PARTICIPLE	PRESENT	IMPERATIVE	IMPERFECT	FUTURE	PASSÉ COMPOSÉ
aller* *to go*	**vais**	**va**	allais	**irai**	suis allé(e)
	vas	allons	allais	**iras**	es allé(e)
	va	allez	allait	**ira**	est allé(e)
allé	allons		allions	**irons**	sommes allé(e)s
	allez		alliez	**irez**	êtes allé(e)(s)
	vont		allaient	**iront**	sont allé(e)s

apprendre *to learn* (like **prendre**)

avoir	**ai**	**aie**	avais	**aurai**	ai **eu**
to have	**as**	**ayons**	avais	**auras**	as **eu**
	a	**ayez**	avait	**aura**	a **eu**
eu	**avons**		avions	**aurons**	avons **eu**
	avez		aviez	**aurez**	avez **eu**
	ont		avaient	**auront**	ont **eu**

comprendre *to understand* (like **prendre**)

découvrir *to discover* (like **ouvrir**)

devenir* *to become* (like **venir**)

dire	dis	dis	disais	dirai	ai **dit**
to say, tell	dis	**disons**	disais	diras	as **dit**
	dit	**dites**	disait	dira	a **dit**
dit	**disons**		disions	dirons	avons **dit**
	dites		disiez	direz	avez **dit**
	disent		disaient	diront	ont **dit**

écrire	écris	écris	écrivais	écrirai	ai **écrit**
to write	écris	écrivons	écrivais	écriras	as **écrit**
	écrit	écrivez	écrivait	écrira	a **écrit**
écrit	**écrivons**		écrivions	écrirons	avons **écrit**
	écrivez		écriviez	écrirez	avez **écrit**
	écrivent		écrivaient	écriront	ont **écrit**

INFINITIVE, PARTICIPLE	PRESENT	IMPERATIVE	IMPERFECT	FUTURE	PASSÉ COMPOSÉ
envoyer *to send* envoyé	**envoie** **envoies** **envoie** envoyons envoyez **envoient**	**envoie** envoyons envoyez	envoyais envoyais envoyait envoyions envoyiez envoyaient	**enverrai** **enverras** **enverra** **enverrons** **enverrez** **enverront**	ai envoyé as envoyé a envoyé avons envoyé avez envoyé ont envoyé
être *to be* été	**suis** **es** est **sommes** **êtes** **sont**	**sois** **soyons** **soyez**	**étais** **étais** **était** **étions** **étiez** **étaient**	serai seras sera serons serez seront	ai **été** as **été** a **été** avons **été** avez **été** ont **été**
faire *to do, make* fait	fais fais **fait** **faisons** **faites** **font**	fais faisons **faites**	faisais faisais faisait faisions faisiez faisaient	**ferai** **feras** **fera** **ferons** **ferez** **feront**	ai **fait** as **fait** a **fait** avons **fait** avez **fait** ont **fait**
lire *to read* lu	lis lis **lit** **lisons** **lisez** **lisent**	lis lisons lisez	lisais lisais lisait lisions lisiez lisaient	lirai liras lira lirons lirez liront	ai **lu** as **lu** a **lu** avons **lu** avez **lu** ont **lu**
mettre *to put* mis	**mets** **mets** **met** mettons mettez mettent	mets mettons mettez	mettais mettais mettait mettions mettiez mettaient	**mettrai** **mettras** **mettra** **mettrons** **mettrez** **mettront**	ai **mis** as **mis** a **mis** avons **mis** avez **mis** ont **mis**
ouvrir *to open* ouvert	**ouvre** **ouvres** **ouvre** **ouvrons** **ouvrez** **ouvrent**	**ouvre** ouvrons ouvrez	ouvrais ouvrais ouvrait ouvrions ouvriez ouvraient	ouvrirai ouvriras ouvrira ouvrirons ouvrirez ouvriront	ai **ouvert** as **ouvert** a **ouvert** avons **ouvert** avez **ouvert** ont **ouvert**

INFINITIVE, PARTICIPLE	PRESENT	IMPERATIVE	IMPERFECT	FUTURE	PASSÉ COMPOSÉ
partir* *to leave* (like **sortir**)					
permettre *to allow* (like **mettre**)					
pouvoir	**peux (puis)**	*(none)*	pouvais	**pourrai**	ai **pu**
to be able	**peux**		pouvais	**pourras**	as **pu**
	peut		pouvait	**pourra**	a **pu**
pu	**pouvons**		pouvions	**pourrons**	avons **pu**
	pouvez		pouviez	**pourrez**	avez **pu**
	peuvent		pouvaient	**pourront**	ont **pu**
prendre	prends	prends	prenais	prendrai	ai **pris**
to take	prends	prenons	prenais	prendras	as **pris**
	prend	prenez	prenait	prendra	a **pris**
pris	**prenons**		prenions	prendrons	avons **pris**
	prenez		preniez	prendrez	avez **pris**
	prennent		prenaient	prendront	ont **pris**
promettre *to promise* (like **mettre**)					
recevoir	**reçois**	reçois	recevais	**recevrai**	ai **reçu**
to receive	**reçois**	recevons	recevais	**recevras**	as **reçu**
	reçoit	recevez	recevait	**recevra**	a **reçu**
reçu	**recevons**		recevions	**recevrons**	avons **reçu**
	recevez		receviez	**recevrez**	avez **reçu**
	reçoivent		recevaient	**recevront**	ont **reçu**
savoir	**sais**	**sache**	savais	**saurai**	ai **su**
to know (how to)	**sais**	**sachons**	savais	**sauras**	as **su**
	sait	**sachez**	savait	**saura**	a **su**
	savons		savions	**saurons**	avons **su**
su	**savez**		saviez	**saurez**	avez **su**
	savent		savaient	**sauront**	ont **su**
sortir*	**sors**	sors	sortais	sortirai	suis sorti(e)
to go oui	**sors**	sortons	sortais	sortiras	es sorti(e)
	sort	sortez	sortait	sortira	est sorti(e)
	sortons		sortions	sortirons	sommes sorti(e)s
sorti	**sortez**		sortiez	sortirez	êtes sorti(e)(s)
	sortent		sortaient	sortiront	sont sorti(e)s

INFINITIVE, PARTICIPLE	PRESENT	IMPERATIVE	IMPERFECT	FUTURE	PASSÉ COMPOSÉ
venir* *to come* **venu**	**viens** **viens** **vient** **venons** **venez** **viennent**	viens venons venez	venais venais venait venions veniez venaient	**viendrai** **viendras** **viendra** **viendrons** **viendrez** **viendront**	suis **venu**(e) es **venu**(e) est **venu**(e) sommes **venu**(e)s êtes **venu**(e)(s) sont **venu**(e)s
voir *to see* **vu**	vois vois voit **voyons** **voyez** **voient**	vois voyons voyez	voyais voyais voyait voyions voyiez voyaient	**verrai** **verras** **verra** **verrons** **verrez** **verront**	ai **vu** as **vu** a **vu** avons **vu** avez **vu** ont **vu**
vouloir *to want* **voulu**	veux veux veut voulons voulez veulent	**veuille** **veuillons** **veuillez**	voulais voulais voulait voulions vouliez voulaient	**voudrai** **voudras** **voudra** **voudrons** **voudrez** **voudront**	ai **voulu** as **voulu** a **voulu** avons **voulu** avez **voulu** ont **voulu**

[4] COMMON REFLEXIVE VERBS

s'acheter to buy for oneself
s'amuser (à) to have a good time, enjoy
s'appeler to be named
se brosser to brush oneself
se coucher to lie down; to go to bed
se demander to wonder
se dépêcher (de) to hurry
se déshabiller to undress
s'ennuyer (à) to get bored
s'habiller to dress
se laver to wash (oneself)

se lever to get up; to rise
se maquiller to put on makeup
se marier avec to get married to
se mettre en route to start out
se peigner to comb one's hair
se préparer to prepare oneself
se promener to take a walk
se rappeler to remember
se raser to shave
se reposer to rest
se réveiller to wake up

[5] COMMON PRÉPOSITIONS

a. Simple prepositions

à to, at, in
après after
avant before

avec with
chez to /at, in the house (place) of (a person)
contre against

dans in, into, within	**pour** for
de of, from	**sans** without
depuis since, for	**sauf** except
derrière behind	**selon** according to
devant in front of	**sous** under
en in, into, as	**sur** on
entre among, between	**vers** toward
par by, through	

b. Compound prepositions

à cause de because of, on account of	**autour de** around
à côté de next to, beside	**avant (de)** before
à droite de on (to) the right	**du côté de** in the direction of, near
à gauche de on (to) the left	**en face de** opposite
au lieu de instead of	**loin de** far from
au milieu de in the middle of	**près de** near

[6] PUNCTUATON

French punctuation, though similar to English, has the following major differences:

(a) The comma is not used before *et* or *ou* in a series.

Elle a laissé tomber le livre, le stylo et le crayon.	*She dropped the book, the pen and the pencil.*

(b) In numbers, French uses a comma where English uses a period and a period where English uses a comma.

7.100 (sept mille cent)	*7,100 (seven thousand one hundred)*
7,25 (sept virgule vingt-cinq)	*7.25 (seven point twenty five)*

(c) French final quotation marks, contrary to English, precede the comma or period; however, the quotation mark follows a period if the quotation mark encloses a completed statement.

Elle demande: **«Est-ce que tu m'aimes?»**.	*She asks: "Do you love me?"*
— **«Oui»**, répond-il.	*"Yes," he answers.*

(d) The ellipsis in French is : **Je pense... donc** (three close dots followed by a space) while in English it is : *I think . . . therefore* (three dots separated by spaces)

[7] Syllabication

French words are generally divided at the end of a line according to units of sound or syllables. A French syllable generally begins with a consonant and ends with a vowel.

(a) If a single consonant comes between two vowels, the division is made before the consonant.

ba-**la**-der   pré-**cis**   cou-**teau**

> NOTE: A division cannot be made either before or after *x* or *y* when *x* or *y* come between two vowels.
>
> **tuyau**   **exact**

(b) If two consonants are combined between two vowels, the division is made between the two consonants.

es-**p**oir   al-**l**er   chan-**t**er

> NOTE: If the second consonant is *r* or *l*, the division is made before the two consonants.
>
> sa-**ble**   pro-**pre**

(c) If three or more consonants are combined between vowels, the division is made after the second consonant.

o**bs-t**iné   com**p-t**er   in**s-t**aller

(d) Two vowels may not be divided.

oa-sis   th**éâ**-tre   es-p**io**n

Nor can there be a division immediately after *l'*, *j'*, *t'*, or *m'*

l'avion   **j'en**-voie   elle **m'en**-chante

[8] Pronunciation

Each syllable in a French word has about equal stress.

Liaison and Elision

Liaison refers to the linking of the final consonant of one word with the beginning vowel (*a, e, i, o, u*) or vowel sound (generally, silent *h* and *y*) of the following word, as in the following example:

nous aimons
 z

Pronunciation of the final "*s*" of *nous* takes on the sound of '*z*' and combines with the pronunciation of the beginning '*a*' of *aimons*.

Elision usually occurs when two pronounced vowel sounds follow each other, one at the end of a word and the other at the beginning of the next word. Drop the final vowel of the first word and replace it with an apostrophe. The two words then simply slide together:

je +aime = j'aime

Note that the final '*e*' sound of *je* is dropped.

Accents

An accent mark may change the sound of a letter and the meaning of a word. It may replace a letter that existed in old French or have no perceivable affect at all. Accents are used only on vowels. Another mark, the *cédille*, can be used under the letter '*c*'.

- An **accent aigu** (´) is used only on the letter '*e*' (*é*) and produces the sound *ay*, as in 'may'. It may replace an '*s*' from old French. When you see this letter, replace the *é* with an imaginary '*s*' to see if its meaning becomes more evident.

    éponge = *sponge*

- An **accent grave** (`) may be used on an '*a*' (*à*) or '*u*' (*ù*) where it causes no sound change, or on the letter '*e*' (*è*), producing the sound of *eh* as in the '*e*' in 'let'.

    là,   où,   très

- An **accent circonflexe** (^) may be placed on any vowel but causes no perceptible sound change, though '*ê*' is usually pronounced like '*è*'. It, too, often replaces an '*s*' from old French, which may give a clue to the meaning of the word.

    hôpital = *hospital*

- A **cédille** (,) is placed under a '*c*' (*ç*), to create a soft '*s*' sound before the letters '*a*', '*o*', or '*u*',

    garçon = *boy*

- A **tréma** (¨) is placed on the second of two consecutive vowels to indicate that each vowel is pronounced independently.

    Noël

Vowels

Some vowels in French have multiple pronunciations determined by specific linguistic rules, letter combinations, and/or accent marks.

Table 1.   Vowels and their Sound

Vowel	Sound	
a, à, â	ah as in *pa*	papa, là, pâte
é, final *er* and *ez*, *es* in some one-syllable words, some *ai* and *et* combinations	ay as in *day*	télé, adorer, arrivez, mes, gai, et
e in one syllable words or in the middle of a word followed by one consonant	uh as in *the*	je, demander
è, ê, and *e* (plus two consonants or a final pronounced consonant), *et, ei, ai*	eh as in *get*	très, fête, est, avec cette, ballet, seize aider
i, î, y	i as in *magazine*	timide, dîne, lycée
ill or *il* when preceded by a vowel	y as in *you* (there are exceptions like ville, village, where *ill* is pronounced *eel*)	fille, détail
o (before *se*), *ô, au, eau* *o* (last pronounced sound of word)	o as in *go*	rose, allô, aussi, peau, stylo

Table 1. (continued)

Vowel	Sound	
o when followed by a pronounced consonant other than *s*	oh as in *dove*	téléphone, opéra
ou, où, oû	oo as in *boot*	toujours, où, goût
oy, oi	wah as in **wand**	toi, voiture
u, ù, û	No equivalent: try saying *ew* with lips rounded	tu, super, une

Nasal Sounds

French nasal sounds occur when a vowel is followed by a single *n* or *m* in the same syllable.

Table 2. Nasal Sounds

Nasal	Sound	
an, en, am, em	like *on* with minor emphasis on *n*	dans, encore, maman, décembre
in, ain, im, aim	like *an* with minor emphasis on *n*	cousin, demain important, faim
ien	like *yan* in *yankee* with minor emphasis on *n*	italien
oin	like *wa* in *wag*	loin, point
on, om	like *on* in *long*	bon, compter,
un, um	like *un* in *under*	un, parfum

The following combinations do not require nasalized vowel sounds:

- vowel + *nn* or *mm*   Example: bonne (pronounced like *bun* in English)
- vowel + *n* or *m* + vowel   Example: mine (pronounced like *mean* in English)

Consonants

The French consonants in Table 3 are pronounced the same way as they are in English: *b, d, f, k, l, m, n, p, s, t, v, z.* Most final French consonants remain unpronounced except for *c, r, f,* and *l* (think of the word **careful**). When in doubt, consult a good dictionary.

Table 3.   Consonant Sounds

Consonant	Sound	
c + a,o,u	c as in *can*	carte, court, document
c + e, i	s as in *say*	ce, ici
ch	sh as in *machine*	chaise, chocolat
g + a,o,u gu + e,i	g as in *good*	garçon, gomme, légume bague, guide
g + e,i,y ge + a,o	zh as in *measure*	âge, girafe, gymnastique mangeais, plongeon
gn	ny as in *union*	montagne
j	zh as in *measure*	jour, je
h	usually silent sometimes 'aspirate' (pronounced)	l'homme, l'herbe le homard, le haut, le huit
q and qu	k as in *kid*	cinq, qui, que
r	no equivalent—the sound is slightly guttural and pronounced at the back of the throat as if gargling	rare, merci, groupe, leur
s between two vowels	z as in *zoom*	rose, musique
t in –tion	s as in *see*	nation, relation
th	t as in *team*	thé, sympathique
x (before vowel)	eg as in *peg*	exact, examen
x (before consonant)	ks as in *excel*	excès, extraordinaire

[9] WEB SITES: A SELECTION OF ADDRESSES ON INTERNET

French Search Engines include:

http://www.yahoo.fr
http://www.google.fr
http://wanadoo.fr/
http://excite.fr/
http://lycos.fr
http://afp.voila.fr
http://francite.com
http://www.msn.fr

French Web sites include:

French online magazines and newspapers:
http://www.lemonde.fr
http://le figaro.fr
http://www.francenet.fr

http://www.liberation.fr
http://www.calvacom.fr
http://www.worldnet.fr
http://www.wunet.fr
http://www.francepress.com
http://www.parismatch.com.fr

French learning programs and exercises
http://www.francepress.com
http://francealacarte.org.uk
http://www.lire-francais.com

French arts, culture, sports, travel, and leisure:
http://www.pariscope.fr
http://www.paris.org
http://www.culture.fr
http://www.francophonie.fr
http://web.culture.fr/
http://www.arts-culinaires.com
http://www.baguette.com/ch

French tourism
http://www.travlang.com
http://www.paris.org/

French-English Vocabulary

The French-English vocabulary is intended to be complete for the context of this book.

Irregular feminine and plural forms are given in full: [**beau** (*f.* **belle**); **œil** (*m.*) (*pl.* **yeux**)], or are indicated by showing the ending that is added to the basic form: [**bon(ne)**; **bateau(x)**], or the ending that replaces the basic form ending: [**généreux (-euse)**; **cheval** (*m.*) (*pl.* **-aux**)]

An asterisk (⋆) indicates an aspirate *h : le haricot.*

ABBREVIATIONS

(*adj.*)	adjective	(*f.*)	feminine
(*adv.*)	adverb	(*m.*)	masculine
(*coll.*)	colloquial	(*m./f.*)	masculine or feminine
(*inf.*)	infinitive	(*pl.*)	plural
	(*p.p.*)	past participle	

à at, to; **à bientôt** see you soon; **à cause de** because of; **à côté (de)** next (to); **à demain** see you tomorrow; **à droite (de)** to the right (of); **à gauche (de)** to the left (of); **à l'avance** in advance; **à l'heure** on time; **à partir de** from; **à peu près** about, approximately; **à pied** on foot; **à tout à l'heure** see you later; **à travers** across, through

abord: d'abord at first

absolument absolutely

académie (*f.*) academy

accepter to accept

accès (*m.*) access

accompagner to accompany

accomplissement (*m.*) accomplishment

accusé(e) accused

acheter to buy

achever to complete, finish

acteur (*m.*) actor

actif (-ive) active

activité (*f.*) activity

actrice (*f.*) actress

admirer to admire

adolescent(e) teen-ager

adorer to adore

aéroport (*m.*) airport

affaire (*f.*) affair; **affaires** (*f. pl.*) business; things

affiche (*f.*) poster

affirmativement affirmatively

africain(e) African

Afrique (*f.*) Africa

âge (*m.*) age

agé old

agent de police (*m.*) police officer

agréable agreeable, nice

aide (*f.*) aid, help

aider to help

aimable friendly, kind

aimer to like, love; **aimer mieux** to prefer

aîné(e) older, oldest

air (*m.*) air; **avoir l'air (de)** to appear, seem; **en plein air** outdoors; **prendre l'air** to get some air

ajouter to add

algèbre (*f.*) algebra

Allemagne (*f.*) Germany

allemand(e) German

aller to go; **aller à la pêche** to go fishing; **aller à pied** to walk, to go on foot; **aller bien** to feel well; **aller en voiture** to go by car; **aller mal** to feel poorly

allumer to light, turn on

alors then, thus, so

amaigrissant reducing

ambitieux (-euse) ambitious

amener to bring; lead to

américain(e) American

ami(e) friend; **petit ami** boyfriend; **petite amie** girlfriend

amitié (*f.*) friendship

amour (*m.*) love

amoureux (-euse) in love; **tomber amoureux** to fall in love

amusant fun, amusing

amusement (*m.*) fun

amuser to amuse; **s'amuser** to have fun

an (*m.*) year; **avoir... ans** to be ... years old

ancien(ne) old, ancient, former

âne (*m.*) donkey

anglais(e) English

Angleterre (*f.*) England

animal (*m.*) (*pl.* **-aux**) animal

animé(e) animated

année (*f.*) year

anniversaire (*m.*) birthday; **bon anniversaire** happy birthday

annonce (*f.*) advertisement; announcement; **petite annonce** classified ad.

annoncer to announce

annuaire (*m.*) phone book

anxieux (-euse) anxious

août (*m.*) August

appareil-photo (*m.*) camera

appartement (*m.*) apartment

appel (*m.*) call

appeler to call; **s'appeler** to be named, call oneself

applaudir to applaud

appliquer to apply; **s'appliquer** to apply oneself

apporter to bring

apprécier appreciate

apprendre (à) (*pp.* **appris**) 'to learn; to teach

approprié(e) appropriate

après after, afterward; **après tout** after all; **d'après** based upon

après-midi (*m.*) afternoon

arbre (*m.*) tree

argent (*m.*) money; silver

armoire (*f.*) wardrobe

arranger to arrange

arrêt (*m.*) stop

arrêter to stop; to arrest; **s'arrêter (de)** to stop

arriver to arrive, to come; to happen

arrondissement (*m.*) administrative district

artichaut (*m.*) artichoke

ascenseur (*m.*) elevator

Asie (*f.*) Asia

asperge (*f.*) asparagus

aspirateur (*m.*) vacuum cleaner; **passer l'aspirateur** to vacuum

assez enough; rather; **assez (de)** enough (of)

assiette (*f.*) plate

assis(e) seated

assister (à) to assist; to attend

astronomique astronomical

attacher to attach

attaquer to attack

attendre to wait (for)

attentif (-ive) attentive

attention (*f.*) attention; **faire attention (à)** to pay attention (to)

attraction (*f.*) attraction; **parc d'attractions** amusement park

au (*pl.* **aux**) at the, to the; **au bas de** at the bottom of; **au contraire** on the contrary; **au fond (de)** in/at the bottom (of); **au haut (de)** in/at the top (of); **au lieu de** instead of; **au milieu de** in the middle of; **au moins** at least; **au rabais** at a discount; **au revoir** goodbye

aujourd'hui today

aussi also, too; as

auteur (*m.*) author

automne (*m.*) fall, autumn

autoriser to authorize

autorité (*f.*) authority

autour (de) around

autre other; another

autrefois formerly

avance (*f.*) advance; **à l'avance** in advance

avancer to advance

avant (de) before

avant-hier the day before yesterday

avec with

aventure (*f.*) adventure

aveugle blind

avion (*m.*) airplane; **en avion** by airplane

avocat(e) lawyer

avoir to have (*pp.* **eu**); **avoir... ans** to be . . . years old; **avoir besoin (de)** to need; **avoir chaud** to be hot (*of persons*); **avoir envie de** to desire, want, feel like; **avoir faim** to be hungry; **avoir froid** to be cold (*of persons*); **avoir honte (de)** to be ashamed (of); **avoir l'air (de)** to appear, seem; **avoir l'habitude de** to be accustomed to, to be in the habit of; **avoir (de) la chance** to be lucky; **avoir le temps (de)** to have the time (to); **avoir mal à** to have an ache in; **avoir peur (de)** to be afraid (of); **avoir raison** to be right; **avoir soif** to be thirsty; **avoir sommeil** to be sleepy; **avoir tort** to be wrong

avril (*m.*) April

bac (*m.*) **baccalauréat** baccalaureate examination / degree

bagages (*m. pl.*) luggage

baguette (*f.*) a long French bread

baigner to bathe

bain (*m.*) bath; **maillot de bain** (*m.*) bathing suit; **salle de bains** (*f.*) bathroom

bal (*m.*) dance

baladeur (*m.*) Walkman

balcon (*m.*) balcony

balle (*f.*) ball

ballon (*m.*) balloon; ball

banane (*f.*) banana

banc (*m.*) seat, bench

bande (*f.*) band, strip; **bande dessinée** comic strip, comic book

banque (*f.*) bank

bas(se) low; **en bas** downstairs; **en bas (de)** at the bottom (of)

bas (*m.*) stocking

basé(e) based

basket (*f.*) basketball sneaker

bateau (*m.*) (*pl.* **-aux**) boat

bâtiment (*m.*) building

bâtir to build

bâton (*m.*) stick, pole; **bâton de craie** stick of chalk

bavarder to chat

beau, bel (*f.* **belle**) beautiful, handsome; **faire beau** to be beautiful (*weather*); **à la belle étoile** outdoors

beaucoup (de) a lot (of), many, much

beauté (*f.*) beauty

bébé (*m.*) baby

besoin (*m.*) need; **avoir besoin de** to need

beurre (*m.*) butter

bibliothèque (*f.*) library

bibliothécaire (*m. / f.*) librarian

bicyclette (*f.*) bicycle; **monter à bicyclette** to go bicycle riding

bien well; **aller bien** to feel well; **bien sûr** of course

bientôt soon; **à bientôt** see you soon

bifteck (*m.*) steak

bijou (*m.*) jewel

billet (*m.*) bill; ticket

biologie (*f.*) biology

bise (*f.*) (*coll*) kiss; **(grosses) bises** lots of love (*in a letter*)

blâmer to blame

blanc(he) white

blanc (*m.*) egg white

bleu(e) blue

bœuf (*m.*) beef

boire (*pp.* **bu**) to drink

bois wood (*m.*)

boisson (*f.*) drink

boîte (*f.*) box, can; **boîte aux lettres** mailbox; **boîte de conserves** can

bol (*m.*) bowl

bon(ne) good; **bon anniversaire** happy birthday; **bon marché** inexpensive; **bonne année** happy new year; **bonne chance** good luck; **de bonne heure** early

bonbon (*m.*) candy
bonheur (*m.*) happiness
bonhomme (*m.*) chap; **bonhomme de neige** snowman
bonjour hello
bord (*m.*) edge; **au bord de la mer** at / to the seashore
botte (*f.*) boot
bouche (*f.*) mouth
boucher (-ère) butcher
boucherie (*f.*) butcher shop
bouger to move
bouillabaisse (*f.*) fish stew
boulanger (-ère) baker
boulangerie (*f.*) bakery
boule (*f.*) ball; **boule de neige** snowball
boum (*f.*) party
bourse (*f.*) scholarship
bouteille (*f.*) bottle
boutique (*f.*) boutique, small store
bras (*m.*) arm
brioche (*f.*) sweet roll
brosse (*f.*) brush; **brosse à dents** tooth brush
brosser to brush; **se brosser** to brush oneself
bruit (*m.*) noise
brun(e) brown, brunette
bureau (*m.*) desk; office; **bureau de poste** (*m.*) post office

ça that; **ça ne fait rien** it doesn't matter
cabine (*f.*) phone booth
cadeau (*m.*) gift, present
cadet(te) younger
cadre (*m.*) setting; frame
café (*m.*) coffee; café
cahier (*m.*) notebook
caissier (-ière) cashier
calculette (*f.*) calculator
calendrier (*m.*) calendar
camarade (*m. / f.*) friend
campagne (*f.*) country
camper to camp
camping: faire du camping to go camping
canapé (*m.*) sofa
cantine (*f.*) cafeteria
car because
car (*m.*) tour bus

caractère (*m.*) character; **caractères gras** boldface
carnaval (*m.*) carnival
carrefour (*m.*) intersection
cartable (*m.*) school bag
carte (*f.*) card; map; **carte d'identité** identification card; **carte de crédit** credit card; **carte postale** postcard
cas (*m.*) case; **en cas de** in case of
case (*f.*) box
casquette (*f.*) cap
casser to break
casserole (*f.*) saucepan
cause (*f.*) cause; **à cause de** because of
ce it, he, she, they; this, that; **ce que** that which, what
céder to yield
cela that
célèbre famous
célébrer to celebrate
cent one hundred
centre (*m.*) center; **centre commercial** shopping mall
cercle (*m.*) club
céréales (*f. pl.*) cereal
cerise (*f.*) cherry
ces these, those
cesser to stop
cet(te) this, that
chacun(e) each one
chaîne: chaîne stéréo (*f.*) stereo; **chaîne de montagnes** mountain range
chaise (*f.*) chair
chambre (à coucher) (*f.*) bedroom
champ (*m.*) field
championnat (*m.*) championship
chance (*f.*) luck; **avoir (de) la chance** to be lucky; **bonne chance** good luck
changer (de) to change
chanson (*f.*) song
chanter to sing
chanteur (-euse) singer
chapeau (*m.*) (*pl. -aux*) hat
chapiteau (*pl. -aux*) circus tent
chapitre (*m.*) chapter
chaque each
charcuterie (*f.*) delicatessen
charmant charming

chat(te) cat
châtain (*m. only*) light brown (hair)
château (*m.*) (*pl. -aux*) castle
chaud warm, hot; **avoir chaud** to be hot (*of persons*); **faire chaud** to be warm / hot (*weather*)
chauffage (*m.*) heating; **chauffage air pulsé** forced air heating
chauffer to heat, warm
chaussette (*f.*) sock
chaussure (*f.*) shoe
chef (*m.*) chef, cook, chief, head
chemin (*m.*) road; **chemin de fer** (*m.*) railroad
cheminée (*f.*) fireplace
chemise (*f.*) shirt
chemisier (*m.*) woman's shirt
chèque (*m.*) check; **chèque de voyage** traveler's check
cher (*f.chère*) dear; expensive
chercher to look for, search
cheval (*m.*) (*pl. -aux*) horse
cheveu (*m.*) (*pl. -eux*) hair (*one strand*)
chez to / at (the house / place of)
chien(ne) dog
chiffre (*m.*) number
chimie (*f.*) chemistry
chimique chemical
chinois(e) Chinese
choisir to choose
choix (*m.*) choice
chose (*f.*) thing
ci-dessous below
cidre (*m.*) cider
ciel (*m.*) heaven, sky
ciné-club (*m.*) film club
cinéma (*m.*) movies
cinq five
cinquante fifty
cinquième fifth
circonstance (*f.*) circumstance
cirque (*m.*) circus
ciseaux (*m. pl.*) scissors
citoyen(ne) citizen
citron (*m.*) lemon
citronnade (*f.*) lemonade
classe (*f.*) classe; **classe de neige** snow class; **salle de classe** classroom (*f.*)

classeur (*m.*) looseleaf notebook
clef (*f.*) key
client(e) client, customer
cloche (*f.*) bell
clown (*m.*) clown; **faire le clown** to clown around
cocher to check
cochon (*m.*) pig
code postal (*m.*) zip code
cœur (*m.*) heart
coiffe (*f.*) headdress
coiffer to do the hair of
coiffeur (-euse) hairdresser
coin (*m.*) corner
collectionner to collect
collège (*m.*) secondary school
coller to paste
collier (*m.*) necklace
colline (*f.*) hill
colonie (*f.*) colony; **colonie de vacances** camp
colonne (*f.*) column
combien (de) how many, much
comédie (*f.*) comedy
comique comical, funny
commande (*f.*) order
commander to order
comme as, like
commencement (*m.*) beginning
commencer to begin
comment how
commercial(e) commercial; **centre commercial** (*m.*) (shopping) mall
commerçant(e) merchant
compagnie (*f.*) company
comparer to compare
complet (-ète) complete
compléter to complete
composer to compose
comprendre (*pp.* **compris**) to understand
compter to count; to intend
conducteur (*f.* **conductrice**) driver
conduire (*pp.* **conduit**) to drive; **permis de conduire** driver's license
confiture (*f.*) jelly, jam
confortable comfortable
congé (*m.*) time off; **jour de congé** day off
congélateur (*m.*) freezer

connaissance (*f.*) acquaintance, knowledge; **faire la connaissance (de)** to make the acquaintance of
connaître (*pp.* **connu**) to know, to be acquainted with
connu known
conscientieux (-euse) conscientious
conseil (*m.*) advice; council
conseiller to advise
conséquent : **par conséquent** consequently
conserves (*f. pl.*) preserves; **boîte de conserve** can
construire (*pp.* **construit**) to construct, build
consulter to consult
contacter to contact
contagieux (-euse) contagious
continuer to continue
contraire (*m.*) opposite; **au contraire** on the contrary
contre against
contribuer to contribute
convenir to fit
copain (*f.* **copine**) friend, pal
copier to copy
corbeille (*f.*) basket; **corbeille à papier** wastebasket
corde (*f.*) cord, rope; **sauter à la corde** to jump rope
cornet (*m.*) cone
corps (*m.*) body
correspondant(e) pen pal
correspondre to correspond; to exchange letters
corriger to correct
costume (*m.*) costume; suit
côte (*f.*) coast
côté (*m.*) side; **à côté (de)** next (to); **de côté** aside; **de l'autre côté** on the other side
cou (*m.*) neck
coucher (*m.*) setting; **coucher de soleil** sunset
coucher to put to bed; **se coucher** to go to bed
coude (*m.*) elbow
couleur (*f.*) color
couloir (*m.*) hallway
coup (*m.*) blow; **coup d'œil** glance; **coup de téléphone**

telephone call; **coup de tonnerre** thunder clap
couper to cut
cour (*f.*) courtyard
courageux (-euse) courageous
courant (*m.*) current
courir (*pp.* **couru**) to run
courrier (*m.*) mail
cours (*m.*) course, subject
course (*f.*) errand; race; **faire des courses** to go shopping
court(e) short
couteau (*m.*) knife
coûter to cost; **coûter cher** to be expensive
couvert(e) covered; **piscine couverte** indoor pool
couvert (*m.*) cover; **mettre le couvert** to set the table
couverture (*f.*) cover
couvrir (*pp.* **couvert**) to couver; **se couvrir** to cover oneself
craie (*f.*) chalk; **bâton de craie** (*m.*) stick of chalk
craquer to crack
cravate (*f.*) tie
crayon (*m.*) pencil
créer to create
crème (*f.*) cream; **crème caramel** (*f.*) caramel custard dessert; **crème solaire** sun-tan creme
crémerie (*f.*) dairy store
crier to shout
criminel(le) criminal
critique (*m.*) critic; (*f.*) review
critiquer to criticize
croire to believe
croisière (*f.*) cruise
croix (*f.*) cross
cueillir to pick (*flowers*)
cuiller (*f.*) spoon
cuir (*m.*) leather
cuisine (*f.*) kitchen; cooking; **faire la cuisine** to cook
cuisiner to cook
cuisinier (-ière) cook; **cuisinière** (*f.*) stove
curieux (-euse) curious
cyclisme (*m.*) cycling

d'abord first, at first
d'accord okay; all right?
d'habitude usually

dangereux (-euse) dangerous
dans, in, into, within
danse (*f.*) dance
danser to dance
davantage more
de of, about, from; **d'abord** at first; **d'après** based upon; **de bonne heure** early; **de côté** aside; **de long en large** back and forth; **de nouveau** again; **de rien** you're welcome; **de temps en temps** from time to time
débarrasser to clear
débat (*m.*) debate
debout standing; up
décembre December
décider to decide
déclarer to declare
décoiffé(e) disheveled
décorateur (-trice) decorator
décorer to decorate
découvrir (*pp.* **découvert**) to discover
décrire (*p.p.* **décrit**) to describe
dedans inside
défendre to defend; to forbid
défi (*m.*) challenge
degré (*m.*) degree
dehors outside
déjà already
déjeuner (*m.*) lunch; **petit déjeuner** breakfast
déjeuner to eat lunch
délicieux (-euse) delicious
demain tomorrow; **à demain** see you tomorrow
demande (*f.*) application
demander to ask (for)
déménager to move (*to another residence*)
demeurer to live, stay
demi(e) half; **demi-heure** (*f.*) half hour
dent (*f.*) tooth; **brosse à dents** tooth brush
dépêcher to dispatch; **se dépêcher** to hurry
dépenser to spend (*money*)
depuis for, since
dérangement (*m.*) trouble
déranger to bother, disturb
dernier (-ière) last
derrière behind

des (some); of the; from the; about the
désastre (*m.*) disaster
descendre to go down; to take down
déshabiller to undress; **se déshabiller** to get undressed
désirer to desire, want
désobéir (à) to disobey
dessin (*m.*) drawing, design; **dessin animé** cartoon
dessiné(e) drawn, designed; **bande dessinée** (*f.*) comic strip, comic book
dessiner to draw
détester to hate
deux two
deuxième second
devant in front (of)
devenir (*pp.* **devenu**) to become
devise (*f.*) motto
devoirs (*m. pl.*) homework
dictionnaire (*m.*) dictionary
difficile difficult
diligent hard working
dimanche (*m.*) Sunday
dîner (*m.*) dinner
dîner to dine, eat dinner
dire (*p.p.* **dit**) to say, tell
directeur (*f.* **directrice**) director, principal
diriger to direct
discuter (de) to discuss
disque (*m.*) record; **disque compact** compact disc, CD; **disque vidéo** laser disc
divan (*m.*) sofa
divers(e) diverse, different
diviser to divide
divisé divided; **divisé par** divided by
dix ten
dix-huit eighteen
dix-neuf nineteen
dix-sept seventeen
docteur (*m.*) doctor
documentaire (*m.*) documentary
doigt (*m.*) finger
donc therefore
donné(e) given
donner to give
dormir to sleep
dortoir (*m.*) dormitory

dos (*m.*) back; **sac à dos** backpack
d'où from where
doucement softly, gently
douche (*f.*) shower
doute (*m.*) doubt; **sans doute** without a doubt
doux (*f.* **douce**) sweet, mild, gentle
douzaine (*f.*) dozen
douze twelve
drame (*m.*) drama
drapeau (*m.*) flag
droit (*m.*) right
droit(e) right; **tout droit** straight ahead
drôle funny; strange
du some, any; of the
dur hard
durer to last
dynamique dynamic

eau(x) (*f.*) water; **eau minérale** mineral water
écharpe (*f.*) scarf
échecs (*m. pl.*) chess
échelle (*f.*) ladder, scale
éclairer to light
école (*f.*) school; **faire l'école buissonnière** to cut classes, play hookey
écouter to listen (to)
écran (*m.*) screen
écrire (*p.p.* **écrit**) to write; **machine à écrire** (*f.*) typewriter
écriture (*f.*) writing
écrivain (*m.*) writer
édifice (*m.*) building
éditeur (*f.* **éditrice**) editor
éducation physique (*f.*) gym
éducatif (-ive) educational
effacer to erase
égal (*pl.* **-aux**) equal
égalité (*f.*) equality
église (*f.*) church
égoïste selfish
élève (*m. / f.*) student
élever to bring up, raise
élire (*p.p.* **élu**) to elect
elle she, it, her,
elles they, them
embarrassé(e) embarrassed
embrasser to kiss

émission (*f.*) program
emmener to take away, lead away
empêcher (de) to prevent (from)
emploi (*m.*) job; **emploi du temps** (*m.*) schedule, program
employé(e) employee
employer to use
emprunter (à) to borrow (from)
en in; to; **en auto** by car; **en avion** by airplane; **en bas** downstairs, **en bas (de)** at the bottom (of); **en cas de** in case of; **en face (de)** opposite; **en haut** upstairs; **en retard** late; **en train de** in the middle of; **en ville** downtown
en about it/them, from it/them, of it/them; from there
encore still, yet, again
encourager to encourage
encre (*f.*) ink
endroit (*m.*) place
énérgie (*f.*) energy
enfant (*m. / f.*) child
enfin at last, finally
enlever to remove, take off
ennemi(e) enemy
ennui (*m.*) boredom, problem
ennuyer to bore; to bother; **s'ennuyer** to become bored
ennuyeux (-euse) annoying, boring
énorme enormous
enseigner to teach
ensemble together
ensuite then
entendre to hear
enterré(e) buried
entier (-ière) entire, whole
entraîneur (*m.*) coach
entre between, among
entrée (*f.*) entrance
entrer to enter, go in
envie (*f.*) desire, want; **avoir envie (de)** to desire, want; to feel like
envoyer to send
épaule (*f.*) shoulder
épeler to spell
épicier (-ière) grocer
épicerie (*f.*) grocery store
époque (*f.*) age, era
épouser to marry
équipe (*f.*) team

erreur (*f.*) error, mistake
escalier (*m.*) staircase
escargot (*m.*) snail
espace (*m.*) space
Espagne (*f.*) Spain
espagnol(e) Spanish
espérer to hope
esprit (*m.*) spirit, mind
essai (*m.*) essay
essayer (de) to try (to)
essence (*f.*) gasoline
essuyer to wipe
est (*m.*) east
estimer to hold in esteem
estomac (*m.*) stomach
et and, plus
étage (*m.*) floor, story
état (*m.*) state; **États-Unis** (*m. pl.*) United States
été (*m.*) summer; **en été** in the summer
étoile (*f.*) star; **à la belle étoile** outdoors
étrange strange
étranger (-ère) foreign; foreigner; **à l'étranger** abroad
être (*p.p.* **été**) to be; **être à** to belong to; **être en train de** to be (doing something)
étude (*f.*) study
étudiant(e) student
étudier to study
européen(ne) European
eux they, them
événement (*m.*) event
examen (*m.*) test
excitation (*f.*) excitement
exemple (*m.*) example; **par exemple** for example
exercice (*m.*) exercise
expérience (*f.*) experience, experiment
explication (*f.*) explanation
expliquer to explain
explorer to explore
exprimer to express
extraordinaire extraordinary

fabriquer to manufacture
fâché angry
facile easy
façon (*f.*) fashion, way, manner; **de cette façon** this way

facteur (-trice) mail carrier
faible weak
faim (*f.*) hunger; **avoir faim** to be hungry
faire (*p.p.* **fait**) to make, do; **faire attention (à)** to pay attention (to); **faire beau** to be beautiful (*weather*); **faire chaud** to be warm / hot (*weather*); **faire de son mieux** to do one's best; **faire des courses** to go shopping; **faire du camping** to go camping; **faire du patin à glace** to go ice skating; **faire du soleil** to be sunny; **faire du sport** to play sports; **faire du vent** to be windy; **faire fortune** to make a fortune; **faire frais** to be cool (*weather*); **faire froid** to be cold (*weather*); **faire (la) connaissance (de)** to make the acquaintance (of); **faire la cuisine** to cook; **faire la vaisselle** to do the dishes; **faire le ménage** to do the housework; **faire mauvais** to be bad (*weather*) **faire partie de** to belong to; **faire plaisir (à)** to please; **faire un voyage** to take a trip; **faire une promenade** to go for a walk
famille (*f.*) family; **en famille** with the family
fanfare (*f.*) band
fatigué(e) tired
faute (*f.*) mistake
fauteuil (*m.*) armchair
faux (*f.* **fausse**) false
favori(te) favorite
félicitations (*f.*) congratulations
femme (*f.*) woman, wife; **femme de ménage** cleaning woman
fenêtre (*f.*) window
férié: jour férié legal holiday
ferme (*f.*) farm
fermer to close
fermier (-ière) farmer
fête (*f.*) feast, holiday, party
feu (*m.*) fire; **feu d'artifice** fireworks
feuille (*f.*) leaf
février (*m.*) February
fidèle faithful

fier (*f.* **fière**) proud
fièvre (*f.*) fever
figure (*f.*) face
fille (*f.*) daughter, girl
fils (*m.*) son; **petit-fils** (*m.*) grandson
fin (*f.*) end
finir to finish
fixé(e) attached
fleur (*f.*) flower
fleuve (*m.*) river
flic (*m.*) cop
fois (*f.*) time (*in a series*); **trois fois** three times
fond (*m.*) bottom; **au fond (de)** at the bottom (of)
football (*m.*) (*coll.* **foot**) soccer; **football américain** (*m.*) football
forêt (*f.*) forest
former to form
formidable great
formulaire (*m.*) form
fort(e) strong; loud (*voice*)
fouetter to whip
four (*m.*) oven
fourchette (*f.*) fork
frais (*f.* **fraîche**) fresh, cool; **faire frais** to be cool (*weather*)
fraise (*f.*) strawberry
franc(he) frank
franc (*m.*) franc
français(e) French
frapper to knock
frère (*m.*) brother
frites (*f. pl.*) French fries
froid (*m.*) cold; **avoir froid** to be cold (*of persons*)
froid(e) cold; **faire froid** to be cold (*weather*)
fromage (*m.*) cheese
fruit (*m.*) fruit; **fruits de mer** (*m. pl.*) seafood
fruiterie (*f.*) fruit store
furieux (-euse) furious

gagner to win; to earn
gant (*m.*) glove
garçon (*m.*) boy; waiter
garder to keep; to take care of
gare (*f.*) train station
gâteau(x) (*m.*) cake; **gâteau au chocolat** chocolate cake
gâter to spoil

gauche left
gaz (*m.*) gas
geler to freeze
généreux (-euse) generous
genre (*m.*) type
gens (*m. pl.*) people
gentil(le) kind, nice
gentillesse (*f.*) kindness
gentiment gently
géographie (*f.*) geography
geste (*m.*) gesture
glace (*f.*) ice; ice cream; mirror
gloire (*f.*) glory
gomme (*f.*) eraser
gorge (*f.*) throat
gosse (*m.*) youngster, kid
goûter to taste
goûter (*m.*) snack
gracieux (-euse) graceful
gradin (*m.*) bleachers
grammaire (*f.*) grammar
gramme (*m.*) gram
grand(e) large, big; tall
grand(e) older (one); grown-up
grand-mère (*f.*) grandmother
grand-parent (*m.*) grandparent
grand-père (*m.*) grandfather
grandir to grow
grec (*f.* **grecque**) Greek
Grèce (*f.*) Greece
grenier (*m.*) attic
grippe (*f.*) flu
gris(e) gray
gronder to scold
gros(se) big; fat; **grosses bises** lots of love
grossir to become fat
guérir to cure
guerre (*f.*) war
guichet (*m.*) ticket window
gymnase (*m.*) gymnasium
gymnastique (*f.*) gym, gymnastics

habiller to dress; **s'habiller** to get dressed
habitant(e) inhabitant
habiter to live (in)
habits (*m. pl.*) clothes
habitude (*f.*) habit; **avoir l'habitude de** to be accustomed to, to be in the habit of; **d'habitude** usually
*****haricot** (*m.*) bean; **haricots verts** (*m. pl.*) string beans

*****haut(e)** high; loud (*voice*); **au haut (de)** in / at the top (of); **en haut** upstairs
herbe (*f.*) grass
heure (*f.*) hour; **une heure** one o'clock; **à l'heure** on time; **à tout à l'heure** see you later; **de bonne heure** early
heureusement fortunately
heureux (-euse) happy
hier yesterday
histoire (*f.*) story, history
historique historical
hiver (*m.*) winter
homme (*m.*) man
honnête honest
honneur (*m.*) honor; **tableau d'honneur** honor roll
*****honte** (*f.*) shame; **avoir honte** to be ashamed
hôpital (*m.*) hospital
horaire (*f.*) schedule
horloge (*f.*) clock
*****hors** outside
*****hors-d'œuvre** (*m.*) appetizer
hôte (*m.*) host
hôtesse (*f.*) hostess
*****huit** eight
humain(e) human
hypermarché (*m.*) large supermarket

ici here
idée (*f.*) idea
identité (*f.*) identity; **carte** (*f.*) **d'identité** identification card
ignorer to ignore
il he, it
il y a there is/are; **il n'y a pas de quoi** you're welcome
île (*f.*) island
illustre famous
ils they
image (*f.*) picture
imaginatif (-ive) imaginative
imaginer to imagine
immeuble (*m.*) apartment building
imperméable (*m.*) raincoat
impressionner to impress
impulsif (-ive) impulsive
indien(ne) Indian
indiquer to indicate
infirmier (-ière) nurse
informations (*f. pl.*) news

informatique (*f.*) computer science
ingénieur (*m.*) engineer
injuste unfair
inscription (*f.*) registration
installer to install
instituteur (**-trice**) teacher
intensité (*f.*) intensity
interdit(e) forbidden, prohibited
intéressant(e) interesting
intéresser to interest
intime intimate
intuitif (-ive) intuitive
inutile useless
inventer to invent
invité(e) guest
inviter to invite
irriter to irritate
itinéraire (*m.*) itinerary

jaloux (-ouse) jealous
jamais never, ever; **jamais de la vie** out of the question; **ne... jamais** never
jambe (*f.*) leg
jambon (*m.*) ham
janvier (*m.*) January
jardin (*m.*) garden
jardinage (*m.*) gardening
jardinier (-ière) gardener
jaune yellow
jaune (*m.*) yolk (*of egg*)
je I
jeter to throw; **se jeter** to empty (*river*)
jeu (*m.*) game; **jeu de cartes** card game
jeudi (*m.*) Thursday
jeune young
jeunesse (*f.*) youth; **jeunesses musicales** (*f. pl.*) musical association
joie (*f.*) joy
joli(e) pretty
jouer to play; **jouer à** to play (*a game / a sport*); **jouer de** to play (*a musical instrument*); **se jouer** to be played
joueur (-euse) player
jour (*m.*) day; **jour de congé** day off; **jour férié** legal holiday
journal (-aux) (*m.*) newspaper; journal
journée (*f.*) day
joyeux (-euse) joyous

juge (*m.*) judge
juillet (*m.*) July
juin (*m.*) June
jumeau(x) (*f.* **jumelle**) twin
jupe (*f.*) skirt
jus (*m.*) juice
jusqu'à until
juste fair; right

karaté (*m.*) karate; **faire du karaté** to do karate
kilogramme (*m.*) kilogram
kilomètre (*m.*) kilometer

la the; her, it
là there
lac (*m.*) lake
laid(e) ugly
laisser to leave
lait (*m.*) milk
laitue (*f.*) lettuce
lancer to throw
langue (*f.*) language
lapin (*m.*) rabbit
lavage (*m.*) wash
laver to wash; **laver la vaisselle** to do the dishes; **machine à laver** washing machine; **se laver** to wash oneself
le the; him, it
leçon (*f.*) lesson
lecture (*f.*) reading
léger (-ère) light (weight)
légume (*m.*) vegetable
lentement slowly
les the; them, to them
lettre (*f.*) letter; **boîte aux lettres** (*f.*) mailbox; **en toutes lettres** in full
leur their; to them
lever to raise, lift; **se lever** to get up
lèvre (*f.*) lip; **rouge à lèvres** (*m.*) lipstick
liberté (*f.*) freedom, liberty
librairie (*f.*) bookstore
libre free
lieu (*m.*) place; **au lieu (de)** instead (of)
ligne (*f.*) line
limite (*f.*) limit
limonade (*f.*) lemon soda
lire (*pp.* **lu**) to read

liste (*f.*) list
lit (*m.*) bed
living (*m.*) living room
livre (*m.*) book
livret (*m.*) booklet
location (*f.*) rental
loi (*f.*) law
loin (de) far (from)
Londres (*m.*) London
long(ue) long; **de long en large** back and forth
longtemps a long time
loterie (*f.*) lottery
louer to rent
loup (*m.*) wolf
lourd(e) heavy
lui he, him, to him, her, to her
lumière (*f.*) light
lundi (*m.*) Monday
lune (*f.*) moon
lunettes (*f. pl.*) eyeglasses; **lunettes de soleil** sunglasses
luxe (*m.*) luxury
luxueux (-euse) luxurious
lycée (*m.*) high school

ma my
machine (*f.*) machine; **machine à écrire** typewriter; **machine à laver** washing machine
madame (*f.*) (*pl.* **mesdames**) Madam, Mrs.
mademoiselle (*f.*) (*pl.* **mesdemoiselles**) Miss
magasin (*m.*) store; **grand magasin** department store
magnétoscope (*m.*) V.C.R.
magnifique magnificent
mai (*m.*) May
maigre thin
maigrir to become thin
maillot (*m.*) jersey; **maillot de bain** bathing suit
main (*f.*) hand
maintenant now
maire (*m.*) mayor
mairie (*f.*) town hall
mais but
maison (*f.*) house; **maison des jeunes et de la culture (M.J.C.)** youth center
maître master; **maître-nageur** (*m.*) lifeguard
maîtresse (*f.*) teacher

mal bad(ly); **aller mal** to feel poorly; **avoir mal à** to have an ache in; **mal de dents** (*m.*) toothache

malade sick

malade (*m. / f.*) patient, sick person

maladie (*f.*) illness, sickness

malgré in spite of

malheureusement unfortunately

malheureux (-euse) unhappy

maman (*f.*) mom

manger to eat

manières (*f. pl.*) manners

mannequin (*m.*) mannequin, model

manquer (de) to be missing, lack

manteau (*m.*) coat

maquiller to apply make-up; **se maquiller** to put on one's make-up

marchandise (*f.*) merchandise

marche (*f.*) walking

marché (*m.*) market; **bon marché** inexpensive

marcher to walk; to work, function

mardi (*m.*) Tuesday

mari (*m.*) husband

marier to marry; **se marier (avec)** to marry

marmite (*f.*) pot

maroquinerie (*f.*) leather (goods) store

marquer to mark

marron (*inv.*) brown

mars (*m.*) March

masque (*m.*) mask

matériel scolaire (*m.*) school supplies

matière (*f.*) subject

matin (*m.*) morning

matinée (*f.*) morning

mauvais(e) bad; **faire mauvais** to be bad (*weather*)

mauve purple

me me, to me

mécanicien(ne) mechanic

méchant(e) naughty, wicked

médecin (*m.*) doctor

médecine (*f.*) medicine

médicament (*m.*) medicine

meilleur(e) best

mélanger to mix

membre (*m.*) member

même same (*adj.*); even (*adv.*)

menacer to threaten

ménage (*m.*) household; **faire le ménage** to do the housework; **femme de ménage** cleaning woman

mener to lead

mensonge (*m.*) lie

mentionner to mention

mer (*f.*) sea; **au bord de la mer** to / on the seashore

merci thank you

mercredi (*m.*) Wednesday

mère (*f.*) mother

merveilleux (-euse) marvelous

mes my

météo (*f.*) weather report

mètre (*m.*) meter

métro (*m.*) subway

mettre (*p.p.* **mis**) to put (on); **mettre la table** to set the table; **mettre le couvert** to set the table; **se mettre à** to begin to; **se mettre en route** to start out

meuble (*m.*) piece of furniture; **meubles** (*m. pl.*) furniture

midi (*m.*) noon; south

mieux better; **aimer mieux** to prefer; **faire de son mieux** to do one's best

milieu (*m.*) center, middle; **au milieu** in the middle

mille (mil *in dates*) (one) thousand

milliard (*m.*) billion

mince skinny

minuit (*m.*) midnight

miroir (*m.*) mirror

mobylette (*f.*) moped

modèle (*m.*) model

moi I, me

moins less, minus; **au moins** at least; **moins (de)** less, fewer

mois (*m.*) month

mon my

monde (*m.*) world; **tout le monde** everybody; **faire le tour du monde** to go around the world

monsieur (*m.*) (*pl.* **messieurs**) sir, gentleman, Mr.

montagne (*f.*) mountain

monter to go up, climb; to carry up; **monter à bicyclette** to go bicycle riding

montre (*f.*) watch

montrer to show

morceau (*m.*) piece

mort(e) dead

mot (*m.*) word

moteur (*m.*) motor

motocyclette (*f.*) motorcycle

mouchoir (*m.*) handkerchief

mourir (*p.p.* **mort**) to die

mousquetaire (*m.*) musketeer

mouton (*m.*) sheep

moyen (*m.*) means; **moyen de transport** means of transportation

mur (*m.*) wall

musée (*m.*) museum

musical musical; **jeunesses musicales** (*f. pl.*) musical association

musique (*f.*) music; **musique rock** rock music

n'est-ce pas? isn't that so?

nager to swim

naïf, naïve naïve

naissance (*f.*) birth

naître (*p.p.* **né**) to be born

natation (*f.*) swimming

nationalité (*f.*) nationality

naturel(le) natural

nautique nautical; **ski nautique** (*m.*) water skiing

ne... jamais never; **ne... pas** not; **ne... personne** nobody, no one; **ne... plus** no longer, no more, anymore; **ne... rien** nothing

nécessaire necessary

négatif (-ive) negative

négliger to neglect

neige (*f.*) snow; **bonhomme de neige** (*m.*) snowman; **boule de neige** (*f.*) snowball **classe de neige** (*f.*) snow class

neiger to snow

nerveux (-euse) nervous

nettoyage (*m.*) cleaning

nettoyer to clean

neuf (*f.* **neuve**) new

neuf nine

neveu(x) (*m.*) nephew

nez (*m.*) nose

noir(e) black; **noir** (*m.*) darkness

nom (*m.*) name

non no

nord (*m.*) north

nos our
note (*f.*) note, grade
noter to note
notre our
nous we, us, to us
nouveau, nouvel (*f.***nouvelle**) new; **de nouveau** again
nouvelles (*f. pl.*) news
novembre (*m.*) November
nuage (*m.*) cloud
nuit (*f.*) night; **table de nuit** (*f.*) night table
numéro (*m.*) number; **numéro de téléphone** telephone number

obéir (à) to obey
objet (*m.*) object
obligatoire compulsory
obliger to oblige, compel
observer to observe
occasion (*f.*) occasion, opportunity
occupé(e) busy
octobre (*m.*) October
œil (*m.*) (*pl.* **yeux**) eye; **coup d'œil** (*m.*) glance
œuf (*m.*) egg
œuvre (*f.*) work
officiel(le) official
offrir (*pp.* **offert**) to offer
oignon (*m.*) onion
oiseau(x) (*m.*) bird
on one, we, you, they, people (*in general*)
oncle (*m.*) uncle
ongle (*m.*) nail
onze eleven
opérateur (-trice) operator
optimiste optimistic
orangeade (*f.*) orange soda
ordinaire ordinary
ordinateur (*m.*) computer
ordonner to order
ordre (*m.*) order
ordures (*f. pl.*) garbage
oreille (*f.*) ear
organiser to organize
orteil (*m.*) toe
orthographe (*f.*) spelling
ôter to remove, take off
ou or
où where
oublier to forget
ouest (*m.*) west

oui yes
ours (*m.*) bear
ouvrier (-ière) factory worker
ouvrir (*p.p.* **ouvert**) to open

page (*f.*) page
pain (*m.*) bread; **pain grillé** toast
paire (*f.*) pair
paix (*f.*) peace
palais (*m.*) palace
pantalon (*m.*) pants
papier (*m.*) paper
paquet (*m.*) package
par by, through, per; **par conséquent** consequently; **par exemple** for example; **par jour** per day; **par rapport à** with regard to; **par terre** on the ground
parapluie (*m.*) umbrella
parc (*m.*) park; parking; **parc d'attractions** amusement park
parce que because
pardessus (*m.*) overcoat
pardonner to forgive, excuse
paresseux (-euse) lazy
parfait(e) perfect
parfois sometimes
parfum (*m.*) perfume
parfumer to perfume; **se parfumer** to put perfume on
parfumerie (*f.*) perfume shop
parisien(ne) Parisian
parler to speak
partager to share, divide
participant(e) participant
participer (à) to participate (in)
partie (*f.*) part; **faire partie de** to belong to
partir to leave, go away; **à partir de** from
partout everywhere
pas not; **pas du tout** not at all; **pas encore** not yet; **ne... pas** not
passé(e) past; **l'année passée** last year
passer to pass; to spend (*time*); **passer l'aspirateur** to vacuum; **passer un examen** to take a test; **se passer** to happen
passionner to interest passionately
patin (*m.*) skate; **patin à glace** ice skate, ice skating; **faire du patin à glace** to go ice skating

patiner to skate
pâtisserie (*f.*) pastry; pastry shop
pâtissier (-ière) pastry maker
patron(ne) boss; patron saint
patte (*f.*) paw
pauvre poor
payer to pay (for)
pays (*m.*) country
paysage (*m.*) countryside; landscape
paysan(ne) peasant
peau (*f.*) skin
pêche (*f.*) peach
pêche (*f.*) fishing; **aller à la pêche** to go fishing
pêcher to fish
pédaler to pedal
peigne (*m.*) comb
peigner to comb; **se peigner** to comb one's hair
peindre (*pp.* **peint**) to paint
peintre (*m.*) painter
pelouse (*f.*) lawn
pendant during; **pendant que** while
penderie (*f.*) closet
pendule (*f.*) clock
penser to think; to intend
perdre to lose; **perdre son temps** to waste one's time
père (*m.*) father
perfectionné(e) perfected, improved
perfectionner to improve
perle (*f.*) pearl
permettre (*p.p.* **permis**) to allow, permit
permis (*m.*) permit; **permis de conduire** driver's license
permission (*f.*) pass; permission
personne (*f.*) person
personne (ne) nobody, no one; **ne... personne** nobody, no one
personnel(le) personal
peser to weigh
petit(e) little, small; **petit ami** (*m.*) boyfriend; **petite amie** (*f.*) girlfriend; **petit-fils** (*m.*) grandson; **petit déjeuner** (*m.*) breakfast; **petits pois** (*m. pl.*) peas
peu (de) little, few; **à peu près** about, approximately; **un peu** a little
peuple (*m.*) people

peur (*f.*) fear; **avoir peur de** to be afraid of

peut-être perhaps, maybe

pharmacie (*f.*) pharmacy, drug store

physique (*f.*) physics

pièce (*f.*) play

pied (*m.*) foot; **aller à pied** to walk, go on foot

piscine (*f.*) swimming pool; **piscine couverte** indoor pool

placard (*m.*) cabinet, cupboard

place (*f.*) seat, place, square

placer to place, set

plafond (*m.*) ceiling

plage (*f.*) beach

plaisir (*m.*) pleasure; **faire plaisir (à)** to please

planche (*f.*) board; **planche à voile** surfboard

plancher (*m.*) floor

plante (*f.*) plant; **plante verte** potted plant

plastique (*m.*) plastic

plat (*m.*) dish

plein(e) full; **en plein air** outdoors

pleurer to cry

pleuvoir (*p.p.* **plu**) to rain

plonger to plunge, dive

pluie (*f.*) rain

plus (de) more; **plus tard** later; **ne... plus** no longer, no more, anymore

plusieurs several

pneu (*m.*) tire

poche (*f.*) pocket

poésie (*f.*) poetry

point (*m.*) point; period; **point de vue** point of view

poire (*f.*) pear

poisson (*m.*) fish

poissonnerie (*f.*) fish store

poitrine (*f.*) chest

poivre (*m.*) pepper

poli(e) polite

policier (-ière) police

pomme (*f.*) apple

pomme de terre (*f.*) potato

pont (*m.*) bridge

populaire popular

porte (*f.*) door, gate

portefeuille (*m.*) wallet

porter to carry; to wear

poser to place; to ask (*questions*)

posséder to possess, own

poste (*f.*) poste office; **bureau de poste** (*m.*) post office

poster (*m.*) poster

potage (*m.*) soup

poule (*f.*) chicken

poulet (*m.*) chicken

poupée (*f.*) doll

pour for, in order to

pourquoi why

pousser to push; to grow; **pousser un soupir de soulagement** to breathe a sigh of relief

pouvoir (*p.p.* **pu**) to be able to, can

pratique practical

pratiquer to practice

précieux (-euse) precious, important

précis(e) precise; **à deux heures précises** at two o'clock exactly

préférer to prefer

premier (-ière) first; **premier ministre** (*m.*) prime minister

prendre (*p.p.* **pris**) to take; **prendre soin** to take care

préparatifs (*m. pl.*) preparations

préparer to prepare; **se préparer** to prepare oneself

près (de) near; **à peu près** about, approximately

présenter to introduce; to offer

pressé(e) in a hurry

prêt(e) ready

prétendre to claim

prêter to lend

printemps (*m.*) spring

privé(e) private

prix (*m.*) prize; price

prochain(e) next

proche nearby

produit (*m.*) product

professeur (*m.*) (*coll.* **prof**) teacher

programmeur (-euse) programmer

progrès (*m.*) progress

projet (*m.*) project

promenade (*f.*) walk; **faire une promenade** to go for a walk

promener to walk; **se promener** to take a walk

prononcer to pronounce; to declare

propriétaire (*m.*) owner

protéger to protect

prudemment prudently

prudence (*f.*) prudence, wisdom

prune (*f.*) plum

public (*m.*) public, audience

publicité (*f.*) publicity

publier to publish

puis then

puisque since

pull (*m.*) pullover sweater

punir to punish

pupitre (*m.*) pupil's desk

qualité (*f.*) quality

quand when

quarante forty

quart (*m.*) quarter

quartier (*m.*) neighborhood

quatorze fourteen

quatre four

quatre-vingt-dix ninety

quatre-vingts eighty

quatrième fourth

que that, whom, which; what; than; **ce que** that which, what; **qu'est-ce que** what

quel(le) what, which; what a

quelque some; **quelques** (*m/f. pl.*) a few, some

quelqu'un someone

quelque chose something

quelquefois sometimes

querelle (*f.*) quarrel

qui who, whom, which, that

quinze fifteen

quitter to leave

quoi what; **(il n'y a) pas de quoi** you're welcome

rabais (*m.*) discount; **au rabais** at a discount

raconter to tell; to describe

rafraîchissement (*m.*) refreshment

ragoût (*m.*) stew

raisin (*m.*) grape

raison (*f.*) reason; **avoir raison** to be right

ramasser to pick up

ramener to bring back

rang (*m.*) row

ranger to put away; to put in order, straighten, arrange, tidy

rappeler to recall; **se rappeler** to remember

rapport (*m.*) report; **par rapport à** with regard to

raquette (*f.*) racket

raser to shave; **se raser** to shave (oneself)

rasoir (*m.*) razor

rassurer to reassure

réception (*f.*) receipt

recette (*f.*) recipe

recevoir (*p.p.* **reçu**) to receive

recherche (*f.*) search

recommander to recommend

récompense (*f.*) reward

refaire to redo

refermer to close again

réfléchir to reflect, think

réfrigérateur (*m.*) refrigerator

refuser (de) to refuse (to)

regarder to look at, watch

régime (*m.*) diet

régle (*f.*) ruler

réglement (*m.*) rules

régler to set

regret (*m.*) regret, sorrow

regretter (de) to regret (to)

regulièrement regularly

reine (*f.*) queen

remarquable remarkable

remercier to thank

remettre (*p.p.* **remis**) to put back; to deliver

remplacer to replace

remplir to fill

rencontrer to meet

rendre to give back, return; **rendre visite (à)** to visit

renoncer (à) to give up, renounce

renseignements (*m. pl.*) information

rentrée (*f.*) return; **rentrée scolaire** return to school

rentrer to return

renvoyer to send back; to fire

réparer to repair

repas (*m.*) meal

répéter to repeat

répondre (à) to answer

réponse (*f.*) answer

reposer to rest; **se reposer** to rest, relax

représenter to represent

résoudre to solve, resolve

respecter to respect

responsabilité (*f.*) responsibility

ressembler (à) to resemble; **se ressembler** to look alike

rester to remain, stay

résultat (*m.*) result

retard (*m.*) lateness; **en retard** late

retourner to return

retraite (*f.*) retirement; retreat

réussir (à) to succeed (in)

réveil (*m.*) alarm clock

réveiller to awaken; **se réveiller** to wake up

revenir (*p.p.* **revenu**) to come back

rêver (de) to dream (of)

revoir (*p.p.* **revu**) to see again; **au revoir** goodbye

revue (*f.*) magazine

rez-de-chaussée (*m.*) ground floor

rhume (*m.*) cold

rideau(x) (*m.*) curtain

rien (ne) nothing; **de rien** you're welcome; **ne... rien** nothing

rire to laugh

rive (*f.*) bank

robe (*f.*) dress

roi (*m.*) king

roman (*m.*) novel; **roman policier** detective story

rompre to break

ronde (*f.*) round; ring-around-a-rosy

rose pink

rôtir to roast

roue (*f.*) wheel

rouge (*m.*) red; **rouge à lèvres** lipstick

rougir to blush

rouler to roll along

route (*f.*) road, route; **en route** on the way; **se mettre en route** to start out

roux (*f.* **rousse**) red (hair)

rue (*f.*) street

russe Russian

sa his, her

sable (*m.*) sand

sac (*m.*) bag, sack, pocketbook; **sac à dos** backpack

sage wise; well-behaved

saisir to seize, grab

saison (*f.*) season

sale dirty

salle (*f.*) room; **salle à manger** dining room; **salle de bains** bathroom; **salle de classe** classroom; **salle de séjour** living room

salon (*m.*) living room; lounge

salut hi

samedi (*m.*) Saturday

sandale (*f.*) sandal

sans without; **sans doute** without a doubt

santé (*f.*) health

satire (*f.*) satire

saucisse (*f.*) sausage

saucisson (*m.*) dry sausage

sauter to jump; **sauter à la corde** to jump rope

sauvage savage

sauver to save

savoir (*p.p.* **su**) to know (how to)

savon (*m.*) soap

scolaire school; **matériel** (*m.*) **scolaire** school supplies; **rentrée** (*f.*) **scolaire** return to school

scotch (*m.*) scotch tape

se (to) himself, (to) herself, (to) oneself, (to) themselves

secondaire secondary

secrétaire (*m. / f.*) secretary

seize sixteen

séjour (*m.*) stay; family room; **salle de séjour** (*f.*) family room

sel (*m.*) salt

selon according to

semaine (*f.*) week

semestre (*m.*) semester

séparer to separate

sept seven

septembre (*m.*) September

série (*f.*) series

sérieux (-euse) serious

serveur (*m.*) waiter

service (*m.*) service

serviette (*f.*) briefcase; napkin

servir (de) to serve (as)

ses his, her

seul(e) only, single, alone

seulement only

short (*m.*) shorts

si if; yes; so

siècle (*m.*) century

s'il te plaît please

s'il vous plaît please

situé(e) situated

six six

sixième sixth

ski (*m.*) ski; **ski nautique** water skiing; **faire du ski** to go skiing

société (*f.*) company; society

sœur (*f.*) sister

soie (*f.*) silk

soif (*f.*) thirst; **avoir soif** to be thirsty

soin (*m.*) care; **prendre soin (de)** to take care (of)

soir (*m.*) evening

soirée (*f.*) evening

soixante sixty

soixante-dix seventy

solaire sun

soleil (*m.*) sun; **coucher de soleil** (*m.*) sunset; **lunettes de soleil** (*f.*) sunglasses; **faire du soleil** to be sunny

somme (*f.*) sum

sommeil (*m.*) sleep; **avoir sommeil** to be sleepy

son his, her

son (*m.*) sound

songer (à) to think (of)

sonner to ring

sorte (*f.*) sort, type

sortir to go out

souhaiter to wish

soulagement (*m.*) relief

soulier (*m.*) shoe

soupir (*m.*) sigh; **pousser un soupir de soulagement** to breathe a sigh of relief

souris (*f.*) mouse

sous under

sous-sol (*m.*) basement

souvent often

spécialité (*f.*) specialty

spectacle (*m.*) show

splendide splendid

sportif (ive) sports, sporty

stade (*m.*) stadium

store (*m.*) shade, blind

studieux (-euse) studious

stylo (*m.*) pen

succès (*m.*) success

sucre (*m.*) sugar

sud (*m.*) south

sud-américain(e) south American

suggérer to suggest

suivant(e) following

suivre (*p.p.* **suivi**) to follow

sujet (*m.*) subject; **au sujet de** about

supermarché (*m.*) supermarket

superstitieux (-euse) superstitious

sur on, upon

sûr(e) sure; **bien sûr** of course

sur on

surtout especially

survêtement (*m.*) warm-up suit

sympathique likable, nice

ta your

table (*f.*) table; **table de nuit** night table; **mettre la table** to set the table

tableau (*m.*) chalkboard; painting; **tableau d'honneur** honor roll

tailleur (*m.*) woman's suit

tant so much / many; **tant pis** too bad

tante (*f.*) aunt

tapis (*m.*) rug

tard late; **plus tard** later

tarif (*m.*) rate

tarte (*f.*) pie

tasse (*f.*) cup

te you, to you

technologie (*f.*) technology

tel(le) such

téléphone (*m.*) telephone; **au téléphone** on the telephone; **coup de téléphone** telephone call; **numéro de téléphone** telephone number

téléphoner to phone

tellement so

temps (*m.*) time; weather; **emploi** (*m.*) **du temps** schedule, program; **de temps en temps** from time to time; **perdre son temps** to waste one's time; **tout le temps** all the time

tente (*f.*) tent

terminer to end

terrasse (*f.*) terrace

terre (*f.*) earth, land; **par terre** on the ground

tes your

tête (*f.*) head

thé (*m.*) tea

thon (*m.*) tunafish

tigre (*m.*) tiger

timbre (*m.*) stamp

timide shy

tirage (*m.*) drawing

tiroir (*m.*) drawer

toi you

toilettes (*f. pl.*) toilet

toit (*m.*) roof

tomate (*f.*) tomato

tomber to fall; **tomber amoureux** to fall in love

ton your

tondre to mow

tonnerre (*m.*) thunder; **coup de tonnerre** (*m.*) thunder clap

tort (*m.*) error; **avoir tort** to be wrong

tôt early; soon

toucher to touch; **toucher un chèque** to cash a check

toujours always, still

tour (*m.*) tour; **faire le tour du monde** to go around the world

tour (*f.*) tower

touriste (*m. / f.*) tourist

tourner to turn

tout everything; quite, entirely; **à tout à l'heure** see you later; **après tout** after all; **tout à coup** suddenly; **tout à fait** entirely; **tout d'un coup** suddenly; **tout de suite** immediately; **tout droit** straight ahead

tout(e) (*m. pl.* **tous**) all; every; **tous les jours** every day; **tout le monde** everybody; **tout le temps** all the time

toux (*f.*) cough

traduit(e) translated

trahir to betray

train (*m.*) train; **être en train de** to be in the process of (do)ing

traiter to treat

tranquille tranquil, calm

transformer to transform

transport (*m.*) transportation; **moyen de transport** (*m.*) means of transportation

travail (*m.*) (*pl.* **-aux**) work; **travaux ménagers** housework

travailler to work

travers: **à travers** across, through

traverser to cross

treize thirteen
trente thirty
très very
triste sad
trois three
trop (de) too; too many, too much
trottoir (*m.*) sidewalk
trousse (*f.*) pencil case
trouver to find; **se trouver** to be (found)
tu you (*fam.*)
typique typical

un(e) a, an, one
unité (*f.*) unit
université (*f.*) university
usé(e) worn
utile useful
utiliser to use

va (*inf.* **aller**)
vacances (*f. pl.*). vacation; **colonie de vacances** (*f.*) camp
vache (*f.*) cow
vaisselle (*f.*) dishes; **faire, laver la vaisselle** to do the dishes
valise (*f.*) suitcase
vallée (*f.*) valley
vanille (*f.*) vanilla
vaporisateur (*m.*) atomizer
veau (*m.*) veal
vélo (*m.*) bicycle
vendeur (-euse) salesperson

vendre to sell
vendredi (*m.*) Friday
venir (*p.p.* **venu**) to come
vent (*m.*) wind; **faire du vent** to be windy
ventre (*m.*) stomach
verité (*f.*) truth
verre (*m.*) glass
vers towards
vert(e) green; **haricots verts** (*m. pl.*) string beans; **plante verte** potted plant
veste (*f.*) jacket
vêtements (*m.pl.*) clothes; **vêtements sport** sport clothes
vêtu(e) dressed
viande (*f.*) meat
vide empty
vie (*f.*) life
vieux, vieil, (*f.* vieille) old
vif (*f.***vive**) lively
ville (*f.*) city; **en ville** downtown
vin (*m.*) wine
vingt twenty
violon (*m.*) violin
virgule (*f.*) comma; point
visage (*m.*) face
visiter to visit
vite rapidly, quickly
vivre (*p.p.* **vécu**) to live
vocabulaire (*m.*) vocabulary
vœu (*m.*) (*pl.* **vœux**) vow, wish
voici here!, here is / are

voie (*f.*) track
voilà there!, there is / are
voir (*p.p.* **vu**) to see
voisin(e) neighbor
voiture (*f.*) car; **voiture de sport** sports car; **aller en voiture** to go by car
voix (*f.*) voice; **à haute voix / à voix haute** out loud; **à voix basse** in a low voice
vol (*m.*) flight
voler to fly
voleur (*m.*) robber
vos your
vote (*m.*) vote
voter to vote
votre your
vouloir (*p.p.* **voulu**) to want
vous you, to you
voyage (*m.*) trip, voyage; **chèque de voyage** traveler's check; **faire un voyage** to take a trip
voyager to travel
vrai(e) true
vraiment truly, really
vue (*f.*) view

y to it/them, in it/them, on it/them; there; **il y a** there is
yeux (*m. pl*) eyes
yogourt (*m.*) yogurt

English–French Vocabulary

The English-French vocabulary includes words that might be needed for exercises requiring students to answer in their own words and is intended to be complete for the context of this book.

Irregular feminine and plural forms are given in full : [beau (*f.* belle); œil (*m.*) (*pl.* yeux)], or are indicated by showing the ending that is added to the basic form : [bon(ne); bateau(x)], or the ending that replaces the basic form ending : [généreux (–euse); cheval (*m.*) (*pl.* –aux)]

ABBREVIATIONS

(*adj.*)	adjective	(*inv.*)	invariable
(*adv.*)	adverb	(*m.*)	masculine
(*f.*)	feminine	(*pl.*)	plural

able: to be able pouvoir
accept accepter
act acte (*m.*)
active actif (-ive)
actress actrice (*f.*)
add ajouter
address adresse (*f.*)
admire admirer
adore adorer
advance avance (*f.*); **in advance** à l'avance
advertisement annonce (*f.*)
afraid: be afraid avoir peur
after après
afternoon après-midi (*m.*)
afterwards après
again encore une fois
age âge (*m.*)
airplane avion (*m.*)
all tout(e) (*m. pl.* tous); **all the time** tout le temps
almost presque
alone seul(e)
along le long de
also aussi
always toujours
A.M. du matin
ambitious ambitieux (-euse)
American américain
amusing amusant(e)
and et
angry fâché(e)
animal animal (*m.*)(*pl.* -aux)
another un autre (*m.*)
answer répondre (à); réponse (*f.*)
any de
anymore ne... plus
anything ne... rien

apartment appartement (*m.*)
apple pomme (*f.*); **apple pie** tarte aux pommes (*f.*)
April avril (*m.*)
arm bras (*m.*)
around autour (de)
arrange arranger
arrive arriver
artiste (*m./f.*) artist
ask (for) demander
at à; **at home** à la maison
attention attention (*f.*); **pay attention** faire attention
attentively attentivement
August août (*m.*)
aunt tante (*f.*)
autumn automne (*m.*)

back dos (*m.*)
backpack sac à dos (*m.*)
bad mauvais(e)
bag sac (*m.*)
baker boulanger (-ère); pâtissier (-ière)
bakery boulangerie (*f.*), pâtisserie (*f.*)
balcony balcon (*m.*)
bank banque (*f.*); rive (*f.*)
basement sous-sol (*m.*)
basketball basket(ball) (*m.*)
bathing suit maillot de bain (*m.*)
bathroom salle de bains (*f.*)
be être; **to be . . . years old** avoir... ans
beach plage (*f.*)
beautiful beau, bel (*f.* belle)
because car, parce que

become devenir; **become fat** grossir
bed lit (*m.*); **to go to bed** se coucher
bedroom chambre (à coucher) (*f.*)
before avant (de)
beginning commencement (*m.*)
behind derrière
bell cloche (*f.*)
between entre
bicycle / bike bicyclette (*f.*), vélo (*m.*)
big grand(e), gros(se)
bird oiseau(x) (*m.*)
black noir(e)
blue bleu(e)
blush rougir
board tableau(x) (*m.*)
boat bateau(x) (*m.*)
book livre (*m.*)
bookstore librairie (*f.*)
boot botte (*f.*)
bore ennuyer; **to get bored** s'ennuyer
borrow emprunter
bother ennuyer, gêner
bottle bouteille (*f.*)
box boîte (*f.*)
boy garçon (*m.*)
bracelet bracelet (*m.*)
bread pain (*m.*)
break rompre, casser
breakfast petit déjeuner (*m.*)
brilliant brillant(e)
bring apporter
brother frère (*m.*)
brush brosser; **brush (oneself)** se brosser

build bâtir
bus bus (*m.*), autobus (*m.*)
but mais
butcher boucher (*-ère*); **butcher shop** boucherie (*f.*)
butter beurre (*m.*)
buy acheter
by par; **by bus** en bus

cake gâteau(x) (*m.*)
calendar calendrier (*m.*)
call appeler; téléphoner (à)
camp camper
can pouvoir
Canadian canadien(ne)
candy bonbon (*m.*)
car voiture (*f.*)
card carte (*f.*); **postcard** carte postale (*f.*)
carrot carotte (*f.*)
cardboard carton (*m.*)
cassette cassette (*f.*)
castle château (*m.*)
cat chat (*m.*)
cathedral cathédrale (*f.*)
ceiling plafond (*m.*)
celebration fête (*f.*)
centimeter centimètre (*m.*)
certain certain(e), sûr(e)
chair chaise (*f.*)
chalk craie (*f.*)
change changer; **change one's mind** changer d'avis
charming charmant(e)
chat bavarder
cheap bon marché
cheese fromage (*m.*)
chicken poulet (*m.*)
child enfant (*m. / f.*)
China Chine (*f.*)
chocolate chocolat (*m.*); **chocolate mousse** mousse au chocolat (*f.*); **chocolate cake** gâteau au chocolat (*m.*)
choose choisir
church église (*f.*)
city ville (*f.*)
class classe (*f.*)
clean nettoyer
climate climat (*m.*)
clock horloge (*f.*), pendule (*f.*)
close fermer
closet penderie (*f.*)

clothes vêtements (*m. pl.*)
club (*m.*) club; **film club** ciné-club
cold froid; **to be cold** (*person*) avoir froid; **to be cold** (*weather*) faire froid
come venir
comfortable confortable
compact disc disque compact (*m.*); compact (*m.*) CD (*inv.*)
concert concert (*m.*); **rock concert** concert de rock
cook cuisiner, faire la cuisine
cookie biscuit (*m.*)
country campagne (*f.*); pays (*m.*)
courageous courageux (*-euse*)
courageously courageusement
course cours (*m.*) ; **of course** bien sûr
cousin cousin(e)
cow vache (*f.*)
criticize critiquer
cross croix (*f.*)
cruel cruel(le)
cry pleurer
cup tasse (*f.*)
cure guérir

dance danser
daughter fille (*f.*)
day jour (*m.*); journée (*f.*)
December décembre (*m.*)
decide décider (de)
defend défendre
delicious délicieux (*-ieuse*)
descend descendre
desk bureau (*m.*), **pupil's desk** pupitre (*m.*)
dessert dessert (*m.*)
dictionary dictionnaire (*m.*)
die mourir
different différent(e)
difficult difficile
dining room salle à manger (*f.*)
dinner dîner (*m.*); **eat/have dinner** dîner
disobey désobéir
dive plonger
do faire
doctor docteur (*m.*), médecin (*m.*)
dog chien (*m.*)
donkey âne (*m.*)
door porte (*f.*)

down: go down descendre
downtown en ville
dozen douzaine (*f.*)
dress habiller; **dress (oneself)** s'habiller
dress robe (*f.*)
during pendant

each chaque
ear oreille (*f.*)
easy facile
eat manger; **eat dinner** dîner
egg œuf (*m.*)
eight huit
eighteen dix-huit
eighty quatre-vingts
eleven onze
empty vider
encourage encourager
end fin (*f.*)
ending fin (*f.*)
enemy ennemi (*m.*)
England Angleterre (*f.*)
English anglais (*m.*)
enter entrer
entire entier (*-ière*)
entrance entrée (*f.*)
equals font
eraser gomme (*f.*); brosse/éponge à effacer (*f.*)
Europe Europe (*f.*)
evening soir (*m.*)
ever (ne...) jamais
every chaque; tout (tous, toute, toutes); **every day** tous les jours
everybody tout le monde (*m.*)
everyone tout le monde (*m.*)
everything tout (*m.*)
exchange échanger; **exchange letters** correspondre
expensive cher (*f.* chère)
explain expliquer
eye œil (*m.*) (*pl* yeux)

face figure (*f.*), visage (*m.*)
false faux (*f.* fausse)
family famille (*f.*)
famous célèbre
far loin (de)
farmer fermier (*f.* fermière)
fast vite, rapidement
fat gros(se); **become fat** grossir
favorite favori(te), préféré(e)

fear peur (*f.*)
February février (*m.*)
field champ (*m.*)
fifteen quinze
fifty cinquante
fill remplir
find trouver
finger doigt (*m.*)
finish finir, achever, terminer
fire feu (*m.*)
fireplace cheminée (*f.*)
first premier (-ière)
fish pêcher, aller à la pêche
fish poisson (*m.*)
five cinq
flight vol (*m.*)
floor plancher (*m.*)
flower fleur (*f.*)
food nourriture (*f.*), aliments (*m. pl.*)
foot pied (*m.*)
football football américain (*m.*)
for pour
forget oublier
fortunately heureusement
forty quarante
four quatre
fourteen quatorze
frank franc(he)
French français(e)
Friday vendredi (*m.*)
friend ami(e) (*m.*), copain (*m.*) (*f.* copine), camarade (*m. / f.*)
friendly amical(e) (*m.pl.* –aux), aimable
from de
front: in front (of) devant
fruit fruit (*m.*); **fruit store** fruiterie (*f.*)
full plein
fun: have fun s'amuser
funny drôle, comique, amusant

game match (*m.*)
garbage ordures (*f. pl.*)
garden jardin (*m.*)
gas(oline) essence (*f.*); **gas station** station service (*f.*)
generally généralement, d'habitude
generous généreux (-euse)
gently doucement
get up se lever
gift cadeau (*m.*) (*pl.* –x)
girl fille (*f.*)

girlfriend petite amie (*f.*)
give donner
glass verre (*m.*)
glasses lunettes (*f. pl.*)
go aller; **go back (home)** rentrer; **go down** descendre; **go out** sortir
golf golf (*m.*) **golf club** club de golf
good bon(ne); **have a good time** s'amuser
good-bye au revoir
grandfather grand-père (*m.*)
grandmother grand-mère (*f.*)
grandparents grands-parents (*m. pl.*)
great formidable, super
grow grandir
guard garder
guitar guitare (*f.*)

hair cheveux (*m. pl.*)
half demi(e)
hallway couloir (*m.*)
ham jambon (*m.*)
handsome beau, bel (*f.* belle)
happy content, heureux (-euse)
hat chapeau (*m.*)
have avoir
he il, lui
head tête (*f.*)
hear entendre
heavy lourd(e)
help aider
her la, lui; son, sa, ses
here ici; **here is, here are** voici
high haut
his son, sa, ses
history histoire (*f.*)
home maison (*f.*); **(at) home** à la maison; **at the home of** chez
homework devoirs (*m.pl.*); **do homework** faire les devoirs
honest honnête
hope espérer
horse cheval (*m.*) (*pl.* chevaux)
hot chaud(e); **to be hot** (*person*) avoir chaud; **to be hot** (*weather*) faire chaud
hotel hôtel (*m.*)
hour heure (*f.*)
house maison (*f.*)
how comment; **how much, many** combien (de)
huge énorme

hundred cent
hurry (up) se dépêcher

I je, moi
ice cream glace (*f.*)
ice skating patin à glace (*m*); **go ice skating** faire du patin à glace
idea idée (*f.*)
if si
imaginative imaginatif (-ive)
immediately immédiatement, tout de suite
in dans, en, à
inexpensive bon marché
instead (of) au lieu (de)
intend compter
interesting intéressant(e)
island île (*f.*)
it il, le, la
Italian italien (*m.*)
Italy Italie (*f.*)

jacket veste (*f.*)
January janvier (*m.*)
job emploi (*m.*)
July juillet (*m.*)
June juin (*m.*)

keep garder
key clef (*f.*)
kind gentil(le), aimable
king roi (*m.*)
kitchen cuisine (*f.*)
knife couteau (*m.*)
know connaître, savoir ; **know how to** savoir

lady dame (*f.*)
lake lac (*m.*)
lamp lampe (*f.*)
large grand(e)
last dernier (-ière); **last night** hier soir
late tard
later plus tard
lawn pelouse (*f.*)
lawyer avocat(e)
lazy paresseux (-euse)
lead mener
leaf feuille (*f.*)
least: at least au moins
leather (goods) store maroquinerie (*f.*)

leave partir
left gauche
lemonade citronnade (*f.*)
lend prêter
lesson leçon (*f.*)
letter lettre (*f.*)
library bibliothèque (*f.*)
life vie (*f.*)
light léger (*f.* légère)
like aimer
listen écouter
little petit(e); peu
live habiter, demeurer, vivre
living room salon (*m.*)
long long(ue); **a long time** longtemps
longer: no longer ne... plus
look regarder
loose-leaf notebook classeur (*m.*)
lose perdre
lot: a lot, lots of beaucoup (de)
loud fort(e); **louder** plus fort
love aimer
loyal fidèle
lunch déjeuner (*m.*)

magazine magazine (*m.*), revue (*f.*)
magnificent magnifique
make faire
make-up maquillage (*m.*); **to put make-up on** se maquiller
mall centre commercial (*m.*)
man homme (*m.*)
many beaucoup (de); **how many** combien (de)
map carte (*f.*)
March mars (*m.*)
marry épouser, se marier avec
matter: it doesn't matter ça ne fait rien
May mai (*m.*)
me me; moi
meal repas (*m.*)
meat viande (*f.*)
mechanic mécanicien(ne)
meet rencontrer, faire la connaissance de
metro métro (*m.*)
Mexico Mexique (*m.*)
middle milieu (*m.*), centre (*m.*)
midnight minuit (*m.*)
mind esprit (*m.*); **change one's mind** changer d'avis
minus moins

mistake faute (*f.*), erreur (*f.*)
modern moderne
Monday lundi (*m.*)
money argent (*m.*)
month mois (*m.*)
moon lune (*f.*)
more plus
morning matin (*m.*)
mother mère (*f.*)
motorcycle motocyclette (*f.*)
mountain montagne (*f.*)
move déménager
movie film (*m.*); **movies** cinéma (*m.*)
much beaucoup; **how much** combien (de)
multiplied by fois, multiplié par
museum musée (*m.*)
my mon, ma, mes

name nom (*m.*)
naturally naturellement
near près (de)
neck cou (*m.*)
need besoin (*m.*); **need** avoir besoin de
neighborhood quartier (*m.*)
nephew (*m.*) neveu
never ne... jamais, jamais
new nouveau, nouvel (*f.* nouvelle)
newspaper journal (*m.*) (*pl.* -aux)
next prochain(e)
nice sympathique, agréable, gentil(le); **to be nice** (*weather*) faire beau
niece nièce (*f.*)
night nuit (*f.*), soir (*m.*); **night table** table de nuit (*f.*)
nine neuf
nineteen dix-neuf
ninety quatre-vingt-dix
ninth neuvième
no non
no longer ne... plus
no one ne... personne, personne
nobody ne... personne, personne ne..., personne
noise bruit (*m.*)
noon midi (*m.*)
nose nez (*m.*)
not ne... pas
notebook cahier (*m.*)
nothing rien
November novembre (*m.*)

now maintenant
number numéro (*m.*); **(tele)phone number** numéro de téléphone
nut noix (*f.*)

o'clock heure (*f.*)
obey obéir
October octobre (*m.*)
of de, (du, des); **of course** bien sûr
office bureau (*m.*)
often souvent
old vieux, vieil (*f.* vieille); **to be . . . years old** avoir... ans
on sur, de; **on time** à l'heure
once une fois
one un(e)
only seul (*adj.*); seulement (*adv.*)
open ouvrir
operator opérateur (*f.* opératrice)
opportunity occasion (*f.*)
organize organiser
our notre, nos
out: go out sortir
over there là-bas

P.M. de l'après-midi, du soir
package paquet (*m.*)
painting tableau (*m.*)
pair (*f.*) paire
palace palais (*m.*)
pants pantalon (*m.*)
paper papier (*m.*)
park parc (*m.*)
party fête (*f.*), boum (*f.*)
passport passeport (*m.*)
pastry pâtisserie (*f.*); **pastry shop** pâtisserie (*f.*)
pay (for) payer; **pay attention** faire attention
peace paix (*f.*)
pen stylo (*m.*)
pen pal correspondant(e)
pencil crayon (*m.*); **pencil case** trousse (*f.*)
people (*m.pl.*) gens
perform jouer
perfume store parfumerie (*f.*)
phone téléphone (*m.*); **phone book** annuaire (*m.*); **phone booth** cabine (*f.*) **phone number** numéro de téléphone (*m.*)

picture image (*f.*), illustration (*f.*), photo (*f.*)
pie tarte (*f.*)
plane avion (*m.*)
play jouer; **play** (*an instrument*) jouer de; **play** (*a sport*) jouer à, faire du
please s'il te plaît, s'il vous plaît
pleased content(e), heureux (-euse)
pleasure plaisir (*m.*)
plus et; plus
police police (*f.*); **police officer** agent de police (*m.*)
pool piscine (*f.*)
poor pauvre
post office poste (*f.*), bureau de poste (*m.*)
postcard carte postale (*f.*)
poster poster (*m.*), affiche (*f.*)
potato pomme de terre (*f.*)
prefer préférer, aimer mieux
prepare préparer
present cadeau (*m.*)
present présent(e)
president président (*m.*)
pretty joli(e)
price prix (*m.*)
principal principal(e) (-aux)
problem problème (*m.*)
programmer programmeur (-euse)
protect protéger
proudly fièrement
punish punir
put (on) mettre

quarter quart (*m.*)
quickly vite, rapidement

rain pleuvoir; pluie (*f.*)
read lire
reasonable raisonnable
receive recevoir
recipe recette (*f.*)
record disque (*m.*)
red rouge
refrigerator réfrigérateur (*m.*)
refuse refuser
remain rester
repair réparer
repeat répéter
respond répondre
responsible responsable

return (*home*) rentrer; **return** (*an item*) rendre, retourner
rich riche
right correct(e)
river fleuve (*m.*)
road route (*f.*), chemin (*m.*)
roof toit (*m.*)
room pièce (*f.*); chambre (*f.*)
route route (*f.*), chemin (*m.*)

sad triste
salad salade (*f.*)
same même
sandal sandale (*f.*)
Saturday samedi (*m.*)
say dire
school école (*f.*)
sea mer (*f.*)
see voir
seize saisir
selfish égoïste
sell vendre
send envoyer
sentence phrase (*f.*)
September septembre (*m.*)
set: set the table mettre le couvert
seven sept
seventeen dix-sept
seventy soixante-dix
shade store (*m.*)
share partager
she elle
shirt chemise (*f.*)
shoe chaussure (*f.*)
shop faire les courses
short court(e)
shorts shorts (*m.*)
show montrer
shy timide
sick malade
sing chanter
sister sœur (*f.*)
six six
sixteen seize
sixty soixante
skate patin; patiner; **to go ice skating** faire du patin à glace
ski ski (*m.*); **ski instructor** moniteur de ski (*m.*); **go skiing** faire du ski
skirt jupe (*f.*)
sky ciel (*m.*)

sleep dormir
sleepy to be sleepy avoir sommeil
slowly lentement
small petit(e)
sneaker basket (*f.*); tennis (*f.*)
snow neige (*f.*) ; neiger
so si
soccer football (*m.*)
sock chaussette (*f.*)
soft doux (*f.* douce)
some du, de la, de l', des, en
sometimes quelquefois, parfois
son fils (*m.*)
song chanson (*f.*)
soup soupe (*f.*)
south sud (*m.*), midi (*m.*)
souvenir souvenir (*m.*)
Spanish espagnol
speak parler
spend dépenser (*money*); passer (*time*)
sporting goods articles de sport (*m.*)
spring printemps (*m.*)
stamp timbre (*m.*)
star étoile (*f.*)
start commencer (à); **start out** se mettre en route
station gare (*f.*)
stay rester
stereo chaîne stéréo (*f.*)
store magasin (*m.*)
story histoire (*f.*)
street rue (*f.*)
strict sévère
strong fort(e)
student élève (*m. / f.*), étudiant(e)
study étudier
subway métro (*m.*)
succeed réussir
success succès (*m.*)
sugar sucre (*m.*)
suitcase valise (*f.*)
summer été (*m.*)
sun soleil (*m.*); **to be sunny** faire du soleil
superstitious superstitieux (-ieuse)
sure certain(e), sûr(e)
sweater pull (*m.*)
swim nager
swim suit maillot de bain (*m.*)

swimming natation (*f.*);
   swimming pool piscine (*f.*)

table table (*f.*); **set the table**
   mettre le couvert
take prendre; apporter; **take a trip**
   faire un voyage; **take a walk**
   faire une promenade, se
   promener; **take care of** garder
tall grand(e)
taste goûter
teacher professeur (*m.*), maître (*m.*)
telephone téléphone (*m.*); **on the**
   telephone au téléphone;
   telephone book annuaire;
   telephone booth cabine (*f.*)
television télévision (*f.*)
tell dire
ten dix
terrace terrasse (*f.*)
than que
thank you merci
that que; qui; ce, cet, cette
the le, la, l', les
theater théâtre (*m.*)
their leur, leurs
them eux, elles, les
then puis, alors, ensuite
there là; y; **over there** là-bas;
   there is / are il y a; voilà
these ces
they ils, elles
thin mince
thing chose (*f.*)
think penser
thirst soif (*f.*); **to be thirsty** avoir
   soif
thirteen treize
thirty trente
this ce, cet, cette
those ces
thousand mille, mil (*in dates*)
three trois
Thursday jeudi (*m.*)
tidy ranger
tie cravate (*f.*)
till jusqu'à
time temps (*m.*); **all the time**
   tout le temps; **from time to**
   time de temps en temps; **have a**
   good time s'amuser; **a long**
   time longtemps; **on time** à
   l'heure

to à; **in order to** pour
today aujourd'hui
together ensemble
toilet toilettes (*f. pl.*)
tomorrow demain (*m.*)
too aussi
tooth dent (*f.*)
tourist touriste (*m. / f.*)
towards vers
tower tour (*f.*)
town ville (*f.*)
toy jouet (*m.*)
train train(*m.*); **by train** en train;
   train station gare (*f.*)
travel voyager
tree arbre (*m.*)
trip voyage (*m.*); **to take a trip**
   faire un voyage
true vrai(e)
truly vraiment
truth vérité (*f.*)
try essayer (de)
Tuesday mardi
twelfth douzième
twelve douze
twenty vingt
two deux

United States États-Unis (*m pl.*)
umbrella parapluie (*m.*)
under sous
undress se déshabiller
unhappy triste, malheureux
university université (*f.*)
upstairs en haut; **go upstairs**
   monter
us nous
useful utile
useless inutile
usually généralement, d'habitude

vacation vacances (*f. pl.*); **to**
   go on vacation aller en
   vacances
vacuum aspirateur (*m.*); **to**
   vacuum passer l'aspirateur
vegetable légume (*m.*)
very très
visit visiter

wait (for) attendre
waiter serveur (*m.*)
waitress serveuse (*f.*)

wake réveiller; **wake (oneself)** se
   réveiller
walk marcher; promener; **to go**
   for a walk se promener; **to take**
   a walk se promener
walkman baladeur (*m.*)
wall mur (*m.*)
want désirer, vouloir
war guerre (*f.*)
wash laver; **wash (oneself)** se
   laver
wastebasket corbeille à papier
   (*f.*)
watch regarder; surveiller
watch montre (*f.*)
water eau (*f.*); **mineral water**
   eau minérale
we nous
weak faible
wear porter
weather temps (*m.*); **bad weather**
   mauvais temps
Wednesday mercredi (*m.*)
week semaine (*f.*)
weekend fin (*f.*) de semaine;
   week-end (*m.*)
well bien
weight poids (*m.*); **to gain weight**
   grossir
west ouest (*m.*)
what que, qu'est-ce que, quoi;
   quel(le); ce que
when quand
where où
white blanc (*f.* blanche)
who qui
whole entier (-ière); tout
whom qui
why pourquoi
wife femme (*f.*)
win gagner
wind vent (*m.*); **to be windy** faire
   du vent
wine vin (*m.*)
winter hiver (*m.*); **winter sports**
   sports d'hiver
wise sage
with avec
without sans
woman femme (*f.*)
wonderful merveilleux (-euse),
   formidable
word mot (*m.*)

work travailler; marcher (*machines*);
   travail (*m.*)
world monde (*m.*)
write écrire

year an (*m.*); **to be . . . years old**
   avoir... ans

yes oui
yesterday hier
yet encore; **not yet** pas encore
yogurt yogourt (*m.*)
you tu, toi, vous
young jeune; **young people**
   jeunes gens (*m. pl.*)

younger cadet(te)
your ton, ta, tes, votre, vos

zip code code postal (*m.*)
zoo zoo (*m.*), parc zoologique
   (*m.*)

Glossary of Grammatical Terms

adjective A word that modifies a noun or a pronoun.

adverb A word that modifies a verb, an adjective, or another adverb.

antecedent A word or group of words to which a relative pronoun refers.

articles Words that precede nouns and usually indicate the number and the gender of the nouns.

auxiliary verb One of two elements needed to form a compound tense. Also called a **helping verb**. *Avoir* and *être* are the auxiliary verbs in French.

cardinal numbers The numbers we use for counting.

cognates Words that are the same or similar in both French and English.

conjugation The action of changing the ending of the verb so that it agrees with the subject noun or pronoun performing the task.

definite article The article "*the*" that indicates a specific person or thing: *the house.*

demonstrative adjective An adjective that precedes nouns to indicate or point out the person or thing referred to: *this, that, these,* or *those.*

direct object Answers the question *whom* or *what* the subject is acting upon and may refer to people, places, things, or ideas. It may be a noun or pronoun.

exclamation A word or phrase used to show surprise, delight, incredulity, emphasis, or other strong emotion.

false friends Words that are spelled the same or almost the same in both languages but have entirely different meanings and can be different parts of speech.

future A tense that expresses what the subject *will do* or *is going to do* or what action *will* or *is going to take place* in a future time.

gender Indicates whether a word is masculine or feminine.

idiom A particular expression whose meaning cannot be readily understood by either its grammar or the words used.

imperative A verb form used to give commands or make requests.

imperfect A past tense that expresses a continuous, repeated, habitual or incomplete action, situation, or event in the past that *was* going on at an indefinite time or that *used to* happen in the past.

indefinite article The article "*a*" or "*an*" that refers to persons and objects not specifically identified: *a house.*

indicative A verb mood that states a fact.

indirect object Answers the question *to whom* or *for whom* the subject is doing something. It may be a noun or pronoun.

infinitive The basic "*to*" form of the verb.

intonation A way of asking a question by inserting a rising inflection at the end of the statement.

inversion A way of asking a question by reversing the word order of the subject pronoun and the conjugated verb within the sentence.

noun A word used to name a person, place, thing, idea, or quality.

partitive The article indicating an indefinite quantity or part of a whole: *some* or *any.*

passé composé A tense that expresses an action or event completed at a specific time in the past.

past participle A verb form expressing an action or a condition that has occurred in the past.

preposition A word used to relate elements in a sentence: noun to noun, verb to verb, or verb to noun/pronoun.

present tense A tense that expresses what is happening now.

pronoun A word that is used to replace a noun (a person, place, thing, idea, or quality).

reflexive verb A verb that shows that the subject is performing the action upon itself.

relative pronoun (*who, which, that*) A pronoun that joins a main clause (a clause that can stand alone) to a dependent clause (a clause that cannot stand alone.)

stress pronoun A pronoun used to emphasize or to replace nouns or pronouns in certain situations.

subject The noun or pronoun performing the action of the verb.

verb A word that shows an action or state of being.

Index

NOTE: For specific verb conjugations, see the Appendix.